eadership helped me to see the unity of all the worlds religions. It helped y own calling. It helped me awaken to the truth that I am not just God's uld become His Daughter. I would recommend this book to everyone; ill speak to everyone; and I know it will help everyone become their d. Not only in heaven, but right here in the earth...

MARIA S. LIS, Senior Citizen & Elder, Calgary, AB

f integrating many disciplines, philosophies and bodies of , *Integrative Leadership* is number one. The book captured my rom the beginning, compelling me to learn about your integrative to the very end. In my daily activities, I found that whenever I mind, heart or thoughts to *Integrative Leadership*, my own life ned for improvement possibilities. Even though I am a novice in s of living an integrative life and far from any official leadership nd your work to be deeply meaningful and personally resonant. It t help in measuring the quality of work situations of which I chose t and the quality of what I would bring to those situations.

N. NASH, Editor, Ottawa, ON

Leadership richly illustrates the principles of compassion and at can serve as a beacon for others, bringing positive, productive any workplace. In demonstrating, through the depth and breadth tensive research, how science and psychology affirm centuries-old he authors inspire us to live, to lead and become the change we e in our world. This work is a powerful, transformative, must-read wanting to lead with integrity in their marriage, relationships, orkplace or community. If consciously and persistently applied, the and practices of integrative life and leadership will help make you, more effective and integrated leader, but a better human being.

V. PETRICH, Director, *Yoga Studio College of Canada*, Calgary, AB

Leadership sheds light into the life-giving forces that inspire and reat leadership. Through extensive research, the authors have and reconciled the often divergent approaches to leadership and p development into one wholistic framework that is simple, and grounded in life experience. They invite us to a higher truth en lacking in leadership literature, which, when embraced, infuses and spiritual energy in one's life, love and work. By consciously n the principles and practices of the path of integration into your ill gain the confidence to rise up to any challenge, grow the capacity aradox, and lead people through change and transition in today's economic, social and political environments. *Integrative Leadership*

What readers (
Integrativ

Every so often a book crosses one's p
inside. Such a book is *Integrative Leac*
when more and more people are searc
in the workplace and in their spiritu
outer worlds and a longing deep v
instinctively know exists, but are unab
many keys to achieving this balance i

M. KITCHEN, President *Yoga*
Chairmar

I loved *Integrative Leadership.* I founc
reflect on my own beliefs about invo
while interacting with the integrativ
the authors. It was wonderful how tl
so many of the world's wisdom ar
psychological and scientific perspec
advance in understanding life and leac
and yet an easy read and should be rea

Integrative Leadership encourages us to
ourselves so that we could become all t
poke and prod us from multiple pers
vast potential that often is hidden witl
combining the wisdom of the ages wit
create a powerful tool for improving o

I. MCNAII

Integrative Leadership challenges each
own lives and in the lives of others.
transcending the *newer* humanistic styl
the concept of the spiritual mystic leade
material, the authors have been succes
leadership. They propose a seven-step p
by anyone, regardless of position or r
following the journey of two coaching c
transform their lives. A must-read for
achieved all there is to achieve in their

L. MASLAK, Presic

Integrative L
me to feel m
child, but c
and feel it
Image of Go

In terms
knowledg
attention f
framewor
turned my
was exam
the proces
roles, I fou
was a grea
to be a pa

Integrativ
wisdom th
change to
of their ex
wisdom,
want to se
for anyon
careers, w
principles
not only a

Integrati
sustain g
captured
leadersh
balanced
that is oft
meaning
weaving
life, you v
to hold p
turbulent

is a unique resource and a must-read for anyone aspiring to be an enlightened, transcendent, visionary leader.

B. Mutwiri, Executive Director, Saskatoon, SK

Integrative Leadership is fabulous! In examining life through the integrative model and framework, I have come to understand that it is we who determine our path by the very way we choose to live our life. Blaming others for how our life is going is not going to get us a better life. *Integrative Leadership* speaks to our responsibility to 'get it right' so that we can enjoy enlightened awareness in life, love and leadership. This book is for all those who have a sincere desire to transform themselves and their world from the mechanistic to the organic paradigm.

L. Friesen, Managing Partner, *Brennan & Associates*, Calgary, AB

I really enjoyed the integrated story telling writing style between the two case studies and the theory, principles and practices of integration. This style allowed me to identify with the main characters as well as experience many awakening moments while reading the theory associated with their personal transformational journeys. For me, *Integrative Leadership* is a continuation of my own journey towards authenticity in life and work that began several years ago and is a *must read* for anyone who is searching for inner and outer peace.

D. Grimbly, Contract Administrator, Calgary, AB

Integrative Leadership has introduced me to several new ideas that have helped me make positive life changes. I recommend *Integrative Leadership* to everyone. Whether you are searching for personal growth or interested in learning about leadership roles in organizations, this book gives you resources that you can apply to all aspects of your life.

A. Charlton, Student, *Mount Royal College*, Calgary, AB

I really enjoyed *Integrative Leadership*. It is an excellent, intelligent, well-researched and thoughtful work. The integrative life and leadership framework and concepts presented resonated with all I have been taught in my secular and religious life. It has prompted me to focus more time on my inner self and I will use it as an ongoing source of inspiration. I believe that *Integrative Leadership* is for all those who desire to develop their inner wisdom and enrich the lives of those who they love and care for in every day life and work.

Dr. Izzat Jiwani, Sociologist, Post Doctoral Fellow,
University of Montreal & McMaster University

I must admit I was surprisingly impressed with *Integrative Leadership*. Rather than reading simply 'another' business and leadership handbook, what I found was an approach to life, to one's self and to other's that was not only applicable to the business world but to life in general. The approach entailed not only becoming a better business executive but also becoming a better person in the process. I would recommend *Integrative Leadership* to individuals interested in expanding their awareness of what it really means to be a leader, the responsibility that entails, and the impact your leadership can have on your company, its employees and your self.

KEVIN J. TODESCHI, ARE Director
and Editor-in-Chief, *Venture Inward* magazine, Virginia Beach, VA

In rare instances in our lifetime we come across an inspiring work that has the potential to change the very fabric of our society. *Integrative Leadership* is one such book. It not only has the ability to awaken us to our own vast and often untapped human potential, but suggests guidelines, principles and practices to ensure that we remain alive and true to ourselves and to our world. *Integrative Leadership* transcends cultures, creeds, languages and promotes the Ideal of one world family. At the same time, it inspires us with the hope that each of us can be that *spirit of unity* that will build a firm foundation for the coming age of integration.

PAT GRECO, Filmmaker, Calgary, AB

As a seeker of the truth for many decades, I have been the grateful recipient of some wonderful knowledge. Recently, two beautiful creations have impacted my world that served to accelerate me along my journey towards higher awareness. The first is a movie entitled, *What the Bleep do we Know?* This amazing film unites science and spirituality and reaffirmed my faith that we are all co-creators on the path of increasing enlightenment.

The second is an incredible book by Richard John and Lillas Marie Hatala called *Integrative Leadership*. Where the movie leaves off, this book begins. It is a manual that helps show us the way to freedom and happiness and a guide for personal transformation and transcendence. The journey of integration that Rick and Lillas so clearly describe, is a scientific, spiritual and artistic dance that draws together the best of our physical, mental, emotional and spiritual domains into one harmonious and collaborative whole. *Integrative Leadership* is a book that has assisted me, and I know will also assist you in your personal journey and help guide you on your path towards radical truth, inner peace and increasing bliss.

CHRIS LEIGH-SMITH, Founder & President, *Tao of Peace Martial Arts School.*
Calgary, AB

Integrative Leadership

©2005 Richard John Hatala and Lillas Marie Hatala

All rights reserved. No part of this publication may be reproduced, stored in a retrieval system or transmitted in any form or by any means — electronic, mechanical, photocopying, recording, scanning or otherwise — without the prior written permission of the Publisher. Requests for permissions should be addressed to the Permissions Department at the following address:

Integrative Leadership Institute
P.O. Box 22204 Bankers Hall
Calgary, AB, Canada T2P 4J5
Direct Phone: (306) 244 • 0934 Fax: (306) 244 • 1379
Toll Free: 1 (866) 616 • 0934
E-Mail: iliinfo@integrativeleadership.ca
Website: www.integrativeleadership.ca

Library and Archives Canada Cataloguing in Publication

Hatala, Rick, 1953–
Integrative leadership: building a foundation for personal, interpersonal and organizational success / Richard J. Hatala & Lillas M. Hatala.

Includes bibliographical references and index.
ISBN: 0–9735351–1–3 (bound). — ISBN: 0–9735351–0–5 (pbk.)

1. Leadership. I. Hatala, Lillas M. (Lillas Marie), 1953– II. Integrative Leadership Institute. III. Title.

BF637.L4H37 2004 158'.4 C2004–904172–X

Technical Credits:
Copy Editing: Susan Bond, *Small Bird Editorial Services*, Saskatoon, SK
Design, Production & Print Management: Jeremy Drought, *Last Impression Publishing Service*, Calgary, AB
Cover Image: Veer.com (hurricane SBP 00227126)
Indexing: Elizabeth Bell, *Pinpoint Indexing*, Calgary, AB and Ursula Acton, *Proof Positive*, Saskatoon, SK
Proofreading: Ursula Acton, *Proof Positive*, Saskatoon, SK and Jennifer M. Hatala
Printing: *Friesens Corporation*, Altona, MB, CANADA

Building a Foundation for Personal, Interpersonal & Organizational Success

Integrative Leadership

RICHARD JOHN HATALA
&
LILLAS MARIE HATALA

INTEGRATIVE LEADERSHIP INSTITUTE
Calgary, Alberta, Canada

The journey of a thousand miles begins with the first step.

Lao Tzu

You will probably find some language baffling, exasperating, even downright meaningless. This alas is not an easy work. It was written, not to instruct, but to awaken.

Anthony De Mello

For a healthy body, you need to learn to drink your food and chew your drink. This principle also applies for a healthy mind. We need to learn to chew on new ideas and drink in their feelings before we can properly assimilate and integrate them within our whole being.

Hugh Vicars

Dedication

To all those who have the insight, strength, courage and willingness to walk the path of integrative life, love, learning and leadership.

Whatever you do, you need courage. Whatever course you decide upon, there is always someone to tell you that you are wrong. There are always difficulties arising that tempt you to believe your critics are right. To map out a course of action and follow it to an end requires some of the same courage that a soldier [or warrior] needs. Peace has its victories, but it takes brave men and women to win them.

Ralph Waldo Emerson

Acknowledgements

WE WOULD LIKE TO THANK ALL THOSE WHO HAVE PREPARED THE WAY for this work — through the ages — in the scientific, psychological, social, wisdom and mystic traditions. Through our work these past years we found that we 'stood on the shoulders of giants' and we are in awe and wonder at all they have allowed us to see. We also thank and acknowledge the following: our mother Maria, who held the loving space for us and supported us during our personal and collective integrative journeys; our five children: Scott, Jennifer, Marie, Andrew, and Michael for engaging and being present with us during our many reflections and introspections in walking this path; the many reviewers who shared with us their comments and constructive critiques and helped our work move from good to great; our editorial and design team who collectively gave our ideas form, clarity and accuracy: Jeremy Drought, of *Last Impression Publishing Service*, our book designer, teacher and coach on all facets of the book design and publishing business; Susan Bond, our sometimes substantive, always copy, and wonderfully stylistic editor who helped to clarify our message and make it more accessible; Ursula Acton for her meticulous proofreading and final indexing, ensuring our message remained precise and accurate; Elizabeth Bell for her initial indexing of our work and helping readers find what we have discovered on our journey of integration; and finally, our special thanks to Jennifer Margaret Hatala for helping our work move, not only from good to great, but from good to grace in her final proofreading of the manuscript for form, meaning and intent.

If I have seen farther than others, it is because I stand on the shoulders of giants.

ISAAC NEWTON (1642–1727)

Contents

List of Tables

List of Figures

Outline of the Journey

The Search for the Foundational Model of Life and Leadership

WHEN WE WERE FIRST CONFRONTED WITH THE COMPLEXITY and many different definitions, models and approaches to the idea of leadership, we began an intensive three-year study of human, management and leadership development to help unravel the mystery and complexity. The purpose of our study was to search for the foundational model of leadership that we felt stood behind and informed all other models. Three criteria guided our search: the model needed to be simple and resonant, unifying and integrative, and of service and additive.

Our search led us first through the past 100 years of leadership development literature, then through 300 years of scientific research, then through 3,000 years of wisdom and mystic traditions externally, while simultaneously deeply reflecting and examining our own 50 years of experience in consciously walking the path of integration internally. Our search resulted in an evolving integrative philosophy, uncovering what we feel is the foundational model that gives rise to all other life and leadership models; and universal laws, principles and practices that guide and inform the journey of integration.

Collectively we have chosen to call our results, Integrative Leadership ™.

What is Integrative Leadership?

Integrative Leadership is a wholistic approach to leading oneself and others in a reflective, conscious, thoughtful and responsive way. The process of integration involves multiple perspectives, four domains of intelligence (physical, mental, emotional and spiritual) and three levels of awareness (personality, individuality, universality) that help build, through the exercise of our power of choice, a foundation for personal, interpersonal and organizational success.

Walking the Path of Integrative Leadership

Integrative Leadership is harmoniously and simultaneously walking the path of the mystic (inner journey) and the path of conventional leadership (outer journey) in every day life and work. It is a way of illuminating the path that would allow individuals to evolve in three ways: from individual contributors and team players to managers; from managers to effective leaders; and from effective leaders to visionary, integrative and enlightened leaders. *Integrative Leadership* provides a method and process for integrating the often-paradoxical duality of involutionary spiritual leadership (inside out) and evolutionary scientific leadership (outside in) within the awakened heart of the Integrative Leader. The Integrative Leader practices, and helps facilitate, extraordinary personal, interpersonal and organizational performance regardless of how that performance is measured.

About the Integrative Model

The model of integrative life and leadership that is presented is not a number of models, but one unified model. If you can imagine, while reading the model-building phase of this work, a crystalline sphere that has within it, depending on your perspective, beliefs and paradigm, a cube, four-sided pyramid (octahedron divided in two), or cone, we are simply rotating the sphere in our writing and examining different aspects, dimensions and perspectives of the same unified model (systems, structures, relationships).

The cubic, pyramidal and conical perspectives can be further separated into three levels of awareness and eight dimensions of universal principles, much like one would separate a stacked deck of cards: one deck, one model, but multiple layers that comprise it.

In our study, we found that this wholistic, universal and unified model of life, love, learning and leadership is found both within us and outside of us, attempts to explain in words, ideas and images what physicists attempt to explain using mathematics, geometry and physics (unified field theory), and is not conventionally deterministic, but rather heuristic in nature.

The model's ultimate value is in how clearly it will reflect back to you your own life and leadership journey and help you to answer "Who are you and what do you want?" from the life you've been given.

Thoughts on Interacting with Integrative Leadership

This book has the potential to be transformative and transcendent. It is meant for those desiring to consciously or unconsciously begin the process of integration. Based on their reactions or responses to this work, readers generally fall into one of four categories.

The first group responded to the book with instant ease and resonance on many levels of their being. They became excited from the very beginning and their excitement built until the very end. They found they were not only captured, but were enraptured by it. They felt that much of what was presented made sense to them and was complimentary to their own inner and outer understanding. In their reading, they found many creative ways to intensively interact with the book in order to make it their own. In that interaction, they experienced resonance, were affirmed and felt alignment with the integrative framework, principles and practices that continued to impact them after they finished the book.

For those in this first group, they fully accepted the invitation, are into self-generation and are well on the path of integration. It is this group that will receive the most benefit from this work. For they were willing to reflect and place the content of their own life, love and leadership journey within the integrative context and concepts we've shared. They were willing to suspend their own beliefs for a time and enter into this work openly and freely. With this openness and willingness, the book came alive for them and continues to be a living companion and source of inspiration on their personal journeys.

The second group was unsure whether to *react* or *respond*. At times they found it to be a slow and difficult read. At other times, they may have been stuck on the words, meanings or a lack of empathy for the main characters.

At still other times, the integrative ideas slipped easily into their consciousness and helped strengthen their emerging awareness.

We have found that the members of this second group were generally less articulate about their intention and desire for integration then the first group. They knew they needed something. They knew they were missing something. But they were not all that sure what that something was.

During portions of their reading, some members became physically, mentally or emotionally uncomfortable to the point of nausea, dizziness and queasiness comparing their reading of the book to riding a roller coaster: up and down, round and round.

If you feel that you fall into this second group, we would like to assure you that the physical symptoms and feelings of uncertainty are a natural process of awakening the four domains and moving your attention through the three levels of awareness. We would encourage you to continue to engage, interact and reflect despite these symptoms. We invite you to persevere if at all possible until the very end.

Afterwards, pause and let yourself return to a place of mental, emotional and physical equilibrium. When you feel ready, get back on the ride and read the book again with an eye towards seeing connections and associations that you had not seen the first time through. It will be easier the second time than the first. Easier the third time than the second.

Members of this second group have shared that their inspirations, insights, intuitions and epiphanies increased ten-fold by their third reading. They likened their first reading to plowing their own inner body mind fields. It felt like hard, slow and tedious work. Their second reading was like walking through their heart mind fields planting seed thoughts of truth. It felt more gentle and relaxed and rhythmic. Their third reading they compared to experiencing the harvest from their soul minds that reverberated and integrated at every level of their beings. See if you can experience the process as others have within this group of readers by engaging and remaining engaged more than once through this work.

The third group found there was no resonance, understanding or comprehension of the nature and intent of the book. Whether they read it, or didn't read it, made no difference to their lives.

Many of the members of this third group are much like the prospective student who sought an interview with a renowned Chinese Taoist Master. After the Master listened for hours to the student expound the depth, breadth and degree of knowledge he had learned to that point in his life that qualified him to be the Master's student, the Master politely asked, while holding a teapot, if the student would like to pause a moment in his discourse and have a cup of tea? The student replied he would while holding out his cup in gratitude at the Master's thoughtfulness.

The Master began to pour the tea into the student's cup, filled it to overflowing, and continued to pour the remaining pot of hot tea onto the students lap, pants and feet until it was empty, all the while ignoring the loud exclamations by the student to stop his pouring. After examining the floor and his tea-stained clothes for a time, the student looked up and asked the Master why he had done that? To which the Master replied:

"Your cup is too full of yourself and your own ideas about the nature of your life, the nature of all life and the nature of the Path. Until you choose to empty yourself, even a little, there is no room in you for my Teaching. So go now. Empty yourself. Then return to me when you are somewhat empty so that we may have a chance to begin our relationship again."

For those who are members of this third group, until you can choose to empty yourself a little, there is no room in you to consider anything new. When you empty yourself a little, either by choice or circumstance, return to this book if called to do so and see if it has more value for you when you are a little empty rather than when you were totally full.

A few readers had fearful, visceral, sometimes violent reactions to some or all of the ideas discussed within this book. For this fourth group, we would suggest cultivating the virtue of patience. In our own life journeys we found that: '*When one encounters a new or original thought that differs from what we already believe, at first it is rejected; then it is ridiculed; and finally it becomes for us and for all, self evident*'. For members of this fourth group, we would suggest that understanding would just be a matter of time, space and patience.

Preface

In the Beginning

In everyone's life at some time, our inner fire goes out.
It is then burst into flame by an encounter with another human being.
We should all be thankful for those people who rekindle the inner spirit.

Albert Schweitzer

When we first met at a Business and Consciousness conference in Acapulco several years ago our inner fires were nearly out. There were a variety of reasons why our fires had been dampened to the point of extinction: taking those closest to us for granted; immersing ourselves in our work to such a degree that our passion had turned into obsession; losing sight of and failing to live our personal mission, vision, principles and values; and finding meaning almost solely as achieving, lonely, fragmented *human doings* while forgetting we had begun our lives many years before as innocent, truthful and whole *human beings*.

During our initial Acapulco encounter we experienced what it was like to share one's whole self with another without fear of judgment, condemnation or rejection. We shared truths with each other that week that we had never shared with anyone else. It was not just an encounter with our public and private selves, but a sharing of our *essence* that few had ever seen. It was not just an encounter as a *conversation*, but was a deep experience of long forgotten *communion*.

Ours was a serendipitous and synchronistic meeting that was born in radical honesty, compassion, wisdom and mutual service that led us to realize what was to become our life's work.

This book is rooted in 3,000 years of wisdom and mystic traditions and in 300 years of scientific research. We have spent the past 50 years of our lives experiencing and the past three years deeply reflecting, researching and integrating our personal histories within the greater context of humankind's. Awakening and understanding these patterns has helped us to successfully navigate the transition from who we were as *personality* to who we are as our *Ideal*.

It is our hope that our experiences, understandings and insights will resonate with you and help you to navigate through your own times of transition and change.

Our life's work has evolved these past three years into a philosophy, a foundational model and a set of principles, processes and emerging practices that we call Integrative Life and Leadership™. We have developed workshops, seminars and retreats based on this philosophy. We have written, taught, coached and spoken to thousands of people sharing with them our integrative approach.

Most importantly, we first walked the path of integration ourselves, then with family and friends, before introducing it to the marketplace. This unique process has moved us more and more from the inside out and not, as we had relied on in the past, from the outside in.

The journey of becoming an Integrative Leader™ is an emergent and *evolutionary* process that is guided by a convergent and *involutionary* process that awakened within us from three fundamental sources.

The first source involved deeply examining our life and leadership experiences with government, business, not-for-profit and academic institutions; our various roles as mother, father, daughter, son, brother, sister, spouse, family member or friend; and our evolving capacities as individual contributors, team players, managers, leaders, entrepreneurs, intrapreneurs, founders, executive directors, presidents and CEOs of a variety of organizations. In the course of our self-examination, we looked for the common ground, common patterns, and common principles and processes that wove through and informed these diverse experiences.

Secondly, we observed some of the same patterns in the literature of various disciplines, including science, psychology, sociology, anthropology, management, leadership and adult education, as well as our research of the world's wisdom and mystic traditions.

Thirdly, we found that our shared interpersonal and intrapersonal experiences were reflected in stories from individuals, organizations, communities and cultures with whom we chose to work these past years. We discovered that our integrative approach helped many people and organizations build a foundation for success on many levels — personally, interpersonally, professionally and organizationally.

We believe these three foundations and resulting multiple perspectives yield insights that will help guide those who choose to step onto the path of becoming an Integrative Leader. It is a journey that will help move your awareness from complexity to simplicity, from analysis to synthesis, and from fragmentation to wholeness.

Many have said that the inner journey of life and leadership is a courageous and mysterious process. We have found this to be true and wish to share with you what we have learned to this point in our journey. Our intent is to be hopeful, helpful, inspiring and challenging to all who choose to apply these ideas in their own lives.

If in your reading you come across an idea that is difficult or a concept you cannot swallow or stomach at this time, we suggest you put the book down and leave it for a while until you feel ready to work with the transformative ideas this work contains.

However, for those who engage and resonate with the ideas within this work and who have the courage to accept the invitation and begin to walk the path of integration, we hope this book will serve to not only nurture you, but feed and sustain you — body, mind, heart and soul — and in some small way help rekindle your inner fire and spirit once again.

Richard John & Lillas Marie Hatala
Integrative Leadership Institute
Calgary, Alberta, Canada
April 20 2004

Foreword

by Joel & Michelle Levey

IN A WORLD FRAUGHT WITH UNCERTAINTY, fragmentation, polarization, and fear, *Integrative Leadership* takes a bold stand in affirming the power and influence of leaders doing the *inner work* necessary to bring a deeper wisdom to their *outer work*. Grounded in science, research, and business, the integral approach of this book invites you to consider the radical possibility that you can live, work, and lead with greater health, balance and vitality, and with greater wisdom, spirit, and effectiveness than you may have ever dreamed of. Given the magnitude of dramatic change, challenges, and unrealized potentials in our lives and world today, it is compelling to take the invitation of this inspiring book to heart.

Over the past three decades we have witnessed first hand the power of an integrative, inside-out approach to leadership. In our work with thousands of leaders in hundreds of diverse organizations around the globe, and from our work and research in medicine and extraordinary human performance, it is clear that the power of the principles and practices of integrative leadership flows from their congruence with natural systems that govern the deep structures and workings of our human nervous system and innermost being. You could say that an integral approach to leadership and organizational performance is compatible with the natural systems, structures, and in-born "operating system" that you were born with. These life-affirming and wholistic principles and practices make sense both rationally and intuitively, and if you apply them you will get positive, immediate, and long-lasting results that will inspire others along the way.

Integral themes are being increasingly addressed and embraced by a diversity of the most influential thought leaders of our times. Most notably, Ken Wilber, Peter Senge, Buckminster Fuller, David Bohm, Fritjof Capra, Margaret Wheatley, Willis Harman, Dee Hock, Parker Palmer, Dana Zohar,

David Suzuki, Reverend Martin Luther King Jr., Archbishop Desmond Tutu, the Dalai Lama, Joanna Macy, and Jane Goodall, to name but a few. They have all helped to advance our understanding of how powerful forces weave us inextricably into the fabric of a many-dimensional wholeness that we share with all beings.

While this may be the first book on *Integrative Leadership*, it will not be the last. You hold in your hands a pioneering work that will play a unique role in advancing our understanding of the integrative qualities of leadership so vital to our success, change resilience, and survival in the complex times to come.

Rick and Lillas Hatala have refined and distilled the knowledge they present here in the laboratories of their own mainstream lives and work as leaders in business, transformative education, and partners in life. They have been rigorous and disciplined in their explorations, and offer you many of their most valuable and illuminating discoveries. Through their writing they provide a wealth of practical guidance to help you replicate their findings in the laboratory of your own life and verify for yourself that by changing yourself for the better you can positively change your personal, interpersonal, and organizational world.

True to their words, the authors' writing style models an integrative approach. For readers who are inspired by the real life examples, learnings, and transformations of others, the stories so poignantly told in these pages bring this book alive in heartwarming ways. For those of us who learn best from visual models, and specific step-by step guidelines, the Hatalas present maps of the "territory" of Integrative Life and Leadership with clear distinctions, principles, and practices for exploring the four domains of intelligence, three levels of awareness, integrative transformative and transcendent practices, and the seven elements of integration that honor the integral weavings of our highest physical, emotional, mental, and spiritual potentials. In these pages you will find many mirrors in which to reflect how these leadership principles and practices apply to the unique bundle of circumstances in your own life and work.

Integrative Leadership is emerging as an evolutionary step toward meeting the needs of our times. The innate wisdom of natural systems reminds us that our survival as individuals and as leaders is found not in the thin veneer of a tough, overpowering presence, but in a deep connectedness to our world, our wholeness in relationship to our world, and our capacity to be aware of and responsive to the needs of other forces in our world so that we can cooperate with them.

Time and time again we have witnessed how the inner state of a leader is telegraphed — for better or worse — to people throughout their organizations. In our rapidly changing and interconnected world, old styles of dominating and intimidating leadership are debilitating, dangerous, short lived, and unsustainable. They require massive amounts of resources and fear to prop them up until they exhaust themselves, falter, and fall. The complexity and pace of our times require leaders who are nimble, responsive, aware, courageous, wise, well-networked, and connected to their people — qualities needed to respond intelligently to the challenges and opportunities of rapidly changing and powerful forces.

Never before have our decisions as leaders had the power and potential to impact the quality of life for so many people throughout the world, or for so many generations into the future.

The growing crisis of leadership in our post-modern world has created many complex problems that will burden humanity for generations to come. The daily news offers a cavalcade of sobering failures about so many of our world's struggling leaders. Taken to heart, these devastating examples of failed leadership compel us as individuals and leaders to affirm our own resolve to live and work with greater integrity, think in deeper, more complex ways, and expand our capacity to become ever more skilful and wise in living our lives and leading those who look to us for guidance. As Einstein so brilliantly stated, "A problem cannot be solved at the same level of thinking that created it.... We shall require a substantially new manner of thinking if humankind is to survive."

After the Cold War ended, Vaclav Havel, then President of the Czech Republic, addressed the United States Congress and called for a global revolution, saying:

> *Without a global revolution in the sphere of human consciousness, nothing will change for the better in the sphere of our being as humans, and the catastrophe towards which this world is headed — be it ecological, social, demographic, or a general breakdown of civilization — will be unavoidable. ... The salvation of this human world lies nowhere else than in the human heart, in the human power to reflect, in human meekness, and in human responsibility.*

As one of our world's most respected living examples of integrative leadership, Havel beckons us all to join this global revolution in consciousness, to bring it alive in our own lives, and to source our guidance from a deeper source of wisdom that will lead us to live together and steward our world in saner, safer, and more sustainable ways.

True regime change begins within, by freeing ourselves from the tyranny of our own confusions, delusions, shortsightedness and myopic concerns. As we steward this r/evolution in our own consciousness, we awaken ever more deeply to our wholeness. We become more aware of the profound interdependence of all things, and the far-reaching influence of our decisions as they ripple out into the world and into the lives of countless beings. And we come to live and lead in ways that encourage confidence in others willing to work with us in stewarding the emergent potentials for a better world.

It is in this evolutionary spirit, that Lillas and Rick Hatala offer to you this treasury of wholistic tools, practices and principles to support a transformation in consciousness in your own life, and through you in the lives of all who are touched, directly or indirectly, by how you lead and ultimately live.

Integrative Leadership invites its readers on a learning journey into a deeper working awareness of the omnidimensional wholeness and extraordinary potential in each of our lives. Through these readings and reflections we hope you will come to discover more degrees of freedom, opportunity, and potential than previously imagined.

It was a great honor to be asked to write the Foreword to this seminal book. May your reading be profoundly inspired, and may that inspiration flow through you to the individuals and communities that you serve!

Joel & Michelle Levey
Founders, International Center for Corporate
Culture & Organizational Health at
InnerWork Technologies, Inc.
Seattle, Washington, U.S.A
October 11, 2004

Background: Models in Motion

The Story of John & the Story of Mary

There was never yet an uninteresting life. Such a thing is an impossibility. Inside of the dullest exterior there is a drama, a comedy and a tragedy.

MARK TWAIN

The Story of John

WHEN WE OPENED OUR DOORS on our Integrative Leadership Development, Consulting & Coaching Company several years ago, one of the first phone calls we received requesting our services was from one of Rick's colleagues. Rick and John* had known each other for fifteen years, first corporately and then as fellow entrepreneurs within the domestic and international energy business.

John had heard about Rick's transition from the energy business into leadership facilitation, consulting and coaching. He had heard about the uniqueness of our integrative approach and decided that he wanted to see both of us as soon as possible. We suggested the following week, but on John's insistence that the matter was urgent — he would not discuss it on the phone — we cleared off our calendars and met him in his 29th floor office building later that same day.

When we first met John, he was polite, greeted us without a smile and asked us into his spacious corner office. John seated us around his meeting table and then got right to the point.

* John and Mary are not separate and specific individuals, but rather an amalgam of clients we have dealt with over the years in our integrative coaching and consulting practice.

"I need some help in finding someone for a senior Executive position in my company. I would like you to look internally first and then externally if you have to. But I would like you to help me fill the position within six weeks. Sooner if at all possible."

We told him that we didn't really do executive placement, but he knew about Rick's experience in his company's international area of operations and of Lillas's expertise in all facets of human resources and felt we would be perfect to help manage the search process for him using whatever resources we needed. We tabled our objections, reserved our decision, and asked him for the specifics about the position.

"I want you to find someone to replace me as President and CEO of my company as soon as possible."

We were surprised. When we asked why so fast, he shared that he had had a meeting with his doctor and specialists that morning. His tests had come back negative. They had found cancer in a key internal organ; it was inoperable and conventionally untreatable and their prognosis was that he had from eight to ten months left to live.

When John had asked his doctors what he should do, they shrugged their shoulders, sat back in their chairs and said he should double his insurance policy, quit his job and do what he had always wanted to do for the time he had remaining. After the initial shock that morning, he followed their advice, called his insurance company and increased his personal and company key man insurance. The second people he called and told about his condition was us. He hadn't spoken to his board, the people in his organization, or his wife and children yet, waiting until he had done what he felt he had to do.

"That is the story of my life," John said with a crooked smile. "Doing what I had to do today so that I could eventually do what I wanted to do tomorrow. And now the funny part is, it looks like there may not be a tomorrow."

He told us that there were two parts to the assignment. The first part was to find a replacement for him to run his company. The second was to advise him in his personal transition over the next several months.

"Perhaps, you can help me understand why this happened to me. Why me? Why now?" he asked, then excused himself to go to the washroom, not expecting an answer. When he got up we both noticed there were tears in his eyes.

In his absence, we talked and agreed to proceed with the assignment to help John through this difficult time in his life. When he returned, we told him of our decision and then, because time was short, we asked him to describe the history, present circumstances, and key people within his organization as well as his personal history for our own understanding and context.

After we heard his story, we code-named the file, and his company, *Crisis Energy*.

The Story of Mary

Mary first came to us by referral from a past participant in our integrative life and leadership programs. Mary wanted a series of integrative coaching sessions that her company was willing to support. After an exploratory interview, we agreed to take her on as a client.

Mary was in her late forties with three children in their teens and early twenties and a husband of 25 years who was an Engineering Manager in a global Engineering, Procurement & Construction (EPC) Company. Mary worked for a large successful retail chain based in western Canada. She was one of the few female senior managers in the corporation's head office that we eventually code named "Sad But True" or *SBT Company*.

Mary had a wonderful personality, bubbly, smiling and optimistic on the outside. As the coaching sessions progressed, we found Mary also had a deep sadness and a lack of fulfillment that smoldered on the inside. There was a disconnect between her inner and outer story. Her present life was not what she had wanted, imagined or envisioned in her youth. She was not living the life of her dreams, but for the past eight years her life was more along the lines of a quiet, fragmented and dissatisfying nightmare.

By our third coaching session, Mary said there must be more to life than what she now knew. She felt she was dying a slow death and asked if we could help her live again. We said that we would try and do the best we could for her sake and also for our own, for we knew, as one of us gets better, so do we all.

Introduction

What is Integrative Leadership?

You cannot teach a man anything;
you can only help him find it within himself.

GALILEO GALILEI

BEFORE WE CONTINUE WITH THE STORIES of John and Mary, we would like to pause and give you some background on our perspective regarding leadership development and the framework we have developed and will use to help guide John and Mary through their life and leadership journey.

Integrative Leadership

Integrative Leadership is a wholistic approach to leading oneself and others in a reflective, conscious, thoughtful and responsive way. The process of integration involves multiple perspectives, four domains of intelligence (physical, mental, emotional and spiritual) and three levels of awareness (personality, individuality, universality). Integrative leadership is an integral philosophy, a framework model, a set of universal principles, and an emerging practice that informs and helps build a foundation for personal, interpersonal and organizational success.

Our Leadership Beliefs

In our years as reflective practitioners of leadership we have come to believe that leadership is:

- Everyone's business, regardless of position or situation. Everyone has the capacity to lead. Leadership is a choice.
- Development of the whole person. All leadership development is ultimately self-development.
- About people and process, whereas management is about the work and goals. Both are needed for sustainable success.
- About meaningful and purposeful relationships with yourself and others.
- About producing transactional, transformational and transcendent change, individually and organizationally.
- About an outside story (actions, behaviors, opinions) and an inside story (intentions, thoughts, feelings) that require balance, truth, compassion and wisdom to be effectively integrated.
- About learning. Leaders are learners who learn by a) experience, b) accessing role models, coaches, mentors, and counselors, and c) education, training and development. We have found that everyone can, through patient and consistent practice, become a better leader.

We believe that the greatest leverage to being a responsive, Integrative Leader is through personal development addressing multiple perspectives, all four intelligences, all three levels of awareness, and through awakening and effectively using our power of choice.

Evolution and Involution

In leadership development we can move from the outside in, which we call *evolution*, or from the inside out, which we call *involution*. These two forces of change and development have been with us since the beginning of time. If we are influenced more by actions, behaviors and our senses, then we are more evolutionary in our approach to life. If we are influenced more by our core values, beliefs, principles and intuitions that can help us reshape our attitudes and emotions and inform our behaviors, then we are more involutionary. [1]

Both these processes are happening for us simultaneously. We will discuss this further in Chapter 1, with two complementary forces—separation and integration—discussed in Chapter 2.

The Coming Age of Integration

We have moved through various ages in the history of humankind. We have evolved from walking on hind legs nearly ten million years ago to being hunters, gatherers, nomads, shepherds, farmers, industrialists, informationalists and knowledge masters. Today, we are entering a new age of wisdom, synthesis and integration. This new age is the subject of debate on how it will impact our global socio-economic framework over the next decade. Integrative Leaders will thrive in this coming time of transition by willingly awakening, developing and utilizing more of their natural human potential. We will discuss this coming *Age of Integration* more fully in Chapter 3.

Building a Model of Integrative Leadership ™

Multiple Perspectives

Integrative Leaders see the world from multiple perspectives. This is fundamental to developing creativity, adaptability and flexibility. Without this ability, we can only see the world through our own narrow perspective. In any exchange, we need to suspend for a moment our own beliefs and attitudes to allow ourselves to see the others. Without this openness and curiosity about life and people, we remain rigid in our thinking. These rigid beliefs act as barriers to seeing the world as it truly is, and move us instead to seeing our world only as we are.

Four Domains of Intelligence

The four domains of intelligence are physical, mental, emotional and spiritual. The physical involves impulsive, instinctive thinking; the mental involves serial thinking; the emotional, associative thinking; and the spiritual, unitive thinking. The latter three all use the physical domain to express themselves in the world. Whereas management primarily focuses on actions and thoughts, leadership also focuses on feelings and intentions. An Integrative Leader awakens, develops and uses all four domains of intelligence to inform their evaluating, decision-making, problem-solving and planning processes.

Three Levels of Awareness

In our work, we also observed that there are three levels of awareness that influence our journey of life and leadership.

The first level is about our *personality*, our *image of self,* or what we call our *Surreal Self* that we publicly show to the world. This level is often superficial and skims the surface of who we really are, and captures much of our waking attention. When this intoxication with our worldly life becomes unfulfilling, our search for fulfillment can move our attention upwards and inwards to more fully engage our second level of awareness.

Level II awareness is about our *Individuality* or *Character,* that is our more private thoughts and feelings about our world and is the home of our *Real Self*. From Level II awareness, our attention can be drawn back to the noise, glamour and glimmer of Level I awareness, or our search for lasting fulfillment can move our attention higher and more deeply inward to fully engage our Level III awareness.

Level III awareness is about our *Universality* or *Essence* and is the home of our *True Self*. It is the level from which wisdom, higher knowledge, genuine compassion, authentic happiness, original inspirations and higher sensory perception flow into our conscious Level I awareness. This flow serves to not only capture, but also enrapture, enlighten and illuminate our attention.

Our *Ideal* is a consciously formulated image of who we would like to become. It can be attuned to and motivated by any of our three levels of awareness. The highest of what we can conceive as the best of human qualities and virtues is our *Ideal Self*. As we attune, apply and embody our Ideal in our daily life, our knowledge and understanding of our Ideal will evolve and in time, will become more and more aligned, harmonious and resonant with our True Self. This is the aim or goal of the journey and process of integration.

When we compare our Ideal Self to our Real and Surreal Selves, we find that there are some alignments, overlaps and areas of strengths upon which we can build. And we also find that there are misalignments, separations and areas for development. The separation between our three levels of awareness we call the *Being-Knowing-Doing* Gap.[2]

Building on our alignments and strengths while reducing and minimizing these gaps is an essential part of the journey to becoming an Integrative Leader.

A Fifth Domain: The Power of Choice

The method for negotiating through the four domains of our intelligence and the three levels of our awareness is awakening and utilizing our power of will, choice and desire.

For the majority, our will is either mesmerized, hypnotized or asleep while immersed in Level I awareness. Awakening our personal will is a step along the path of integration that is first seen as negation, then negotiation and finally affirmation. The phase of affirmation leads to full conscious, responsible and accountable development of our personal will. The final step on the path towards integration is to allow our personal will to be informed and transformed into our *Higher Will* so that more of our True Self can be embodied in our world.

We will deal more fully with the four domains of intelligence, three levels of awareness and the power of choice in Chapter 4, *Building a Model of Integrative Leadership*.

The Process of Becoming an Integrative Leader

The journey of becoming an Integrative Leader can be described in various ways. It is about making the unconscious conscious. It is about balancing and harmonizing our inner and outer stories. It is about integrating our various personality roles into a more congruent and cohesive whole among many other similar perspectives.

Each leader has a unique path to walk for personal and professional development and integration. However, there are some patterns, perspectives and processes that seem to be the same for all who have successfully walked the path of integrative life and leadership, involving change, choice and approach.

There are three processes of change: transactional, associated with Level I awareness; transformational, associated with Level II awareness; and transcendent, associated with Level III awareness. All three processes are evident in the journey of integrative life and leadership.

There are fundamentally two choices before us in every situation we encounter. We can either react from our past habits and image of self, or respond in accordance with our Ideal Self. One choice leads to sameness and mediocrity and the other to growth and adventure. Cultivating the practice of reflection becomes a key that will help to inform our choice in the present moment.

Just as there are two fundamental choices, there are also two fundamental approaches to the journey of integration. One is the path of struggle. The other is the path of flow. The path of struggle has been called the 'crucible of leadership'[3] and is often characterized by crisis, drama, loss and trauma. Currently, 85% of the world walks the path of struggle. The path of flow has been called 'awakening the soul of leadership' and is characterized by peak experiences, awe, wonder, grace and adventure. Currently, 15% of the world walks the path of flow.[4] Cultivating the practices of awareness and attention will help you apprehend the messages from your inner and outer life that will in turn help your journey of integration have more flow and less struggle.

Chapter 5, *The Process of Becoming an Integrative Leader,* will move into more detail about these aspects of the journey as well as the seven elements of becoming an Integrative Leader.

Guidelines for Becoming an Integrative Leader

The foundational guidelines for the integrative journey are Universal Laws that operate everywhere, all the time, on everyone and everything. They are beyond belief because whether or not you believe in the law of gravity, it still works. Awareness of these Universal Laws and seeking to align, apply and understand them will help you successfully navigate your personal journey of integration.

The eight Universal Laws, twelve principles for strengthening relationships, and twelve Integrative, Transformative & Transcendent (ITT) Practices, if habituated, become a natural life-giving response to the ever changing events of your life.

We will share our understanding of these Universal Laws, principles and associated practices more fully in Chapter 6.

Organizational Integration ™: Building a Living Organization

For an organization to be alive, its constituents must number among the *living* as opposed to the *living dead*. The process of integration is one that helps renew and awaken new life in individuals, and by association, the organizations they serve.

Applying the integrative leadership philosophy, principles and practices to an organization can help its culture transform from a surviving to a thriving one. This process, which we call *Organizational Integration*, will allow the organization to be engaged, enthused and inspired to make a meaningful difference. We will share some further thoughts and ideas about *Organizational Integration* and *Building a Living Organization* in Chapter 7.

An Emerging Integral Philosophy

Over the past three years, Integrative Leadership has evolved into a philosophy, a worldview or an integrative paradigm. The key points that comprise this philosophy are:

- Everybody and every body of knowledge contain a portion of the truth, but no one body at this time contains it all.
- Life is our teacher and our Ideal Self is our guide. Our life provides our life and leadership curriculum.
- Everyone can become their Ideal Self by having the courage to experiment and practice new behaviors.
- The process of becoming our Ideal Self is as important as the goal. Balance between our process and goal orientations is important for successfully walking the path of integration.
- An unreflective life is not worth living. Without regular periodic life reviews, we tend to repeat the mistakes of our past *image of self*.

- We are more than our actions, thoughts and feelings. Within us resides a vast untapped and unexplored sea of energy, information and potential. Tapping into this sea of energy and information and allowing it to move with us and through us becomes the path of flow.
- Higher-order integrative thinking can solve old problems in often unique and surprising ways.
- There is a shadow side and a light side within every leader. Acknowledging and dealing with our shadow side while emphasizing the light side are necessary parts of the process of becoming an Integrative Leader.

We hope that you see a reflection of your own life and leadership journey in John's, Mary's and our own, and that it will give you more clarity, new insights and a heightened awareness of who you are and what you want to do with this gift of life we have all been given.

Summary

Integrative Leadership at a Glance

Introduction:

Integrative life and leadership is a philosophy or approach to living a conscious life. It is about rekindling the curiosity to know yourself (*attitude*), what you are made of (*model*), where you are going *(Ideal)* and discovering what you are here to do (*purpose*). It is a foundational model that draws on the best from scientific research, the best of the wisdom and mystic traditions (*spirituality*) and our own life observations and experiences. It is a set of Universal Laws that frame the process we call walking the path of integration.

The Foundational Integrative Model:

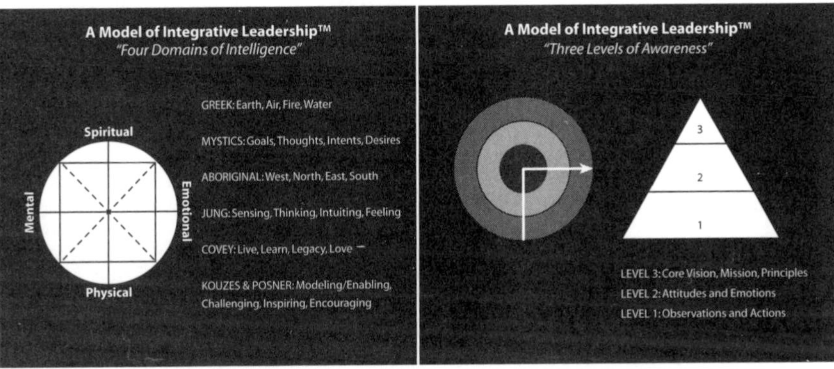

The Process of Walking the Path:

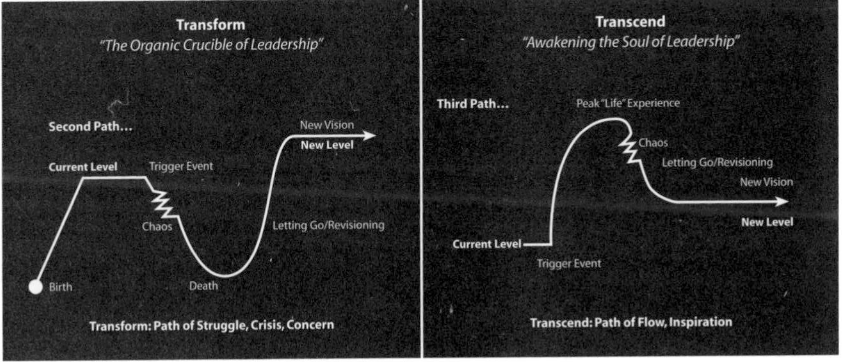

Integrative, Transformative and Transcendent (ITT) Practices:

- **Formulation:** Ideal, Personal Vision, Intent
- **Observation:** Witnessing your life drama
- **Self Awareness:** All domains
- **Relaxation:** Stress Management
- **Concentration:** The Power of Focus
- **Visualization:** Images and Association
- **Meditation:** Inner Power of Silence
- **Contemplation:** Leading a Reflective Life
- **Interpretation:** Nightly Dreams, Visions and Intuitions.
- **Integration:** Attunement, Alignment, Embodiment
- **Application:** Knowledge to Understanding; Understanding to Wisdom

The Seven Elements of Integration:

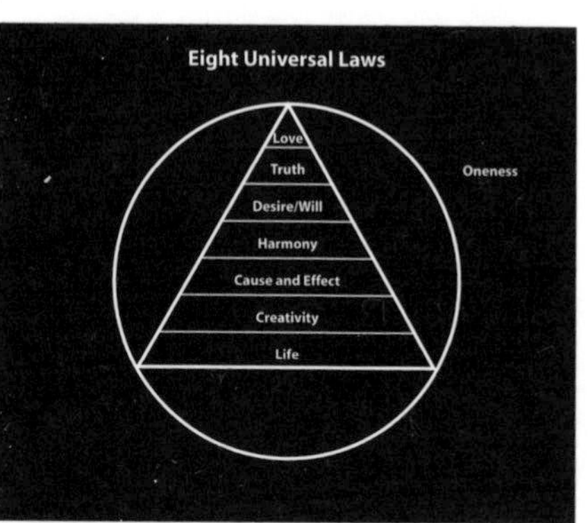

1. **My Ideal** (*Secret*) **Self:** Who do I want to be? What is my vision?
2. **My Mission:** What is my purpose? What do I want to do and whom do I want to serve?
3. **My Surreal** (*Public*) **Self:** Who am I as personality? What are my strengths and gaps?
4. **My Real** (*Private*) **Self:** Who am I as character or individuality? What are my strengths and gaps?

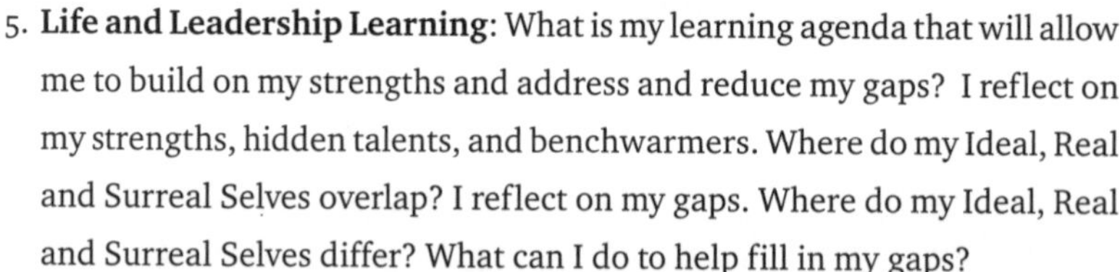

5. **Life and Leadership Learning:** What is my learning agenda that will allow me to build on my strengths and address and reduce my gaps? I reflect on my strengths, hidden talents, and benchwarmers. Where do my Ideal, Real and Surreal Selves overlap? I reflect on my gaps. Where do my Ideal, Real and Surreal Selves differ? What can I do to help fill in my gaps?
6. **Application and Experimentation:** I practice new behaviors, beliefs, feelings and values on the road (preparation, awakening, transforming, transcending, integration) to Mastery
7. **Relations and Associations:** I develop supportive and trusting relationships that make my personal, interpersonal and organizational change possible. Who will support and encourage me as I walk this path of integration?

Chapter 1

Evolution and Involution

"Much as we might wish to believe otherwise, universal love and the welfare of the species as a whole are concepts which simply do not make evolutionary sense."

RICHARD DAWKINS

"God created a number of possibilities in case some of his prototypes failed — that is the meaning of evolution."

GRAHAM GREENE

John's Initial Conditions

JOHN'S LAST QUESTION TO US BEFORE LEAVING HIS OFFICE that first afternoon was to ask how he should tell the news of his condition to others. During our discussion, a communication plan evolved and it was decided his wife should be first to receive full disclosure. Together, they would discuss how to tell their children, who were 16 and 19 years old. His board would then be given full disclosure and, through discussion, would determine the level of disclosure to the rest of the organization.

John committed to beginning the communication process immediately, gave us his organization chart and key personnel files, and penciled in a meeting with us for the following afternoon to formally begin our assignment.

When we returned to our offices, we decided that Rick would be the lead contact with John, while Lillas and our other associates would act as backup and support.

Late that afternoon, Rick opened a file on *Crisis Energy*, combined their meeting notes and under *Observations* wrote:

> John is physically in bad shape. He looks far worse than when I saw him several years ago. He has deep lines under his eyes, a pale complexion, graying hair and appears not just overweight but puffy. I feel these are symptoms, not just of his physical illness, but of a mental, emotional and spiritual illness as well.
>
> John was understandably acting distraught given the morning's diagnosis and prognosis. During our three-hour conversation, he had become more and more animated and agitated, periodically getting up to pace around his office, waving his arms and telling the floor — rather than looking at and telling us — his personal and corporate story. It was all very dramatic....
>
> While our conversation was taking place, secretaries and other employees kept interrupting us to get his opinion, signature or what seemed to us trivial advice, even though we had heard him tell his assistant that he did not want to be disturbed during our meeting. John had to take two urgent phone calls from his people overseas who were a third of the way around the world and nine hours distant in time. The telephone conversations lasted nearly 40 minutes while Lillas and I patiently sat waiting for him to continue his background story.

"From the little I've observed, John has created a totally dependent and tightly controlled organization that cannot make a move without him." Rick said to Lillas on their way home that night.

"I agree," Lillas replied. "Which means we probably won't be successful in finding a replacement for John within his current organization." After a pause, she added, "More importantly than John's replacement, do you think, given his prognosis, that there is anything we can do to help him get better?"

"I do." Rick affirmed. "But any option we suggest has to speak into his listening, be understood and leave him with a deep sense of hope. In the end, it will take courage for him to consider walking another path than the one he is currently on." After investing time in discussing various perspectives, they both agreed their strongest argument about inviting John to walk the path of integrative life and leadership was, "*What has John got to lose?*"

Mary's Initial Conditions

In a similar way to John and his *Crisis Energy* assignment, we agreed the lead with Mary's coaching would be Lillas, with support from Rick and our other associates.

In the first two sessions of Mary's integrative coaching, much effort was spent on understanding where she was in her journey. Like consulting a map, any journey begins first by finding out where you are on multiple levels and from various perspectives, then deciding where you would like to go in terms of an Ideal, and finally mapping out an optimum route on how best to get there.

To find her "*You are Here*" arrow, Lillas had Mary fill out a number of in-depth situational questionnaires, personality profiles, emotional and social intelligence tests, and spiritual intelligence assessments. She also asked probing and open-ended questions during their coaching sessions.

From the results of the assessments and conversations, Lillas felt that she had a good understanding of Mary as *personality*, Mary as *individuality* and Mary as *universality* and the Ideal she desired to become. From those same assessments, Lillas had also identified some key issues and gaps within her four domains and three levels of awareness that needed more open discussion.

Lillas knew from experience that one aspect of the journey was to help awaken Mary consciously to what was driving her actions unconsciously, and she felt this was the time to bring up Mary's issues.

"Mary, in our first session I asked you what you wanted to be different in your life. Do you remember how you answered?" Lillas asked, looking up from her notes at the beginning of their third session.

"Yes. I said on the outside everything was fine. I said I loved my Human Resources work and felt I was making a positive difference in people's lives, despite disagreeing with many of my company's methods. I said I have a good husband and three incredible young adult children who are managing to find their way in the world."

"So what's the problem?" Lillas asked innocently. "It sounds to me like you're living a wonderful life."

"It sounds like it, doesn't it?" Mary agreed, looking away. "That's one perspective on my life. But another perspective is that I feel exhausted all the time. I've been suffering from adult onset of asthma and sinusitis for the past eight years. That could be part of it. But there are times when I stop doing and doing, when everyone is out and I'm home alone, that I'm overcome with feelings of sadness, loneliness and despair. In those times it's as if I've lost something, but I don't know what it is. I'm confused. I'm not clear. I try and think and feel and reflect and journalize, but in the end I don't know what it is that is troubling me. It's as if there's a big hole in my heart or a deep pit in my stomach that I can't fill. When I begin to feel myself moving into that state of confusion and despair, I've learned to busy myself into forgetfulness and start *doing* all over again." Mary paused and looked up, "And I feel exhausted all the time, Lillas."

"What have you done about these feelings in the past?"

"I've consulted with my Doctor. She prescribed anti-depressants, but I've never taken them," Mary said. "It seems that half the people in our company are on some form of anti-depressant just to keep them working. I don't think that people should be drugged into doing their work and being only half-alive in their lives. That may be what they want, but that isn't what I want." Mary concluded.

"And what is it you want, Mary?"

"I want to be healthy and happy. I want to feel energy and vitality, not just on the outside but on the inside as well. I want a softer, gentler and more balanced life," Mary said raising her arms questioningly. "Why is it that my life, from one perspective, is so rich and full and from another perspective so poor and unfulfilling?" Mary paused, looked deeply at Lillas and asked, "I feel like I'm dying, Lillas, and have been for a very long time. Can you help me to live again?"

Growth, Crisis and Renewal

The central problem in unstable organizations in turbulent environments is that the situations in which managers find themselves are not just uncertain, they are equivocal.

David K. Hurst

As Rick waited in the 29th-floor reception area the following afternoon for his meeting with John, he reviewed his notes, thoughts, and strategies, and John's history and involvement with *Crisis Energy*.

John had started the company more than three years earlier with two partners: a well-connected financial person he knew in Toronto and an in-country specialist on the Former Soviet Union (FSU). Together, they had accurately surmised that the domestic market was overheated. Prices for oil and gas were high and, in their opinion, not sustainable. They felt they should try to position their start-up company in the FSU because of the availability of proven undeveloped reserves and prices that were low and controlled, but rising to meet world market prices in a predictable fashion.

With that strategy in mind, John had managed to find an opportunity in the FSU, had raised private funds from high net-worth individuals and institutions with his Toronto partner, and assembled people to help them develop and operate the opportunities in-country with his FSU advisor and partner.

John felt that the first year was his best year, with all the excitement of building a Value Centered International Energy Company while drawing on his previous domestic company-building experiences. The second and third years were the hardest times John had ever experienced in his life, and both Rick and Lillas felt it was this past circumstance that had contributed to his present illness.

In year two of *Crisis Energy*, things had started to go badly on many levels.

Technically, the project that they initially acquired did not work, and they had to scramble to find another project to develop in the western region since they had already invested in the infrastructure but now had no project to support it. Competitively, one of the major global fully-integrated energy companies was encroaching on a property on which they had made a deal and felt was theirs in the eastern region of the country.

"In the Former Soviet Union, you have to understand that each country was historically run like a giant centralized company, with divisions in agriculture, energy, industry, services and education," John had explained. "Without government support in a command-and-control economy, nothing in private business happens. FSU governments prefer to deal with major foreign energy companies, and not the minor ones like us, and that is why we were in danger of losing the deal on that significant eastern oil and gas property."

Economically, their prediction of overheated oil and gas prices was correct, but no one had foreseen the depth of the crash when prices rapidly descended to their lowest levels in twelve years.

"We had raised money in year one in the belief that we had a foundation in the West and a major project in the East, and now we were in danger of losing it all due to early technical failures, collapsing prices and major foreign competition," John said.

Rick had remembered, as John was relating his story, that at that time entire economic regions were collapsing due to low world commodity prices, from Asia to Latin America, with only North America and Western Europe (the major energy consumers) maintaining any sense of economic stability.

To capture the eastern opportunity, which was his operational hope, John needed more money than he had raised to date. With the technical and economic failure in the west, his initial cash in the company was running out. He needed to slow down spending while continuing to raise additional funds, which was a delicate balancing act.

"It was like walking a tight rope. On one side was the devil of personal and family bankruptcy, on the other was the deep blue storm-tossed financial sea in which the global economy was drowning entire regions of the world, and in front of me was a dark and mysterious abyss that was the future of the company," John said.

John rose to the challenge, set an almost impossible goal for himself and his company, and made a Herculean effort to raise the funds his company needed in an unfriendly environment.

In that final financing campaign, John felt alone, alienated and abandoned by everyone in his life. His partners had walked away, deeming the project to be hopeless in that financially toxic environment. His board members felt that he had done enough and recommended that he simply let the company go into bankruptcy. His friends could not understand his passion and energy for keeping the company alive, but also noted the toll it was taking on his life. And his wife shook her head in shocked disbelief at the rare times he made it home from his globetrotting financing campaign.

"No one could understand why I did what I had done," John had said.

But against all odds, he had persevered. He was determined to achieve his goal of saving the company, or die trying. Despite three failed attempts within eighteen months, *Crisis Energy* was one of only two companies in the world to successfully raise funds during that desperate time. He had won the game, raised the funds needed for the company to survive and now managed and led his company with an iron fist. And the final irony was that although his company had survived, it looked like John would not. He had won the *battle,* but in the end was in serious danger of losing the *war.*

A Story of Evolution and Involution

> *Supermind is the vast self-extension of the Brahman that contains and develops.... It possesses the power of development, of evolution, of making explicit, and that power carries with it the other power of involution, of envelopment, of making implicit. In a sense, the whole of creation may be said to be a movement between two involutions, Spirit in which all is involved and out of which all evolves downward to the other pole of Matter, Matter in which all is involved and out of which all evolves upwards to the other pole of Spirit.*
>
> Sri Aurobindo

Rick had reflected on the presenting situation and subsequently discussed the strategy for approaching John with Lillas. Their initial assessment of John was that he was a curious mix of leadership styles—visionary, inspiring and forward-looking on one hand, and balanced by a very pragmatic action orientation on the other. His current mental model for management and leadership had worked to this point in his life.

For John to begin to see another approach to life and leadership, Rick felt he needed to share their research on two crucial forces that seemed to weave their way through history. One force was evolution and the other was involution.

When Rick finally met John that afternoon (John was predictably late for their meeting), they first discussed the effectiveness of the communication strategy. In John's opinion it had not gone well with his wife and children the previous night, or with some of his board members that morning. John was not all that concerned about the board members' reactions, but he was with his wife's.

"It was odd, Rick. Diane was not emotional about my health crisis, not like our kids, but took the news quietly and calmly. It was as if she knew or had been expecting it," John said, a bit puzzled.

After his discussion with the board, they had decided that the rest of the organization would be told that John wanted to spend more time with his family and would be moving away from an active Executive role in the company, while not disclosing his illness to employees at this time. The company, in order to fulfill John's wishes, would begin searching for his replacement immediately, and Rick and Lillas's firm had been hired to handle that task.

John and Rick discussed key board members and internal personnel who Rick wanted to interview as part of the Executive placement assignment.

With immediate business out of the way, Rick focused his attention on how to help John in his personal transition.

"John, do you believe that life is purposeful and meaningful, or random and accidental?" Rick asked, which made John think before he answered.

"I would say it's a bit of both. The things I can control, like the financing campaign, capital expenditures or operations of the company, are purposeful and meaningful to me. The things I can't control—like the price of oil and gas, government policies and my illness—I would say were more accidental," John replied, sipping his afternoon coffee.

"Most people would agree. Rather than two perspectives, purposeful or accidental, they end up with a third, which is a blending of the two that sounds something like, 'Life is purposeful, but shit happens.' I think that is the first confusion in terms of your beliefs and something I would like to discuss with you."

"Are you going to get philosophical on me, Rick?" John asked narrowing his eyes. "I don't have time for this."

Rick smiled at John's reaction and said, "One of the reasons you called us was to help you try and understand what has happened to you, John. We thought about it and felt this is the best way to start. And I assure you, my story won't take nearly as long as yours did yesterday afternoon!"

That brought a smile to John's face, and he relaxed and allowed Rick to continue.

Rick described their work the past few years in which they had recognized recurring patterns or themes in their own lives that they also saw in the lives of others. In their research they had taken a step back in order to gain perspective and could see similar patterns, themes and stories recurring throughout history.

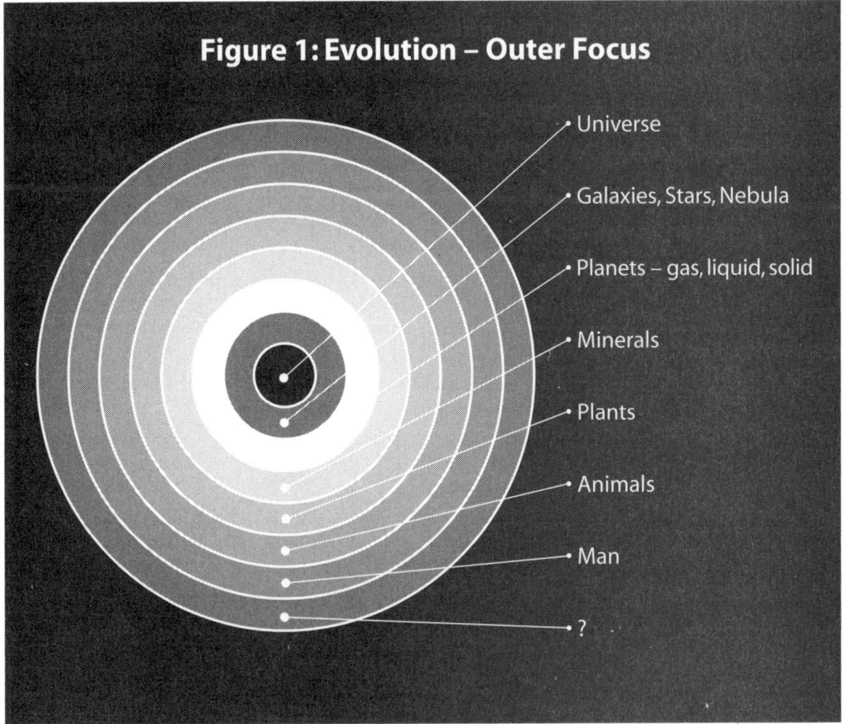

"One is a familiar story that is grounded in scientific inquiry, empiricism and observation, which is the story of *evolution*. The other is not as familiar. It is grounded in the world's wisdom and mystic traditions and is called *involution*," Rick said, reaching into his briefcase and placing several pictures on the conference table before them. "Each story influences the way we see our world and our place in it. In our work on integrative life and leadership, this is where we sometimes begin our conversations, asking which story you believe. You told me John, that you believe in both."

To which John nodded, leaned forward and studied the pictures of concentric circles that lay on the table in front of him.

"Evolution is a perspective that describes how events happen to us from the outside in, John.

"The inner ring is the 'Big Bang' theory Edwin Hubble first proposed in 1929 that is still upheld by the scientific community.[1] The 'Big Bang', which happened some 12 billion years ago, scientists believe was caused by a singularity—an accidental coming together of initial conditions at the beginning of time—that formed high energy particles which eventually

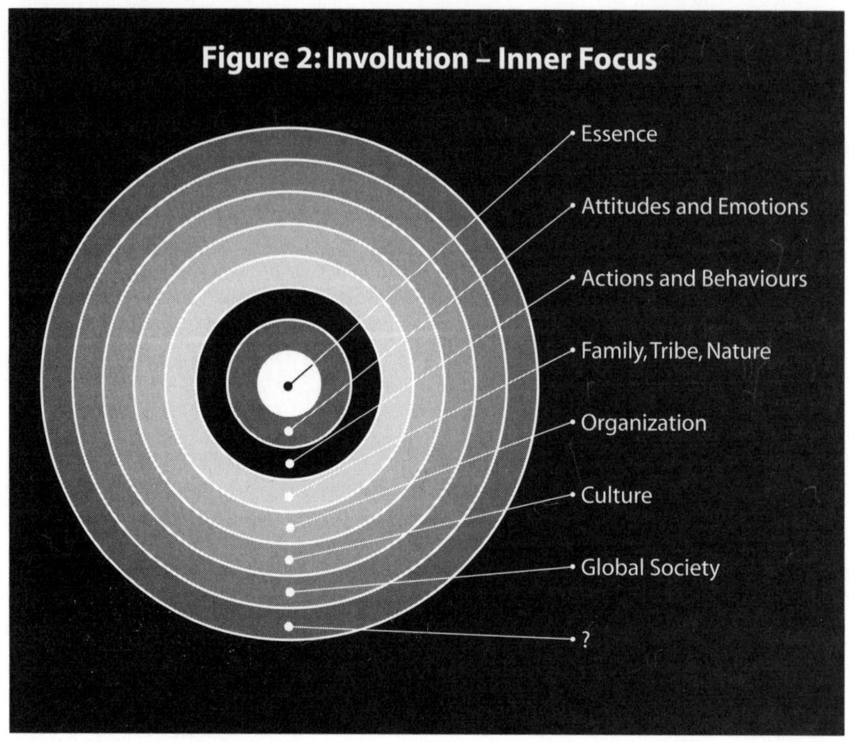

condensed into galaxies, stars and nebula," Rick said pointing to the second ring. "The third ring is where the planets further condensed from gas to liquid to solid. The fourth ring is minerals, the fifth is plants, the sixth is animals and the seventh ring is the evolution of humankind."

"Those would be the four kingdoms that at one time or another ruled the earth; mineral, plant, animal and today, humankind," John said.

"Exactly," Rick replied, looking pleased. "And each one of those kingdoms is with us and within us."

He then pointed at the rings again. "Now, the time between the third ring, or Earth's formation, and today is about 4 billion years. The time between the sixth and seventh rings, or humankind's evolution, is about 10 million years. The time that we have a historical record of us being around as we are today is perhaps 10,000 years."

"Not a very long time to make such a mess of things on Earth," John said. Then he pointed to the question mark on the outer ring. "What's the eighth ring?" John asked. "Is that where man evolves into superman?" Rick smiled and suggested they leave that discussion for now, and continued.

"You can see evidence of this grand evolutionary story everywhere as Darwin, Sedgwick and Henslow did nearly 150 years ago.[2] Darwin felt, in his principle of natural selection, that 'it was not the strongest of the species that survives, nor the most intelligent, but the one most responsive to change.' This story of evolution is replayed on the stages of human, management and leadership development. It is replayed in the environmental forces that shape and reshape natural ecological systems. It is replayed in our culture, community and organizations.

"And," Rick said with emphasis, pausing to look into John's eyes, "we see this grand story reflected in our own lives."

"For example, the story you shared with us yesterday, John, has elements of evolution where the environment was adversely effecting your company with low oil prices, foreign government policies and non-supportive internal relationships. You chose to become the hero of your own crisis drama. You responsively adapted your company to survive the crisis and then, against all odds, you raised the necessary funds to allow it to possibly thrive once again. It might not have been the smartest thing you could have done, according to your partners, board, friends and family, but it was the way you responded to the external threat, managed the change, and in the short term won the battle."

John leaned back in his chair and nodded reflectively, saying, "I understand. This macroscopic evolutionary force for change, as you call it, affects and impacts on our relatively microscopic lives."

"Exactly," Rick said. "The macro story effects our micro story. The wisdom traditions would say, 'As above, so is it below. As without, so is it within'. But they also say, 'As within, so is it without' that leads us into the second, less familiar story."

"This second picture is an involutionary perspective that describes how events happen to us from the inside-out. Given your applied science and engineering background, it may be a bit harder to swallow, so I would suggest we take this one slowly," Rick said with some concern.

"The inner ring is where someone or something, which most traditions refer to as the Creator, said 'Let there be light' in the universe, and there was light. The second ring is the formation of the patterns, ideas and thoughts we call *mind* and the desires that are often contained within emotions. The third ring is an expression of light from the first ring with patterns and desires from the second ring, both of which form our physical bodies in the third ring that is the Earth." Rick paused and asked, "Are you still with me, John?"

"I've heard this story before, when they read Genesis to us in Sunday school," John replied sitting back, "but not in the way you are describing it."

"What I am saying, according to many of the wisdom and mystic traditions—not just Christianity—is the first creation is in spirit; the second is in the mind which is shaped by desire, and the third is the physical expressions, actions, behaviors, and opinions that we can see, hear, touch, taste or smell while we are here on Earth," Rick said tapping his finger on the table. "The fourth ring is our family of origin and tribe that establishes our initial relationship with nature. The fifth ring is our principle organizational affiliation. The sixth is our culture and the seventh is our global relationship as citizens of the earth."

"If I put these pictures of evolution and involution side by side, then you can see more clearly the relationship between these two stories." Rick said moving them together.

"What we are suggesting is that at some level, by journeying inward towards what we are calling our *Essence*, we can understand the very beginning of the universe. This is what the mystics have been saying for thousands of years. To be 100% objective, we need to become 100% subjective, where our inner and outer stories become reconciled.

"This is the philosophy behind the journey of integrative life and leadership," Rick concluded, and reached down to set a diagram beside the pictures. "This is what these two forces look like when we've tried to translate them into words and ideas."

John examined the table that illustrated the differences between the story of evolution and the story of involution and discussed the specific choices of words, categories and meanings. Satisfied with their discussion, he said, "What you're saying is that by moving inside I have a chance of changing my outside. This is not new, and the fact is, it has been done many times and in many places before."

"Exactly right, John." Rick continued, "A way to see the relationship between spirit, mind and body in this involutionary story is to imagine yourself in a movie theater. Your attention is focused on the drama in the film: you may feel a rush of emotions; you may get challenged by ideas and try to figure out the plot; you might even learn something from the

Table 1: Comparison of Evolution and Involution

Type	Evolution	Involution
Creation	Big Bang Theory	'Let There Be Light'
Paradigm	Western	Eastern
Influence	Outside In	Inside Out
Approach	Hierarchy	Community
Desires	Embodiment	Attunement
Preference	Creativity	Receptivity
Thinking Style	Analysis	Synthesis
Type	Objective	Subjective
Perspective	Scientific	Spiritual
Orientation	History	Possibility

experience. But if you took the time to refocus your attention, disengage and turn around, you would see that a beam of moving light was creating the picture on the screen which for that moment was your reality. And you would see that the patterns on the film were transforming the light into your mental movie images. Now, if you were to back up one more step, you would then see that behind the film was a pure white light or essence that projected through the film and caused the moving pictures that shaped your reality. Without the light from your essence, you have no life. To change your life, you must change the belief patterns in your own mind."

John nodded and summarized his understanding: "In your evolutionary story, cause and effect happens from the outside in. You are suggesting, in your involutionary story, that cause and effect happens from the inside out." John was thoughtful. "What you are *really* suggesting, Rick, is that somehow I am the cause of my own illness."

Rick was silent, watching John's reaction to his own insight. When he seemed calm and thoughtful rather than angry or defensive, Rick felt it was safe to continue. "From the involutionary perspective, that is true, John. I heard Stephen Covey say it this way: 'In all my experience I have never seen lasting solutions to problems, lasting happiness and success, that came from the outside in.'[3] Many great ideas, philosophies, inventions, innovations and discoveries that we have researched these past three years began from the inside out through visions, dreams, inspirations and intuitions, and not from the outside in. I know that you've had them too, John, while building your own businesses." John nodded.

"What is also interesting in our research is that for the past hundred years, many scientists, psychologists and philosophers in the West—even with their predominantly external scientific focus—have championed bringing knowledge and practices from the East—with their predominantly internal spiritual focus—and have endeavored to combine these two paradoxical paradigms into a third higher order, wholistic and integrative paradigm.

"If you choose to walk the path of integration, John, I can assure you from personal experience that at some level of your own awareness, involution and evolution will be reconciled."

Rick paused as John sat digesting and reflecting on their conversation. During the pause, Rick went within himself and felt confirmation that it was the right time to ask the question he had come to ask that afternoon.

"John, are you willing to try on an involutionary belief that your *whole* life is purposeful and meaningful, and not just part of it? If you can do that for a time, then our job together is to help you find that purpose and meaning for yourself. And, in the process, we just might be able to help positively influence your prognosis by working with you from the inside out."

Rick waited as John sat quietly looking at the concentric circles and the diagram for what seemed like a very long time. He could see the internal struggle play itself across John's face.

Finally John shrugged, looked up and said, "What have I got to lose?"

• • •

A Chance to Live Again

I knew the work was suffocating my soul,
but to admit it would be too devastating;
it would mean that I had to do something about it.

John Izzo & Eric Klein
[testimony from a client]

Lillas looked compassionately at Mary and said that she would do everything she could to help her to live again if Mary was willing to do the same for herself. "We were all innocent at one time in our lives. Part of the process of integration, wholeness and healing is about reclaiming that innocence."

Lillas brought out a chart that described involution and evolution and placed it on the coffee table between them. "This is one way that we see the world, Mary. There are two forces that seem to interplay in our lives. One is evolution and the changes that we make to adapt to our external environment. The other is involution, which is the changes that we make to adapt to our internal environment. One of these approaches is your preferred way to be in the world. Which would you say it is in this present moment?"

Mary looked at the chart and asked for an explanation of some of the words and then said, "I think I am more internally than externally oriented. At this time I feel more connected within and less connected without. So I would have to say that I believe more in involution than evolution, in community rather than hierarchy, in bringing things together in some form of relationship rather than breaking them apart in analysis."

Mary paused in her examination of the chart pointed to a word and asked, "What do you mean by spirituality, Lillas? Is that the same as being religious?"

"No, spirituality and religion are not necessarily the same thing. Religion is primarily about beliefs, whereas spirituality is primarily about experience. I once heard someone say religion was for people who were afraid to go to hell. Spirituality is for people who have been there," Lillas said with a smile.

"In that case, I must be very spiritual," Mary said with a laugh, "because it feels like I've been in my own version of hell for a very long time."

"At one time or another, we all have been there. But the good news is that in this integrative journey we have the chance to invite a portion of heaven into our earth," Lillas added with another smile.

"We feel, Mary, that spirituality honors our personal experience and helps reshape our beliefs to align with those experiences. Religion often is in opposition to personal or objective experience, honoring beliefs and suppressing, repressing or discarding our personal experience. This has been the struggle between science and religion, reality and superstition since the Age of Enlightenment 300 years ago.

"The process of integration, as we have experienced it, is about alignment so that our intentions, beliefs, desires and actions become congruent. As Integrative Leaders, we don't say one thing and do another, feel one thing and think another, purpose one thing and act another." Mary nodded and Lillas continued.

"Your profile suggests that you have an introspective, intuitive and feeling personality, Mary, which suggests, as you have said, that you tend toward an involutionary approach to life in which you pay attention to your intuitions and feelings, which are internal, more than to your external sensory experiences.

"With your type of profile, it is easy and natural for you to meditate, contemplate and attune to your Ideal Self, but it is much more challenging for you to embody it. In other words, you know what you should be doing, but you are having difficulty doing it.

"In order to unify these two forces in the journey of integrative life and leadership, we need to balance our conscious *evolutionary attunement* with our *involutionary embodiment*. We know from experience that this integration can only happen through an awakened heart that is the home of our emotional intelligence."

Lillas leaned forward. "All of my observations and your assessments are telling me that somewhere within you, you already know what the problem of the missing piece of your life truly is. What do you feel intuitively it could be? Are you willing and ready to name it, Mary?"

Mary looked away from Lillas, bit her bottom lip and remained silent, playing nervously with the molding that outlined the love seat in which she sat. After what seemed a quiet eternity, she looked up at Lillas with moist eyes and said slowly and deliberately, "I'm missing love in my life. I don't feel I love my husband anymore, and haven't for a long time. And he doesn't really love me, and maybe never has."

After she spoke her truth, Mary covered her face with both hands and sobbed.

Chapter 2

Separation and Integration

The mind is involved in analysis where things are broken down into pieces and examined. The heart on the other hand deals with bringing the pieces together.

CARL JUNG

AT THIS STAGE, we were pleased with where Mary and John had chosen to be in their journeys. Their recent breakthroughs, we felt, were not just steps, but more like leaps along their personal paths towards integration.

John had willingly chosen to re-evaluate his long-standing beliefs about the world and try out a new belief, model or paradigm in which he was willing to consider his life and all events in it as meaningful and purposeful. Mary, in naming a long-standing issue that she knew unconsciously had been there all along, was now in a position to begin to consciously and thoughtfully deal with it.

We felt that John, who was very externally focused in his life and work, needed to begin his journey within, become aware of his Real Self and make efforts to come to know and attune to his *Ideal Self*. Mary, who was very internally focused, needed to begin to express and embody her *Ideal Self* and be willing to inform her individuality and reshape her personality to allow her Ideal Self to more fully express itself.

From experience, we knew that neither process would be easy. John and Mary would need courage to try out new beliefs and behaviors and establish new habits that would allow them to walk their personal journeys successfully.

At this point in our consulting and coaching of John and Mary, we wondered whether we should openly introduce into their sessions two complementary, supportive, emergent and resultant processes to involution and evolution — separation and integration — or if we should simply highlight them when they occurred.

We allowed ourselves two days to connect, reflect, intuit and introspect on this question before we decided exactly what each of us should do.

Separation and Integration

> *There are no grounds for believing that the movement of conjoining and dispersing is either with or without purpose. Nor are there any grounds for commenting on whether those movements are the mischief of blind, mechanical, physical nature or the wonderful creation of an artistic, universal mind. It is all the same when one has the insight to see the deep nature of things. It is different when one is bewildered by the diversified movements on the surface of reality.*
>
> LAO TZU

We had experienced the processes of *separation* and *integration* playing out in our own walks along the path of integrative life and leadership and in the lives of others who had chosen this journey. We also saw these processes operating in the history of humankind as meta-forces that played a role in the cycles of growth, decline and renewal within societies, cultures and civilizations. We saw them again, operating under different names, in the hard and soft sciences, wisdom and mystic traditions and in personal and organizational development.

In science, the ultimate form of separation is called reductionism, which is the sequential breaking down of things or problems in order to understand the whole. This analytical paradigm has led to the fragmentation and compartmentalization of many scientific disciplines. Today there is a growing need for an Integrative Science that will assist in the transition from the Age of Reason to an Age of Synthesis or Integration.

In the two-thousand-year history of Christianity and the Church, forces for integration were evident in the early conversion of the Roman Empire, institutionalization and the eventual evangelization of the new worlds of Africa, North and South America, India, China and Japan. The forces of separation were also evident and variously described as the great Schism,

Reformation, Age of Enlightenment and Communism that resulted in the splitting of the one original Christian root into thousands of Christian sects now operating all over the world. Today, there is a growing movement to search for an integration of these various divisions and fragmentations, described as Ecumenism within Christianity, and Spirituality within congresses of the world's wisdom traditions

In Communism, the forces of *integration* that brought the USSR together nearly a century ago gave way to the forces of *separation* with the fall of the Berlin wall in 1989. Subsequently, the forces of integration were active in the reunion of Eastern and Western Germany.

The United Nations (UN), European Economic Community (EEC) and North American Free Trade Agreement (NAFTA) are examples of a global force of international *integration*, just as the World Bank, International Monetary Fund (IMF) and World Trade Organization (WTO) are forces of global economic *integration*.

In organizations, we see these two forces operating as acquisition and divestment, consolidation and diversification, centralization and decentralization, creation and dissolution, or death and renewal.

What was intriguing was that wherever we looked — science and technology, spirituality and religion, philosophy and psychology, governments, organizations and individuals — there was a motivation, need and desire for integration that pulsed and throbbed at the very heart of our current time of transition.

What was also intriguing was that we observed two constants that appeared against a background of the rise and fall of empires, cultures, societies, ideologies and civilizations.

The first constant was an upward growth — what Jacob Bronowski eloquently called the *Ascent of Man* — as the primary forces of evolution and involution positively influenced the development of humankind.[1] Even though, from a limited perspective or a short cycle of time, we could see evidence of decline, in the long run the gains achieved exceeded the losses grieved.

The second constant was that all revolutions, all changes brought on by the secondary forces of separation and integration, first began with an individual, then with a group, and then among the masses and classes. We see that Christianity arose from the teachings and spirit of Jesus Christ. Communism arose from the philosophy, thoughts and ideas of Karl Marx.

The theory of evolution arose from the studies of Charles Darwin. The League of Nations arose from the inspiration of Woodrow Wilson. Buddhism arose from the life of Siddhartha Guatama, the original Buddha. Islam arose from Mohammed, Judaism from Abraham, and so on.

So to effect meaningful change within the life and leadership of an organization, that change must first begin with the individual.

First to the Individual

To put the world right in order, we must first put the nation in order; to put the nation in order, we must first put the family in order; to put the family in order, we must first cultivate our personal life; we must first set our hearts right.

CONFUCIUS

The State is to make what is useful. The individual is to make what is beautiful.

OSCAR WILDE

From the evolutionary perspective, our first separation — from integrative union with our mothers in the womb — activated within us a yearning and desire to return to that same feeling of peace, nurturing and safety we had known in the beginning. The Yin of our first separation (birth) yearned for the Yang of our first integration (mother's womb) in order to once again feel balanced and whole.

From the involutionary perspective, our first separation (either by choice, necessity or desire, depending on the creation myth) from the pulsing, rhythmic and nurturing spiritual womb that is the One Source or First Cause gave birth to our *Soul*. Within us is an often unconscious yearning and desire to return to that same feeling of peace, joy, love, wonder and bliss that our Souls had known in the very beginning. The Yin of our Soul is searching for the Yang of our Spiritual Source so that we might once more become fully integrated, balanced and whole.

The purpose of both internal and external processes was to come to know ourselves as unique and individual, yet at one with the collective whole of humanity, nature and all things sacred and secular. Our separated selves and our separated souls have a natural yearning to return to that same sense of oneness or integration that we remember from the beginning.

From the involutionary perspective, confusion arises at our birth into the physical world when our growing ego that informs and shapes our personality, seeks the fulfillment of its natural desires externally and falls asleep to its supernatural desire for union and integration with a Higher Order Essence, or True Self, internally.

At the physical birth of our conscious awareness in the earth, we often become conditioned to satisfy our desire for integration through external relationships, challenges and achievements. We are motivated by security, social acceptance and self-worth. We become intoxicated with ourselves, relentlessly seeking sensual gratification through sex, money, earthly influence and power. We fall asleep, become mesmerized or hypnotized by the allure of our own self-created reality, a personal drama that is projected through our often-limiting and unaligned beliefs, and repeated like old worn-out movies onto the screen of our life.

In this process, we often forget our True Self — which by choice could become our Ideal Self — and also forget that the only path to true and lasting health, happiness, wealth, wisdom and abundance is not found externally, but is found by awakening and consciously beginning our journey within.

Separate to Integrate and Integrate to Separate

I have of late grown intrigued by the idea that separating out the elements of an experience, then putting them together again, may help me understand other things that seem impossibly, dauntingly difficult. I am trying to grasp what is at the essence of things that have already happened, of historical events. This strikes me as important, even urgent, because what we believe about our past dictates what we think about the present, and our expectations about the shape of the future.

Erna Paris

During our time on this Earth, we enter into many different kinds of interpersonal relationships: from the superficial to the sublime, from the imposed to the invited, or from the fully human to the fully divine.

In our experience, there is no greater opportunity for growth and development than when we choose to enter into an intimate relationship with ourselves and with others.

We found our experience reflected in the ancient Hindu wisdom traditions, where it is suggested that in order to successfully walk the path of enlightenment, the process is not to *separate* oneself from family and society and seek inner communion in a desert, cave or mountaintop alone; rather, the advice is that if one truly desires to attain a state of integration and enlightenment, one should enter the marketplace and get fully involved in intimate relationships. In this resulting crucible of life and leadership, the behaviors, beliefs, attitudes and unhealed emotions that stop you from fulfilling your desire for integration will be fully revealed.

When we chose to consciously embark on our personal journeys of integration and strove to align with our True Selves by becoming our Ideal Selves in the world, when we eventually entered fully into an intimate relationship with one another, we found that we would *integrate in order to separate* and *separate in order to integrate*.

Our Ideal for entering an intimate loving relationship was to help each other become the best we could be for ourselves, each other and the world. In making that choice, we agreed to act as a mirror for each other, reflecting back to one another our own illusions, shadows and false beliefs that were the blocks that prevented us from becoming our Ideal Selves. Without an intimate relationship, born of a mutual desire for growth and support, neither one of us would have been able to so quickly and clearly see and deal constructively with our own self-created blocks to integration.

In this way, we chose to *integrate* within our relationship in order to effectively separate the wheat from the chaff, life-giving from death-dealing beliefs, and constructive from destructive attitudes we had clung to in our past.

In the journey of integrative life and leadership, in our daily transactions, our transcendent peak experiences, and through the crucibles of transformative learning, we discovered also how to separate in order to effectively *integrate*.

When we separate, we may choose to analyze rather than synthesize for a time. We may break things apart in an effort to understand before putting them back together. We may leave existing relationships with family, friends or work or in turn they may choose to leave us. We may choose a "time out" if we find ourselves in the midst of an emotionally charged encounter by taking a walk, pausing for reflection, journalizing our thoughts and feelings, or meditating to gain perspective.

In experiencing the processes of separation and integration, an emergent guiding principle for us became "life is our teacher and our Ideal is our guide." Another aspect that emerged was a series of Integrative Transformative & Transcendent (ITT) practices that helped us walk this journey of integration successfully.

The path of integrative life and leadership is about bringing our inner and outer stories together in alignment, balance and harmony. It is about awakening to the importance—for those immersed in an Evolutionary Western paradigm—of our search within, just as those immersed in the Involutionary Eastern paradigm need to be of more service and make a meaningful and purposeful contribution without.

Our natural and supernatural desire for integration is the result of our initial separation. Our desire for growth, harmony and balance leads us on an evolutionary path that, if we awaken and choose, may be informed and guided by an involutionary path. One path is characterized by struggle. The other is characterized by flow.

The choice of which path you choose to walk is up to you.

Preparation or Emergence

> *It is from the numberless diverse acts of courage and belief that human history is shaped. Each time a man [or woman] stands up for an Ideal; or acts to improve the lot of others; or strikes out against injustices; they send out [from themselves] a tiny ripple of hope [into our world]. And crossing each other from a million different centers of energy and daring, these ripples [at first] build a current, [then a wave], which can sweep down even the mightiest walls of oppression or resistance.*
>
> Robert F. Kennedy

We met two days later at our favorite coffee house to discuss the benefits and challenges of preparing John and Mary for the concepts of *separation* and *integration*, versus simply waiting until these processes emerged in their own journeys and highlighting them.

We felt that John was already in the process of *separation* by voluntarily leaving his position as Chief Executive Officer of *Crisis Energy*, so for John, beginning his inner journey was of more practical value than sharing another aspect of integrative philosophy. Mary, in speaking her truth about the lack of love in her intimate relationship, had set the course for coaching that would naturally include separation and integration — divorce or recommitment, death or renewal — as part of her process, and that meant there was no need to bring them up as a separate issue.

Feeling satisfied with our decision, we speculated on the many possible outcomes of our integrative coaching and consulting sessions. We knew from personal experience, that as one person changes in a relationship, all people that surround and support that relationship also feel the impact and have an opportunity to change. Like a stone thrown into a still-calm pond, the resulting ripples flow, touch and affect the whole pond and not just a portion.

And, we wondered what impact John's and Mary's changes would ultimately have on all the intimate and distant others in their lives.

Stepping on the Path

[...if you live in truth,] you will know the truth and the truth will set you free....
And they that practice the truth move towards the light
so that all their actions may be seen.

John 8:32, 3:21

After Mary named her lack of loving intimacy as the missing piece in her life, Lillas had suggested that she take a few days to reflect on how this lack had impacted upon and influenced her life decisions. They agreed to accelerate their next session for later that week rather than waiting for the following week.

"The first step on the path of integration, Mary, is radical honesty," Lillas began. "Because you were able to name the issue that has troubled you for so long, we can begin to openly deal with it and see how it has influenced all the decisions you have been making in your life."

Mary then shared her journal reflections from the past two days: How she and her husband had married quite young while they were both in University. How her husband, Ron, had a wonderful sense of humor that tempered Mary's seriousness and determination and made them come together as a couple. Early in their marriage, they had focused their attention on their education and then their careers; but this had been individual self-development, not cooperative and collaborative mutual development.

"I see now that we never had any real guidelines for what an Ideal interpersonal relationship should be like," Mary said. "We only had whatever had been modeled by our own dysfunctional parents and caregivers, married friends and associates, or what we had read in books or seen on television."

Mary thought that children would help them experience another dimension of life and love as family, and Ron had reluctantly agreed. "He had always been overly conscious about money, seeing things as expenses rather than investments, and focusing on the future rather than living in the present. That was why he was initially reluctant about having a family," Mary said, looking up from her journal. "I see now that my intent in having a family was to bring us closer together but I think in the end it has pushed us further apart."

"Why do you feel that, Mary?' Lillas asked.

"Ron loved the kids in his own way but always seemed jealous of the attention I focused on them. It was as if he had a missing piece that he wanted my attention to fill. He felt jealous about the time I invested in my work, in gaining a Masters in Organizational Development, in my friends and in self-development. The more he demanded my attention, the more I found reasons not to give it to him. I invented one excuse after another until we arrived at where we are today: two independent people who are cohabiting, but not really living and loving one another."

"It seems you have worked very hard at avoiding the key issue in your life," Lillas observed.

"I worked hard all my life, Lillas, and have achieved and been recognized for it. I have created an image of myself that is very rewarding on many levels. People look at us and think that Ron and I are the ideal couple, but that is not the truth," Mary said, closing her journal. "We tried counseling and it hasn't helped, so both of us have chosen unconsciously to live this kind of compromised life."

"Are you willing to share with Ron what you have just shared with me?" Lillas asked.

"No," Mary said immediately, then softened, "Not now. I am concerned about the consequences of disclosure. We have our kids to think of, their futures and their education." Mary paused, swallowed, and then said, "I guess I think that having a family like ours for our children to grow up in is better than not having a family at all."

Lillas was thoughtful about how Mary had just named *her chief misunderstanding about life.*[2] She was choosing the "devil she knew rather than the devil she didn't." This belief was holding her in fragmentation and separation, rather than allowing her to move into wholeness and integration.

"Mary, we've found that there are several ways that people step off the path of integration. The first is avoidance. The second is, when they cannot avoid a relationship — like you can't with Ron — they suppress and repress their true thoughts and feelings when they are with each other. These thoughts and feelings don't go away, but are emotionally swallowed and form a part of the shadow side of our natures, psychologically, and they block assimilation and circulation, physiologically.

"I would suspect that some of your physical symptoms of asthma and sinusitis could be the result of this kind of swallowing, blockage and lack of circulation.

"Sometimes when we can't avoid a person or situation, suppression does not work. In those times, we publicly blurt out the truth about what we think and feel. Afterwards, we feel guilty about having spoken. We are overcome with fear or guilt over unwittingly speaking our truth. And that leads us further into a state of compromise. We have found in our journey, Mary, that compromise is a lose-lose proposition that may work for the short term but in the end is unfulfilling and dissatisfying for all involved.

"Finally, we end up in abdicating responsibility for our lives and blaming others or blaming external circumstances for our unfulfilling life," Lillas concluded. "Does this story sound familiar?" Mary nodded that it did.

"The first step on the path is radical honesty. You have already taken that first step by sharing your truth with me this week. I respect that you are not ready to deal with Ron at this time, but I also would suggest that in the other areas of your life that involve your family, social, work or community, you are also avoiding people or situations just like you are avoiding Ron.

"Would you take a moment and reflect on whether this is true or not for you, Mary, while I get us some tea?" Lillas went to make them some tea. When she returned, Mary agreed that she was avoiding others in different areas of her life as she was avoiding Ron.

"I would like you to try an experiment this coming week. Choose one of the safe segments of your life and find someone with whom you can share your truth. Then tell them what you have observed, what you think about them, how you feel about them, and what you have wanted from your relationship with them in the past, now and in the future."

Lillas then explained the details of a model of integrative communication that they had used successfully in the past as a guide for Mary to use in planning her truthful encounter.

"I would like you to do this as a life experiment, Mary, and see what happens when you witness to the truth of your experience with someone, rather than avoiding, suppressing, compromising or abdicating responsibility for yourself and others."

"Lillas, I don't want to hurt anyone by sharing my truth," Mary said shaking her head in concern.

"I understand your perspective," Lillas said, and then replied: "There is a Sufi story about three gates that any communication needs to pass through before being spoken. The first gate is the gate of truth, including hard or difficult truths. The second gate is higher intent or purpose; your communication must be selfless rather than selfish, constructive rather than destructive, life-giving rather than death-dealing. The third gate is compassion, which means you must communicate in a way that shows you care about the other person and your relationship. If what you want to communicate does not pass through these three gates of truth, selflessness and compassion, then it shouldn't be said."[3]

"I understand," Mary said reluctantly, "but I am still concerned. What if my message aligns with the three gates of communication, but in sharing the truth of my experience, my listener gets angry, walks away and rejects me?"

"Let me share what we have experienced in our own process," Lillas replied.

"There is a pain that leads to growth and expansion, and a pain that leads to decline and contraction. The confusion for most of us is that these two pains feel the same. I have experienced the kind of truth that is shared with a malicious intent which made me feel hurt and smaller. I have also experienced the kind of truth that is shared with a virtuous intent that still hurt just the same but which, through reflection and over time, made me feel more alive and bigger.

"Whenever you speak the truth of your experience to someone with compassion and constructive intent, you need to cultivate the faith that the kind of pain you may cause will lead to growth — not necessarily in the moment, but over time."

"I am not sure I understand, Lillas," Mary said.

"There is a universal principle that says, 'like begets like.' A tomato seed will grow into a tomato, not a potato. An acorn will grow into an oak tree, not a willow. So in a similar way, a seed thought of truth planted in wisdom and service in another's heart will in time yield more truth and wisdom in their life and in yours. It must happen in time, even though we may not see it nor understand it in the moment, for the law works whether we believe in it or not.

"In our journey, there were people whom we thought we knew who in fact chose to walk away from us when we shared the truth of our experience. Then there were others whom we did not know well, who chose to walk closer to us. And we never knew in the beginning who would be left with us in the end. So you see, Mary, we can resist this process and struggle against it or we can accept, allow it, and flow with it. That is your choice.

"The price of admission on the path of integration is to begin to tell the truth. Tell it first to yourself, and then to those others in your life. I am suggesting that you can build up small successes and experiences of the truth during this process, in safe segments of your life. But ultimately, Mary, you will need to face your issue with Ron and what you are consciously willing or not willing to share in truth with him.

"That is the price of stepping on the path of integration. Are you willing to pay it?" Lillas asked while looking deeply into Mary's eyes.

Mary looked away for a time, then looked back, nodded and said that she was.

Chapter 3

The Coming Age of Integration

Men and Nations behave wisely once they have exhausted all the other alternatives.

ABBA EBAN

RICK THOUGHT THAT JOHN WAS IN SHOCK AND DENIAL, Elisabeth Kübler-Ross's first of five stages of response to death and dying.[1] What else would explain why John, 21 days after receiving his death sentence from his team of doctors, still came in to work early every morning and left late at night with an attitude of "business as usual"? John was protecting his image of self and Rick had concluded, after their initial discussions, that John would not seriously examine his transitional journey until he knew his company was in good hands. Without a named successor, John was unable to move his attention inward from its current outward fixation. Habit and inertia, despite his wake-up call three weeks earlier, were conspiring to keep John confined within his current life and leadership paradigm.

Rick and Lillas's one small victory was that they had suggested, early in their assignment, that John seek out options for healing his illness through the Integrative Medical Institute (IMI). The IMI provided conventional Western medical services as well as alternative healing modalities such as Naturopathy, Acupuncture, and Ayurvedic Medicine. The IMI would at least give John another perspective on his illness and at most give him a hopeful protocol for treatment that he could choose to follow. After their discussion, John had once again reluctantly agreed by shrugging his shoulders and saying, "What have I got to lose?"

To move forward on finding John's replacement, Rick had interviewed prospective internal candidates and met with selected board members within the first week. As Rick and Lillas had suspected, the internal candidates were either unwilling to assume or unsuitable for the top position, so Rick had recommended broadening their search externally, and received approval to do so.

With Lillas's help, Rick had sourced his energy network, tapped into several reputable International Executive Recruitment firms and compiled a list of candidates. He conducted interviews, checked references and had reduced the hopefuls to three primary candidates. All three candidates were very competent and available, but each possessed a very different outlook on life and leadership, and would move the company to different marketplace positions in the next decade.

John had blocked off his late afternoon and early evening so that he and Rick could discuss the selected candidates. Rick felt this would be an opportunity to share more integrative research and philosophy by introducing John to the ideas that emerged from the coming *Age of Integration*.

The Winds of Evolutionary Change

In describing today's accelerating changes, the media sends blips of unrelated information at us. Experts bury us under mountains of narrowly specialized monographs. Popular forecasters present lists of unrelated trends, without any model to show us their interconnections or the forces likely to reverse them. As a result, change itself comes to be seen as anarchic, even lunatic.

ALVIN TOFFLER

The most exciting breakthrough of the 21st century will occur not because of technology, but because of an expanding concept of what it means to be human.

JOHN NAISBITT

John and Rick spent the late afternoon discussing the specific experience, competence, profiles and perspectives of the three candidates. By the end of the first half of their meeting, John and Rick had tentatively ranked each candidate and an interviewing strategy and process was established for the forthcoming week. After a refreshment break, Rick opened the second half of their meeting by recapping the first.

"As you know, John, leadership is part art and part science. So is the process of replacing a leader. We've done the best we could with the time we've had, compiling background and current information on our short list of candidates. All three rate highly on the key characteristics we've identified: honesty, authenticity, competence, forward thinking and motivating. All three rate highly on their past knowledge and experience in managing and leading groups and companies in the Former FSU. Each candidate has the content and specific context to potentially be your replacement.

"However, each of the three have very different leadership paradigms and world views. These differences in concept and global context may change our rankings of the three candidates as they now stand." Rick paused and obtained John's agreement before proceeding.

"There are a number of questions that leaders have asked us over the years that I want to share with you, John. They've asked: How do I consciously and consistently lead in times of increasing chaos, complexity and uncertainty? How do I move to prioritizing people over profits from our current profits-over-people culture and environment? How do I effectively lead a virtual *hi-tech* organization while still maintaining a *high-touch* sense of community? How do I simultaneously embrace both individual uniqueness and corporate unity? How do I give a sense of meaning and purpose to individuals without sacrificing corporate performance and profitability?

"Each of these questions expresses a paradox: stability or uncertainty; people as expense or people as investment; high-tech or high-touch; diversity or unity; individual uniqueness or organizational collective; complexity or simplicity.

"From my conversations with you and your key people, I know you have wrestled with similar questions in *Crisis Energy* these past few years. We feel that how well leaders can hold and deal with these paradoxes will determine how successful their companies will be in this decade of transition."

"Decade of transition?" John asked. "What do you mean by that?"

"A decade of increasing change as we move our awareness and understanding from where we are today to where we may be going tomorrow. We see it as an evolutionary and accelerating rate of change," Rick said pulling out a picture from his briefcase and setting it on the table in front of them. "This picture should be familiar to you."

John nodded and said, "Yes, I've seen it many times."

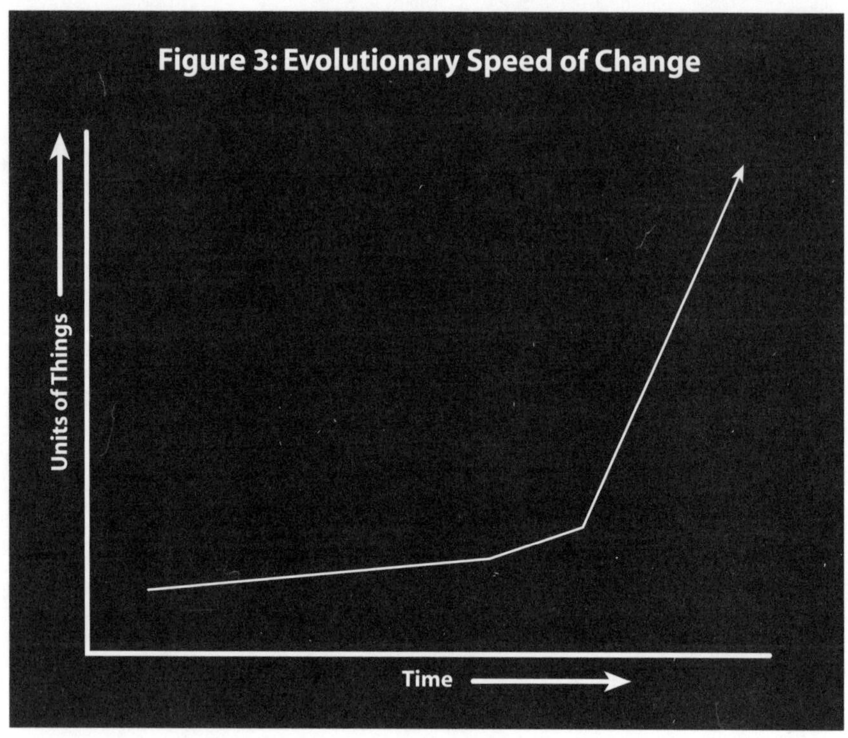

"What do you think it represents?" Rick asked.

"It could be a picture of the growth of Earth's population over the past 2,500 years from 100 million to 6.3 billion. It could be the number of McDonald's hamburgers sold each year, the number of computer chips manufactured worldwide since 1960, or the growth in the number of items we can choose from in an average North American grocery store," John said sitting back.

"Absolutely," Rick said. "People see this evolutionary speed and rate of change in many different ways. What we find interesting is that the amount of change that you and I experienced in the year 2000 was estimated to be 40 times the amount of change we experienced in the year 1960. According to some futurists, in the 21st Century, humankind will experience 20,000 years of change as we experienced in the year 2000."[2]

"So this picture could represent the advancements in science and technology during the past hundred years that have accelerated over the past fifty," John offered.

"Yes, and many are concerned that our hearts and souls—our morals, ethics and principles—are still trying to catch up with that technological driver," Rick replied. "Technology is a great servant, but a poor master. That's why we feel it is imperative at this time for Western society to turn inward, to help balance and mitigate our relentless outward-bound journey."

"Regardless of the source," John said pointing to the figure, "I want this to be a picture of Crisis Energy's production, profits and dividends over the next five years." John's half-smile turned to half-sadness when he remembered he may not be there to see it. He swallowed hard and continued, "So for Crisis Energy to be successful, our top candidate must be able to adapt to this kind and rate of change."

"From an evolutionary perspective, that's right. But I would like to suggest that our top candidate must be able not only to initiate, manage and lead himself or herself and the company to proactively respond rather than react to environmental change, but also must be able to simultaneously provide a personal and corporate environment of rock solid foundational stability and integrity. In our opinion, that is the only path that will lead to sustainable personal and organizational success in this decade of transition."

Rick went on to give example after example of how this seeming paradox of *change in stability* and *stability in change* was reconciled in a wide variety of companies, institutions and organizations with long-term success on multiple levels.[3]

"You are saying that these organizations were able to combine and reconcile evolution with involution," John said, after Rick finished presenting his examples. "Do you think any one of our three candidates has the ability to handle this kind of paradox for *Crisis Energy* as skillfully as the other leaders and organizations you mentioned?"

"Not fully as yet," Rick replied, "but one of the three candidates we feel could do the job with minimal integrative coaching, the second with a lot of coaching and the third most likely not at all."

"Which of the candidates would require only minimal integrative coaching?" John asked.

"Marilyn Taylor Sprott, the only woman and the one of the three candidates whom you ranked lowest earlier this afternoon, saying she was the least likely to succeed in an energy company, especially one based in the FSU," Rick calmly replied, while John's eyes opened wide in surprise.

A Brief History of Human, Management and Leadership Development

Before we can arrive at the Age of Integration, we must become more sophisticated in our thinking. Specifically, we must come to learn how to think paradoxically. Translating directly from its Greek root, paradox literally means 'contrary to reason'. Perhaps the greatest [intellectual] problem in this country is how 5 percent of us who comprehend paradox can communicate with the 95 percent who don't.

M. Scott Peck

At their next coaching session, Lillas asked Mary how she was applying the principle and practice of *telling the truth* in her life, which they had discussed in their last session as well as her progress applying other Integrative Transformative and Transcendent (ITT) practices from earlier sessions.

Mary shared her progress—her thoughts, feelings, experiences and observations—about speaking her truth during a relatively safe social segment. She had chosen Laura, her friend of fifteen years, and was pleasantly surprised by the results.

"Laura thanked me and was totally unaware of how her actions and behaviors had negatively affected me and our relationship. She knew there was something wrong, but until I shared my truth using the integrative communication method you taught me, she did not know what it was. As a result, we've become closer and I would have to say that the life experiment in sharing my truth was a success," Mary said, smiling. "And you'll be pleased to know that I am currently applying a 'tell the truth' experiment on a target relationship at work that has been troublesome for some time. I will let you know how that experiment works out."

Lillas was pleased with Mary's success and asked about the other ITT practices Mary had added to her daily routine since they began their coaching weeks before.

"The one practice I am having difficulty with is embodying my Ideal of loving relationships. I have been affirming, concentrating and visualizing my Ideal in my daily meditation practice, but when I am in a difficult, emotionally charged circumstance, I tend to *react* the way I always have rather than *respond* in accordance with my Ideal." Mary then described some specific instances where she was reactive rather than responsive at home and work that previous week.

Lillas reflected on Mary's difficulties in embodying her Ideal and altered her plan for their current session. Perhaps what was needed was a broader perspective, and stepping back to gain perspective on Mary's story might be the best thing they could do in the moment.

"Mary, as someone who has worked in the field of human resources for the past 20 years, you must have seen some significant changes in human, management and leadership development."

"Of course, I have..." Mary said thoughtfully. "When I first started in Human Resources, it was called Personnel & Payroll. Back then, everything was based on productivity and profits. We planned, organized and controlled the work and directed the people for that purpose. Today we can talk about people's attitudes and feelings a lot more openly, even though in SBT Company we still do little about it. Productivity and profitability is still primary, and people and process are secondary."

Lillas nodded and then said, "In our research of integrative leadership we have found that there are many different ways to divide the stages and phases of evolutionary development of people, organizations and cultures. With your permission, I would like to take a moment to introduce you to our way of describing these stages. My intent is to create a common language that will help our future work together." Mary was agreeable to this suggestion and so Lillas proceeded.

"Humankind has been on the planet for perhaps 10 million years. Presumably for much of that time we were slowly evolving through the hunter-gatherer-forager phases. About 25,000 years ago, we began to domesticate wild animals. About 10,000 years ago, we domesticated plants and gave birth to the *Agricultural Age*. About 200 years ago, the *Industrial Age* was born in Great Britain and spread at different times and different rates to different countries all over the world. About 40 years ago the *Information Age* began, prompted by the advent of digital computer technology in the 1950s. About 10 years ago, society found itself drowning in a sea of information that was so deep, people began yearning for a simpler way to handle the deluge. That desire gave birth to what some call the *Knowledge Age*.

"In this procession of the ages, the first thing many noticed is that the time between the stages, ages or paradigm shifts in human thinking and behavior

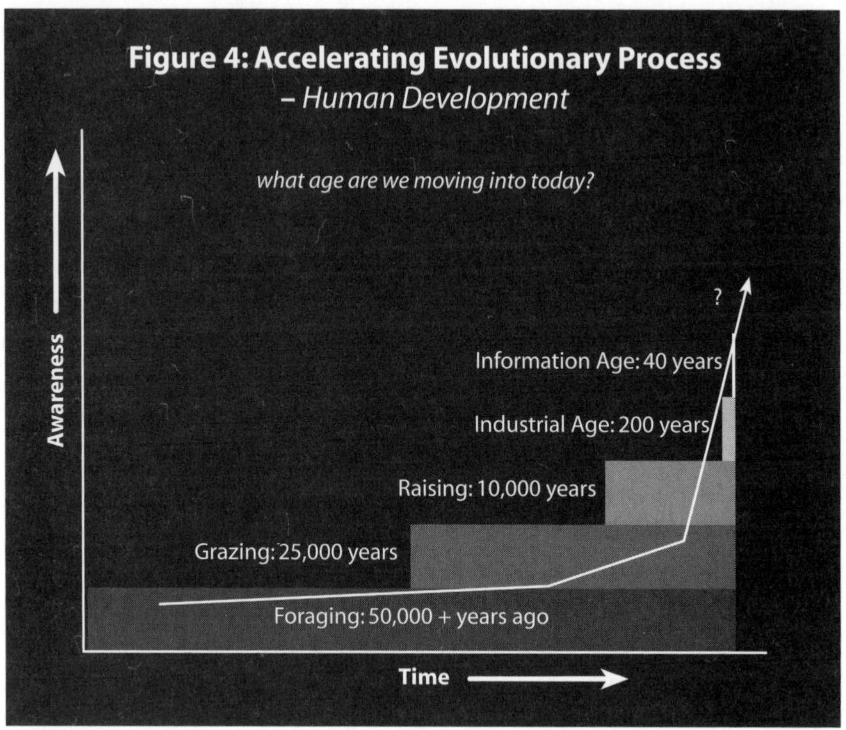

were getting shorter and shorter: 25,000, 10,000, 200, 40 then 10 years. The second thing many noticed was that the entire sum of human information and knowledge was doubling every decade, with doubling expected to happen faster and faster in the future. The third thing they noticed was that all the ages of humankind — foraging, grazing, raising, industrial, information and knowledge — exist somewhere and in some form in the world today.

"Now we're beginning to see the dawning of yet another age. People have not yet agreed to its name, but we've seen it referred to as the Age of Synthesis, Age of Wisdom, New Renaissance and New Enlightenment. In the context of our work on integrative life and leadership, we have chosen to call it the *Age of Integration*.[4]

"Within this grand story of human evolution, we can look at the smaller story of personal, cultural, management and leadership development.

"Leadership is not new, Mary." Lillas said, as an aside. "It has been around since the beginning of time. The ancients have been talking and writing about it for thousands of years, whereas we moderns have only seriously examined it over the past century.

"A hundred years ago, we hired hands or laborers to do our work. Fifty years ago, after World War II, we started to hire heads with those hands that allowed people to think while at their jobs. About ten years ago, with the popularization of emotional intelligence, we began to hire hands, heads and now hearts, that allowed people to discuss and learn how to appropriately use and express their feelings at work.

"Today, another Age is dawning that will recognize whole people who are comprised of hands, heads, hearts and souls. We are discovering our spiritual intelligence; an intelligence we feel represents the last untapped frontier of human potential and the next step in our evolutionary and involutionary journeys.

"It is the awakening and embodiment of our natural spiritual intelligence that will help establish the coming Age of Integration."

Paradoxes and Paradigms: Mechanistic, Organic and Wholistic

John wanted a time-out to return some phone calls, including one to his wife, to review Marilyn's file a second time and to reflect on Rick's recommendation before returning to their discussion. When he sat down again about forty minutes later, he looked tired, a little angry and a bit distracted. "All right, what's next?"

"The final thing I want to share with you this afternoon, John, is about three different paradigms that are currently working their way through our global socio-economic framework. We have found these three paradigms to be a simple way to discuss changes we are observing in people, organizations and cultures.

"The first is what we call the *mechanistic.* The second is what we call the *organic*. And the third is what we call the *integrative* or *wholistic*," Rick said, pulling out a final chart titled "The Coming Age of Integration" from his briefcase and laying it on the table in front of John.

The Mechanistic Paradigm

"The mechanistic paradigm is the one that is predominant today, with about 85% of the world belonging in this group. It has emerged and developed

Table 2: Mechanistic, Organic and Wholistic Paradigms

Type	Mechanistic	Organic	Wholistic
Relationship	Competition	Cooperation	Collaboration
Thinking	Serial	Associative	Unitive
Personal	Image	Character	Essence
Change	Transact	Transform	Transcend
Process	Knowledge	Understanding	Wisdom
Governance	Rules	Practices	Principles
Communication	Debate	Discussion	Dialogue

over the past 300 years, originating during the time of Isaac Newton with his proposal of the laws of mechanics, optics and gravity. This was the first stirring of the Age of Reason, also known as the Age of Enlightenment, that flowered in the 18th Century and heavily influenced western society to believe in the powers of observation, experimentation, reason and critical thinking.

"Mechanistic is the world view that people are like machines and are repairable or dispensable. Within this paradigm, our business focus is on competition, with a war-like metaphor that suggests elimination, subjugation or defeat of our perceived marketplace enemies at all costs.

"Mechanistic thinking is about physical and left-brain mental intelligence and is serial in nature. Logic is important; it is a conceptual place where 1+1 will always and forever equal 2. Our attention in mechanistic thinking is focused on our *image of self* and external appearances and behaviors. In this paradigm we are constantly afraid of losing our *image of self* and will defend it to the death, whether in homicide or suicide, on multiple levels.

"The management and leadership style and the change process within this paradigm is transactional, where if you do something for me, I will in turn do something for you.

"In the mechanistic paradigm, knowledge is power that is to be protected and guarded and rules, policies and procedures govern individuals, companies and countries.

The Organic Paradigm

"The second evolutionary paradigm is the organic in which people are treated like people and not like machines. This is the second-most predominant paradigm and includes about 10% of the world's population. It re-emerged during the past 100 years and its spirit is contained in Einstein's theory of relativity in which everything is said to be relative rather than absolute. Organic thinking involves harmonizing our left and right brain patterns. It engages and develops emotional and social intelligences that are associative rather than serial: where logic and feelings, head and heart, reason and passion, words and images can be blended together in higher order balance and harmony.

"In the organic paradigm, 1+1 can equal 8, 10, 50 or 100, depending on the nature of each 'one'. If we have 'one' male rat plus 'one' female rat, the answer would be up to 22 baby rats every month. If we have 'one' male rabbit plus 'one' female rabbit, the answer could be 64 baby rabbits every year. If we have 'one' wheat seed planted in 'one' fertile field, then the answer could yield 30, 60, or up to 100 times the weight of that original seed.

"The organic paradigm is the paradigm of transformative management and leadership change, in which the heart is engaged and learning is emotionally charged. Here, *Character* is more important than our *image of self* and we can let go of beliefs and feelings about our image for the sake and in support of our Character.

"Because only 10% of our current population has self-awareness, and self-management, social awareness and relationship management skills, those who are naturally organic are also seen as natural leaders. Organic people can also be mechanistic if they choose, playing the game by the rules made up by a mechanistic culture, but they are innovative and not just mechanistically imitative.

"Organic is also the paradigm of best practices as opposed to blind rules, and is where knowledge is transformed through application into understanding.

The Wholistic (Integrative) Paradigm

"The third evolutionary paradigm is the wholistic or integrative. In this paradigm, people are treated not just like people, but also as sacred spiritual beings. Less than 5% of the population currently belongs in this paradigm.

This is where the paradox of the organic paradigm's duality and the multiple forms and situations of the mechanistic paradigm can be easily understood and reconciled.

"Integrative thinking is unitive and engages our whole psycho-neuro-endocrinology and our four domains of intelligence: physical, mental, emotional and spiritual. This is the paradigm of original inspiration, rather than organic innovation or mechanistic imitation. The Integrative paradigm is about our Essence taking precedence over our *Character* and image of self. It is a paradigm in which the understanding of the organic becomes the wisdom of the wholistic through deep connection and reflection. It is where mechanistic rules and organic practices are informed by universal laws that act as guidelines and help us play the game of life and leadership successfully.

Emerging Trends in the Coming Age of Integration

"Each of us has all three paradigms within us at various stages of development, awareness, or degree.

"One way to look at that is: where do we focus our attention? How much time do we spend externally focused and feeding the mechanistic paradigm within us, and how much time do we spend internally focused and feeding our organic and wholistic paradigms? This applies to the individual as well as to the team, group, or organization. For example, an individual could be organic in nature, working within a mechanistic organization, but be a member of a wholistic and very creative family or team.

"On average, as I shared earlier, the global population is currently estimated to be made up of 85% mechanistic (or traditional), 10% organic (or modern) and 5% wholistic (or integrative) people, but this is expected to change dramatically in the next decade.

"Our feelings are that the mechanistic paradigm will decrease from 85% to 50% of the population. The organic paradigm will increase from 10% to 30%, and the wholistic from 5% to 20%. This will happen only if some form of Integrative Transformative and Transcendent (ITT) practices are adopted and utilized by a growing percentage of the population.

"If this degree of change occurs as forecast, it will have a dramatic impact on our global socio-economic framework and the future of *Crisis Energy*."

"So what am I supposed to do with this information?" John asked impatiently.

"I have rated the three candidates for your position using our integrative assessment tools. Fred is the consummate mechanistic, Thomas is a higher order mechanistic, and Marilyn Taylor Sprott is a very centered organic who can also function very well in the mechanistic paradigm.

"This is why I suggested earlier that Marilyn has greater ability to handle paradox than the other two. She has more flexibility, adaptability and access to her creativity as inspiration and innovation than the others. On this basis, I would rate Marilyn first, Thomas second and Fred third. Earlier we rated them on purely conventional assessment scales, as Fred first, Thomas second and Marilyn last and least likely to succeed.

"So I need your thoughts on context, John, for it will influence our final ranking of the three candidates. What is the governing paradigm for the FSU today? Which paradigm is predominant and where and when do you think it might evolve to higher order thinking?"

"The FSU won't be evolving in my lifetime, Rick," John said acidly, then got up and quickly left the conference room without saying another word.

Rick smiled, inwardly thinking—as he cleaned up the boardroom and put his meeting notes and charts back in his briefcase—that John's reactionary behavior felt very mechanistic.

• • •

The Three Paradigms and Intimate Relationship

The highest understanding of love lies in its power to transform lives, restore health, and bring about a sense of total well-being. It is the other end of the spectrum, which is directed by desire—the limited contracted form of love—that has a tremendously destructive potential.

SWAMI CHETANANANDA

When Lillas had finished describing the mechanistic, organic and wholistic paradigms that followed her story about the evolutionary growth of humankind, she asked Mary if she could place her relationships with her husband, children, family, friends and organization into these three paradigms. After some thought, Mary responded.

"I would like to think of myself as an organic person who is working in a mechanistic company. My husband is mechanistic, which makes it difficult for me. He and I never seem to be on the same wavelength. My oldest daughter takes after her father, but our youngest daughter and middle son are organic in their orientation and take after me. I have several women friends who are mainly Organic, but Laura sometimes acts very mechanistic, which is what our truth-telling session was all about the other week. I don't think I have any wholistic or integrative relationships in my life at the moment." Mary thought for a moment, and then smiled, "Except maybe you, Lillas."

Lillas smiled her thanks. "So within these three paradigms, there are different types of love we call, from the original Greek, Eros, Phillia and Agape.

"The mechanistic kind of love, we call Eros. Joseph Campbell, who wrote *The Hero of a Thousand Faces* and *The Power of Myth,*[5] described Eros as two overheated sweating inflamed glands meeting one another. The mechanistic paradigm is about control, manipulation and self-gratification, which affect how we express and satisfy our sexuality, physical needs and bodily desires.

"Organic love, we call Phillia. It means fraternal love or a love of the heart in fellowship with others. Philadelphia, for example, has its root in Phillia, meaning, the city of brotherly and sisterly love. The organic paradigm is about balance, harmony and cooperation in terms of learning, living and loving one another.

"Wholistic love, we call Agape. Agape means Divine Love, which is an unconditional love that comes from our spirit or soul. The wholistic paradigm is about collaborating and seeking the best for others by allowing Divine Love to be involved and embodied through us.

"We see these three as the primary colors of love: red for Eros, yellow for Phillia, and blue for Agape. When we blend these three colors on the pallet of our life and leadership journey, we end up with all the various colors and shades of love. However, there are times when we have layered so much paint on our memories that we can no longer see the original colors that are hiding beneath them.

"What I would like to suggest as an experiment is for you to explore your memories and creatively work with your imagination to rekindle the truth about all the loves you have experienced in your life.

"For our next session, Mary, I would like you to reflect and do a life review exercise. The subject of this life review is all the elements—all the good, bad and ugly faces—of love that you have ever experienced. What were the peak experiences or high points of Agape, when you felt whole and pure? What were the low points of Eros where you sometimes felt like an object, fragmented and incomplete? When have you felt Phillia, or a love of friends and family in a balanced and harmonious way?"

Mary jotted down Lillas's suggested exercise in her journal and said, "You want me to describe all my experiences about love for our next session?"

"Yes, that's partly right. But not just describe them. I want you to first mine your memories about love and remember all the faces of love you have experienced in your life. Have you ever had a special toy, doll or pet that you loved? What was your favorite poetry, music or prose about love when you were a young adult, in later life, and today? Have you ever painted or sketched anything about love? Have you ever danced so effortlessly and beautifully that it felt like an experience of love in motion? Did you read about love and romance or see romantic comedies and weep at different times and places, not just in sadness, but also in joy? Have you ever painted, cooked or sung in the shower with love?

"Secondly, I want you to engage your creative imagination about love and think about all the ways that you can embody it. Think about painting or making a sketch or drawing about love. Think about writing an essay about love. Think about composing a poem about love, or dancing, singing and acting with love. Be creative. And bring some of your creativity with you to our next session.

"Finally, and perhaps most importantly, Mary," Lillas said leaning forward for emphasis, "I want you to fully remember: When was your heart first broken? And when was your heart first awakened? These two defining moments set the framework and sound the note for love in your life.

"For we know that in the journey of integrative life and leadership, where you choose to focus your attention with intention, there will your heart be also."

Chapter 4

Building a Model of Integrative Leadership

The process of becoming a leader is much the same as becoming an integrated human being.

Warren Bennis

Following their afternoon conversation on paradoxes and paradigms, John moved rapidly into the anger stage of death and dying (E. Kübler-Ross), bypassing the bargaining stage altogether. During Rick's last presentation, John had realized he was very mechanistic and did not like seeing himself and his world that way. He had not always been like that, he had reasoned, but had fallen into the mechanistic paradigm under intense external financial and corporate pressures. His initial anger at recognizing his own fall from grace was first directed at Rick, as the messenger, and then later at himself.

Rick did not ask for details about the phone call John had had with his wife during the last coaching session, but knew intuitively that it also had a bearing on John's angry reaction.

From that paradoxical afternoon on, John began letting go of his need to focus on his replacement, became satisfied that the process was in capable hands, openly questioned his further day-to-day involvement in *Crisis Energy* and refocused more and more of his attention on his own personal life-and-death journey. All of these were positive signs, in Rick and Lillas's opinion, and they felt that afternoon may have been a turning point for John.

Mary was becoming more able to clearly describe and attune to her Ideal Self and was busy applying integrative practices to different safe segments of her life in an effort to build her strength and confidence along her integrative journey. She was preparing herself with small successes for the eventual truth-filled encounter with her intimately unaware husband, while simultaneously wrestling with her fears, doubts and worries about the possible outcomes of that encounter.

Rick and Lillas felt that John and Mary would benefit from a more in-depth review of the integrative framework they were using than they had previously provided. They prepared a handout for them to read before their next coaching and consulting sessions, one that they called, "Building a Model of Integrative Leadership."

A Brief History of Leadership

If you want to understand today, you have to search yesterday.

Pearl S. Buck

In 1977, when Abraham Zaleznik first suggested a difference between managers and leaders, the North American fascination with leadership development was born.[1] Since that time, thousands of books, tens of thousands of articles and millions of sites on the Internet have become available for those interested in pursuing the subject of leadership.

The concept of leadership appears on the surface to be very complex. So great was the complexity that Warren Bennis often lamented that there are as many theories and definitions of leadership as there are authors of leadership books. In an attempt to simplify this apparent complexity, management and leadership researchers from the past 50 years have categorized the hundreds of theories available into three approaches: trait, behavior and contingency.

The "Great Man" (trait) theory observes leaders' traits, characteristics and competencies, with an underlying belief that natural leaders are born and not made. To become a great leader, such as Winston Churchill or Eleanor Roosevelt, you can try to imitate their traits and characteristics and you may become better, but you will never be quite like them, for great leaders are born and not developed.

The "Adaptive Man" (behavioral) theory notes that leaders learn, change and adapt their behaviors in response to changing environments. The underlying belief in this theory is that leaders are bred and not born. To become an adaptive leader, such as Harry Truman or Abraham Lincoln, you need to be acutely aware of and responsive to external change.

The "Emergent Man" (contingency) theory advocates that leaders rise to the occasion, circumstance or situation as required. The underlying belief is that the right leader will emerge as and when needed. To be a successful emergent leader — such as Rudolpho Giulliani, the former mayor of New York City during the 9/11 World Trade Center tragedy — you must always be prepared and have practiced a plan for every foreseeable contingency within your area of influence.

Beyond these three principally humanistic and scientific theories of leadership lies a fourth spiritual and sacred theory, contained in the thousands-of-years-old histories, parables and myths of the world's wisdom and mystic traditions. Wilber defines *wisdom traditions* as non-dual philosophies that are built on Oneness that is evident in Christianity, Islam, Buddhism, Hinduism, Taoism and Judaism, among others. These wisdom and mystic traditions gave birth to many of the world's greatest visionary, inspirational and universal principle-centered leaders whose enduring impact continues to ripple and influence the world today.

In our experience, there appeared to be something essential missing in the scientific (outside-in) approaches to leadership development. There also appeared to be something practical missing in the spiritual (inside-out) approach to leadership development. Although the parallels and connection points had been observed and documented, there still appeared to be a discernible gap that served to separate rather than integrate these two fundamental perspectives.

The intention of our work has been to uncover and discover a simple foundational leadership model that reconciles these two basic approaches to leadership development.

This foundational approach to leadership development is what we call Integrative Leadership™.

Building a Model for Integrative Leadership

A leader is a person who has an unusual degree of power to project on other people his or her shadow or his or her light. A leader is a person who has an unusual degree of power to create the conditions under which other people must live and move and have their being-conditions that can either be as illuminating as heaven or as shadowy as hell. A leader is a person who must take special responsibility for what's going on inside him or her self, inside his or her consciousness, lest the act of leadership create more harm than good. The problem is that people rise to leadership in our society by a tendency towards extroversion, which means a tendency to ignore what is going on inside themselves. Leaders rise to power in our society by operating very competently and effectively in the external world, sometimes at the cost of internal awareness.

PARKER PALMER

The first step in our search for leadership simplicity was to adopt the hypothesis that all theories and models of leadership we had observed and experienced contained a portion of the truth, but no one theory as yet contained all of the truth. The second step was to capture these multiple perspectives and step back far enough to see the underlying patterns or processes that informed them, with a focus on similarities (integration) rather than differences (separation). The third step was to build an Integrative Leadership model that captured more of these common patterns and processes than what we had seen or noted in any other model before.

The truth, in our experience, is always simple. The information we gathered was external (historical and current research) balanced by our internal perceptions (experiences, evaluations, intuitions, and imaginations) of the life and leadership journey. The resulting information, through evaluation, became a body of knowledge. Through application, we transformed this body of knowledge into understanding. Through deep self-reflection and introspection, we endeavored to integrate our understanding into wisdom.

In this process of sifting and panning for golden nuggets of common truth, we experienced many "ah-ha" moments intellectually, "ha-ha" moments emotionally, and "ahhh" moments spiritually.

We measured the success of our model-building approach by how well the evolving integrative model clearly reflected and illuminated the life and leadership journeys of others. The greater the resulting clarity and simplicity, the happier we were with our emerging results.

We found, in the building process, that an enduring truth is one that — when spoken, seen, heard or read — awakens, resonates and integrates from within. For the participating listener, the truth becomes self-evident. It is as if it had always been there, hidden, forgotten or blended into the background of their lives. But when it is unearthed and returned to conscious awareness, it becomes a self-generating touchstone around which the process of integration can take place.

The presence of integrative resonance continues to be a standard for measuring our success, as we continue our ongoing research in building, refining and communicating the Integrative Leadership model to individuals, groups and organizations.

Multiple Perspectives

Creativity is not just a way to make things better. Without creativity we are unable to make full use of information and experience that is already available to us and is locked away in old structures, old patterns, old concepts, old perceptions.

EDWARD DE BONO

As we examined the two historical approaches of scientific (evolutionary) and spiritual (involutionary) leadership, we observed more similarities than differences. What has kept these two approaches apart historically was the respective beliefs and perspectives held by each position.

We found that developing a natural capacity to see multiple perspectives — on any given subject, object, problem, situation or decision — is essential for successfully walking the path of integrative life and leadership. This capacity enhances personal and organizational creativity, flexibility, and adaptability in times of change and transition.

Each individual has a preferred way of viewing the world, which is their own mental model of how things work. This mental model can be like moist clay that can be reshaped with each new life experience, idea or belief; or, it can be like hardened pottery that has been fired in the crucible of life's emotionally charged events. For those of us still willing to learn from life, the more perspectives that are brought to our mental table, the more flexibility we have in seeing the world through different eyes, and the more truth we may potentially uncover and add to our integrative knowledge and resources.

There is much in leadership literature that advocates this multiple-perspective approach. Ken Wilber's Four Quadrant Model of "I-It, We-Its" is an elegant and integral way of discussing objective and subjective, structure and culture, body and soul, to capture four essential perspectives.[2]

Edward de Bono's "Six Thinking Hats" is a technique of deliberately adopting a variety of perspectives on a single subject that may be different than the one you would naturally hold. The method is to try on a role represented by one of the six hats and discuss the subject from that perspective. The six roles include: objective (facts — white hat), subjective (feelings, intuitions — red hat), creative (inspirations, possibilities, vision — green hat), optimistic (benefits, advantages, value — yellow hat), pessimistic (detriments, criticism, devil's advocate — black hat), and witness to the process (management, control — blue hat).[3]

Others call this capacity for multiple perspectives re-framing, re-engineering, or re-imagining styles and roles.

What we have found most useful has been to examine the subject of life and leadership from four conventional perspectives: *intrapersonal*, interpersonal, group and organization. The first and most important perspective in Integrative Leadership is intrapersonal, since we believe that all meaningful change first begins with the individual, then the group, and then the organization, community and nation.

Intrapersonal perspectives include four domains of intelligence — physical, mental, emotional and spiritual — and three levels of awareness that are seen by the individual as conscious, unconscious and superconscious, and by the culture as mechanistic, organic and wholistic paradigms.

Four Domains of Intelligence

> *So there are four Atmas — the life, the mind, the soul, the spirit. The ultimate force which lies at the root of macrocosmic power of the manifestations of soul, mind, and the life-principle, is the spirit.*
>
> RAMA PRASAD

The first commandment of life and leadership development is to "know thyself". But the truth is that few of us know who and what we truly are. Early in our lives we were haunted by questions such as: Who am I? What do I want? What am I made of? Where have I come from? Why am I here? Where am I going? These questions are not new or uniquely our own, for they have been part of humankind's journey since the beginning of time. Some of us have searched for the answers to these questions all of our lives, others have given up, forgotten or were lost along the way, while still others have been fast asleep, not even aware there are any questions.

Historically, the ancients observed themselves and the natural world and were creative in developing stories and myths that would help them answer these age-old questions. Mystics observed their inner world and also created stories, myths and parables to assist in understanding what they had inwardly experienced in order to help answer these questions.

In examining these inner and outer stories, we saw recurring patterns that related to the number four: four directions, four primordial elements, four spirits, four bodies, four states of consciousness, four derivatives in science, and so on, that were cross-cultural, across all disciplines and across all of time.

For example, Egyptian creation mythology was not just about nine (the original Egyptian Pantheon) and three (Father, Mother, Son), but also contained the four. Their creation story suggests that in the beginning there was only Ocean, and it filled all of space and all of time. Then suddenly, from the ocean there arose an egg from which the Sun God Ra emerged. Ra brought forth from himself four god-like children. One became the earth, two became the air and the fourth became the sky. The ancient Greeks were influenced by Egyptian mythology and went further to suggest that the four primary elements of earth, air, fire and water, when combined together, made up all things and all people. Pythagoras, who many consider to be the father of mathematics, referred to four in terms of the four operations (addition, subtraction, multiplication, division) and in geometry in terms of the four principle ways in which all physical shapes manifest themselves (point, line, plain, solid). The Chinese consider the sacred four, the *Hong Fen,* as metal, water, fire and wood. Aboriginal people in different regions of the world speak of the four primary directions that relate to the four natural divine elements within the medicine wheel.

In the past 100 years, Carl Jung used the four domains in his explanation of personality types as sensing, thinking, feeling and intuiting.[4] Today, there is a growing awareness that as human beings, we have four fundamental intelligences — physical, mental, emotional and spiritual — from which all other intelligences may be derived.[5]

In modern leadership development these past 25 years, the perspective of the four was evident in many models either implicitly or explicitly. Leadership models we reviewed that did not contain this four-fold perspective we felt missed something essential and did not resonate with us.

We found so many associations, through historical and current research, that contained the concept of four in describing the dimensions of human nature, that we considered it to be a foundational building block for seeing and understanding ourselves and our world. To acknowledge the many associations, we suggest that they are more like *Domains* or *Archetypes* than isolated characteristics or processes, and we have incorporated them into our Integrative Life and Leadership Model as the *Four Domains of Intelligence*. Tables 3 & 4 show a brief correlation of our work to date.

We encourage you to examine the tables, reflect on them, and see if you can find, as an amateur symbologist, patterns of the four in your own experience.

In our model-building process, there were times when we needed to separate and times when we needed to integrate, in order to facilitate our own understanding. Although we were aware these four domains of intelligence wove together to form an unbroken tapestry of our life and leadership journey, separating them and examining each of them gave us a different way in which to know ourselves.

Table 3: Correlating the Four Domains of Intelligence (in no particular order)

Type	Physical	Mental	Emotional	Spiritual
Renaissance	Body	Mind	Heart	Soul
Greek	Earth	Fire	Water	Air
Aboriginal	West	North	South	East
Jungian/MBTI	Sensing	Thinking	Feeling	Intuiting
Integral Psychology	Body	Mind	Soul	Spirit
Mystic	Action	Thought	Desires	Intention
Psychological	Behavior	Cognitive	Empathic – Gestalt	Transpersonal
Yogic Traditions	Karma	Jnana	Bahkti	Raja
Four Destinations	Law	Truth	Love	God
Four Approaches	Scientific	Occult	Psychic	Mystic
Young's Levels	Sensation Motor Output	Thinking Ratiocination	Feeling Motivation	Purposive Action Pure Potential
Pythagorean	Solid	Plane	Line	Point
Four Derivatives	Position	Velocity	Acceleration	Control
Neo-Pythagorean	Matter	World Reason	World Soul	God
Body of Buddha	Physical Body *(Rupa Kaya)*	Apparition/ Growth Body *(Nirmana kaya)*	Bliss Body *(Sambhoga kaya)*	Essence Body *(Dharma kaya)*
Hindu Vedanta & Tibetan Buddist	Gross Body *(Sthula-sarira)*	Subtle Ether Body *(Suksam-sarira)*	Causal Astral Body *(Karana-sarira)*	Absolute Being *(Atman-Brahman)*

The Physical Domain

We are not human beings having a spiritual experience;
we are spiritual beings having a human experience.

PIERRE TEILHARD DE CHARDIN

In evolutionary theory, a male's sperm cell and a female's egg cell join together under the right conditions and are guided by the program found in

Table 4: Four Domains and Contemporary Models of Leadership

Model	Physical	Mental	Emotional	Spiritual
Integrative	Action	Mission	Passion	Vision
Covey Needs	Live	Learn	Love	Leave a Legacy
Covey Balance[1]	Discipline	Mission	Passion	Conscience
Covey Leadership[2]	Aligning	Pathfinding	Empowering	Modeling
Kouzes & Posner[3]	Model the way and enable others to act	Challenge the process	Encourage the heart	Inspire a shared vision
Kyle's Four Powers *(Archetype)*	Presence *(Sovereign)*	Wisdom *(Magician)*	Compassion *(Artist)*	Intention *(Warrior)*

[1] Covey uses an elegant example for the existence of the fourth spiritual domain by asking participants to compare the leadership style of Gandhi and Hitler. (See Chapter 7, "Building a Living Organization" for details.) To fit within the integrative framework, we would substitute mission for the mental and place vision in the spiritual. What differs is not just their conscience, as Covey suggests since conscience can be informed from different levels of awareness, but their intention: constructive or destructive, selfish versus selfless, personal power or Higher Power.

[2] Covey's Four Roles of Leadership, given the words used to describe them, would better fit within the integrative framework as follows: physical (modeling), mental (aligning), emotional (empowering), spiritual (pathfinding). The confusion within the complexity of leadership is the shifting terminology does not always align with the four domains.

The integrative framework is an attempt to unify and clarify intention, evaluation, intuition and action of the various leadership models.

[3] For the Kouze & Posner and Kyle models, we have placed the five practices and four powers notionally into the domains on a best-fit basis. Kouze & Posner and Kyle have not done this categorization.

their combined DNA. Then, 50 cell divisions and 270 specialized cells later, new life is born into this world. During nine months of growth, the fetus has moved through stages that reflect those of fish, amphibia, reptiles, and mammals to eventually become human prior to birth.

From birth onward, the body grows and develops through various stages, lines and developmental cycles (that depend on the perspective of the observer), from baby to toddler, adolescent, youth, young adult, adult, mature adult, senior and eventually, death. This cycle of birth, growth, maturity, decline, death and decay is observed in all of nature of which we are an integral part.

The body is made up of systems that work in relative harmony and balance (homeostasis) with each other, without our conscious direction. These systems include: skeletal, muscular, nervous (including the brain), circulatory, respiratory, immune, digestive, reproductive, endocrine and sensory. We are informed about the nature of our world through our sensory systems of touch, taste, smell, hearing and sight, all of which send signals back to our nervous system that we perceive as images, sounds, smells, tastes and body sensations.

The conventional medical model views the body as a machine, believing that if the body is fed the right fuel (diet), is regularly maintained (exercise and relaxation), and continues to perform its processes of respiration, digestion, assimilation, circulation and elimination, it will continue to function, support and sustain life normally. According to this theory, all of our awareness, reason, feelings, instincts, needs and desires are woven into the body so that all concepts of mind, memory and soul die when the body dies: ashes to ashes and dust to dust.

According to involutionary theory, the wisdom and mystic traditions suggest a much less familiar story of physical birth and development.

The intention, attitudes and emotions of the male and female as the two contemplate bringing a child into the world send a signal into higher levels of awareness that there is a channel or doorway opening which may provide a soul with an opportunity to be born on Earth. The circumstances, conditions and opportunities for growth are evaluated and assessed collectively at higher levels. One soul, out of many competing for the channel, chooses and is chosen, then descends and observes the creation of the opportunity. If conception occurs as foreseen (for there is always choice), the soul influences the program within the fertilized egg's DNA to match its needs and desires. It further influences the growth of the fetus during gestation, and finally partially inhabits the new body with its life force[6] near the time of physical birth.

The physical birth of the body is followed by a period of transition. In this transition, the soul spends as much time in higher levels of consciousness as it does in earthly awareness (which is why babies sleep a lot). At some time within the first seven years, the soul descends into and fully engages with the body. In many traditions this point is referred to as the embodiment of the soul. At the point of embodiment, soul awareness awakens in the body, the veil that separates conscious awareness from higher awareness is drawn, and life and learning begin along what is objectively seen as ordinary evolutionary lines.

The relationship of the soul — and the spark of spirit that is the life force within it — and the *body-mind* is continual during evolution, learning and growth. However, like many of our autonomic systems of breathing and respiration, heartbeat and circulation, eating and digestion, we are consciously unaware of this spiritual presence. In order to become aware, we must choose to journey within and seek to awaken to the active presence of our soul in our life.

At the body's death, either through accident, decline or design, the soul and its life force are released to continue the journey in other realms, dimensions and levels of awareness.

Evolution and involution create two very different perspectives and paradigms regarding physical intelligence. One is mechanistic and the other is wholistic.

In the mechanistic perspective, the body is viewed as a machine that performs for a time before it declines and fades away. In this view, consciousness is centered in the nervous system and brain, and determines who and what we think we are, but only while the body is alive.

In the wholistic perspective, the body is viewed as a temple that for a time is the residence of our essence or soul. In this view, consciousness exists in each of the trillions of cells that make up our body that collectively contribute to who and what we are, although we may not be aware of it.

The Mental Domain

Mental Intelligence is an excellent servant, but a very poor master.

John Stillman

The intuitive mind is a sacred gift and the rational mind a faithful servant.
We have created a society that honors the servant and has forgotten the gift.

Albert Einstein

From an evolutionary perspective, the mental domain of intelligence contains our cognitive processes that describe how we come to know what we know. The process of knowing is still a scientific mystery that is thought to involve three fundamental areas: memory, reasoning and imagination.

Memory has four levels: sensory, short-term, working and long-term. The ability to reason includes attention, learning, thinking, interpretation, judgment, evaluation, assessment, self-talk, problem solving, decision-making and planning. Imagination includes visualization, creativity, daydreaming and night dreaming.

The modern metaphor for mental processes is a computer. The hardware is like our nervous system, with the brain and its network of 100 billion neurons, axons and interconnected dendrites. Software is similar to our ability (consciously or unconsciously) to program experiences (thoughts, beliefs, feelings, values) that collectively comprise our situational mental model. Our mental models can be changed and periodically updated, whereas our "hardware," beyond a certain chronological age, is felt to be fixed or in decline.

Memory is intimately associated with learning and is often used to define who and what we are. In sensory memory, there are fleeting sensations that move through our minds and wash over our bodies in fractions of a second. Our short-term memory (RAM) processes 125 bits of information per second (which is very small), can handle about 7 discrete packets of information and is principally electrical in nature. Depending on our focus and attention, cognitive theorists suggest that we use our short-term memory to transfer our perceptions, evaluations and learning in the present moment to our huge but passive long-term (ROM) chemical storage.

To access our long-term memory we need to simply ask a question that activates our internal search engine which in turn seeks to provide us with an answer. More information about what we have learned and experienced is stored in our unconscious long-term memory than we consciously realize.

Another aspect of the mental domain is that our mind does not make a distinction about whether the input it receives comes from our external world of sensory stimulation or from our internal world of creative memory or imagination. External experience and internal visualization produce similar sensations, feelings, thoughts and evaluations. So, for the mind, the inside story and the outside story are not differentiated as to their source.

The mind grows and thrives on challenge and change. What allows us to fall asleep, become mesmerized or hypnotized in the course of our lives is the natural process of habituation.

When we first learn an activity, such as walking or riding a bicycle, it requires a conscious focus of our attention and repetitive effort for a period of time. After we learn a new skill, that network of physical, mental, and emotional memories are bundled together and relegated to unconscious control. The ability to walk or ride a bicycle eventually becomes the same to us as breathing or the beating of our hearts.

This delegation of responsibility from the conscious upwards to the unconscious naturally frees up our short-term memory so it can handle any changes in our environment. When there is no change, there is no focus, no attention and no learning. When there is change, we often react to that change, according to past habits of our *image of self* that are contained within our situational mental models, rather than align the change with our *Ideal Self*.

One way of ensuring that habits within our models support us on our journey of life and leadership is to periodically shake up, reflect and reprogram our situational mental models. This helps move us towards the possibility of our *Ideal Self* rather than thwarting, opposing and limiting ourselves to our history within our past *image of self*.

In the involutionary theory, consciousness is the intelligence, energy and spirit that resides in everything from the smallest particle conceivable to the largest universe imaginable. What changes, develops and evolves during our journey of life and leadership is our awareness of the existence of that consciousness. From this perspective, the domain of mind is a distributed phenomenon that involves and weaves together our body, heart and soul. Mind is not localized in the brain, but distributed from the tips of our toes to the top of our head and can exist outside the confines of the body.

Mind is the medium through which all four domains can effectively communicate and coordinate with one another *intrapersonally*, and is also the medium through which we can effectively communicate *interpersonally*, organizationally and globally.

Mind is not tangible in the same way that we normally view objects in our world, but is more like a field of intelligent vibrational energy. Our "mind field" can be compared to radio, television or communication waves that are passing through us at any given moment, carrying information — present, but invisible. If we have the right instrument and attune it to the right channel, we can decode this information for our own use and pleasure. In the involutionary view, the body, much like a radio or television, is not the source of information, but rather the receiver or transmitter of it.

The mind, it is said, is a great servant, but a very poor master, because if we allow it to become the sole lead in our lives and our only voice, the medium of mind limits us to itself and becomes our only guiding message.

In the involutionary view, we live not only in a sea of materiality, but also in a sea of thought. At each moment, our intentions, thoughts, feelings and actions are either adding to this collective field (collective unconscious)[7] of intelligence, or else taking from it. Moment by moment, we are plugging in and attuning to this field at the very same time that it is plugging in and resonating with us. Creativity and receptivity become simultaneous ongoing processes.

Mind inhabits a body, but an aspect of mind has an existence that is separate from the body and can access information that is beyond our personal experience or knowledge.

Mind is also considered to be the builder, where whatever we focus our attention on will be built for us, for better or worse. Thoughts — according to involutionary theory — are as important and as real as things, because the mind does not distinguish between external and internal realities. In our earlier example of a projector, film and movie screen, the mind is the film that shapes the light of our essence into our reality. In this way, our thoughts eventually become our perceptions that are the substance of our reality that in turn, shapes our world.

In the involutionary view, there are three stages of thought: perception, reflection and opinion. In our fast-paced culture, we often perceive an event or situation (such as reading a story in a newspaper) and move directly to an opinion (by sharing the story writer's opinion as if it were our own) without investing any time to first reflect upon it. The lack of a habit of reflection is a recipe for fragmentation rather than integration. Through reflection, the isolated and hardened islands of long-term memory and perception have the ability to move and come together in often surprising ways. Reflection is the catalyst and lubricant that becomes integration in motion.

Integrative Leaders develop the mental domain of intelligence through study and education. They learn through teaching and experiencing, cultivating their abilities, talents and skills, and adopting mental attitudes that are positive and constructive rather than negative and destructive. The needs of the mental domain are stimulation and challenge. Without them, a leader will become autonomic, hypnotized, mesmerized, habituated or asleep. The purpose of the mental domain of intelligence is growth — through learning, awakening, cultivating and maintaining conscious awareness.

The Emotional Domain

Emotion is the chief source of all becoming conscious.
There can be no transforming of darkness into light
and of apathy into movement without emotion.

CARL JUNG

The emotional domain of intelligence is the realm of body sensations, feelings and emotions. We need healthy bodies and alert minds in order to accomplish our goals and play our roles in life and leadership. However, we are often not aware of the role that emotions play in supporting or thwarting our journey towards integration.

Emotions are defined as a 'strong surge of feeling that is marked by a desire to express outwardly what we are feeling inwardly, often accompanied by strong and complex bodily reactions.'

Feelings involve body sensations such as hot or cold, pain or pleasure, tension or release. Examples of emotions are: joy, anger, surprise, happiness, friendliness, anxiety, desire, shyness, loneliness, embarrassment, hurt, tiredness, confidence, energy and sadness.

Sensations are like words, feelings are like sentences and emotions are like paragraphs that form the story of our heart's needs and desires.[8] If we can learn to listen, decipher and interpret the voice of our emotional domain, we will gain a formidable companion on our journey of integration.

An Evolutionary Perspective on Emotions

While, according to Western conceptions, the brain is the exclusive seat of consciousness, yogic experience shows that our brain-consciousness is only one among a number of possible forms of consciousness, and that these, according to their function and nature, can be localized or centered in various organs in the body.

LAMA ANAGARIKA GOVINDA

From an evolutionary perspective, the reptilian brain (the brain stem) — that controls our autonomic functions such as breathing, circulation and digestion

— is the part of the brain that evolved first. The mammalian brain (the mid-brain or limbic system), that contains our long-term memory patterns and stores emotional memories, evolved second. The human brain (the cerebrum), that contains our intelligence, ability to reason and imagination, evolved last. The three levels of the brain may also be seen in relation to the four domains of intelligence, if the two hemispheres of the cerebrum are considered as logic and reason (left brain) and imagination and emotion (right brain).

As humans evolved over 10 million years, the body's needs and appetites took the lead. Feelings were believed to be sensate, instinctual and impulsive. As we evolved further and developed intelligence and the ability to reason, emotions — which some consider to be a way to organize feelings — evolved as well. In human evolution, emotion overtly relinquished leadership to the domain of mind, but covertly continued to influence, through the unconscious, our every decision, problem or plan.

Today, there are times when our reason leads and our emotions follow. Other times, our emotions lead and our reason follows.

In situations we perceive as threatening, our instinct for self-preservation overrides our reason, and our emotions govern and control our reactions. Daniel Goleman, who popularized Emotional Intelligence over the past decade, coined a phrase that described this process as an "Amygdala Hijacking."[9]

In an "Amygdala Hijacking," sensory signals from the body pass through the thalamus on the brain stem and are routed to the Amygdala (the center of emotion) at the base of the brain and then to the Executive Control Centre (ECC) in the prefrontal lobes (the center of reason) of the brain. The Amygdala associates past memories with the current sensory event. If the current event matches something we had experienced before that was frightening or of concern, it sets off an alarm which activates our fight-or-flight sequence that releases a flood of adrenalin that causes us to react to the situation from our past memories, as opposed to responding to the situation in the present. The flood of emotion overwhelms our working memory and becomes the lead for that moment in our life.

The result is an outburst of emotion and a bodily reaction to either fight and get angry or run and stay afraid. There are times when this reaction is completely appropriate, but there are more times when we react emotionally and impulsively, when we're not sure why this happened, and later regret having acted as we did.

Self-control and self-management are a part of developing our emotional intelligence.

For the majority, self-control consists of suppression and repression as opposed to appropriate expression. Tactics often used to control strong emotional reactions include avoidance, suppression, compromise, abdication or medication. Each of these has a negative impact on our mental, emotional and physical well-being.

For example, our desire to express an emotion on the one hand, and our mental evaluation that it may be inappropriate to do so on the other, causes a conflict within the body that is known as a "muscle lock." Muscle lock can exist in our legs, stomach, back, chest, throat, neck, head or other body areas and may inhibit proper functioning of the systems of the body and eventually lead to disease. Muscle lock is one of many somatic indicators that an emotion desiring to be expressed is being consciously or unconsciously suppressed.

Learning to align our intentions, thoughts and actions with our expressed emotions is one way to move from a fragmented to an integrated physiological and emotional condition.

The limbic system operates on *fuzzy logic*, which means that emotional situations and states from the past will evoke a similar emotional reaction through projection and transference in the present. Seeing a German shepherd dog today could cause a reaction of fear or anger if as a child you were bitten, mauled and hospitalized by a German shepherd. The unresolved issue of the past event is projected onto the dog in the present, even though logic and reason recognize they are not the same dog. Being unreasonably upset and angry with your daughter today for not keeping her word is linked in memory to the unresolved anger you still hold towards your husband for not keeping his word many years before (transference).

Emotions travel across time, linking emotional events together in memory using fuzzy logic. In this way, emotionally charged and unresolved issues from our past continue to influence our present.

Resonance is a concept which describes how vibrations are shared between two or more objects or systems. The concept of resonance is found as an observable principle in acoustics, physics, chemistry, medicine and biology, among others. An example of acoustic resonance can be observed in a tuning fork. One tuning fork, that is struck and is vibrating, will cause a second tuning fork some distance away (that is tuned to a similar frequency) to sympathetically vibrate. Everything has a natural resonant frequency that, if struck, may be constructive and add value to a thing, system or relationship; or, it may be destructive.

Researchers wondered if, since resonance was a phenomenon observed physically and electro-magnetically in circuits and energy fields, could this resonant idea also be applied to the field of intrapersonal, interpersonal and group communications and interactions? The concept of resonance, and its associated principles, may help explain what we all have observed and experienced in ourselves and with others. For instance: Why do you dislike some people almost instantly (dissonance)? Why is there a connection, a similar wavelength, or an ability to see eye-to-eye and communicate on multiple levels with someone you've just met (resonance)? Why do you sometimes have to listen and converse with someone for a long time before you finally click and connect (searching and finding attunement)?

Emotions travel across space and distance and are infectious. This phenomenon may be explained by applying concepts and principles of resonance, not only to the physical, but also the mental and emotional domains.

If our receptive system becomes dampened by muscle locks, physical contractions and mental models of resistance to sensations, feelings and emotions, we cannot experience the resonant emotional vibrations of others. If this practice of shutting down becomes a habit, then we also remove our ability to become aware, experience and deal with our own emotional states. Resonant attunement, awareness, allowance and acceptance are methods that help us begin to understand the language of our own heart which then allows us to empathetically understand the hearts of others.

Short-term strategies for dealing with an "Amygdala Hijacking" include withdrawing from the situation, pausing for reflection, journaling about the issue, sitting in silence, going for a walk, and having a discussion with someone. These strategies may deal with the moment, but they don't resolve the original emotionally charged memory. The process of integration suggests that we choose to deal with the shadow side of life and leadership resident within our own bodies, hearts and minds, and to return that shadow side to the light of conscious awareness.

We will discuss the transformative and transcendent processes more fully in Chapter 5.

Endocrinology and Emotions

In man, soul and body touch each other only at a single point,
the pineal gland in the head.

RENEE DESCARTES

From the scientific evolutionary perspective, if the body is comprised of multiple physical systems and processes that sustain life, and if mental consciousness is related to our nervous system that includes the brain, current research suggests that emotions are highly involved with our body's endocrine system.

The endocrine system is a series of ductless glands that secrete powerful mood-altering and character-shaping hormones which in turn affect the well-being of our body and mind. Lacking their own system of distribution, these glands are called endocrine or 'ductless' because they inject their secretions directly into our blood stream for circulation throughout the body.

Hormones are comprised of proteins, steroids and chemical compounds called *amines*. A very small amount of hormones has a significant effect on the body, emotions and mind.

The existence of these glands was first noted in ancient Greece in the fourth century B.C. They were rediscovered in sixteenth-century Europe; then, in the twentieth century, anatomical investigations evolved into the specialization of endocrinology, a branch of modern medicine that is devoted to the study and treatment of the endocrine system.[10]

There are seven principle glands or tissues in our endocrine system, situated from the top of the midbrain (the pineal gland) to the base of the pelvis (the gonads). Our seven glands from top to bottom are: pineal, pituitary, thyroid, thymus, adrenals, pancreas and gonads (ovaries and testes).

The three upper endocrine glands are the pineal, pituitary and thyroid. The pineal gland is situated in the top of the midbrain, is about the size of a pea and is thought to be photosensitive. The pineal gland produces the hormone melatonin, a derivative of tryptophan and serotonin, during the night. Melatonin influences our natural biorhythms and other glands and systems of the body. The pituitary gland is comprised of three lobes, is situated at the base of the brain (a line from the top of our head intersecting with another from between our eyebrows) and is considered to be the master gland of the body. The pituitary secretes hormones that stimulate all the other endocrine glands, and it also produces natural opiates that act on the nervous system to reduce pain. The thyroid gland is situated at the throat around our larynx (voice box) and regulates our growth, maturation, metabolism, and physical and mental alertness. The parathyroid, which is embedded in the thyroid gland, produces hormones that regulate calcium and phosphorus in the blood and enhance bone resorption.

The middle endocrine gland is the thymus. This gland lies behind the sternum (breastbone), which is located in the upper chest. It is made up of mostly lymphatic tissue, grows until puberty is complete, and then slowly involutes (or shrinks), replacing lymphatic tissue with fat as we grow older. The thymus gland produces lymphocytes and antibodies and has a positive impact upon our immune system.

The three lower endocrine glands are the adrenals, the pancreas and the gonads. The two adrenal glands sit on top of the kidneys and are comprised of the medulla (inner gland) and the cortex (outer gland). The adrenal glands produce adrenalin and noradrenalin, used to arouse and activate the body during acute emergencies. The pancreas injects digestive juices directly into the upper small intestine and also produces insulin and glucogen.[11] The gonads manifest as ovaries in females and testes in males. The ovaries produce eggs, progesterone and estrogen in the female body. The testes produce sperm and androgens, the most important of which is testosterone.

Hormone levels in our bloodstream are controlled by individual glands, groups of glands working in cooperation, the master gland of the body (the pituitary) and the central nervous system.

The easiest gland for us to sense is the adrenal gland. When we perceive a threatening or stressful situation, adrenalin is pumped into the bloodstream that is first felt in our stomach, then by our accelerated heart and breathing rates. The adrenalin makes the body ready, in multiple and complex ways, to either face the situation (fight) or run away (flight). This is a physical or somatic reaction to a feeling of fear. If the choice is to fight, our fear may turn to anger. If the choice is to flee, our fear helps propel us from the situation. The effects of this adrenalin injection into our bodies may last up to 20 minutes and be retriggered if we reflect on the original situation, since mind does not distinguish between external reality or internal memory and imagination.

The search for natural hormones during the past 30 years has stemmed from the following hypothesis: "If external drugs — such as pharmaceutical drugs, hallucinogens, heroin and opium—were able to find natural receptors in the body, then the body must also produce natural substances that safely connect with these same receptors." Candace Pert, in her book *Molecules of Emotion*, documents a quest that ended in her successfully finding natural opiates in the body that she called endorphins.[12] Endorphins can reduce pain without side effects and, gram for gram, are tens of thousands of times more powerful in suppressing pain than is morphine.

A little natural inner hormone seems to go a very long way.

The endocrine system has a significant effect on our moods, emotions, motivation and well-being. The emerging Integrative Science of Psycho-Neuro-Endocrinology brings together Cognitive Psychology, Neuroscience, Neuropsychology, Neurobiology and Endocrinology, in an effort to more fully understand the relationships between the body, brain, mind and emotions.

An Involutionary Perspective on Emotions

...It is possible now to conceive of mind and consciousness as an emanation of emotional information processing, and as such, mind and consciousness would appear to be independent of brain and body.

Candace Pert

The relation between virtual particles and the vacuum is an essentially dynamic relation; the vacuum is in reality a 'living Void', pulsating in endless rhythms of creation and destruction. The discovery of the dynamic quality of the vacuum is seen by many physicists as one of the most important findings of modern physics. From its role as an empty container of the physical phenomena, the void has emerged as a dynamic quantity of utmost importance. The results of modern physics thus seem to confirm the words of Chinese sage Chang Tsai: 'When one knows that the Great Void is full of Ch'I [vital energy] one realizes that there is no such thing as nothingness.'

Fritjof Capra

From an involutionary perspective, emotions existed from the first moment of creation. A typical creation myth sounds something like this:

In the beginning was the primordial womb of Oneness that throbbed and pulsed within itself and was an Ocean of Being that filled all of space and all of time. And in infinite time, it decided within itself to move. And in that movement, a desire was born within itself that knew itself to be Love that said, "Let there be Light" and there was light, not of the body, but the light that is and ever will be the Light of the Mind of the Divine. And the light of awareness and the all-knowing darkness desired to dance, one with each other as One. And in that dance they sang the song of first creation for an eternity and a time. And after a time a thought came and it was this: "With whom can we share the joy of this song and dance of Creation?" And the thought reflected back from itself and to itself that it would share the dance with itself and for itself, but not as the One, but in the desire born from Love, as the many. And souls were born, each made in the Image of the First Cause and All That Is. And each soul had an equal portion of spirit; each had an

> equal portion of mind; and each had an equal portion of free will and desire so that each could choose which note it could play in the music, which step it could make in the dance, and which lyric to sing in harmony, balance, love and joy, in the Song of Divine Creation.

In this creation myth, there are three aspects to All That Is: Spirit, Mind and Desire. The spirit is life that through desire born of love gives birth to the mind that is light. These two primordial parents, Mother Life and Father Light, give birth in love to our souls and made each one of us in their Image, each carrying a portion of their original divine elements — Spirit, Mind and Desire.

> Because of the gift of free will, some souls, as is the way with children, chose not to play harmoniously in the original Song of Creation, but to go and sing a song that they composed themselves.

This was the original separation (or fall) from a place of harmony and integration (such as heaven) into a place of discord and fragmentation (such as Earth).

> In the course of time the fallen souls became so enmeshed in their own physical creations that each forgot who they truly were.
>
> From the center of Divine Love there arose a desire to help those who were lost by giving them an opportunity to return to the whole. To accomplish this task, the One Light divided itself into seven lesser lights and placed them each within the body of these lost souls. These seven are the seven connections, the seven laws, the seven motivations, the seven lamps, the seven eyes, the seven ears, the seven churches and the seven seals of the body that when opened, would allow the body that held the soul, if it chose, to remember its relationship with the One that is, All That Is.
>
> Then Teachers, Sages and Enlightened Ones were sent by the One to all places and all times to help awaken the lights of awareness within these sleeping bodies and their unawakened souls. These promised ones came to help those who had forgotten who and what they truly were. They came to remind them that they were Children of the First Cause: Sons and Daughters of All That Is.

> However, the forces for separation bound these forgetful ones with fear, lies and disharmony to keep them in blinding darkness. In the midst of the ignorant darkness, these Enlightened Ones who embodied love, truth and harmony, invited each forgetful soul to walk towards the light; to move towards the love; to flow towards the peace.
>
> Many separated ones were deaf or chose not to hear. Many were blind or chose not to see. Many were in struggle and chose not to feel the peace of the Divine invitation. And so many remained in fear, lies and darkness till the end of their time, not from a choice born of knowledge, but from a choice made in ignorance and forgetfulness.
>
> But there were some, although not many, who chose to hear. There were some, just a few, who chose to see. And there were some who chose to face the light, remember themselves, and walk the path that illuminated the darkness within and without, and freed them from bondage, allowing them to return to the Source as fully individual and unique, and yet one with the Whole.

The seven points of connection are the seven centers or *chakras* (Sanskrit for "wheels") that were placed, according to Yogic wisdom tradition, within the body of humankind as a path that would allow us to remember and return to the Source. The seven points of connection are also found in Jewish mystic traditions as the symbol of the Sefirot, in which the ten limbs can be reduced to the seven candles of the menorah. They may also be found in Western Christian Traditions as the seven churches, seven sacraments and seven seals mentioned in the Book of Revelation.[8, 13]

The seven centers represent universal levels of consciousness and motivation that are correlated to positions in the spine and head. The physical order of these seven centers from top to bottom are: the crown, brow (the point between the eyebrows above the bridge of the nose), throat, chest, belly, navel, root (tail bone or coccyx). The highest level is experienced — as *being* — as a state of cosmic universal consciousness, and the lowest level is experienced — as *doing* — as a state of earthly consciousness.

The three lowest centers or chakras are related to the mechanistic paradigm. The fourth or heart chakra is related to the organic paradigm (with influences from the third and fifth chakras). The three highest chakras are related to the wholistic paradigm.

Table 5: Seven Centers and Various Correlations

Center	Name	Modified Maslow	Cultural Paradigms	Universal Principals	Hawkins Emotions – Motivations
7	Crown	*Enlightenment*	WHOLISTIC	Love	Bliss
6	Brow	Transcendence	WHOLISTIC	Truth	Joy
5	Throat	Self-Actualization	WHOLISTIC	Desire	Serenity
4	Heart	Transformation/ Relationship[1]	ORGANIC	Harmony	Love – Hope – Peace
3	Belly	Self Esteem[1]	MECHANISTIC	Cause & Effect	Courage – Pride – Power
2	Navel	Safety	MECHANISTIC	Creativity	Fear – Anger – Hate
1	Root	Physiological	MECHANISTIC	Life	Guilt – Shame – Despair

[1] Maslow related Self Esteem to the 4th center and Relationship (Belonging) to the 3rd center. We have modified them as shown. Center's 3 and 5 are zones of overlap between Mechanistic – Organic and Organic – Wholistic.

Abraham Maslow related his "needs hierarchy" with six of the seven centers.[14] David Hawkins also related the seven centers to his map of consciousness and, in his book *Power vs. Force,* further suggests that there is a hierarchy among emotions and motivations.[15] Fear, guilt and shame are lower or heavier emotions that are negative attractors which lower our awareness downwards to the mechanistic paradigm, whereas love, peace, hope and joy act as positive attractors that lift our awareness upwards towards the wholistic paradigm.

There is an ongoing search in psychology for the "primary color emotions." These are emotions from which all other feelings and reactions when combined are sourced. Early tests conducted by John Watson, the father of behavioral psychology, focused on love, anger and fear as candidates for "primary color emotions."[16] We discovered recurring patterns in the creation myths, from diverse cultures worldwide, that support Watson's ideas but suggest an even simpler explanation.

In the primordial dance of integration and separation, the original divine emotion and motivation for integration was Love. The original self-created emotion and motivation for separation was Fear. [17]

Within our hearts we have a choice between Doubt — which is born of ignorance rather than the all-knowing darkness — and Faith, which is born of the illuminating light of awareness. If we choose to live in Doubt, then Doubt becomes the father, Fear becomes the mother and their children of darkness are shame, guilt, worry, disgust, pride, anger, rage, mistrust and avarice.[18] If we choose to live in Faith, then Faith becomes the father, Love becomes the mother and their children of light are peace, kindness, gentleness, hope, patience, compassion and longsuffering.[19]

One choice allows us to remain as we are. The other choice allows us to move across the gaps that exist between our *image of self* and *Real Self*, and between our *Real Self* and our *Ideal Self*. The choice of which inner emotional children we choose to play with in our journey of life and leadership is up to us.

Integrative Leadership is about awakening the heart. It is about cultivating awareness of our sensations, feelings and emotions while learning to listen and interpret the language of the heart. It is about being willing to deal with inhibiting, limiting or negative emotions that keep us bound to our *image of self* and prevent us from walking towards our Ideal Self. It is about aligning the energy of our emotions with our actions, thoughts and intentions in a way that supports us in life and leadership.

And it is a way of awakening from the *living dead* by choosing to live life fully once again.

The Spiritual Domain

> *As from its fineness, the all-pervading ether is not touched, so the soul, located in every body, is not touched. As the one Sun illumines all this world so He, that abideth in the body, lights up the whole field. They, who with the eye of Wisdom perceive the distinction between the field and the Knower of the field, and the liberation of being from nature, go to the Supreme.*
>
> BHAGAVAD GITA, XIII, PP. 32, 33, 34.

Whereas the home of the Scientist is the physical domain, the home of the Psychologist is the mental domain, and the home of the Artist is the emotional domain, we suggest the home of the Mystic is the spiritual domain. All of the wisdom and mystic traditions point to this domain as an aspect of our Divine nature that is often unacknowledged, undeveloped and remains invisible and unknown.

In the past, the ordinary person with a burning desire to awaken, embrace and experience the spiritual domain would have chosen to separate from the marketplace in order to integrate. Some would have chosen to be alone on their inner journey. Others would enter monasteries and convents, deserts and mountain caves, or islands and retreats in search of an external silence that would allow them to connect with their inner *Essence*. Their hope was to reach a state — with persistence, practice and patience — of nirvana, enlightenment, illumination, self-realization, universal cosmic consciousness or divine inspiration.

Many of these ordinary people who reached extraordinary states of awareness never returned. But a few did return to share their inner mystical experiences as best they could. They would often have difficulty communicating their experiences in a way that could be understood, for the mystic experience is often ineffable. They would live it and *be* it, teach it and *do* it, but rarely did they themselves write about it, often leaving that task for those whom they taught.

In the third millennium, the ordinary person with a burning desire to awaken, embrace, experience and develop their spiritual domain can separate and integrate within their current life, family, friends and organizations. They don't have to go anywhere. They can remain in the marketplace, for all the knowledge and secrets of the wisdom and mystic traditions can come to them in various ways: orally (through seminars, workshops, or retreats), in written form (in books, magazines, or newspapers), ritually (in churches, temples, mosques, synagogues or gathering places) and electronically (through television, radio, telephone or the Internet).

One aspect of integrative life and leadership is understanding that the sacred is present in everyday life.[20] All we need do is to become aware of it, choose to experience it, and then have the courage to authentically act like it in the moment.

Leadership and the Mystic Path

> *There is an understanding and practice of leadership that elevates spirit, honors the whole self, and encourages us to use all of our energies in the activities of leadership. There is an understanding and practice of leadership that taps into the best that is within us, that gives each of us an opportunity to be involved and engaged. There is an understanding and practice of leadership that helps us discover meaning in our work, that helps us live out our vision and make our mission manifest. It is an understanding that makes use of our spiritual energy, and it is understood as a spiritual experience. It leads to inspired performance.*
>
> Russ S. Moxley

There are similarities between the path of leadership and the path of the mystic. Both paths involve self-development, self-awareness and self-management. Both paths honor personal experience over preconceived beliefs. Leaders have mentors, and mystics have teachers; both study their role models in order to clearly define the practices they need to develop that will allow them each to move from good to great.

A good leader is one who is willing to move through the "crucible of leadership" in order to achieve a new vision of himself or herself. A good mystic is someone who is willing to move through the "dark night of the soul" in order to achieve a new vision of themselves.[21] Great leaders have an Ideal to which they aspire, and mystics have an Image of God by which they are inspired. Each has developed a personal vision, mission, passion and discipline with which to achieve their goals.

And our belief is that everyone can become a leader, and everyone can become a mystic.

Historically, there are also differences. Mystics, in the past, have been content to remain separated from organizations and society. Leaders are fully involved with their organizations and society. Mystics often walk alone. Leaders always walk with others and have a bias for outer action. Mystics have a bias for inner action. And the intent for each may be different. One may be seeking power on the earth while the other may be seeking power from the heavens.

Today, in this time of transition, a movement is emerging to integrate the path of leadership and the path of the mystic. The method of integration is to focus on similarities while situationally adapting differences. Gay Hendricks & Kate Ludeman, in their book *The Corporate Mystic,* give numerous examples of senior leaders, presidents and CEOs of large corporations who have woven what was formerly seen as mystic practices — daily meditation, introspection, and a weekly day of contemplative silence — into their work schedules.[22]

Integrative Life and Leadership is the process of integrating these two paths into daily life. It shows how to balance the inner journey of the mystic with the outer action-orientation of a leader. It teaches how to take the time to *separate,* in daily inner reflection, and also how to *integrate* within the marketplace.

Integrative Leadership is about service and contribution in honoring our individuality and uniqueness, while also honoring the individual and collective contributions and uniqueness of others.

Perspectives on Spiritual Intelligence

> *Spiritual Intelligence is the ultimate intelligence with which we address and solve problems of meaning and value, the intelligence with which we can place our actions and our lives in a wider, richer, meaning-giving context, the intelligence with which we can assess that one course of action or one life path is more meaningful than another.*
>
> DANA ZOHAR & IAN MARSHALL

The simplest definition of spiritual intelligence is that it is the intelligence of our soul. The soul is defined as 'the animating and vital principle in humankind credited with the faculties of thought, action and emotion and conceived as forming an immaterial entity distinguished from but temporally coexistent with the body.'

There has been much written concerning spiritual intelligence since the dawning of the third millennium.[23] Some perspectives that have emerged are:

- Those who have spiritual intelligence have the capacity for transcendence. They have a heightened consciousness and a capacity to endow everyday activity with a sense of the sacred; they use spiritual resources on practical problems, decisions and plans; and they engage in virtuous behaviors (forgiveness, gratitude, humility, compassion and wisdom) (Robert A. Emmons).

- Spiritual intelligence is the ultimate way of understanding life. We use it to envision unrealized possibilities and to transcend the methodical plod of life. We also use it to understand pain, to answer basic philosophical questions about life and to find meaning both temporally and existentially (Cynthia R. Davis).

- Spiritual intelligence is "the human capacity to ask ultimate questions about the meaning of life, and to simultaneously experience the seamless connection between each of us and the world in which we live" (Richard N. Wolman).

- Spiritual intelligence is not necessarily religious, or even dependent upon religion as its foundation. It can be defined in relation to or observed through some telling criteria such as truthfulness, compassion, respect for all levels of consciousness, constructive empathy, a sense of being a player in a large whole, generosity of spirit and action, an ability to be 'in tune' or 'in synch' with nature, and an ability to be comfortably alone without being lonely (Clive Simpkins).

- Spiritual intelligence "is the clear-lucid-loving-radiant Presence that is the deepest sense of identity within all beings and the organizing field that weaves a myriad of frequencies of energy into the complex and dynamic patterns of forms of all creation." Spiritual Intelligence of an individual or group of people is a reflected by the degree to which they are consciously aware of their multidimensionality and of their profound and complex interdependence with all living beings across those multiple dimensions and the degree to which they have integrated this wisdom-insight-understanding-intuition into how they live their lives. Spiritual intelligence is reflected in action by living with kindness-compassion as expressions of a wisdom that directly or intuitively beholds and honors the profound and intimate interdependence of all living beings across space and time, in this world and time, and in countless others (JOEL & MICHELLE LEVEY).

- The ten characteristics of spiritually intelligent people are: being flexible, being self aware, having a vision, using adversity positively, being wholistic and a synthesist, being open to diversity and difference, being field independent, asking why, reframing situations, and practicing servant leadership (DANA ZOHAR & IAN MARSHALL).

- The characteristics of spiritual intelligence are: an awareness of others, wonder, awe, a sense of the numinous (astronomy, microbiology, cosmology), wisdom (proverbs, sages), perspective, an ability to listen ("Be still and know that I am God"), comfort with chaos, with dichotomy and with paradox, commitment, dedication, faith, and a promise of hope and fulfillment (ILLINI CHRISTIAN FACULTY).

Evolution and Spiritual Intelligence

Beyond treatment of specific conditions, institutions such as Harvard University's Mind/Body Clinic have known for years that spirituality is hard-wired to health, that the brain has enormous influence over all other organs, that people who have a sense of oneness of body, spirit and mind are healthier people gamboling down the path to a longer and happier life.

JAMES HITT

From an evolutionary perspective, there are three relatively recent scientific events that suggest a neurobiological basis for emotional and spiritual Intelligence.

- Damasio and Ledoux have mapped neural pathways between the amygdala, the thalamus and the executive control centers located in the prefrontal lobes of the brain and have charted the possible connections between the limbic system and emotional intelligence.[24]

- Persinger and Ramachandran have shown that within the temporal and parietal lobes of the brain, magnetic resonance can be emitted when one ponders the larger questions of life. Participants in their experiments have also had seemingly mystical experiences under the influence of magnetic resonance fields imposed on them. Some have popularized Persinger and Ramachandran's work as having uncovered the "G-Spot" or "God Spot" within the brain.[25]

- Singer and Llinas et al. have shown that there are periodic, 40 Hz oscillations that occur in the brain. Understanding how these oscillations work could be the key to unlocking how we perceive both external events, during the waking state, and internal events, during the dreaming state. The 40 Hz oscillations appear to help integrate information at all times and at all levels of the brain.[26]

Involution and Spiritual Intelligence

The soul of man is the sun by which his body is illumined,
and from which it draweth its sustenance, and should be so regarded.

Baha'u'llah

The temple of man is like unto a mirror, his soul is as the sun,
and his mental faculties even as the rays that emanate from that source of light.

Abdu'l-Baha

In his book, *Liberating the Corporate Soul*, Richard Barrett defines consciousness as:

> A state of awareness of self (thoughts, feelings, ideas) based on a set of beliefs and values through which reality is interpreted. A shift to a higher state of consciousness involves a change in beliefs, values and behaviors. The values at the higher level of consciousness promote greater inclusiveness and connectedness and less separation and fragmentation.[27]

The process of *evolution* is a movement of awareness upward from fragmented and limited states of consciousness towards more expansive and integrated states of consciousness. The process of *involution* is the descent of higher, more expansive states of consciousness into our limited awareness.

There are higher states of consciousness beyond even the eight that comprise our current framework. In this view, the process of involution will continue to inform our soul so long as there is a desire to evolve and grow.[28]

Evolution and involution are never-ending stories of spiritual emergence and growth that are the ascent of the Soul of Humankind into the Mind of the Divine and the descent of that One Mind into the Soul and the body that it has chosen to inhabit for a time.

Integrative Perspectives on the Spiritual Domain

> *In Soul Consciousness, the separation between the ego and the soul disappears as we release the fears concerning our physical and emotional needs. Carl Jung called this process individuation—the integration of the unconscious content of our minds into our conscious awareness.*
>
> RICHARD BARRETT

From the scientific perspective, there is an underlying sense of order to the universe that is governed by natural laws. The discovery and application of these universal natural laws is science's greatest contribution to the story of the ascent of humankind.

Science has moved from the Laws of Mechanics (body) 300 years ago, to the Theory of Relativity (mind and heart) 100 years ago, to the field of Quantum Mechanics (spirit) that was popularized in earnest about 30 years ago. As a result of this movement, our understanding of the universe from a scientific perspective has changed dramatically.

There are times when light paradoxically acts as a particle and other times when it acts as a wave. Recent experiments that highlight an aspect of this emerging Quantum Mechanical (QM) perspective have shown that the intentions and beliefs of the observer influence the results of experimental observations. Subjective and objective perspectives are becoming blurred, implying that at the most fundamental level we shape and create our own reality. The QM perspective affirms what Socrates said 2,500 years ago: "we do not see things as they are, but rather as we are." [29]

The framework of the Universe is now seen by some as having various levels of energy, with the particle — that is the building block of the material Universe — as the photon of light. In this perspective, through the process of involution, light condenses first into charged particles, then into atoms that, when combined, form all known light and dark matter that comprise the known Universe.

The question, "Who are you?" might be answered from the perspective of the New Physics as, "You are light." Condensed light perhaps, but light nonetheless.

We do not understand the sources of life, light or energy, although we know their components and the laws that seem to govern their use and manipulation.

Biologists can manipulate and control life through genetic research and by engineering the laws of life, yet no biologist can clearly say what life is. A physicist can explain the properties, spectra, laws and constituents of light, but in the end cannot say exactly what light is. A power engineer can build machines to generate, transmit and use electricity for humankind's convenience, but cannot explain precisely what electricity is.

In each case, there is a mystery about life, light and energy that continues to elude the purely rational scientific perspective.

• • •

From the perspective of the wisdom and mystic traditions, the spiritual domain is the source of all energy and life. It is the womb of all knowing and original darkness from which all light was born. It is the One Source from which all life and true creative expression was born. It is the framework that defines the levels of consciousness and the universal laws and principles that govern them. And it is the breath that maintains our life which in turn gives us an opportunity to sound our unique note and sing a melody in harmony — or in discord — with the Song of Creation.

The spiritual domain is both *transcendent,* meaning outside of us, and *immanent,* meaning within us. If we view the spiritual domain as transcendent, then there is a need to discover it through external exploration. If we view it as immanent, then there is a need to seek it through internal exploration. We have found both these perspectives to be valid on our integrative journey.

If from the *transcendent* perspective we define "us" as our personality, then the spiritual domain exists outside of our own view of reality, even though it may be fully present and evident for those who have eyes to see.

Like the story of a seeker fish who asked a passing sage fish, "Excuse me sir. I am looking for the Ocean. Can you help me find it?" To which the sage fish replied, "You're swimming in it. It's all around you. You are breathing and living within it right now." With a look of sadness and disappointment, the seeker fish responded, "And I thought you were a sage fish. You don't even understand my question, do you?" And the seeker swam quickly away from the sage to resume its quest for the Ocean. There were times when we felt much like the seeker fish: misunderstood and determined to complete our quest, only to find — like Dorothy in the Wizard of Oz — that the tools to take us home were with us from the very beginning only we weren't aware of them.[30]

If from the *immanent* perspective we define "us" as our universality then, from our personality's perspective, we need to look deeper within ourselves in order to find it.

The transcendent view would suggest that the drop of water that is our individuality merges with the Ocean of Being. The immanent view would suggest that the Ocean of Being descends and enters the drop of water that is our individuality. We have found that the drop does merge with the Ocean, but it also feels that the Ocean merges with the drop that is our individuality synchronously.

From an integrative perspective, the only way we can become 100% objective is to become 100% subjective so that these two views of transcendent and immanent, evolution and involution, inner and outer become one. Without this blending, there is a disconnection between our inner and outer stories.

The spiritual domain is the home of our True Self, of which our conscious Ideal Self is but a reflection. It is the source of Truth of which our personal truth is but a reflection. It is the source of Love, Wisdom and Service of which our conscious love, understanding and service is but a reflection.

The Spiritual domain is the custodian of our true Mission, Calling or Purpose. Within this domain reside the collective knowledge and wisdom of universal laws that can guide and inform our journey towards integration.

Although there are times in life when our body leads, and other times when it is our mind or heart, our desire in walking the path of Integrative Life and Leadership is that our soul will assume more of the lead in our life. In this way our body, mind and heart will follow and in time become willing servants of our soul and the *spirit of life* that resides within it.

The process of integration then involves three paths: the path of transactional development of our *image of self*, the path of transformation from our image of self to our *Real Self*, and the path of transcendence from our Real Self to become our *Ideal Self*.

• • •

Relating the Four Domains of Intelligence

If we are to make progress in managing learning in organizations we desperately need contributions from fields which already have a Wholistic understanding of people and human systems. We need to understand much more the interconnectedness of emotional, physical and intellectual effort; we need help in seeing management holistically. Nobody can manage successfully if they use only a part of themselves ...managing is a whole person activity, demanding emotional [and spiritual] maturity at least as much as cerebral competence...relationships are at the heart of managing and at the heart of relationship is the key proposition of self-awareness.

David Casey

The mental, emotional and spiritual domains all express through the physical domain while we are in the waking state. The relationships among these domains are polarized along vertical and horizontal continuums. Schematically this is shown in Figure 5 as a cross with the physical-spiritual as the vertical and the mental-emotional as the horizontal.

Ideal Platonic forms or archetypes can be used to relate the four domains within a circle, square or triangle, which are two-dimensional projections of a sphere, cube, pyramid or cone.[31] Within a circle, the four domains represent four segments of Divine perfection (circle and cross) that is the ancient astrological symbol for the earth. Within a square, the four domains represent the four corners of the earth and the four elements of earth, air,

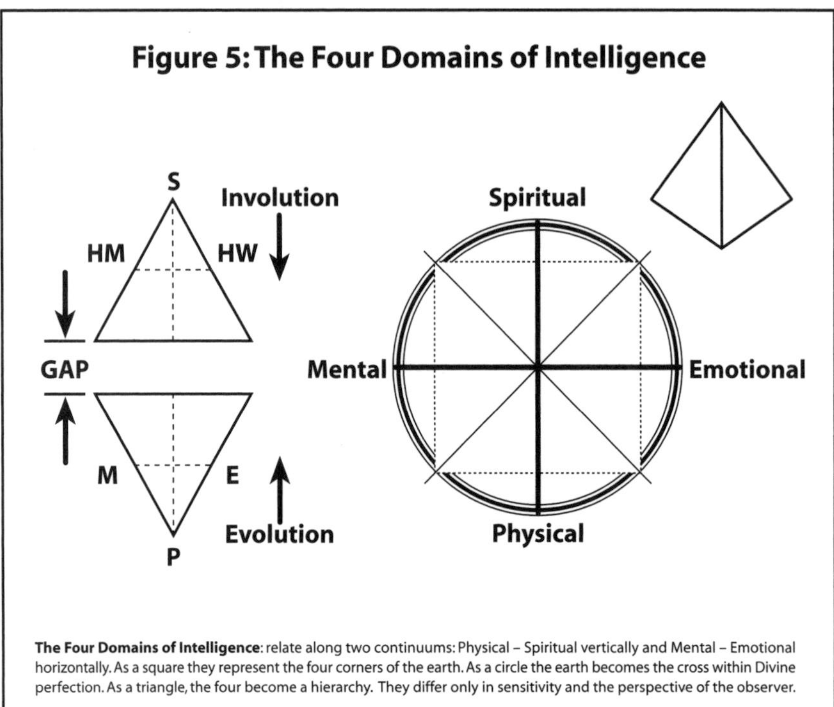

The Four Domains of Intelligence: relate along two continuums: Physical – Spiritual vertically and Mental – Emotional horizontally. As a square they represent the four corners of the earth. As a circle the earth becomes the cross within Divine perfection. As a triangle, the four become a hierarchy. They differ only in sensitivity and the perspective of the observer.

fire and water. Within a triangle, the four domains represent a hierarchy where Spiritual (S) is above physical (P) and the Higher Mental (HM) and Higher Will (HW) are separated from the lower mental (M) and emotional desires (E) by a gap that resides in the core of our being. The journey of integration is one method of bridging this gap. All three perspectives of the four domains are foundational Mandela that in one form or another are reflected in symbols that are found in many of the world's wisdom and mystic traditions.

Everyone has the same capacities resident within the four domains, but each person develops those capacities differently. Athletes have a well-developed physical intelligence. Scientists have a well-developed mental intelligence. Artists, painters and poets have a well-developed emotional intelligence, and sages and saints have highly developed spiritual intelligence (soul mind).

The process of becoming an Integrative Leader is a process that allows us to awaken and develop all four domains of intelligence and to align and focus them in an integrative approach to solve problems, make decisions and carry out plans in our daily life. In this way, inspiration is balanced by action, and reason is balanced by compassion.

An integrative approach to life and leadership that utilizes the four awakened, emerging and developing domains will in time result in the apprehension and realization of the gifts of wisdom, creative inspiration, intuition, clarity, balance and harmony in all that we think, do, say and feel.

In Search of the Perfect Metaphor

Our ordinary conceptual system,
in terms of which we both think and act,
is fundamentally metaphorical in nature.

George Lakoff

A Matter of Perspective

To perceive means to immobilize…we seize in the act of perception,
something which outruns perception itself.

Henri Bergson (1859–1941)

Rick and Lillas met at their favorite coffee shop after work one night. Luck was with them, for their usual table by the fireplace was empty. When Rick returned with Lillas's coffee and his tea, it was Lillas who opened their conversation.

"I'm having doubts about the usefulness of giving John and Mary our 'Building a Model of Integrative Leadership' paper." Rick looked up, surprised by her comment. "All day I've been trying to put into words why I'm feeling uncomfortable," Lillas continued. "I think my first discomfort is that John and Mary are both in crisis."

"Maybe Mary knows she is in crisis, but someone really should tell John. I don't think, despite our conversation about paradox and paradigms the other day, that he fully knows it."

"Maybe so. But whether they are aware or unaware, we know their physical, mental and emotional houses are on fire. They're burning from the inside out. Their world is changing as we speak, whether they know it or not. So as their coaches, our solution to their crisis was to tap them on the shoulder and say, 'Here, read this paper. Trust me. It'll help you.' I don't feel, in retrospect, that what we did makes much sense."

"Point taken," Rick said, acknowledging her perspective.

"Secondly," she continued, "I'm not sure if John or Mary will understand the model even if they've taken the time to read it. It's a very dense read. It would be difficult for the uninitiated, without discussion. I gave our paper to a friend to read last week. She called this morning and said, among other things, that reading our paper was like climbing Mount Everest. It was a long, slow, difficult, uphill climb."

"It is condensed reading," Rick nodded in agreement, finally understanding the source of Lillas's doubt. "But we did add lots of endnotes to help lighten the theoretical load."

"I'm not sure if anyone reads endnotes, Rick."

"Reader's choice," Rick shrugged. "They are very readable endnotes. Anyway, my feeling is that even if John and Mary don't understand our paper on one level, I know they will understand it on another. Giving them the paper, in my opinion, has done no harm and might lead to some good."

"Today, I'm even questioning our intent," Lillas continued, undeterred. "Did we give them our paper to show how smart we are, or to genuinely help them in their journey?" She paused. "What was your intent?"

"My intent? To give them some background and a way to rediscover who they are; to give them an internal and external road map; to share with them the integrative model of life and leadership that we've uncovered; to alert them to the next steps we will use, if they are willing, in their personal process of integration. That was my intent."

"So what did you feel was important for them to know that we haven't already shared with them?" Lillas asked disarmingly.

"In my mind, the first significant step into the model is to cultivate the ability to see yourself and your situation from multiple perspectives. If you are an extrovert, try being an introvert for a while. If you are always in your head, try being in your heart for a while. If you only see solutions to your health problems in conventional western medicine, try out alternative healing modalities for a while — or vice versa. If you're an evolutionist and think life is accidental, then try out involution for a while where life is purposeful. Many of us have forgotten that life is an experience, but it is also an experiment. We are trying to help them remember that. "

"But you've already done that with John in your coaching sessions."

"True, but I'm not sure he got it. It's one thing to believe something in your head. It's quite another to believe it in your heart. I don't feel any emotion behind his statement about adopting an involutionary belief. It was mechanical and not organic, just words without energy. And I see no evidence in John's behavior to indicate a meaningful change in perspective.

"Despite your friend suggesting our model-building paper is complex, we both know from experience that the first step into the model is simple. We've learned that without cultivating an ability to see multiple perspectives, without deeply listening and trying to walk in the other person's shoes for a time, without a willingness to experiment with life, we can only see a portion of the truth and not its full measure. John can only see at the moment one segment of truth, one model, one paradigm, one perspective about his current life-and-death health crisis: his own."

"Like the old story of the three blind men and the elephant," Lillas offered.

"Exactly," Rick said leaning forward. "The first blind man is hugging one of the elephant's legs, saying an elephant is like a tree trunk. The second blind man is patting the elephant's side saying no, an elephant is not like a tree trunk, but more like a hairy wall. The third blind man is holding onto the elephant's tail saying, no, an elephant is not like a tree trunk, nor is it like a wall—it is more like a living rope or a moving snake. Which perspective is right?"

"They all are. Each one has a portion of the truth, but none of the three have it all."

"But that is where I feel John is in his process. He is desperately hugging the elephant that is his work, family and illness, saying it is like a tree trunk and refusing to listen to the other perspectives that are all around him. He is unwilling to take advice or change places with the guy in the middle or the guy at the end of the elephant in order to experience for himself what their truths are like," Rick concluded.

"There is another way," Lillas suggested. "John can decide to trust the other two blind men, sit down with them, and respect their stories enough to understand that the truth of their experience — although very different from his own — may be an aspect of the truth, just the same.

"I remember someone sharing with me that 'the truth is not spoken until many voices are heard'. The three blind men could choose to form what Parker Palmer calls a community of truth.[32] They could listen deeply to each other and in that way learn more about the truth, shared in radical honesty, than any one of them experienced separately. Each piece of the truth that they share openly, if accepted, could be used to put together a puzzle showing a more wholistic view of truth for their mutual benefit."

"In John's frame of reference, I'm one of those two other blind men," Rick replied. "Even though John believes that I have at least one eye open enough to be his coach, I haven't won his complete trust. Our relationship is superficial, business as usual, and not real. He talks. I listen. I reflect back to him what I have heard. I share with him a different perspective on his story. He listens politely. In the end, nothing meaningful happens. At this stage of our relationship, our conversations are transactional, not transformational."

"But John is getting your message at some level of awareness," Lillas said, reflecting back to Rick his earlier comment about their model-building paper, "even if it's not exactly what you want in this moment. We know from experience on our own journey that no constructive effort done with good intention is ever wasted." Lillas paused, "I think that you and John have formed a community of truth, even though he may not be aware of it. As his coach, your job is to invite in the right spirit, and hold the constructive belief and trusting space so that John's transformational journey has an opportunity to begin."

"You're right," Rick said gently taking Lillas's hand. "Thank you for reminding me of my purpose." They sat there enjoying the spirit of mutual understanding that had joined, like the unexpected warmth of a Chinook wind in winter, their conversation.

"Although," Rick continued more peacefully, "no matter how strongly I hold the trust within the space between us, I am also sensing that for meaningful change to happen, John will need an emotional wake-up call. He will need to experience a deep visceral gut-level reaction to help move him out of his present limited perspective.

"Unlike the blind men and the elephant, John is not physically blind, but he is blind emotionally and spiritually. The eyes of his heart and the eyes of his soul are sealed shut, either by habit or through lack of use. I'm trying to encourage him to willingly open his eyes so that he can see another perspective, but I'm not sure he wants to.

"So to answer your question, Lillas, I gave John the model-building paper with the hope that he might read it. If he reads it, then he might understand some of it and that might help him. If there are parts he doesn't understand, then he might ask me about those parts. If he asks, then there is the hope of us engaging in a more meaningful dialogue than we've had to date. I gave him our paper with the intent to help him, not to hurt him."

Rick paused then looked directly into Lillas's eyes.

"So in John's mind, he is right. And from his current perspective, I would have to agree. He *is* right. The only thing that saddens me is that if he continues on his current path, if he insists on seeing his world from his limited perspective, then I know from personal experience that it's only a matter of time before he's *dead* right."

The Perfect Metaphor

Metaphors are much more tenacious than facts.

PAUL DE MAN

Rick and Lillas lightened their conversation by taking some time to discuss each of their children, family and friends in the context of upcoming social events. When it felt right, Lillas steered their conversation back to their model-building paper.

"The way we've written our paper is more like textbook than story. I think it will be a difficult read and maybe hard for some people to understand. I feel we need to link the model with a good analogy, allegory or metaphor. Your diagrams relating the four domains of intelligence, using circles, squares, crosses and triangles, don't make a lot of sense without some kind of image that will make them come alive in the reader's imagination. What do you think?"

"Who is talking now? Is it you or your friend on Mount Everest?" Rick asked with a smile.

Lillas smiled in return and admitted it was primarily her friend, but she thought she did have a good point and had promised herself she would raise the issue with him sooner rather than later.

"The diagrams relating the four domains of intelligence as two-dimensional projections of three-dimensional Platonic forms — that include spheres, cubes and various octahedral views — are universal perspectives," Rick said, noting the puzzled look on Lillas's face.

Knowing that a picture is worth a thousand words, he took out a pen and sketched on a napkin the shape of an octahedron, two four-sided pyramids joined at the base, then separated them and placed them both individually then together within a sphere. He then rotated the sphere in a series of sketches to show Lillas how the different perspectives, projections and dimensions produced by that sphere's rotation was dependent on the observer's beliefs. It was in fact the observer's belief system or mental model that changed the perspective of the model as circles (which implied community) or triangles (which implied hierarchy). When he finished his sketches, Lillas graciously nodded, but Rick could sense she had disengaged. Despite his inner sense, he continued his monologue to its conclusion.

"These geometric shapes are a simple way of viewing consciousness from a hyperspace perspective.[33] Those drawings are also in alignment with our research and understanding of the world's wisdom and mystic traditions.[34] I don't think there's anything fundamentally wrong with them just the way they are. They are defendable as an integrative model from many different disciplines and perspectives."

"Your models and drawings may be perfect intellectually, but I don't think we can speak just to people's heads. We also need to cultivate the ability to speak to their hearts. You can use mathematics and geometry to appeal to reason all you want, but I believe you also need to stimulate and engage the listener's imagination," Lillas said that made Rick pause and reflect on her wisdom.

"We have about an hour before our supper engagement. My suggestion is that we play a little game before supper."

"What kind of game?" Rick asked, brightening.

"Why don't you and I agree to move into our creative imaginative roles, put on our green thinking hats [35], and search for the perfect metaphor to describe the four domains of intelligence not just for ourselves, but for others in our family, circle of friends, or the marketplace."

"What are the rules of the game?"

"Let's see," Lillas said thoughtfully, "why don't we keep it simple. This game is not about the number of metaphors we can come up with in the next hour, but the highest quality of metaphor. The highest quality metaphor would include one that is resonant with the most number of people, is clearly understood, and links with as many integrative concepts as possible without disengaging the listener's imagination. How's that for a spontaneous set of rules?"

"Sounds good," Rick said with a smile, standing up. "Let me go buy some refills for your coffee and my tea. When I get back, let the games begin!"

Dreaming of the Four Domains

When Rick returned, he agreed to be the first one to start.

"In my dream work over the past 30 years, I've seen common themes running through my own and others' dreams. From an evolutionary mechanistic perspective, dreams are simply a product of our physical processes, like digestion, or a rehashing of our waking life experiences."

"You mean like Ebenezer Scrooge in Dickens's *A Christmas Carol*[36] where, when the ghost of his former business partner, Jacob Marley, visits him on Christmas Eve and asks Scrooge what he thinks is going on, Scrooge answers that he is only having a dream — or more like a nightmare — that was most likely caused by something disagreeable that he had eaten, like a piece of cheese gone bad, or perhaps a bit of undigested beef," Lillas offered.

"Yes. That is the evolutionary perspective on dreams and many have advocated this view in past centuries. *A Christmas Carol* is a wonderful story that shows the involutionary power of dreams to be transformative and transcendent. [37] In one evening, Scrooge undergoes a total personality change from his false self to his True Self. I've heard that Charles Dickens wrote that story in one night of inspiration and laughed and wept continually as the insights flowed to him and through him. When he finished writing the manuscript, Dickens also experienced transformation. His life was changed. Writing that manuscript was the transformational catalyst that allowed him to move from a lower to a higher level of awareness. His gift and legacy to us was a universal parable about the soul's journey that resonates at a place deep within.

"From the involutionary perspective, the soul is independent of the physical body and occupies it for a time. Our body is the vehicle that allows us to experience the world. So in my dreams, I've been either an observer or a participant in the dream drama. As a participant, I would find myself in a house, building, city, countryside or an unfamiliar foreign land. I would find myself alone, or with a group of people I knew or did not know. The people and the situation formed a context that could — from one perspective — be interpreted as extensions of my own level of awareness."

"Didn't Jesus say, 'In my Father's house there are many mansions'?"[38]

"Exactly," Rick agreed. "Many mansions, many states of consciousness or levels of awareness that we can explore either in the waking, dreaming or deep sleep stages that are considered universal. So, one of the recurring themes I've observed is that people find themselves in their dreams in different vehicles that are, on analysis, representations of the four domains of intelligence and their life journeys.

"Some dreamers find themselves hiking in a river valley, by a beach, or up a mountain. Others find themselves on bicycles, motorcycles, cars, buses, boats, planes and trains. Each situation and associated dream symbol represents their soul's vehicle and its relationship with them at that time in their life. Carl Jung has suggested that one of the purposes of a dream is to give us another perspective on our life, one that we may not be consciously aware of.

"So one metaphor that would resonate with this universal involutionary theme would be to see our 'body vehicle' as an automobile.[39]

"Now let's imagine that riding in the car are a woman and a man, and in the backseat, a young adult child. This *family* has decided to take a trip. They have a goal to reach somewhere by a certain time in order to fulfill some purpose. Say they are visiting someone who is important to them, such as a parent or somebody significant. It is an important occasion, and they don't want to miss it. So they've plotted out their route. They make sure the car is well-maintained and filled with fuel in the tank, water in the radiator, air in the tires and oil in the engine. They have a good idea about where they're going. And that morning they embark on their journey. Initially the man is driving, the woman is in the passenger seat with the map, navigating as needed, and the quiet, innocent, young adult child who has been with them from the very beginning is in the back seat, watching and observing all that is happening. There's the scene and the situation."

Rick paused and asked, "Are you imagining this scene with me, Lillas?"

"It's pretty familiar. You and I have experienced it many times in the past," Lillas agreed with a smile.

"Good," Rick said, satisfied. "Now if this were a dream, and we adopted the perspective that it was all about different aspects of who we are internally and not about things externally, who or what could the symbols, situation and images in the dream represent? Wait, let's make this more personal. If this was *your* dream, Lillas, who would the various characters represent for *you*?"

Lillas reflected for a moment. "Well, you already suggested that the car would be our physical body, so that is fairly clear. The car, made up of trillions of cells, would be our physical intelligence. I suppose the man might represent the male perspective within us: the part of us that is analytical, left-brained, logical and reasoning. So the man would represent our mental intelligence. The woman might represent the female perspective within us: the part that is associative, right-brained, imaginative and intuitive. The woman would represent our emotional intelligence. That leaves the young adult in the back seat, who has been quietly with us since the beginning and who represents our spiritual intelligence, the part that is witness to our life's drama." She looked up and asked with a smile, "Did I get it right?"

"Absolutely! So where the family is going could be a goal, a heartfelt desire, a physical need, or an Ideal. Now that we've set the stage and the scene and have an understanding of the characteristics of our main players in this drama, we can develop a situation and ask questions about it.

"For example, who is usually the driver of your vehicle? Is it the logical male part of us, the emotional female part of us, or the spiritually intelligent part of us?"

"I guess it depends on the situation," Lillas replied. "If we were into plans and implementation, then the man would be driving. If we were in need of intuition and creative imagination, the woman would be driving..."

"And if the car had a flat tire, or the red warning light came on, then the vehicle would be in the lead in that moment," Rick added.

"I'm sitting here making a connection from this imagined dream scenario into my daily life. It is interesting to note that whenever we go anywhere, habitually I let you drive."

"Why is that, I wonder...?" Rick asked sitting back.

"I'm not sure. Perhaps its because I do enough activities during my day. When you drive, I'm giving myself permission to be a passenger and to follow your lead for a while. In the role of passenger, I can relax from having to be a human doing and rest in becoming a human being," Lillas said thoughtfully. "I feel that I trust you and your abilities, whether it's driving, co-parenting or co-facilitating. My trust in you allows me to experience peace and simply enjoy the journey."

"So at those times, you are letting me be the driver and the lead in your life and are satisfied with playing the role of follower," Rick reflected, then added thoughtfully, "Even though I do enjoy driving, there are times when I want you to lead and drive our life for a time, Lillas. I also want to rest and move into my heart and out of my head. In this way, I, too, can taste an inner peace that is beyond understanding. At those times, I am totally comfortable and content following your lead for our life ..."

They sat for a time in the unexpected place where the metaphor had led them before resuming their conversation.

"We have several choices," Rick continued quietly. "We can be totally *un*clear about our, goals, vision and Ideal; we can be clear about our goals and our vision, but not our Ideal; or, we can be totally clear about all three of them."

"We can be confident about where we're going in life, or we can be lost, habituated and mechanized about life," Lillas added, building on the metaphor. "It's been my experience that when the man is driving, rarely does he ask for directions, believing that he can think his way into getting to wherever it is he needs to go. Whereas when a woman is driving, she's not afraid or ashamed to ask someone to show her the way."

"I agree. So if the male principle that exists within us finally gives up and suggests that they are lost and don't know where to go with their life anymore, that what they've been doing isn't working or leading them to their image of success, then one way is to allow the female principle within to lead them," Rick added.

"This scenario only works if they've had some meaningful relationship as male and female in the past. Without that, they'll be like two strangers co-habiting in the same vehicle, but with no connection to one another," Lillas qualified. Then she suggested, "However, let's assume that they have a relationship. In that case, the feminine principle can look externally for advice from a counselor, therapist, mentor, trusted friend or associate. Or she can simply turn around and ask their young adult passenger for his or her advice. After all, as the witness and observer, that person has seen your entire life—the good, the bad and the ugly—and can render an impartial opinion and suggest new and surprising options objectively."

"And that is the key issue," Rick said. "For most of our lives, we've been looking for answers to the questions within our heart of hearts outside of ourselves, in other people, books, seminars and workshops. The decision to turn around and look within is fundamental to successfully walking the path of Integrative Life and Leadership."

"Because," Lillas suggested, "our ageless soul, that young adult in the backseat, has been with us all the time, but we seldom notice because we are so focused on our goals looking outside and not within. By looking within, it gives a chance for our inside story and our outside story to become one."

"I like this metaphor," Rick said enthusiastically. "We've been able to connect the four domains and view them not as abstract concepts, but as a family that lives within us. This family can either be working together for a common goal, vision or Ideal, or they can be at war with each other. This Vehicle-Family metaphor is also a way to probe deeper into our existing inner relationships to ask, 'Who is leading me at this moment in my life?'"

"And if your intentions, mission, passions and actions are focused on one goal, vision and Ideal, nothing can stop you from manifesting them in the world," Lillas concluded.

The Four Domains as Life Forces

They continued their dialogue about various scenarios involving their co-created Vehicle-Family metaphor.

"I would like to extend this metaphor about the four domains of physical, mental, emotional and spiritual intelligence and link it with the engine of our vehicle," Rick said. "In this way, the engine of our vehicle could be considered the engine of our life. The four domains could be directly related, by analogy, to the four cylinders in the engine.

"We can then use this analogy to divide up the population into four groups that represent the four domains and three cultural paradigms."

"OK, I'm with you," Lillas said. "You want to extend our metaphor to link the four domains of intelligence to a car engine while weaving in the mechanistic, organic and wholistic paradigms."

"Exactly," Rick began. "Some of us are totally unaware that we even have these four domains under the hood of our car that are the engine of our life. All that these unaware people care about is getting in, turning the ignition key, starting their car and using it as a means to an end."

"You're saying they consider their vehicle as only a way to get from here to there," Lillas said.

"Right. So this first group would represent those who have not thought about who and what they truly are and have no desire to begin that process. The inner journey is irrelevant to them and holds no meaning. So long as their vehicle starts in the morning, they are fine with living their life in an unaware way. This group would be firing primarily on one physical cylinder with the occasional second mental cylinder kicking in every once in a while to give them a moment of fleeting happiness."

"You're suggesting the members of this group are blissfully ignorant?" Lillas offered.

Rick nodded. "This first group represents about 10% of the world's population. Now, the second group has some degree of self-awareness. They have explored inwardly a little. They realize that there is a lot going on inside of them and life is not all about what happens outside of them. They know they have a body and a mind and also know that one impacts on and influences the other. Our thoughts impact on our body, and our degree of health and physical well-being affects our mind. These are the people who are firing on two cylinders, physical and mental, and who are subject to impulsive as well as serial thinking. Occasionally they can have a peak experience of associative thinking that gives them an 'Ah-ha' moment, but it doesn't last. Culturally, we would see this second group, along with the first group, as mechanistic. Together they make up about 85% of the people in the world at this time in our evolution.

"The third group is more self-aware and has explored inwardly more than the members of the second group have. These are the ones who have awakened their emotional intelligence genetically, voluntarily or through life circumstances and are firing on three of their four cylinders. They are more passionate and higher powered than the first or second groups. They have drive and ambition. Their ride through life is smoother and more effortless than the first two groups.

"The third group represents only 10% of the world's populations at this time in our evolution. Because this group is high on personal, emotional and social intelligence, they are also natural leaders. However, they are still missing something. They are not working to their full potential and, because they are operating in the organic paradigm, they are self-aware enough to know it.

"The fourth group has significant self-awareness, self-actualization and self-realization. This group is firing on all four cylinders or domains of intelligence. They are the emerging enlightened, visionary and integrated leaders who can help change our world and move our collective awareness from the mechanistic to the organic paradigm."

"Not a bad metaphor, Rick," Lillas said nodding appreciatively. "However, I think you were successful in alienating 50% of the world's population with your engine analogy."

"Really? I didn't realize I was doing that," Rick said, taken somewhat aback.

"It might be the right metaphor for John, but I don't think it'll work for Mary. Even I don't know how many cylinders are in the engine of my car. So I think you lose points for this metaphor because it won't work for everyone. However, I did like how you wove in the mechanistic, organic and wholistic paradigms and related them with the four domains of intelligence. That was nicely done."

The Four Domains as Archetypes

"Thanks," Rick said relaxing into his chair. "Now it's your turn."

Lillas rearranged herself, folded her hands on the table and began: "I've always loved Carl Jung's work. His personality-type polarities of thinking, feeling, sensing and intuiting can be associated with the four domains as well as with the archetypes stored within our collective unconscious.[40]

"My preference would be to relate the four domains of intelligence to the archetypal roles of Queen, Lover, Warrior and Goddess. I think this will help make the four domains come alive in the hearts and minds of our participants."

"How would you relate your four archetypes with the four domains?"

"I would associate the Queen with physical intelligence. I imagine the Queen archetype as having nobility, core strength and a tangible presence that can be felt when you are with her. When I think of the Queen archetype, I think of Queen Elizabeth I, Queen Victoria or Catherine the Great.

"The Warrior archetype I associate with mental intelligence. Joan of Arc[41] comes to mind as a historical role for this archetype. Joan followed her intuitions, led France to victory over the English, but was, in my opinion, unjustly tried and condemned by the Inquisition. Despite the abuse she suffered during her trial and imprisonment, she held her ground, speaking and witnessing to her truth until her bitter end. She stood for something, and had found in her life something she was willing to die for."

"I remember a story about Joan of Arc," Rick added. "During her trial, the Chief Inquisitor from Rome asked her, 'How do you know that God, and not just your imagination, is speaking to you?' Her thoughtful response was, 'How could God speak to me if it were not for my imagination?' I always thought that was a fabulous answer. But in the end it made no difference. They burned her at the stake anyway."

Lillas nodded and continued. "The Lover of course, represents emotional intelligence. When I think of great lovers, oddly enough, I don't think of Marc Antony and Cleopatra, but rather St. Francis and St. Clare of Assisi or St. Teresa of Avila and St. John of the Cross."

"That *is* interesting..." Rick said, storing away Lillas's association for future discussion.

"Then there's the Goddess archetype, which is about our spiritual intelligence."

"The archetypes fit within the context of your life, but they are also a frame of reference," Rick suggested. "What frame of reference do you feel would be most appropriate for your Goddess archetype?"

"That is an interesting question," Lillas mused. "I think I really resonated for a time with Greek mythology and their pantheon of gods and goddesses. As a new mother many years ago, I identified with family, marriage and all the good qualities of Hera, the wife of Zeus, as my archetypal ideal for she was the patron of marriage, home and family.

"During most of my professional career, I identified with the goddess Athena who was the Warrior and the patron of battle and much later, wisdom. I associated Athena with all the qualities of mental intelligence, especially truth and honor. That was how I led my corporate and academic life.

"However, since we began our journey of integration years ago, I've let go of Athena as an ideal and am experiencing more and more of the Aphrodite archetype. Aphrodite is the goddess of love and compassion that for me is more of the heart as Phillia than of the body as Eros.

"Today, I would resonate most closely with the Divine Mother archetype," Lillas said.

"I would agree. There are different perspectives in the wisdom and mystic traditions on the Divine Mother. The aboriginal would view her as Mother

Earth or Mother Nature with the male counterpart as Father Sky. The Hindu would see her as Shakti with her male counterpart as Shiva. Which one resonates most for you?" Rick asked.

"These past years, it has not been a spirit — as in a goddess, diva or angel. I would say my goddess archetype is more aligned with the Christian traditions. It is the Divine Mother Mary who was the completion of the cycle begun by Eve, and her male counterpart as Jesus who was the completion of the cycle begun by Adam..."

Lillas suddenly looked at her watch in mid-sentence, let out a gasp, stood up and said, "Rick, we're late. We both lost track of time in our discussion. We've got to go. Now."

She stood up without further discussion as Rick quickly grabbed their coats and followed her, saying, "But we haven't finished our search for the perfect metaphor. The game isn't done. We haven't dealt with our three levels of awareness..."

"We'll do that later," Lillas said, walking quickly ahead of him through the door and down the steps of the coffee house, saying as she went to no one in particular, "For now our conversation is over. For the continuation, it's just a question of time..."

• • •

Three Levels of Awareness

The most puzzling thing about developing awareness
is, how can you ever become aware of what you aren't aware of?

EDWARD DE BONO

In our search for the answers to our ancient questions of *Who am I? Where did I come from? What am I made of?* and *Where am I going?* we also saw in our life experiences and in the stories, myths and parables we researched, recurring patterns that related to the number three: three levels of consciousness, three aspects to divinity, three perceptions, three states of matter, and three stages of thought that reached across all disciplines, cultures and time.

The three as manifestations of the One were seen in the wisdom traditions as the Father, Son and Holy Spirit in Christianity: Brahma, Vishnu and Shiva in the Hindu traditions; Crone, Daughter and Mother in the Celtic traditions; and as the three syllables of AUM and the three states of development of Tamasic, Rajasic and Satvic in the Yogic Traditions. The same resonant three was observed in Jungian psychology as conscious, subconscious and collective unconscious; in the writings of the scientist and theologian Tielhard de Chardin, as conscious, unconscious and superconscious, and in Wilber's three universal altered states of consciousness, of waking, dreaming and deep sleep. The pattern of three was also evident in the natural sciences as: the three phases of matter — solid, liquid and vapor — and the three levels of the brain — reptilian, mammalian and human. As well, we see a grouping of three in our concept of time — past, present and future.

In the Western philosophic and scientific traditions, consciousness is a mystery of life. We really don't know what it is, but we do know through our own experience that it does in fact exist.

Consciousness is often defined, as Richard Barrett did earlier, as a level of self-awareness. The word "awareness" does not add value to the word "consciousness". That is why we often use them interchangeably. He was "unconscious" and she was "unaware" mean virtually the same thing.

The Eastern traditions have an inner science of consciousness that has been built and tested for thousands of years. These inner scientists distinguish between these two words by suggesting that all things animate and inanimate, all processes and all cycles have Consciousness (oneness). What changes as we evolve and grow — or decline and descend — is our level of awareness of that ever-present Consciousness.

The law of gravity articulated by Isaac Newton in the 17th Century, for example, existed and operated long before he discovered and named it. However, he awakened us to its existence as a universal principle of nature and gave us the tools to predict its performance. The law of gravity was always there in the background doing what it was meant to do, just like Consciousness. What changed for us, due to Newton's falling apple inspiration, was our awareness of it.

Table 6 shows a sample selection of relationships to our three levels of awareness. These levels are qualitative associations in that Level I is low-level, Level II is mid-level and Level III is high-level awareness. Just as Tables 3 & 4 "Correlating the Four Domains of Intelligence" were intended to do, Table 6 relates ideas, themes and concepts to bodies of knowledge and to disciplines, allowing the opportunity for personal breakthrough, creativity and integration. For example, the three scientific phases of matter, solid (ice), liquid (water) and gas (vapor) can be related to the mystic trinity of Body, Mind and Spirit through three levels of mind: conscious, unconscious and superconscious.

The physical body, for example, is more like a solid. Level I awareness could be called *body-mind* when the conscious level of mind is considered. This line of association led us to a 100-year-old medical theory suggesting the existence of an abdominal brain, which might be the mind, that stands behind our instinctive "gut feelings".[42]

Where we might associate mind with coolness and electricity, we associate heart more with warmth and fluidity. Level II awareness is associated more with the heart than with the head, more with fluidity than with electricity, and with the unconscious level of the mind. We wondered if there could be something called a *heart-mind* at Level II awareness. Historically, this was Aristotle's argument: that the seat of man's knowledge was not in the head, as Plato had suggested, but rather in the heart. This line of association also led us to uncover that, in 1997, medical researchers discovered 40 thousand neurons in the heart, which supports the idea that the heart has a mind, and that mind itself may well be a distributed phenomenon across the entire body and not just localized in the brain.[43]

Table 6: Correlating the Three Levels of Awareness

Source	Level I Awareness	Level II Awareness	Level III Awareness
Christian	Father	Son	Holy Spirit
Celtic	Crone	Daughter	Divine Mother
Hindu	Brahma	Vishnu	Shiva
Mystic	Space	Time	Patience
de Chardin	Conscious	Unconscious	Superconscious
Yogic	Tamasic	Rajasic	Satvic
Greek on Love	Eros	Phillia	Agape
Creativity	Instinct	Intuition	Inspiration
Renaissance	Hell	Earth	Heaven
Image /Character	Public Self	Private Self	Secret Self
Aikido	Creation	Pattern	Light
Jungian	Personality	Individuality	Universality
"	Conscious	Subconscious	Collective Unconscious
Perception	Literal	Meaning	Purpose
Three Levels	Doing	Knowing	Being
Physiological Systems	Central Nervous System	Autonomic Nervous System	Endocrine Glandular System
Species	Animal	Human	Divine
Matter States	Solid	Liquid	Vapor
Leadership	Knowledge	Understanding	Wisdom
Integrative	Multiple/ Myriad Forms	Duality	Unity
Philosophy	Image of Self	Real Self	Image of God
Levels	Surreal	Real	Ideal
Nervous System	Reptilian	Mammalian	Human
Seven Centers	1, 2, 3	3, 4, 5	5, 6, 7
Cultural	Mechanistic	Organic	Wholistic
Mystic Universal	Body	Mind	Spirit

The spiritual body can be associated with something vaporous, gaseous and invisible and may be called the *soul-mind*, at Level III, which is further associated with the superconscious. This led us to Michael Persinger and his work on magnetic resonance, the brain and mystical experiences.

In summary, we can relate the body-mind to the reptilian or impulsive brain, the heart-mind to the mammalian or emotional brain, and the soul-mind to the human brain.

As an amateur symbologist, how have you experienced the pattern of three on your own personal journey?

A Dialogue on the Three Levels of Awareness

> *So the soul, born on Earth, contains three beings: the angel, the jinn and the human. According to the depth of the impressions received in the different planes he or she shows the qualities of the angel and the jinn. The impressions received from returning souls in the jinn sphere give the individual specific qualities and tendencies. In addition, he or she receives the heritage of his or her earthly ancestors.*
>
> H.J. Whitteveen, *Universal Sufism*

When Carl Jung first sought a metaphor for the mind, he thought of an iceberg, where 10% was visible on the surface with 90% invisible below the surface. The visible was our conscious mind, and the 90% invisible was our subconscious, which was large and powerful, but hidden where it could not easily be seen. Later, he felt that each of us was interconnected through the medium of the "collective unconscious", which became the ocean in which our individual icebergs floated. Floating in this ocean, we at times willingly gave our thought-fluids to this collective sea of thinking, while at other times we took from it. The message from this metaphor was that in order to probe the depths of who you truly are, you need to go deep and uncover what lay hidden beneath your conscious awareness.

This metaphor reflects the structure of the brain where our humanity is contained in the top area called the cerebral cortex which drapes over the cerebrum like a swimmer's bathing cap. The corrugations, valleys and hills of the cerebral cortex, if flattened, would form a sheet 16 square feet in area.

Many people are disconnected from and lack awareness of their physical bodies and therefore, their emotions. Yoga instructors who are walking the path of integrative life and leadership have commented to us that 85% of the people in their beginner classes are "dead" from the neck down. The practice of Yoga is one way to help people increase their mental, physical, emotional and body awarenesses.

To be able to explore themselves and fully answer the question "Who are you?" the iceberg metaphor would suggest a journey down into the hidden long-term memories stored in the mammalian brain, and the primitive and often-frightening impulses and drives of the reptilian brain, before full integration could occur. This is the meeting of our shadow side, psychologically and neurologically, and requires significant effort to allow the unconscious drives and impulses to become conscious.

In our own experience of the integrative journey, our awareness has risen and fallen in a cyclical process that reflects our present understanding of the forces of evolution and involution, of separation and integration.

If words are the language of the mind, and emotions the language of the heart, then images are the language of the Soul — whether imagined, visioned or received in a dream. A recurring image or dream about the path of integration was that of ascending a mountain in order to find the Source of Life. In our metaphor:

> Our awareness was at first a living creature, curled up in fear and lost in the closeness and confines of the conscious mind. It was dark outside, threatening, and there were many things to fear, many things to battle in anger, worry and doubt, but somehow, through all its trials and tribulations it survived. It had built and fashioned a strong house to protect it from the danger and harm it had once experienced. But after a time it was lonely and the loneliness was not satisfying. After a time, there was nowhere to go. The jungle was so dense, and the area it had fashioned so small, that after a time there was nothing left to experience and it was lonely.
>
> A river ran by its safe and secure home and served to give this awareness the waters of life. And it wondered, "What is the source of these waters of life?" After years of quietly reflecting on this question, of watching the river and wondering, the awareness decided it was time to leave its safe and secure home and begin to seek the Source of the river of life. The awareness's habit

of sameness was overcome by a desire for newness and it chose to move beyond itself for the first time in a long time.

As the awareness began its journey, it found the jungle dark and unfamiliar. There were many things the awareness encountered that it did not recognize as it moved beyond its familiar spaces. There were strangers, plants, reptiles, lions, tigers and bears that kept it from making good time as it hid and watched them pass by. But after a time and a half-time, the journey slowly became an adventure. The awareness awakened further and looked forward to each new day's discoveries, no matter how small, as it walked the path beside the river.

Then, one day the river rose and moved the awareness above the trees and it saw the sun for the very first time. It was warm, round, good — even perfect — though to look at it for long would have hurt its eyes. There were decisions to be made, here above the jungle and the trees, but somehow they seemed clearer, less confusing, uncomplicated. Finally, one morning, after a long time walking beside the rising river, climbing the mountain, sleeping in caves, and smelling the mountain flowers; finally, one morning above a rise in the cliff beside the cool mountain stream, there opened a vista and before it lay a blue-green mountain lake, shimmering like crystals in the sunlight.

The lake was nestled among seven high snow-capped peaks. The awareness held its breath at the beauty of that lake, the mountains, the sun and the crystal blue sky. In the cradle of the three tallest mountains was a glacier that shone white as the Sun. And as the awareness approached the blinding white light that was the refection of its Source, it remembered many things—the jungle, its fears, its illusions, its doubts, and its adventures—and it smiled, for here in this space and in this place, all was good with the hope of greatness.

From here we took what we knew from our peak experience and descended back into the marketplace (our jungle) and found a community with whom we could share our newfound awareness. In turn, that community helped us gather all the other forgotten parts of who and what we were and held a space for integration of truth, compassion, wisdom and common understanding.

In this story, our awareness had to cut its own path, struggle up a mountain and eventually find its Source — which is the path of self-development and self-realization. This is the process of struggle and integration that feels like moving from darkness into the light of hard-fought and hard-won peak life-giving experiences.

From another perspective, our awareness — every once in awhile and quite unexpectedly — was given a ride in a spirit-filled hot air balloon that moved it from the jungle into the cool crystal blue air, high above the jungle. It was marvelous to see the vista from that higher perspective. It was wonderful to view the sun and to journey to the mountaintops without pain or struggle. It was so effortless that we would smile and laugh in our spirit-filled balloon as it elevated our awareness from the gravity of whatever situation we were in at the time, to the joy of flying freely and effortlessly to our Source.

This was a path of flow and integration that also ended in a peak experience. The journey, however, was one of wonder and surprise, and a sense of moving from light into more light, rather than from darkness into light. We will talk more about the journey of integration and these two paths in Chapter 5.

Our struggle was to learn how could we transfer these deep inner and outer experiences into a model that resonated with the sciences and with wisdom and mystic traditions and yet could be, at the same time, easily, simply and clearly communicated?

Our best understanding at this time of the Integrative Model of Life and Leadership is shown in Figure 6. The two triangles (upper left) of involution and evolution (inverted) represent the framework of three levels of Consciousness. The arrows define a spiral, which represents the path that awareness moves within the framework of Consciousness. The upright and inverted triangles are the perspectives gained by our awareness as it moves through or along that path. In the evolutionary spiral, there is movement from the many, found in the conscious level, upward to the One, found in the superconscious level. In the involutionary spiral, awareness moves from the One, found in the superconscious level, downward to the many, found in the conscious level. One ascends and the other descends, on the path that connects the levels of consciousness.

If you choose to climb the mountain of evolution (upright triangle), what you would observe externally is the right triangle (inverted) and your perspective would become broader and wider with each step (divergence and integration) until you became fully individual and yet one with the Whole. If

Figure 6: The Three Levels of Awareness

Involution

Evolution

Three Levels of Awareness: The Involutionary and Evolutionary triangles are two-dimensional projections of either a cone or pyramid. As a cone, the three circles represent the first three rings of the eight ring involutionary model. These rings are the core as Universality (Superconscious), the inner ring as Individuality (Subconscious), and the outer ring as personality (Conscious). The descending and ascending arrow is the movement of our awareness through the levels of consciousness that define the inner framework. As a pyramid, each of the four domains of intelligence are present at each of the three levels of consciousness, but will only be activated by our motivations. If we were entrained in a Mechanistic paradigm, for example, only the Level I Awareness would be available to us as an experience. A pyramid projects a series of squares whereas a cone projects a series of circles. This illustrates the paradoxical nature of leadership when lower order thinking (2-D) is projected into higher order thinking (3-D).

you were spiraling down the involutionary mountain of Consciousness (upright triangle), you would perceive internally a movement from the simple in being one with the Whole to the complex (divergence and separation).

The paradox is that the hierarchical triangle is a two-dimensional representation of a three-dimensional object. Each triangle could be a projection of either a three-dimensional cone or a three-dimensional four-sided pyramid.

The four-sided pyramids, like those at Giza in Egypt or the Pyramids of the Sun and the Moon at Teotihuacán in Mexico, sit on a square base that is one projection of the Four Domains of Intelligence (See Figure 6). The Four Intelligences — physical, mental, emotional and spiritual — are present on the earth at its base, but also at every one of the three levels of awareness.

At the top of the pyramid is a capstone that represents the four noble virtues that guide the four paths and illuminate the four faces of integration.

In this way, the four domains of intelligence are always present as potential, but perhaps not active at every level of awareness until we awaken, develop or invite them into our consciousness.

This three-dimensional pyramidal perspective can visually (for image is the language of the soul) and simply unite the four domains of intelligence and our three levels of awareness.

The Wheel of Life

All people have a personality for it is essential to exist and express who they are. But unfortunately in the course of their lives, most people are being had by their personality.

Bob Blanton

By using the three dimensional cone as a projection, there is a suggestion that at each level of hierarchical awareness, there is also the presence of community in the form of a circle.

The three-ringed circle is extracted from the core of the eight dimensions that form a part of *Involutionary Theory* (see Chapter 1). These three inner rings we call the Wheel of Life, and understanding this wheel is key to understanding *intrapersonal* life and leadership.

At Level I awareness, our personality is often fragmented into different roles of father, mother, sibling, husband, wife, family, work, social, organizational, and self, among others. The inner ring is the place where our attitudes and emotions about those specific roles are lodged. The core of the wheel is where our purpose, principles, core beliefs and values that support each personality fragment reside.

If we are operating from a mechanistic and materialistic Level I awareness, then our Ideal would be associated with our *chief misunderstanding about life,* such as "peace at all costs" or "no one understands me". If we are operating from an organic and relationship-focused Level II awareness, then our Ideal would be humanistic, in terms of core values and beliefs. If we are operating from a wholistic and integrative Level III awareness, then our Ideal would be spiritual, in terms of virtues and strengths, and be the highest we could

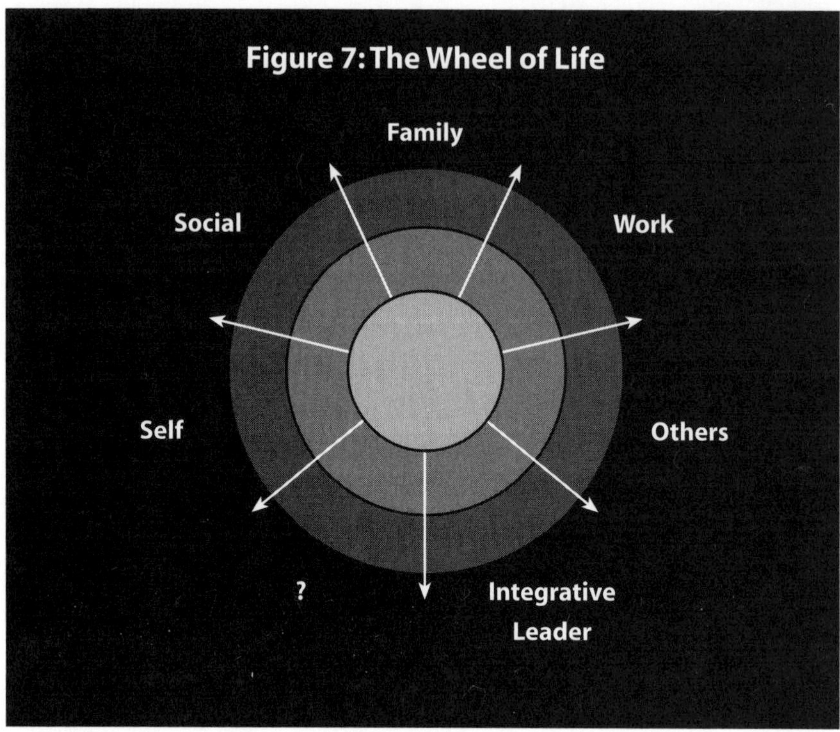

consciously conceive. In this third way, we consciously engage all three levels of awareness in the process of integration.

Only by formulating an Ideal that resonates with Level III awareness, can we consciously engage all three levels of our being within the process of integration.

Without embarking on a journey within, our Level I awareness will begin to spin ever faster in this time of increasing change and transition, eventually overwhelming our fragmented personality and breaking us apart; a breaking that could lead to spiritual, mental and physical illness.

It is interesting to note that an object in two dimensions can produce multiple solutions in three dimensions, each three-dimensional solution having the ability to replicate the two-dimensional object. This suggests that only when we are able to access higher-order thinking through embarking on the journey of integration will we have access to multiple options and creative ways to solve our "lower order" problems. As Einstein once said, 'We can't solve today's problems with the same level of thinking and consciousness that created them.'

In walking the path of integration, you will encounter every part of your personality and individuality that is out of alignment with your Ideal Self on the way to discovering your True Self (universality). This is unavoidable if your desire is to become integrated and whole. How you choose to meet your old self, whether in pain and struggle or in peace and the spirit of adventure, is up to you.

As Warren Bennis suggests, "...one of the most reliable indicators and predictors of true leadership is an individual's ability to find meaning in negative events and to learn from even the most trying circumstances."[44]

We will discuss the three levels of awareness from an evolutionary perspective, beginning with Level I. We understand that all three paradigms (mechanistic, organic and wholistic) and all three types (personality, individuality and universality), as well as all three levels of awareness are within us and emerge at various times in our life and leadership journey.

Level I Awareness: Personality and Multiple Forms

If your world view is that reality is comprised only of what you can see, hear, touch, taste and smell, then that paradigm confines you to Level I awareness and binds you to your personality or body-mind. Level I awareness is the level where the Taoists speak of "ten thousand thousand things"; Buddhists refer to a place of suffering, pain, sickness and death; Hindus speak of Maya or illusion, and Christians describe a world ruled by the prince of darkness; psychotherapists refer to fragmentation and disassociation; and social scientists speak in terms of materialism and self-interest.

The four domains are primarily expressed at Level I as follows: mentally, as beliefs in rules and regulations; emotionally, as fear, anger, worry and doubt; spiritually, as the lust for propagation, sensuality and power; and physically, as preoccupation and intoxication with our *image of self*.

At this level, you understand yourself, others and the world very literally. Self-awareness, at this level of leadership, is focused principally on the cult of image, personality and ego. Level I leadership is reactive leadership that focuses attention on the craft of power [45] and the mastery of gamesmanship. If there are moments of happiness, satisfaction and fulfillment within this level, they are fleeting and temporal, requiring more adventures and more stimulation to maintain mental interest.

The laws that govern this level are mechanistic and ruled by a belief in cause and effect. The leadership styles are commanding ("Do what I say"), pacesetting ("Do what I do") and transactional ("Let's make a deal").

In order to solve the problems and dilemmas created at Level I awareness, there is a need to move to Level II, but only if a leader has not permanently fallen asleep. If they choose to focus their attention once again on the search for meaning, purpose and truth, then their awareness moves to the second level, which is the realm of the heart-mind.

Level II Awareness: Individuality and Duality

At Level II awareness, things are seen in simple dualities: light and darkness, yin and yang, masculine and feminine, reason and intuition, rational and irrational, good and bad, self-interest and selflessness, good and evil. These are the dance of paradox of Level II awareness.

At this level of awareness, the search for deeper meaning can serve to simplify life in the face of complexity. Leadership is focused on individuality, or building character, and on behaviors that integrate with Level I awareness when in alignment with practices at Level II.

This is the level of transformational learning and leadership that takes place within the heart.[46]

At Level II awareness, leaders have an opportunity to model reflective and responsive rather than reactive leadership. Their choice, in a given moment, is to react from personality, or to respond in accord with their Ideal Self.

At Level II, the Four Domains express mentally as a belief in good practices grounded in experience; emotionally, as a heart awakening to fellowship, caring and compassion for others; spiritually, as intentions that are value-centered; and physically, as an awakening to balance life across common meaning rather than common activities.

The law that governs this level is, "Do to others as you would have them do to you." The principle styles of leadership of this level are democratic ("What do you think?"), affiliative ("How do you feel?") and transformational ("Let me empower and encourage you").

If the leader in Level II awareness has formulated and is living an Ideal that provides personal satisfaction, achievement and gratification, then they remain in their organic paradigm. However, if they feel that something is missing, a haunting lack of fulfillment that originates from their Soul, then they can reformulate their Ideal in such a way that would lead them to Level III awareness.

Level III Awareness: Universality and Unity

Level III is the home of our soul-mind, of superconsciousness and universality. At this level there is an awakening sense of the interconnectedness and unity of all things and an ability to handle the diversity that underlies the drama of creation.

This is the level of artists, mystics, saints, inventors and enlightened leaders from all traditions and all cultures. The concepts at this level are a source of inspiration and creativity, of unity and oneness, and they offer resolutions to the problems of duality in Level II, as well as add clarity to the multiple forms and expressions that are so confusing in Level I.

Level III is the place of pure potentiality that is accessed through selfless intentionality.

The desire for resolution of dualities at Level II awareness is evident in philosophy and psychology, as well as physics and spirituality. The discovery of a unifying paradigm that unites spirit and matter, and involution and evolution, would result in universal principles that could guide leaders who have chosen to walk the path of integration.

The formulator of one such comprehensive and unifying paradigm was Arthur M. Young, philosopher, cosmologist, and inventor of the bell helicopter. In his words, written 30 years ago:

> Both religion and science have a common origin in the search for truth, but have approached this goal differently. Religion depends on revelation or inspired teachers, science on experiments and theories. It would appear that religion has declined in dignity and importance from those early times when all art was dedicated to it and architecture created its temples and cathedrals. Science, on the contrary, began humbly and piece-by-piece constructed an edifice, which is yet to be completed.
>
> The investigations I have made into these subjects indicate that these two quite different endeavors tell the same story, reach the same conclusions.

The agreement to which I refer is to be found between the ancient myths and the most recent findings of quantum physics....

It is because science became the Scientific Method and ceased to be the search for truth that it lost relevance and, like a time bomb ticking in an airliner, is dangerous because it is cut off from our control, following its own dictates. It is because the institutionalized churches have taken little cognizance of scientific discoveries and have insisted on a literal reading of all sacred writings that they have become irrelevant and have had their traditional teaching dismissed as superstition. Nor do the presumably humanistic types of social reform fare better, for despite daily trips to the psychologist, himself floundering in uncertain doctrines, social reform has no notion of man's true nature and has created more discontent than it relieves.

In earlier times there were those who went into the desert to discover within their own depths, or to the mountaintop to commune with god, and returned with a teaching for their followers. But that is all past. Twentieth century humanity has come of age. It is not to be led, but must draw out of itself the wisdom it needs. That is why I say we must look at what we already have in the earliest and undistorted traditions. It needs no new doctrine because the printed word makes available today the accumulated wisdom of all ages and of all teachings, which, with the help of science, we can now sort out and interpret. By science, I do not mean cultural anthropology but the ontology provided by Quantum Physics... .

In short, we have no need for more "isms" and schisms, movement to left or right. These divisions are the cause of our splitting up and can hardly lead to its cure. We need a new, integrating direction, but we cannot discover an integrating and unitary theory common to science and religion without postulating the unity of all things.

In sum, then, our thesis is: we inhabit a universe, and this implies one universal set of principles or of truth. To discover these principles or truth, we must enlist both religious and scientific inquiry, and, recognizing the variety of expressions of both, be prepared to seek out the unity in its true implication and significance.

While science as it is presently represented is fragmented into a number of disciplines, and these disciplines seem not necessarily to indicate a common truth, we must look for their connection. Likewise religions, which

> for thousands of years have been manufacturing schisms often merely to justify self-determination, need that overall survey that can see them as the various expressions of one truth.
>
> For just as the world with its oceans, continents, and nations presents many facets, yet is one body of matter, so does our culture with its religions and sciences present many facets, yet is one body of life. Our task then is to seek out this unity.[47]

The four domains express at Level III mentally as Truth and Wisdom; they express emotionally as Agape or Divine Love; spiritually, as Enlightenment and Wholeness; and physically, as understanding and working with universal laws in service to ourselves, others and our Ideal.

The law that governs this level is "unconditional compassion" for all people and all things. Level III is the realm that informs enlightened leaders who are inspired to make a difference and to change a paradigm or world view, with the courage and desire to allow that changed paradigm to manifest graciously in the world.[48]

This is the realm that informs Visionary Leaders, Inspirational Leaders, Virtue Centered Leaders, Servant Leaders, Transcendent Leaders, Integrative Leaders and Level 5 leaders: As Jim Collins states in his book, *Good to Great*, Level 5 leaders are "a paradoxical blend of personal humility and professional will". Those who have worked with or have written about "good to great leaders" use words such as quiet, humble, modest, reserved, gracious, mild-mannered and self-effacing.[49]

Integrative Leadership is about seeking to understand and experience oneness with all four domains of our intelligence and all three levels of our awareness, for as one of us gets better, through the principle of resonance, so do we all.

A Fifth Domain: The Power of Choice

Fatalism, whose solving word in all crises of behavior is 'All striving is vain', will never reign supreme, for the impulse to take life strivingly is indestructible in the race. Moral creeds, which speak to that impulse, will be widely successful in spite of inconsistency, vagueness, and shadowy determination of expectancy. Man needs a rule for his will, and will invent one if one be not given him.

William James

You are what your deep driving desire is. As your desire is, so is your will. As your will is, so is your deed. As your deed is, so is your destiny.

Brihadaramyaka Upanishad IV, 4.5

The model of integrative life and leadership involves four domains of intelligence and three levels of awareness. The final dimension of the Integrative Model is the fifth domain of *Will* that is our ability and power to choose how we will negotiate our journey of life, love and leadership.

Free will is a mystery thought to be one of the three foundations of human existence, with energy and mind as the other two. If energy is the spirit, or light, and mind is the pattern in our mental film, then *will* is the choice and the desire to move energy through the pattern of mind to create our reality. Without will, which is of the soul, choice, which is of the mind, desire, which is of the heart, or need, which is of the body, there would be no reality. Nothing can occur unless one of the four aspects of will is activated and used. Without will, there is no movement and no journey, either towards integration, or away from it towards separation.

From this perspective, we are the sum of our exercises of will, choices, desires and needs.

Will is stronger than nature or nurture, than genetics or environment, than internal or external influences. Through its activation, extraordinary handicaps may be overcome, and through its lack of use, extraordinary gifts and talents may never be realized. Will is the difference between a mundane, mediocre and unfulfilling life, and one that is filled with happiness, excellence and adventure.[50]

From the point of view of the mechanistic paradigm, our will is said to be sleeping, mesmerized or hypnotized. We have conscious, volitional will that we use to make choices in imitation of what we have experienced that often trap us and bind us to an illusion of freedom. We are controlled by our internal habits and conditioning, and we're influenced by external opinions to such a degree that there is no free will, but only repetition of what we have chosen in the past that influences our decisions in the present, that brings to us our past in the form of our future. This process serves to bind us to our wheel of life. With a sleeping will, there is no growth and no life, just a form of *living death*.

From the perspective of the organic paradigm, our will is awakened as personal will when used to align, attune and influence our unconscious will. In this alignment, personal will becomes a potent force for reshaping our mechanistic personality to align with our individuality.[51] In this paradigm, relationships become important, and we move from self-centeredness, in Level I awareness, to thinking, empowering, and enabling others and ourselves in our life and work, in Level II awareness. Our decisions become innovative rather than imitative, and simple rather than complex in that we begin to see the yin and yang of life and death, light and darkness, universality and personality.

The organic, heart level, or Level II awareness is the most difficult level to transform and transcend, for the allure of personal power, self-determination, self-development and intimate relationships often makes for a very challenging choice: whether to let go of the comfort and familiarity of the second level or to choose the mystery and wisdom of the third level.

This is the level at which the battle between selfishness and selflessness, achievement and contribution, and personal will and Higher Will take place.

From this Level II awareness, we can choose to focus our empowered personal will and integrate our mechanistic paradigm within it and live as best as we can, or we can evolve towards the wholistic paradigm by surrendering our personal will in preference and deference to our Higher Will.

From the wholistic paradigm perspective, our will becomes Free Will when aligned and attuned with our superconscious. This is where transcendence of the two lower levels of awareness takes place and it is a choice point for our soul to assume more of a lead in our life.

For those who choose this higher path, the qualities of enlightened awareness — through the process of involution — will descend and reshape their beliefs and attitudes of Level II individuality, then further descend to alter the actions, behaviors and opinions of Level I personality. In this way, many who have walked this path of integration feel that they have been reborn and are no longer alone. They sense and feel the presence of inner guidance; they come to know their Essence and to live in a state of co-creative companionship.

Our conscious or sleeping will is characterized by being immediate, goal-oriented, or logical and requires conscious persistent effort in the frame of "doing." Our empowered personal will — in harmony with our unconscious mind — is seen in retrospect through reflection; is process-oriented, more effortless, and linked to the frame of "knowing." Our superconscious, integrative, Higher Will is seen as "being," and as having conscious and unconscious processes, characteristics and abilities, used as required, to accomplish whatever we need at whatever level needed to aid us in our integrative life and leadership journey.

In the Model of Integrative Leadership, the final question then becomes: "What are you willing and not willing to do in your personal process of integration?"

Conceptions, Projections and Time

Indeed, man has always been seeking wholeness—mental, physical, social and individual.... It is instructive to consider the word 'health' in English is based on an Anglo-Saxon word 'hale' meaning 'whole': that is, to be healthy is to be whole. Likewise the English 'holy' is based on the same root as 'whole'. All of this indicates that man has sensed always that wholeness or integrity is an absolute necessity to make life worth living. Yet, over the ages, he has generally lived in fragmentation.

David Bohm

After Rick and Lillas said good night to their dinner guests, they decided to have one more cup of tea before going home for the evening. Rick seized the opportunity to continue their search for the perfect metaphor conversation that had been curtailed earlier.

"Well Lillas, I think you were successful in alienating 50% of the world's population when you related the four domains to your four archetypes earlier this evening."

"What do you mean?" Lillas asked. "I didn't realize I was doing that..."

"In your story, you illustrated the archetypes of Queen, Warrior, Lover, and Goddess all with examples of mythic or historical *women*: Hera, Athena, and Aphrodite, followed by Queen Victoria, Joan of Arc, St. Claire of Assisi and Divine Mother Mary. Without changing, varying or balancing your associations with these four domain archetypes, your examples would appeal to most women but end up alienating most men."

"Good point," Lillas smiled. "I feel I'm experiencing instant karma for my earlier criticism of your metaphor of the four domains as four cylinders in an engine. I guess 'like really does beget like' doesn't it?' Lillas paused to sip her tea and reflect on the life lesson then looked up. "So how do you suggest we make my archetypal metaphor more universal?"

"Well, the all-male conception of the four archetypes could be King, Warrior, Lover, God-Man. But that perspective won't work either, since I would be doing the same as you in using male mythic and historical figures with whom I would identify, but most women wouldn't."

"How about if I present two archetypes and you present two archetypes?" Lillas suggested.

"That would be a more balanced approach," Rick reflected. "You could keep your Queens and Goddesses and I could describe William Wallace and his Scottish fight for freedom from English rule as the Warrior archetype with some male like Casanova as the Lover archetype."

"Yes, something like that. Only I'm not sure I approve of your choice of Casanova as an example of the Lover archetype. I would prefer you use the Buddha of Compassion over someone like Casanova," Lillas said.

"Maybe we should look for genderless archetypes such as Sovereign that would represent the Queen or the King. Warrior is a good archetype since it can be both male and female. Lover is genderless, so it too could be male or female. But God-Man or Goddess, Divine Mother or Heavenly Father, Mother Earth and Father Sky needs some work."

After some discussion, they decided to reflect on the archetypes and the four domains and come up with a more universal archetype that would be genderless as a representation and illustration of the spiritual domain.

Projecting our Levels of Awareness

> *All the world's a stage, And all the men and women merely players; They have their exits and their entrances; And one man in his time plays many parts, his acts being seven ages.*
>
> William Shakespeare

> *Illusions commend themselves to us because they save us pain and allow us to enjoy pleasure instead. We must therefore accept it without complaint when they sometimes collide with a bit of reality against which they are dashed to pieces.*
>
> Sigmund Freud (1856–1939)

"So what about the three levels of awareness?" Lillas asked. "Any thoughts on the perfect metaphor that might capture the imagination?"

Rick nodded. "Historically, Plato's 'Parable of the Cave' has been the best illustration, suggesting that humans are multidimensional beings. Through his parable, Plato suggested that we, and all things in our world, are simply projections of higher-level awareness into lower-level awareness."

"Remind me again of what Plato's 'Parable of the Cave' [52] was all about, Rick."

"In his parable Plato asked us to imagine — illustrating our limited perception of reality — that we are chained to the ground with our head fixed in such a way that all we could see was the back wall of a cave. Behind us are real three-dimensional people, animals, trees and plants that, via sunlight in the day and fires at night, cast shadows of their shapes and create movements on the wall in front of us. From that chained position, we only see the shadows, which leads us to determine — with good reason, based on our experience — that reality is two dimensional, indistinct, black and white. That would be our world. That would be the sum of the way things are for us. And we would be in a state of blind or conscious acceptance of what comprised our limited view of reality.

"But at another level, our two-dimensional world would only be a fragment of the true three-dimensional reality with all its people, animals, plants, colors, shapes and textures that — while in bondage and chained to a past belief, or through reinforcing a habit or practice of seeing the world from one perspective — we could never know.

"Only if you were freed from bondage, either voluntarily or involuntarily, could you turn around and see for yourself what the world was really like. By turning around — by going within — you would then know more about the truth of your experience. And it would be this inner awakening to truth that would help set you free of your illusions."

"Your modern version of Plato's parable of the cave is the movie projector, film and screen," Lillas suggested. Rick nodded again.

"Absolutely. An even more updated version of the metaphor would be to use a hologram. By projecting the laser through the hologram, we see a three-dimensional picture of an object that can be viewed from many different perspectives. However, when you look at the film of a hologram with the naked eye, all you see is a series of interference patterns.

"In the holographic metaphor, the light of the laser is our essence, moving through the patterns of our mind as the hologram that produces a three-dimensional image that we believe is the reality of our life.

"The other fascinating aspect of the hologram metaphor is that each portion of the patterns on the film contains a portion of the whole hologram. David

Bohm [53] suggests that every piece of the universe contains a portion of the whole of the universe. Since we are a natural part of the universe, the pattern of the entire universe is within us too. This affirms the wisdom and mystic traditions when they say, "As above, so is it below. As within, so is it without." Bohm also suggests that one aspect of the universe is explicate and unfolded and can be seen, while the other aspect of the universe is implicate and enfolded and hidden. Our outside story that is *un*folded and our inside story that is *en*folded, in the context of the new physics, are really one."

"Only most of us are unaware of it," Lillas concluded, then paused before she spoke. "I guess one aspect of a holographic universe is when a biologist suggests that our DNA — the pattern that exists in every one of the trillions of cells of our body — has a code that contains all of our humanity locked within it."

"Or an acupuncturist suggesting that our whole body is represented by acupressure points defined by the energy meridians passing through our ear.[54] Or an iridologist suggesting that our whole body is represented and can be diagnosed by examining the detailed patterns in our irises,"[55] Rick added.

"Or a reflexologist suggesting that our whole body is represented and can be treated by massaging our feet. [56] The natural conclusion, using a holographic perspective, is that everything contains everything else within it."

"That's it exactly, Lillas," Rick said, pleased with the evolution of their conversation.

"So getting back to Plato's 'Parable of the Cave,' if a three-dimensional object casts a two-dimensional shadow, then what do you think is casting our three-dimensional bodies?"

"A fourth-dimensional object…" Lillas suggested tentatively, to which Rick nodded. "So share with me an example of a fourth-dimensional object."

"A good example of a fourth-dimensional object would be a thought or an idea. You don't know its beginning. You don't know its end. You just know that it's there. It can travel in you and through you. It comes at a time when you need it and at other times when you least expect it. In my mind, the fourth dimension would be the realm of thought."

"So if mind is projecting our three-dimensional reality, than what is projecting the mind?" Lillas asked.

"Spirit, purpose, intention is what projects the mind that in time and in turn, projects the body. So there we have our three levels of awareness as conscious, unconscious and superconscious or, culturally, as mechanistic, organic and wholistic paradigms.

"But some advocate that the first creation is in the mind with a second creation as the body," Lillas said. "They use the example of an architect imagining a house, constructing the blueprints based on his imagination, then physically constructing the house."

"That perspective is true when viewed from the organic paradigm, but not true when viewed from the wholistic paradigm. In involutionary theory, first creation is not in the mind, but in the spirit. It is our intention that sets the entire law of manifestation in motion. The second creation is in the mind. The third creation is in our physical world. As Morihei Ueshiba, the founder of Aikido stated after his spiritual awakening in the 1920s, 'Spirit goes first, then the mind, then the body'.[57]

"Those experienced in the martial arts know this to be true. These martial artisits seem to counter their opponent quickly and with ease when viewed with mechanistic eyes.

"The average martial artist fights battles physically. The good martial artist fights battles first mentally and then, physically. The great martial artist fights battles first spiritually then mentally, and then they may not even need to battle physically. These great Masters have developed an ability to sense their opponent's intent even before it is manifested as thought and can often subdue their opponent even before a mental or physical fight begins.

"Therefore, working with our three levels of awareness is simply a matter of perspective and a question of time."

A Question of Time

And of time you would make a stream, upon whose bank you would sit and watch it flowing. Yet the timeless in you is aware of life's timelessness, and knows that yesterday is but today's memory and tomorrow is today's dream, and that which sings and contemplates in you is still dwelling within the bounds of that first moment which scattered the stars into space.

KAHLIL GIBRAN (1883–1931), *The Prophet*

"What do you mean by a question of time?" Lillas asked.

"In the mechanistic paradigm we are always dealing with the past. In the organic paradigm we are dealing with our near or more distant past, or our imagined future. In the wholistic paradigm, we are dealing with the eternal now. That is why to understand the power of the eternal now is to understand the wholistic paradigm and its implications for the organic and mechanistic paradigms." [58]

"OK, I'm lost. Can you give me a concrete illustration of this concept?" Lillas asked. "But before you do, what do you mean we are living in the past?"

Rick reflected for a moment. "When you look up at a clear night sky, what do you normally see?"

"The moon, the planets, the stars," Lillas replied.

"Now the closest star to the Earth is Alpha Centauri. It's about 4.5 light years away. So when you look up in the night sky, the closest starlight you see is 4.5 years old. In the present of Alpha Centauri, it could have gone supernova and disintegrated three years ago. In our present, it is still there as it always was and will be that way for three more years until the light of the cataclysmic event reaches us. Only then will we become aware that Alpha Centauri does not really exist anymore, but was only an illusion. So our present awareness is Alpha Centauri's past. This is what Einstein was trying to tell us with his theory of relativity: everything is relative depending on your point of view within space-time.

"So by analogy, everyone and everything within the mechanistic paradigm that is governed and subject to the speed of light is living in the past. Does this make any sense to you?"

"Not fully as yet, but let's continue. I understand the stars, but what about the planets?"

"The closest planet to Earth is Mars, at about 35 million miles [59] away which, at the speed of light, is a little over three minutes away. The same reasoning applies for planet light as it does for starlight. What we presently see of Mars is already in the past."

"So how do we move closer to the present and away from the past?" Lillas asked.

"To move into Mars's present, we have to move our attention into another level of awareness. This relatively higher level of awareness has to have an opportunity to travel faster than the speed of light. One level beyond the mechanistic that is defined by the speed of light is the organic paradigm that is defined, according to the mystics, by the speed of thought."

When Rick observed the puzzled look on Lillas's face, he paused and asked a passing waiter if there was a flashlight in the restaurant that he could borrow for a moment. While he waited for the flashlight, he folded the red napkins into thin rectangles and laid them end-to-end in a straight line that bisected the table from left to right. Just as Rick completed his line of napkins, the waiter returned with a long-handled flashlight.

"All right," Rick said examining the flashlight. "Let's build another metaphor that relates the four domains and three levels of awareness to the concept of time."

"Imagine that this round table top represents all of space, and that this line of red napkins is a time line. So this is our two-dimensional table of space and time. In the middle of the table is the present moment that we are experiencing. To your left is the past and to your right is the future. Are you with me?"

"I'm with you," Lillas said, rescuing her tea from his table of time.

"In this long-handled flashlight are four batteries. Let's imagine that each battery represents one of our physical, mental, emotional and spiritual domains. The light bulb of the flashlight represents the intensity and focus of our attention. When all four batteries are charged or developed, then energy is flowing and the light of our attention is strong. When one or more of our batteries is weak or undeveloped, the light of our attention is weak."

"So to develop strong self-awareness and the ability to focus our attention, all four of our domains need to be developed and fully charged," Lillas said, building on his metaphor.

"Right," Rick said, looking pleased. "Now, the only real choice we have, once we have developed and activated our four domains and turned on the light of our attention, is where should we shine it? On what or on whom will I focus my attention?" Rick asked, shining his flashlight out the window, on the wall, on Lillas, and then on a passing waitress before Lillas interrupted him, saying:

"May I suggest that you focus it on me and our conversation at this present moment?"

"Good point," Rick said sheepishly. "So this is what most people think is living in the present moment." Rick placed his illuminated flashlight in the middle of the table, facedown and with the handle sticking up. "Now, what can you tell me about this situation?"

"Well, there is no light that I can see. So I would not be able to tell if the flashlight was on or off in that position," Lillas suggested. "I wouldn't know if the person was awake or asleep."

"You're right. Also, they may be blinded by the present moment, self-absorbed and self-centered because they are choosing not to share the light of their attention with anyone else," Rick added. "So this would be an illustration of someone choosing to live in the mechanistic moment.

"Now if we lift our attention to the organic paradigm, let's see what happens." Rick then lifted the flashlight about two feet off the table. "So, what's the organic perspective like when compared to the mechanistic perspective?"

"Well, that person's attention is now illuminating more of their past and their future while still focusing the majority of their attention in the present moment. The light of their attention is also now visible to others, whereas in the mechanistic paradigm it wasn't. So, someone in the organic perspective values relationships because they are willing to share their organic light with others[60] whereas those who are mechanistic — out of fear, worry, doubt or ignorance — refuse to share the light of their attention with anyone but themselves."

"In the mechanistic paradigm everyone is suffering from 'lights on, but nobody's home' syndrome," Rick said with a smile, "which is why many philosophers have suggested that we are asleep, drunk or hypnotized while supposedly living in the mechanistic world. Whereas, in the organic paradigm, their eyes are half open as opposed to mechanistic eyes that are fully shut," Rick said, then added, "Now, I don't mean the eyes of the body that are shut, but I do mean the eyes of their hearts and souls..."

"It seems that the organics," Lillas said, while pointing at the time line and the wider circle of light that illuminated it, "rather than being stuck in the mechanistic moment, have cultivated the ability to travel in time by reflecting and recalling some of their past memories or by connecting and imagining their future possibilities."

"Exactly. Now let's raise the flashlight one more level to simulate the wholistic paradigm," Rick said standing up. "Now what can you observe about the wholistic versus the organic perspectives?"

"The wholistic perspective allows you to see the very beginning and the very end of the time line. It is like seeing the alpha and the omega of our universe, its beginning and its end, in the context of eternity. The majority of the light of our attention is still in the present moment, but the whole table is illuminated with a wider vision afforded by the circle of light." Lillas paused, "So the wholistics have widened the context of their mechanistic and organic moments to view it in terms of all of history and all of possibility..."

Lillas suddenly stopped in mid-sentence, looked up at Rick and said, "Is this what you meant when you said the wholistic paradigm is about living in the eternal now?"

"Absolutely," Rick said, sitting down and turning off the flashlight. "The only way that we can really live in the present moment is to turn that moment into a present sacred moment. How we do this is by elevating our attention first into our organic and then into our wholistic levels of awareness in order to get a wider and broader context for our present moment's decision. If we don't, we are stuck with our mechanistic perspective and with assuming that it is the only one that is valid and true."

"So this is an illustration of the old saying that, in order to forgive and let go in the moment, we need to widen our view and broaden our perspective to set our present moment situation in a fuller and richer context," Lillas said reflectively. "Like the awakening that comes when you hear the saying, 'I was sad because I had no shoes and then I met a man who had no feet'."

Rick nodded. "In their desire to embody their Ideal and move their attention to the highest level of awareness they can conceive, Integrative Leaders would experience what the mystics have promised for ages which is '...all things will be brought back to your remembrance, from the four corners of the earth and the very beginning of time'."

"So the question becomes, for John and Mary," Lillas concluded, "Where will they choose to focus the light of their attention? Will it be in the past mechanistic moment, the relative organic moment or the eternal now?"

Chapter 5
The Process of Becoming an Integrative Leader

I shall be telling this with a sigh
Somewhere ages and ages hence:
Two roads diverged in a wood, and I—
I took the one less traveled by,
And that has made all the difference.

Robert Frost

Reflecting on Our Life's Journey

Despite Rick's recommendation of Marilyn Sprott for the top spot in *Crisis Energy* with quiet support from John, the board voted to offer the position to Thomas Sarkov. After contract offer, negotiation and acceptance, Thom wasted no time in taking full control of *Crisis Energy* and moving into John's 29th floor corner office.

Seven weeks into the Executive placement process John had spiraled down into sadness and depression. Nevertheless, he offered to stay on as an advisor for his remaining months. Thom insisted that the board and senior executives of the company would shepherd him through the transition, and he suggested strongly that John take time to focus on his own personal health crisis.

"You've done enough John," Thom had said. "In reviewing the corporate history, I know that without you at the helm in those years of crisis, there would be no company today. You've done your job. Now you have your own crisis to manage and I hope you do as well for yourself as you did for the company."

It was hard for John to let go of his position, his creation and his work. And it was this moment of realization—that he no longer had his work to sustain him and give his life purpose—that led him into the fourth stage of death and dying: sadness, grief and depression.

"I've done everything I can do to make the family and the company survive without me," John said one morning during a coaching session in Rick's office. "There is nothing left for me to do."

"There is if you are willing, John. We can reflect together on how you got to this peculiar place in space and time. A life review may allow you to see how your past has influenced your present. But only if you are willing," Rick added.

After a time, John looked up sadly and said, as he already had several times before, "What have I got to lose?"

For the first time during their conversations together, Rick finally felt that John meant it.

• • •

Experiencing Divine Love on Earth

Without experiencing human love and happiness,
it is not possible to know Divine Love.

B.K.S. Iyengar

Mary was excited at the beginning of the next coaching session, indicating to Lillas that she had several breakthrough experiences to share.

The first was that she had tried the 'telling the truth' experiment with her work colleague and it was successful for the second time. She learned to *hold her space*—not just the spirit nor the idea of the relationship, but her space. She had spoken clearly and calmly about what she had observed in several incidents in the past, and about what she had thought, felt and now wanted.

Her colleague had at first reacted defensively in an effort to protect his past *image of self*. When Mary uncharacteristically held her ground, rather than compromising as she had done in the past, her colleague finally admitted his part in their unsavory past encounters and committed to wanting what Mary wanted — a more collaborative rather than competitive working relationship in the future.

"I am two for two, in two different segments of my life. And to date, neither one of my targets has walked away in anger, doubt or fear from the truth of my experience," Mary said. "You would have been proud of me, Lillas. I held the space between us and invited in love, truth, trust and wisdom and held it, regardless of the arguments and debates designed to take it away."

"How did holding your space make you feel, Mary?" Lillas asked.

"It made me feel freer to be who I really am. I don't feel as fragmented or like a part-time actress in my personal wheel-of-life drama," Mary said with a smile. "And I'm becoming more comfortable with the idea of risking, speaking my truth and accepting whatever consequences may follow from it.

"The second great thing, Lillas, was that I had a breakthrough in terms of feeling—not just thinking—my Ideal of *loving relationships*. Your exercise of reflecting on the faces of love I had experienced in my life unearthed memories I had long forgotten."

Mary then went on to describe childhood memories: her parents who, even though she felt were mechanistic, gave her love as best they could; her first love of her pet cat, Boots, who was with her for years and died of old age on her sixteenth birthday; the love she felt as the oldest sibling for her younger brothers and sister; the dolls she loved and kept to give to her oldest daughter when she was eight; her first puppy love in elementary school; her first crush in high school; and her first taste of genuine romance in University before she met Ron.

"Before Ron, I had felt immature love, parental love, love for my siblings, and a special love for my grandmother on my mother's side. She and I were true friends. She felt free enough to tell me about all aspects of her life and I felt free enough to tell her all my experiences, hopes and dreams that I could not share even with my own mother. When she died, she was over a 100 years old and willed her engagement ring to me." Mary said holding out her hand and showing the diamond solitaire ring to Lillas. "I will always treasure it in remembrance of the specialness of her.

"With Ron, I've experienced, lust, physical sex, sensuousness, romance and, I believe for a time early in our relationship, a love of the heart.

"In my life review, one of my peak experiences was that I felt the awakening of a mother's love for each of my children when they were born. When I was first given them to hold and place on my breast, the pain of labor and delivery was instantly forgotten. When I saw how perfect they were, felt their breath and heard their first sounds, there was a stirring deep in my heart that has never gone away," Mary said recalling her three birthing experiences.

"I was not sure if what I had felt for them was a love of the heart, which you said was Phillia, or a love of the soul, which you called Agape. So I struggled with trying to understand Agape, or Divine Love, and fellowship, or heart love.

"In the midst of my struggle, I reread your paper on 'Building a Model of Integrative Leadership' focusing on the emotional domain. What caught my attention was where you described a story in which Faith was the father and Love was the mother. From their union they created children of light that were called gentleness, kindness, generosity, patience that I recognized as some of the fruits of the spirit.

"It was when I read and reflected on that section of your paper that I remembered Paul."

"Who is Paul?" Lillas asked making a note in her journal.

"I don't think that I have ever shared my relationship with Paul with anyone," Mary said thoughtfully. "Who was Paul? I think he was a living saint. He was the most generous man I have ever met. He had a magical way about him that made everyone attracted to him for his insights and advice. I can't explain it, really. I think a perfect blend of Faith and Love resulted in him embodying the light of spirit in his life that he shared freely.

"I met Paul when I first joined *SBT Company* ten years ago. He was a manager in Human Resources and a colleague. He was the first on the management team to step forward and offer me assistance. He said he wanted my experience with SBT to be 'the best of my career' and would do what he could to make it so. I found him to be genuine and authentic, and he always walked his talk.

"Very early in our relationship, whenever I entered his office or he entered mine, there was a resonance between us that would make my heart skip with excitement and I would flush with expectation like I was young and innocent again. In his presence, I would stop worrying about the future or fearing the past and simply live in the present moment that was between us. When we were together, time seemed to pass without either of us noticing its movement. It was magical.

"Paul was a very spiritual man, but I would not call him religious or dogmatic for he respected everyone's perspective, even when he did not agree with them. He was an empathetic listener with an ability to focus his whole attention on your conversation in a way that made you feel important. I found him to be something of a paradox—overpowering, challenging and freeing all at the same time. I had never experienced that kind of charisma, magnetism and chemistry ever before with another human being.

"When I thought about the fruits of the spirit in your paper, I remembered that he possessed many if not all of them," Mary paused to look away, "and he had such an impact on me back then, I'm not sure how I ever could have forgotten him."

"You speak so admiringly about Paul's life and leadership. It sounds like you really loved him."

"Oh yes, I loved him. I think I fell in love with Paul in my first few months with SBT. Or maybe I fell in love with the idea of loving him, I am not sure. What I am sure about is how he made me feel. I felt free to be me. I felt totally accepted, trusted and supported. I felt special to the very core of my being. I think my relationship with him is the closest I have ever come to experiencing Agape."

Mary sat up in her chair, "Lillas, I even remember that he had a beautiful atmosphere around him. It was like the smell and odor of fresh cut flowers that had nothing to do with his cologne. It was very puzzling."

Mary looked down, "Ron and I were having troubles ten years ago. I would lay in bed late at night with Ron sleeping beside me and fantasize about having an affair with Paul. I would wonder what it would have been like if we had met earlier, married and had children? I knew in my heart with the right companion I would be able to fly. With Ron, right from the beginning, my life seemed like such a struggle. Paul felt like the companion I had always yearned for that could help me soar and secretly I wanted to be with him."

"Did you have an affair with Paul?"

"No. Never. Paul was happily married to his wife, Susan, whom I also knew. They had two beautiful children who were the same ages as my two oldest.

He was honorable and would never break his word or his marriage vows and neither would I. So nothing of a physically romantic nature ever came between us.

"But I think, now that I've recollected our relationship, that our minds, hearts and souls were having an affair at some level of our being."

"Do you still keep in touch with Paul?"

"No," Mary replied with tears welling up in her eyes. "Paul died suddenly of a heart attack in my second year with SBT Company. He was on a business trip and died alone in his hotel room. His death was a shock to everyone and it was as if a light in SBT was extinguished.

"He was so young, Lillas. I found it so unjust that such a beautiful, spiritual, kind, strong and openhearted man could die of a heart attack alone, suddenly and while separated from those who loved him," Mary said through freely flowing tears.

"I think Paul's death made me doubt the existence of a Higher Power. How could a loving and wise Creator allow that kind of injustice? Why does evil persist and yet the good like Paul are taken from us?"

Lillas got up to sit beside Mary on the loveseat and placed her arm around her to comfort her.

"When Paul died I think that something died within me too," Mary said holding her hand to her heart and leaning on Lillas. "I must have suppressed my memories about him these past years and now they've come back to me."

They sat together for a time while Mary re-experienced her sorrow, sadness and grief over the loss of Paul. When she stopped weeping and was calm and present once again, Lillas spoke.

"We have found in our work, Mary, that there is no possibility of experiencing Divine Love in your life unless you have had an experience of a natural heart love in your life. I feel that you shared a natural love of the heart with Paul that opened the door of your heart to allow you to experience the presence of your own soul.

"Your reflection on your past loves this week was the trigger event and catalyst that allowed you to recall your True Self. Agape is the face of love that is magical, mysterious, wondrous and free.

"Mary, I would like to suggest another experiment as part of your emerging ITT practice. When you concentrate, meditate and contemplate your Ideal, remember Paul and the loving thoughts and feelings you associated with him. After a time, let the image of Paul go, but hold onto the feelings that naturally come from your association with him. In holding that feeling in the silence, adopt an attitude of quiet expectation that through your Ideal Self, your True Self will visit, speak and be present with you again.

"By doing this, I would expect the process of integration will begin to accelerate and self-generate for you."

They discussed other aspects and issues that arose from Mary's life review and saw that Mary's physical issues around the onset of asthma and sinusitis, her mental issues that caused her to choose immersion in work, and her emotional issues of growing separation from her husband Ron, were all linked in time to an impact that was made by the 'Loss of Paul' trigger event in Mary's life.

At the end of their coaching session, Mary took a deep breath and exhaled slowly, shaking herself and smiling. "I feel lighter than I have for a long time, Lillas. I'm even feeling that I'm almost ready to have my encounter with Ron and share the truth of my experience of him with him. What do you think, Lillas? Am I ready?"

Lillas smiled. "Ask your heart, Mary. Go into the silence and ask your heart."

Stages of Maturity

The first step to becoming is to will it.

Mother Theresa

John had called Rick early the following week and asked if they could spend the day together in the mountains, rather than having their weekly session in Rick's office. Memories and thoughts were surfacing for John as he was doing his life review, and he wanted to discuss them outside the city while walking and talking in nature. Rick had agreed, rearranged his schedule and picked John up early the next morning.

On their drive westward John asked, "So how does one really live an integrated life?"

"From our experience, the process is pretty simple, John. First, you consciously formulate an Ideal of the kind of person or leader you want to be. Second, you spend some time finding out who you really are—what we call the Real Self, as opposed to your Surreal Self, image of self or Personality. Third, you choose to start acting and behaving in a way that moves you from your Real to your Ideal."

"Sounds simple," John said quietly looking out the window.

"It is simple in concept. But we've found it very difficult in practice. Did you read that briefing paper I gave you on 'Building a Model of Integrative Leadership' some time ago?" When John nodded that he had, Rick asked what he thought of it.

"There were things that made sense, but with all due respect, Rick, a short while ago I would have said most of your briefing paper was a lot of metaphysical bull. I would have had trouble seeing how your integrative life and leadership ideas could have helped me in building my energy companies or my personal life in practical ways. I just didn't see life and leadership then the way you do now."

"What about now, John? How are you feeling about these integrative ideas today?"

"Now I'm not so sure," John said quietly. "I think life is a bigger mystery than I ever thought it was. Things were so cut and dried, black and white, yes or no for me for such a long time. The doctors at the Integrative Medical Institute (IMI) are suggesting that I had a part to play in the cause of my own illness. They talk, like you do, of the relationship of spirit, mind and emotions on the body and vice versa. If their perspective is true, then I am partly the cause of my own illness. If this is true, then I could also be a part of the cure." John shook his head and said, "Life used to be so simple, Rick, and now I just don't know anymore..."

Rick reflected on John's comments for he knew from his own experience that being ready to step onto the path of integration depends upon your personal level of maturity.

They had learned about four initial stages of maturity on the road towards Abraham Maslow's concept of self-actualization: blind acceptance, conscious acceptance, questioning, and accepting personal responsibility for one's life.

As children, we *blindly accept* nurturing and support from our caregivers or family members. As we mentally and emotionally awaken into Level I awareness, we *consciously accept* the story of how and why things are the way they are. When things don't seem to be working for us anymore, when the old patterns and beliefs no longer serve to lead us towards our *image of success*, we begin to *question* the values and beliefs previously formed, accepted and relied upon to that point in time in our life. Finally, there comes a time when we do not blame others, nor do we take 50 percent responsibility for an event, but we assume 100 percent responsibility for our actions and decisions and the consequences that follow from them, which is the awakening of *personal responsibility* and personal will in our life.

All four stages of maturity are within us at all times, for there are elements in our lives that we either blindly accept, consciously accept, question, or fully accept in terms of personal responsibility and accountability.

Voluntarily choosing to walk the path of integration is determined by readiness, and readiness occurs when one is in the questioning stage of maturity where we begin to wonder what it truly means to develop our body, mind, heart, and soul at higher levels of awareness.

"I think, John," Rick said into the silence, "you are finally ready to walk the path of integration."

Four Faces of Integration

And every one [of the angels] had four faces, and every one had four wings. As for the likeness of their faces, they four had the face of a man, and the face of a lion, on the right side: and they four had the face of an ox on the left side; they four also had the face of an eagle.

EZEKIEL 1:6, 1:10

And all the angels stood round about the throne, and about the elders and the four beasts, and fell before the throne on their faces, and worshipped God.

REVELATION 7:11

Brahma, the Creator, is traditionally depicted with four heads, faces and arms. Each head recites one of the four Vedas (Rig, Yajur, Sama, Athar). The hands hold a water-pot used in creating life, a string of rosary beads used to keep track of the Universe's time, the text of the Vedas, and a lotus flower.

THE FREE ENCYCLOPEDIA

Relating to the four domains of intelligence, Integrative Leaders may develop, if they choose, their four faces of integration by becoming:

- **Spiritually intelligent** and connecting to their Ideal Self, leading authentically and ethically from the Essence of who they are. "Spiritual Intelligence is the necessary foundation for the effective functioning of mental and emotional intelligence."[1]
- **Emotionally intelligent** "and creating a reservoir of positivity that inspires, arouses passion and enthusiasm, instills trust and creates a climate that fosters innovation, all-out performance, and warm lasting customer and employee relations."[2]
- **Mentally intelligent** with heightened awareness, mindset and consciousness. "The true enemy for a leader is resistance to awareness and being on automatic pilot."[3]

- **Physically intelligent** with behaviors and actions congruent with his or her heart, mind and soul. "Leaders who engage in exemplary leadership practices are more likely to have a positive influence on others and significantly impact the organization."[4]

• • •

Less than an hour from the city, Rick stopped at a resort in the Rocky Mountains that was noted for its brunch buffet. Over breakfast they continued their conversation.

"Tell me again—how do the four domains of intelligence relate to one another?" John asked over his morning coffee.

Rick thought for a moment. "Imagine if you had a desire to bake a loaf of bread. We would say that your intention would be of the spiritual domain. Your recipe for the kind of bread you wanted to bake would be the mental domain that provides the tools, techniques and methods for how to bake the bread. Gathering the ingredients for the type of bread you want to bake would be the physical domain, which provides the discipline, behaviors and actions that you need to make your intent and thoughts a physical reality. But without the heat of the oven—that is, without the warmth of the heart—you can stir the ingredients around all you want, but in the end nothing meaningful happens.

"Without the heart, there is no bread, just a kind of primordial dough. If you choose to eat it, it may sustain you for a time, but it won't be very satisfying or nourishing and in the long run, will give you a belly ache," Rick said pointing to John's stomach, "like the kind you have right now."

John was quietly reflecting on Rick's comments. Then he shook his head and said, "I've made things happen in my life without consciously involving my heart, Rick."

"Everyone has. There is no question we can develop mentally and physically; we can transact and even manage transitions from one state to another as you did in *Crisis Energy*, but you can't transform or transcend from a lower to higher level of awareness without an awakened heart. You can't turn a caterpillar into a butterfly, a tadpole into a frog or primordial dough into the bread of life without an awakened heart. From our experience and understanding, it just can't be done.

"That is why we think that awakening and nurturing the emotional domain is at the heart of successfully walking the path of integrative life and leadership."

"So this is like your version of Napoleon Hill's law of manifestation?" John asked.[5]

"Exactly. The process of becoming an Integrative Leader involves aligning our intent, thoughts, desires and actions. If we could do that, nothing would stop the object of our desires and the focus of our attention from manifesting in our world," Rick replied.

"What about if I was baking bread only for me to eat, and not for anyone else?" John asked. "Would this law of manifestation as you've described it still work if my intent is selfish?"

"Yes it would still work. The four domains of intelligence operate at every level of awareness from Level I to Level III with each level activated by your intention and motivation. However, there is a difference in terms of life results; one leads you into the path of struggle and the other onto the path of flow.

"Each of the three levels of awareness is governed by a different core understanding about life. Level I is about Variables. It is about situational life and leadership where you change your personality fragments on your wheel of life to match and accommodate the circumstances and situations in your life. Level II is about Values that are important to you, like family, work, happiness, health, honor, wealth or love of self and others, that seek to unite some of your personality fragments into something called character. Level III is about Virtues and principles that can inform and guide your every life decision in a way that eventually unites your personality fragments and aligns them with your Essence.

"In the process of becoming an Integrative Leader, your Variables, Values and Virtues need to be aligned for this law of manifestation to work naturally in all four domains of intelligence and three levels of awareness.

"So a key question for you, John, would be about your intent: Why did you sacrifice so much of yourself to keep *Crisis Energy* alive? What do you love in your life in this moment?

"And perhaps most importantly: Why do you want to die and what would make you want to live again?"

• • •

Rebirthing Intimate Relationships

For here we are not afraid to follow the truth, wherever it may lead…

Thomas Jefferson

One can have no smaller or greater mastery than mastery of oneself.

Leonardo da Vinci

Mary began her next coaching session by sharing her success at being able to empathetically visualize, during her daily meditation practice, the feeling of Agape she had first felt with Paul and had suppressed for so many years.

"It was like a key that opened the door of my heart and allowed my True Self to pay me a conscious visit," she had shared. "I could feel the depth of that Presence." In that state of attunement, she asked her heart about her readiness to share her truth with Ron and it felt somatically, reasonably and intuitively right.

Mary then became excited about her 'tell the truth' session with her husband, Ron. "I wanted to be mindful, thoughtful and careful about setting the stage for our encounter."

Mary had begun by inviting Ron to spend an intimate relationship weekend with her at home. Initially Ron was surprised at her invitation, then suspicious and somewhat resistive, and finally agreeable. With his agreement, Mary asked him to reflect on what he thought about their intimate relationship in the past and what he wanted in the future. She then managed to eliminate all their social commitments and arrange for their two young adult children (who still lived at home) to be with friends for the weekend.

In preparation for their encounter, Mary used the integrative communication model as a framework, and reflected and wrote in her journal the key points she wanted to communicate to Ron. This was so that if she became emotional, she could refer to her written notes and not forget or lose herself in a debate.

On the Friday night after supper, Mary introduced the session by sharing experiences, experiments and her integrative journey of the past several months that she had not shared with him before. Then she reviewed her history of the many faces of love she had experienced before Ron, her experiences of love with Ron for the past 25 years, her special past relationship with Paul, and where she felt they were currently, which was in the body-mind and not in the heart or soul.

"What was Ron's reaction to your sharing?" Lillas asked.

"At first Ron was shocked and surprised. He had not really known or been aware of how I had truly felt or thought about our intimate relationship since I had withheld for so long. He was angry about my disclosure regarding Paul, feeling that I had somehow dishonored my relationship with him. When I assured him I had not dishonored him, Paul, or myself, he then tried to reason with me and talk me out of my perspective. I held my space and suggested to him that this was the way 'I' was observing, feeling, and thinking about our past relationship. I also suggested that he was free to not agree with me about the way I viewed our past relationship, that it was OK. However, would he be willing to share his private perspective with me?

"After avoiding the question for some time, Ron finally admitted that he too was feeling sad, lonely and fragmented. That he had felt that way for many years and did not know what to do about it."

"That sounds like a breakthrough for Ron from his Surreal Self to his Real Self," Lillas said.

"It was," Mary said excitedly. "He asked me many questions about the integrative journey, philosophy, process, principles and practices. I started teaching him what I had learned about radical honesty, compassion and connecting with inner wisdom which piqued his curiosity to such a degree that over the weekend I taught him the way you taught me how to meditate."

"Really?" Lillas asked with a smile.

"Really! We spent the whole weekend in our intimate relationship intensive session just getting to know each other from different perspectives. I learned things about Ron he had never shared with me before and I with him. Rebirthing our relationship in radical honesty was very freeing for both of us. He asked about how I had come up with my Ideal of loving relationships and I shared with him the process we went through to find it. He then asked if I could help him find his Ideal, and I did."

"What was Ron's Ideal?" Lillas asked.

"His Ideal centered around the virtue of justice, including fairness and equity. Since his father died when he was 11 years old, he always felt that life was unfair. Ron was the oldest and had to grow up quickly with the burden of responsibility for his mother and siblings. This belief hardened over time and became his chief misunderstanding about life around which all his personality fragments revolved. We discussed what justice would look like from several perspectives: mechanistically, which for me was too black and white and harsh; organically, which was more harmonious and compassionate; and wholistically, which was merciful but too mysterious.

"After much discussion, we found a common ground of understanding in the organic paradigm of *compassionate justice* from which we combined my Ideal of *loving relationships* and mutually built an Ideal by which we could measure our intimate relationship."

"Sounds like you made fabulous progress in a very short time," Lillas said. "Ron must have been ready to move positively and constructively toward rather than away from you."

"He was. And it doesn't stop there," Mary continued with a growing smile. "When the kids came home for Sunday night supper, we shared with them all we had discovered and wanted for each other in our intimate relationship. They were initially skeptical, then intrigued and finally happy for us. They were so interested in our process that we have a date to explore Ideals, integrative processes, principles and practices for each of them and our family this coming weekend."

"I am so happy for you, Mary," Lillas said with a broad smile.

"And finally, there have been only a few times in our relationship that Ron has sent me flowers. After our intimate weekend, Ron sent me flowers nearly every day. The last bouquet came with a beautiful card in which he wrote me poetry. He has never done that before and I would like to share his poem with you, which he called 'Oneness'."

She reached into her purse, pulled out a card and read it to Lillas.

I in you and you in me.
Together you and I will be.
Truthful. Joyous, Peaceful and Whole
When, my love, we know our Soul.

"Isn't that a beautiful poem?" Mary said as she quietly wiped tears from her cheeks.

Lillas was very touched, and nodded. "I think, Mary, that our time together is nearly over. The process of integration is becoming self-generative for you. By coming to know your *Real Self*, by allowing an experience of your *Ideal Self* and, with universal laws, principles and practices as your guide, I know you will be fine on your own, in your journey of integration.

"This is especially true now that you have chosen to share your integrative experience with your husband and family and invite them into the process. One coal that is lit and alone will often go out. But if there are many coals gathered together, each lit coal helps keep the others enlightened."

Lillas then stood and they hugged. "It has been a pleasure being with you on this part of your integrative journey, Mary."

Touching Your Real Self

You can fool all of the people some of the time.
You can fool some of the people all of the time.
But you can't fool all of the people all of the time.

Abraham Lincoln

"I am not so sure I have chosen to die," John said unconvincingly.

"One of the first steps onto the path of integration is to get real. That means you need to be able to tell the truth about your past, accept it, forgive it if necessary and then carry on. Without that admission and acceptance, you will continue to dance with your own self-created illusions about who and what you think you are, never admitting who you really are, not even to yourself. So the first step is to get real, John."

"What do you mean 'get real'?" John asked.

Rick took a long deep breath, sipped on his cup of orange pekoe tea and quietly reflected within before beginning what he knew would be a difficult conversation.

"John, I looked at your company's mission, values and principles from over three years ago. They were very good and well thought-out with trust, honesty, justice, honor, excellence, and learning from past mistakes all being part of your personal and corporate credo. I heard that you went to the trouble of getting every board member, employee and consultant to sign the company mission, principles and values before allowing them to work for the company. Is that true?"

John agreed that it was true, but looked uncomfortable in saying so.

"In my interviews with your board members and senior people during my internal search for your replacement, they told me stories about you and the company history, especially your actions during and after the corporate crisis. I would like to share some of them with you to gain your perspective on their validity."

John shrugged his shoulders. "Everyone makes up stories, Rick, especially in the absence of facts. That is human nature."

Rick smiled knowingly and began. "In the first year of the company's existence you were untouched by your position and power. Everyone thought you walked your talk, were fair, and almost too compassionate and generous with personal and company resources.

"Somehow, that all changed in the second and third years as CEO. You attracted the nickname 'King John' whenever you visited the FSU. Apparently, while in that country, you had chauffeurs, limousines, private airplanes, beautiful Executive Assistants, a palatial suite for your accommodations, a dacha on the Black Sea, and staff and servants to satisfy your every need, all paid for corporately. Wasn't that part of the reason why the company was in dire need of financial resources?"

"That is partially true. In the FSU you had to maintain an image of power, strength, wealth and decisiveness when dealing with the post-communist government leaders and in-country oligarchs. Otherwise, they would sense your weakness and not respect you, nor would they make a deal with you."

Rick continued. "When you returned from your kingdom in the FSU, you were just plain John again and in this way, you were living a double life. Here, you initially adhered to your personal and corporate values. There, you bent the truth, weren't always honest, and didn't always act with honor. And, you changed like a chameleon to suit each particular and peculiar situation. You moved from a value-centered approach to leadership here, and descended into a variable-centered approach there for so long, you got the two approaches confused.

"It is one thing to play the role of King John. It is another to begin to believe you are the King."

Rick let his comment hang in the space between them while he sipped his tea and then continued, "Four words that people shared with me, time and again, in describing your management and leadership style during and post corporate crisis were: authoritarian, duplicity, corruption and infidelity.

"*Authoritarian* because you adopted a siege mentality during the corporate crisis, in which you assumed total control of all decision-making in the company without delegation to your senior people, which rendered them impotent. That made you unjust. *Duplicity* because you were saying one thing with your corporate values and doing another in your life. That made you dishonest. You were accused of *corruption* because it was believed you had made payments to senior government officials to secure the eastern property away from your senior energy company competition. That made you untrustworthy. And *infidelity* due to your countless adulterous affairs while in the FSU that made you dishonorable.

"These stories suggest that, by your own actions and behaviors, you seemed to violate every value and principle that a few short years ago you held sacred. You signed those values and principles yourself, didn't you, John?"

John was quiet and did not respond. Rick could see his face was flushed and his jaw muscles were clenching and unclenching spasmodically.

John raised his head and was beet red with anger. It looked for a moment as though he would violently and physically react to Rick's comment. As John looked up with 'hard eyes' and locked onto Rick's, he saw only compassion and not judgment. After a moment of trying to hold onto his anger, he slowly unclenched his fists, softened, and then saddened. After a time he said quietly, "You are right Rick. There is a truth in the stories you've heard about the company and me. I think I've swallowed these events, denied that I could have done them, and held them in my belly for several years without admitting that I had done them. Not even to myself." John looked down and was quiet for a very long time. When he looked back at Rick he said, "Maybe these memories are part of what is killing me."

With his admission, John exhaled, his face turned pale and his body went limp. "I am not feeling very well, Rick. I think I am going to be sick." John stood up and was visibly shaking. "Would you mind helping me to the bathroom?"

To Tell the Truth

There is no defeat in the confession of one's error. The confession itself is victory.

MOHANDAS K. GANDHI

The disclosures of Divine insight are often painful to worldly ears.

PARAMAHANSA YOGANANDA

Afterwards, Rick obtained a day room at the resort for John to have a nap and recover from his breakfast evacuation and wave of physical weakness. When he awoke, Rick ordered up some hot herbal lemon tea and John, a perennial coffee drinker, accepted it without question.

As Rick listened, John talked about never wanting to be the way he had become. He was a man of high ideals and integrity who had lost himself somewhere along the way. He wasn't sure if it was fear, greed, or power that led his downward descent; all he knew was that down he went. He did not like himself anymore and did not know how to break the habits he had acquired in his emotionally charged time of personal and corporate crisis.

"So where do I go from here?" John asked.

"The first step is to admit the things that you thought and did that were out of alignment with your Ideal of living integrity. The second step is to accept them as part of your personality, or as an actor in your life drama, but not as your Director nor your Producer or Essence. You acted like an idiot, John, but you are not an idiot. I know that in your core, you are a good and honest man. The third step is to forgive yourself and ask forgiveness from the spirit that stands behind your Ideal.[6] The fourth is that you should ask forgiveness from all those others you consciously or unconsciously hurt along the way."

"Are you saying I have to admit my affairs to Diane?" John asked.

"Integrity means 'to thine own self be true.' If you would like to have the hope of living and beginning your relationship with Diane again, or of dying and leaving a legacy based on honesty and truth rather than lies, I would suggest that you have no choice but to share the truth of your experience with her. If you want to die while living a lie, then you don't have to tell her. You can take your illusions with you to your grave."

"What if I lose her in the truth-telling process?"

"I suspect, judging by her reactions to the news of your illness and her behavior towards you this past eight weeks, you have all ready lost her on some level. There is a part of her that knows the truth of your infidelity. All you are doing by speaking *your* truth is helping the part of her that knows that truth to reconnect and align with the part of her that consciously doesn't."

"That sounds risky," John said. "I know it will have a negative impact on our relationship."

"Telling the truth is risky. But by doing so, you align with your Ideal of living integrity. By doing so, you give Diane a chance and the freedom to walk toward you — or away from you — in truth. Telling the truth gives both of you a chance at life. Not doing so binds both of you to an illusion which I suspect will continue to lead, one way or another, to your death.

"If you are going to die anyway, John, would you like to die while moving toward your Ideal of integrity or die while holding onto your lies and illusions? Your choice."

"I think I'm beginning to see," John said leaning back and closing his eyes.

"Now, if you choose to do the first four steps in this process of letting go of the past, then the fifth step is to find something in your life that you are willing to die for. For that is the only way that you will give yourself permission to live again."

After a time, John said softly through closed eyes, "I *want* to change, Rick. I am *willing* to change. I'm just not sure I know *how* to change."

"You rest now, John. Later this afternoon, if you're feeling better, we'll go for that walk you promised me, and we'll talk about change."

• • •

Three Paths of Integration: Transaction, Transformation & Transcendence

If there are any universally valid principles in psychology, one of them must be the importance of integration: the fitting together and balancing of the various elements of the psyche to make a complete, harmonious whole. A faulty or pathological psychic system is almost always described with terms that connote division and fragmentation, such as "repression," "dissociation," and "splitting." Health, on the other hand, is usually specified with terms that imply integration and union, such as "insight," "assimilation," and "self actualization." Many religious philosophies also emphasize the attainment of connectedness and unity as the major theme of spiritual development. The whole is greater than the sum of its parts [and] greatness can only be realized when the parts are joined together.

J. Suler

Developmental change means improving through training or skill development. *Transactional change* means changing systems and processes, externally, and changing beliefs, mental models and mind maps internally.[7] *Transitional change* is the ability to manage, from one state to another, in the process of fixing a problem.

Transformational change is about survival (change or die) or the breakthrough (heart-mind) needed to pursue other opportunities.[8] *Transcendent change* is a shift in paradigm to a higher-order consciousness.[9]

Management is primarily involved with developmental, transactional and transitional change (physical, mental), whereas leadership is primarily involved in transformational (heart) and transcendental (soul) change.

• • •

By mid afternoon, John was physically feeling better but mentally and emotionally subdued. They went for a walk on mountain paths that encircled the resort and overlooked a shimmering river valley. The sun was shining and the sky was a clear springtime blue. There was snow on the ground beneath the shade of the evergreen trees, but most of the paths were clear enough for them to walk without encountering mud.

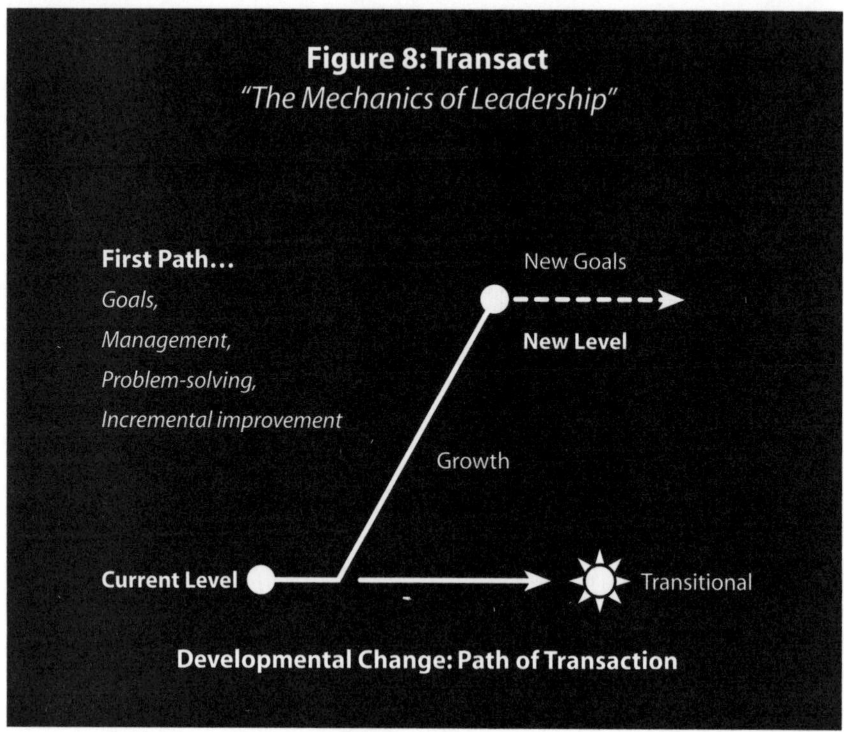

"You talked about the games people play at different levels, Rick. What do you mean by that? Are your 'games' the same as your levels of awareness, consciousness and paradigms?" John asked.

"In a way, they are all associated. Everyone, for example, is familiar with the rules of the mechanistic game," Rick said. "This is where if you do something for me, I will do something for you. It is about contracts, legal and literal interpretations, and the philosophy of quid pro quo. This is what we mean when we say 'reactive transactional leadership' because it is based on learning from past precedents that govern our present actions, just like psychoanalysts search out past emotional traumas that have an unconscious effect on our present life drama."

"Transactional change is about our learning, knowledge, skill and talent development. It is driven by a system of education that prides memory and evaluation over intuition and imagination.

"Fewer people are familiar with the rules of the organic game which involves the heart-mind, or involves bringing our unconscious beliefs and desires into conscious awareness. This game involves 'doing to others what

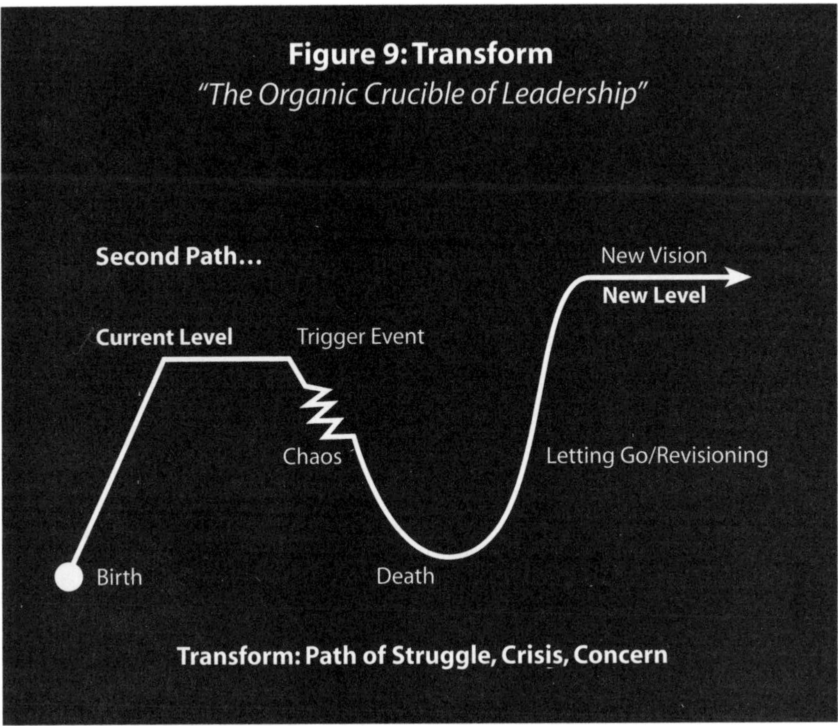

you want them to do for you.' It is hard for people living in a mechanistic family, organization or culture to apply the Golden Rule in their life, love and work. The Golden Rule simply means, if you want friends, be friendly; if you want kindness, be kind; if you want love, be loving. Regardless of what people do to you, treat them in the way you would like to be treated.

"The organic game is the reason why it is said that you can only keep what you are willing to freely give away."

"That is a very difficult thing to do," John said shaking his head. "That is not the way the world works. Actions always cause reactions. Punishment is tailored to suit the crime. Fear creates rules, regulations and codes to protect the many against the few that can violate our rights and freedoms. Justice and vengeance become two sides of the same coin."

"You're right," Rick said with a smile. "That is what makes this process of integration so difficult and why we admire those who are living examples of this value-centered style of reflective transformational leadership.

"Transformational learning, leadership and change is of the heart. We have experienced it as six steps. First, there is a trigger event usually

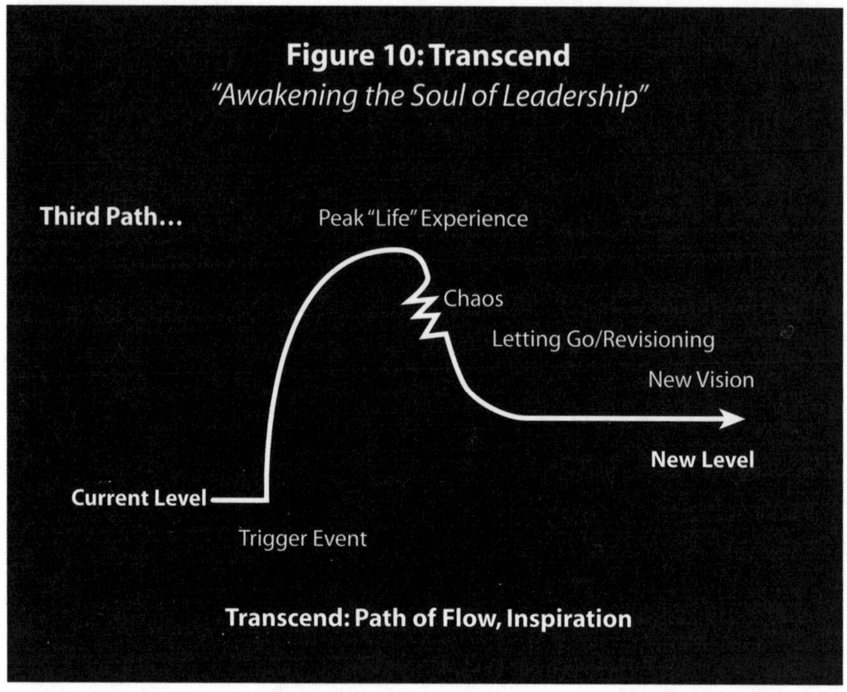

accompanied by a strong emotional visceral reaction like the one you had this morning. Second, there is time for reflection about when you felt this way before: What is the recurring theme? When did it begin? How has it affected your life? Third, there is time for integrative evaluation — thoughts, feelings, desires, wants. What would my Surreal Self do in this situation? What would my Ideal Self do in this situation? The fourth step is making a decision about which part of your self you will align and support? Will it be the Surreal or the Ideal? Fifth, you apply that decision in your life and, to the best of your ability, engage all four domains. Sixth, monitor and observe what life is trying to teach you with the cycle beginning all over again. If your decision was aligned with your best understanding of your Ideal then you move upward on a growth spiral. If it's not aligned, then you move around like a merry-go-round and get to do it all over again!

"Often, people are confused between 'doing unto others' and 'cause and effect.' There is a belief that if I am kind to you, then you will be kind to me. That is not necessarily so in the mechanistic realm, so people doubt the validity of this organic rule and fall back into transactional and away from transformational leadership.

"Finally, even fewer people are familiar with the rules of the wholistic game which involves bringing our True Self into conscious awareness. This game involves 'unconditional compassion' for the Divine in all things, in ourselves and in others. This is the level of virtue-centered responsive transcendent leadership, where your Ideal—when aligned and resonant with your *True Self*—involves itself and descends and reshapes your *Real* and *Surreal Selves*."

What are You Willing to Die for?

If you don't know what you are willing to die for, your spirit is already dead...
For a just cause, you must be willing to die.

Martin Luther King, Jr.

On their way back into the city that evening, John sat quietly digesting the day's events as Rick drove. Finally he said, "I used to say that you never know anyone until you work or live with them. And you really never know anyone until you see them in crisis. If life is purposeful and meaningful as you suggest, then I guess my personal and corporate crisis was an opportunity to get to know who I really was at a very deep level."

Rick smiled. "That's it exactly, John. From an integrative perspective, we would say that when you live or work with someone, you eventually are exposed to their *Private Self* and not just their persona or *Public Self*. In crisis, you get to see their *Secret Self,* which often holds their chief misunderstanding about life that they want no one else to see. Life conspires to make us aware of the things we may not be aware of. It does this through internal or external life events, circumstances and situations. The key is paying attention, staying awake and being aware. We've found it is a lovely and natural process that aids integration, but only when we are aware of it."

"That is why you said in your 'Building a Model' paper 'may life be your teacher and may your Ideal be your guide'," John added.

"Exactly. Your Ideal that we uncovered is living with *integrity*. Integrity comes from the Latin *integrare* which means 'to make whole.' If for every situation you face, you pause, reflect, and get in touch with your four domains by reflecting and expressing your observations, thoughts, feelings and intentions, and if you respond to that situation in accordance with your Ideal rather than react to it in accordance with your past *image of self*, then you can get out of the body-mind (belly) and move into your heart-mind. That is the path of transformation.

"Eventually if you can stay in your heart-mind more than in your body-mind and habituate some of the ITT practices we've discussed into your daily routine, you will establish an intimate relationship with the wisdom, truth, compassion and selfless service that naturally resides within your own soul. That is the path of transcendence."

John was quiet for a time. "I've been thinking about what I am willing to die for, Rick. I would die for my kids. I know I would die for my company because I almost did. But I am not sure if external things feel like the right motivation anymore. I am not sure if I would be willing to die for a principle like integrity, freedom, truth or love. They all seem so, well, idealistic to me." John turned to Rick and asked, "What are you willing to die for?"

"The 'work' that Lillas and I have done these past years in integrative life and leadership is what I would be willing to die for."

"You would be willing to die for what you do?" John asked.

"No, we would be willing to die for who we are. We would be willing to die for the principles, mission and core values that define the Essence of our being. On our integrative journey, what we do is becoming more aligned with who we truly are every moment of every day."

"What are you and Lillas getting out of it?" John asked.

"Didn't Winston Churchill once say, 'You measure a living by what you get. You measure a life by what you give'? We are measuring our lives by what we are giving, not getting, John.

"To see people awaken, connect to their True Selves and begin to walk the path of integrative life and leadership gives a joy to us that is indescribable. It is the virtue of selfless service and contribution in action that resonates throughout our four domains and three levels of awareness and is the spirit that resonates, unites and helps us integrate them all into one.

"We do this 'work' not as a job, but as a calling and vocation. We eat, live and breathe it, for we know that our daily experience of the 'work' becomes food for our minds, hearts and souls. Through our mutual 'work,' we have had so many experiences of heaven on earth, that if either one of us were to die tomorrow, we would feel complete, satisfied and fulfilled.

"Our 'work' is not just about satisfaction that is fleeting and momentary. It is not just about the gratification of achievement, which lasts a little longer but still fades away. It is about experiencing authentic happiness based on the joy and bliss of doing, living and loving for Love's sake alone. It is not just about being still and quiet, but about experiencing a peace that passes understanding. It is not just about being good, but about being good for something.

"It is accepting, allowing and expecting the best from everything that we do and everyone that we encounter.

"That is what we are willing to die for, John. It has allowed both of us to live our lives to the fullest once again. We are living our dream and our Ideal, and we decided some time ago that if we were to die we would rather do it while walking towards our dream rather than walking beside or away from it.

"So, what is your dream, John? What have you been walking away from rather than towards? What have you dropped from your life that you might want to pick up again? What are you willing to die for that will allow you to live your life again, even if it is only for a short time?"

John was quiet for some time. "When I was young I loved music. I played piano, guitar and even played in a band I organized for several years in high school. In University the workload was so hard, I gave up my passion for music. Then I got a job, married Diane, had children and it seemed I never had time to get back to it."

"What was music like for you?" Rick asked.

"When I played my music, I would get lost in it. I would lose track of time and just flow effortlessly into it. Some of the best times I remember from my youth were jamming with my friends on a Sunday afternoon that would often go late into the night. My compositions were generally poor, but some were not bad. Musicians don't make a lot of money. When I chose a career in applied science and engineering, I put my music on the back shelf of my mind and never looked at it again. I never listen to music and don't even know what kind I would like anymore."

They rode in silence for the remaining part of the trip back to the city. As they entered the city limits, it was John who broke the silence. "Rick, I was wondering if you could drop me off at the IMI? I would like to set up some more appointments with them about their suggested diet and alternative healing methods. I'll find my way back home from there."

"It would be my pleasure, John," Rick said and then added, "I also noticed that within a block of the IMI there is one of the best music stores in the city. I'll point it out to you as we get nearer to the IMI. I am thinking that maybe you might want to browse and see if any of those musical instruments will speak to you today like they once did years ago. What do you think, John?"

John said nothing but simply smiled for the first time that day.

The Elements of Becoming an Integrative Leader

> *As for the best leaders, the people do not notice their existence. The next best the people honor and praise; the next the people fear; and the next the people hate…when the best leader's work is done, the people say 'we did it ourselves.' So to lead people, you must walk behind them.*
>
> Lao Tzu

We agree with Goleman *et al* that, "The crux of leadership development that works is self-directed learning; intentionally developing or strengthening an aspect of who you are or who you want to be or both."[10]

Integrative Leadership development involves the whole person that leads to whole leaders and whole organizations. Our approach to self-directed life-long leadership learning comes from our experience and education in adult learning and development. We believe, as did Socrates, that "the unexamined life is not worth living." It is a process of ever-new growth, transformation, and transcendence.

The process of integration is a journey about finding and experiencing a life of purpose, reaching one's full potential, and discovering a deeper relationship with all of life. It is about heightening and expanding our level of awareness. It is about making choices in the present moment that contribute to creating a more fulfilling life, and about experiencing balance and integration and a day-to-day quality of the journey that is peaceful, loving and joyful.

The integrative journey requires a commitment to take time for reflection. Most leaders are caught in their own busyness and over-commitments, with no time for the deep inner work of being the best leader, not just *in* the world, but *for* the world. It takes courage to develop an intimate relationship with your *True Self*. But we have found that integrative personal development, which awakens the emotional and spiritual domains, is the greatest leverage to becoming a better leader.

The process of integration is challenging and most often overlooked in a culture that focuses almost exclusively on intellectual and physical development. The wisdom of walking the path of deep inner work can be found in recent leadership studies as well as in the ancient wisdom traditions.

Integrative Leadership is leading from the Essence of who and what you truly are. So, who are you and what do you want to do with this precious life you've been given?

The following are the seven elements that comprise self-directed, lifelong, Integrative Leadership learning:

1. **My Ideal (True, Universality, Superconscious) Self:** Who do I want to be? What is my personal vision? What are my hopes, wishes, dreams and desires for myself?

   Spending time reflecting and getting a clear perspective on our Ideal Self and our personal vision evokes hope, passion and energy to create and live the life of our dreams. What is our intent for our lives? What is it we most want for our life?

   Our personal vision expresses the direction of our life and is a hopeful, optimistic and positive view of our future. Our Ideal expresses the highest concept of the kind of person and leader we want to become and is a guide and standard for our life decisions and a barometer of our sense of satisfaction with life.

   Our Ideal Self is seen as our "Image of God" in the mystic traditions, and the best of what we can conceive ourselves to be in the secular traditions, and is anchored in virtues. Our Ideal Self is consciously formulated to resonate our Level I awareness and help it attune to our True Self that resides within our Level III awareness. This practice forms the path and initiates the process of full integration. We view our True Self as synonymous with our Essence that is the essential, intrinsic, fundamental and foundational aspect of our Being.

   Many people are involved in vision and mission work in their organizational life, yet few do it for themselves. A compelling personal vision and living Ideal helps transform a lifetime of limiting habits to supportive habits on our journey of integrative life and leadership.

2. **My Mission (Purpose, Calling, Vocation):** What is my purpose? What do I want to do and whom do I want to serve? How do I best use my gifts, abilities and talents to achieve my goals, aims or aspirations and make a purposeful and meaningful contribution?

   We believe everyone has a shared or collective mission and also a personal or unique mission. These missions are two sides of the same coin. On one side is our collective mission that could be phrased: "to be of selfless service with unconditional love and compassion to the spirit of our Ideal, ourselves and others". Our personal mission within this overarching mission would be to "know ourselves, to be ourselves, and yet be One with All That Is". On the other side of the coin is our unique mission that expresses our personal sense of purpose, meaning, talents, gifts and creativity.

   Our mission affects every aspect of our life. Kouzes and Posner feel that, "Burnout is not a lack of energy. It is a lack of living our life purpose."[11] We have found that even if we are close to living our life purpose, burnout can still occur if we continually give to others and neglect to connect, awaken and nurture our inner selves.

   There are excellent resources available to help uncover your personal vision, Ideal, mission and core values and virtues. Some that we have found helpful are shown in the Endnotes.[12]

   Our process of uncovering your life's mission uses an integrative approach that engages the four domains of intelligence, the three levels of awareness and the fifth domain of choice. The process of integration helps to evolve our awareness from viewing our life mission as our job (Level I), to seeing it as our vocation (Level II), to finally arriving at our Calling (Level III).

3. **My Surreal (Public, Personality, Conscious) Self:** Who am I as personality? What are the behaviors, thoughts and emotions I express publicly in my daily life? What are my preferences? What are my strengths, blind spots, and areas for development? What are

my constructive habits that allow me to realize my Ideal and personal vision? What are my destructive habits that are limiting my development as an Integrative Leader?

We have chosen to describe our Public Self using the expression Surreal Self. Surreal means "beyond real," where our life events take on a dreamlike quality. We have chosen this descriptor based on the Eastern wisdom traditions that suggest that our earthly life is an illusion; that we are all actors and actresses within a cosmic dream. From this perspective, what we consider real (materiality) in our mechanistic paradigm is unreal in the wholistic paradigm and what we consider unreal (spirituality) within the mechanistic paradigm is considered the only true reality in the wholistic paradigm. For some this descriptor might be paradoxical, which is our intent.

Personality is defined as "the pattern of collective qualities, traits, behaviors, temperaments, emotions and mental traits of a person". From our Integrative perspective, personality belongs to Level I awareness that is informed by emergent and evolving Ego. It is also the home of our *chief misunderstanding about life*. Personality is divided into many segments or sub-personalities each playing a role within our personal wheel of life. The collection of all sub-personalities we call our *image of self,* which is associated with the body-mind (navel).

The fundamental personality profile assessment tool that we use that most closely aligns with our Model of Integrative Leadership is a Modified and Integrated Myers Briggs Type Indicator (MBTI) with integral interpretations of the foundational eight resulting personality types.[13] There are other tools and assessments that we may utilize depending on the specific need and application. The purpose of these assessments is to foster self-knowledge and self-awareness and promote self-development.

4. **My Real (Private, Individuality, Unconscious) Self:** Who am I as character or individuality? What are my strengths and my gaps?

   We have chosen to describe our Private Self as our Real Self. Our Real Self is about our Character that evokes an image of moral and ethical strength. Character is viewed as the combination of traits, qualities and features of a 'group'. The 'group', in our Model of Integrative Intrapersonal Life and Leadership, resides within us and is made up of at least two or more of our sub-personalities or personality segments. Our Character resides in Level II awareness and seeks to act as a positive attractor with the potential of informing, unifying and partially integrating our various personality segments through common values. Character and Individuality are used synonymously within the Integrative Model.

Character is associated with the unconscious or heart-mind (chest). Character resonates with Maxwell Maltz's Psychocybernetic Self-Image Psychology where our Self-Image, held in the unconscious or heart-mind, has a profound effect on our image of self held by our conscious mind.[14]

Character development is done through awakening and exercising personal will. Level II awareness involves emotional and social intelligence. There are many SI and EI assessment tools ranging from Cooper and Sawaf's EQ Map, Baron's EQi, and Goleman and Boyatzis's EIC, among others, to help initially assess the nature of your Real Self.[15] In the process of integration, we become real as people and leaders when we begin to have the courage to speak and act in truth the thoughts, feelings and desires of our Private Self.

5. **Integrative Leadership Learning Plan:** What is my learning plan that will allow me to build on my strengths and address and reduce my gaps? Reflect on your strengths. Be open to surfacing hidden talents, and benchwarmers (talents in waiting that haven't been used to full potential). Where do my Ideal, Real and Surreal selves overlap? Reflect on your gaps. Where do my Ideal, Real and Surreal selves differ? How can I build on my strengths? What can I do to help fill in my gaps? What are my learning preferences?[16] Some people will set specific measurable goals, develop practices and values, or use universal principles and a mission or vision statement to guide them toward a meaningful and desired future.

6. **Application and Experimentation:** Practicing and experimenting with new behaviors, beliefs, feelings and values that build on our strengths and minimize our gaps will allow us to move from our Surreal to our Real Self, and from our Real to our Ideal Self.

   A curiosity and a willingness to experiment (as we once did as children) with life are essential ingredients in allowing us to overcome past habituation and in moving us towards life-giving habits and practices. We have identified 12 Integrative, Transformative and Transcendent (ITT) practices that are helpful in the process of integration. The ITT practices are sourced from our own journey and experience of integration as well as from the scientific, wisdom and mystic traditions. These are developed further in Chapter 6.

   Another essential ingredient is a desire to apply what we know and have at hand in the moment. Only through application can we move our knowledge to understanding. And only through reflection and connection can we move our understanding to wisdom. The evolution theory would also suggest that an experience of our knowledge forms our beliefs. And an experience of our beliefs supports our Faith.

   Application is the embodiment of our attunement and an essential ingredient for the process of integration.

7. **Relationships and Associations:** Develop supportive and trusting relationships that make your personal, interpersonal and organizational change possible. Who will support you on your integrative life and leadership journey? Who will help you identify your strengths and gaps? Who will support you in your life experiments, applications and practices?

   We have found that it is very difficult to walk this path of integration alone. As Bodhidarma suggested 1500 years ago, it is one in a million who can attain Level III awareness without a mentor, coach, teacher, therapist, counselor or guide who has experienced the challenges and opportunities of the path of integration.[17]

   Without being able to associate with others who choose to remain awake, aware and attentive, the overwhelming allure of Level I awareness will draw you downwards and away from your True Self.

Associating within an Integrative Support Group (ISG) is something which we found to be very helpful.

The final choice for you to make is: Who or what will you serve on your life and leadership journey? Will it be your Surreal Self? Will it be your Real Self? Or will it be your Ideal Self?[18]

Chapter 6

Guidelines for Becoming an Integrative Leader

Building character and creating quality of life is a function of aligning our beliefs and behaviors with universal principles. These principles are impersonal, external, factual, objective, and self-evident. They operate regardless of our awareness of them, or our obedience to them.

STEPHEN COVEY

THE FINAL ASPECT OF 'Building our Model of Integrative Leadership' was to determine the *universal laws* that define the framework for walking the path of integrative life and leadership. From these universal laws, principles and practices, we can suggest guidelines for those desiring and choosing to embark on their personal journey of integration.

Our search for these fundamental and foundational universal laws involved the scientific, psychological, social, wisdom and mystic traditions externally, and our own personal observations, experiences, experimentations, evaluations, intuitions and inspirations internally.

It is important to distinguish universal laws from man-made moral, social, and legal laws, traditions or customs. Universal laws can be defined as laws that are unchangeable, immutable and which operate on everyone and everything, everywhere, all the time.[1] These laws are *descriptive* and not *prescriptive*, which means they don't instruct you to do anything but simply exist, whether you are aware of them and believe in them or not.

An example of a universal law would be Newton's law of universal gravitation. Gravity is unchangeable and immutable. It operates dispassionately on everyone regardless of gender, age, race, color, creed, position or power. It operates everywhere on the Earth, the moon, and our solar system, galaxy and universe. It operates all the time, every second of every day, since the beginning of time. The law of gravity passes no judgments, but simply exists for us to use or abuse as we see fit. Whether we are aware or ignorant, believe or not believe, it continues to inexorably operate, for our benefit or detriment, depending on our motivation and perspective.

As a result of our search, we have identified eight universal laws that govern the framework of consciousness in which humankind plays out its evolutionary and involutionary dramas. We also describe twelve Integrative Transformative & Transcendent (ITT) practices which will assist those choosing integration to move onto the path of flow versus the path of struggle—and twelve principles that are prescriptive in successfully co-creating or strengthening intrapersonal and interpersonal relationships. In addition, we suggest ten ways that indicate you are on the path of integration (Integration Indicators) and five ways that indicate you have wandered off the path of integration (Separation Indicators).

Universal Laws

Though the works of the human race disappear tracelessly by time or bomb, the sun does not falter in its course; the stars keep their invariable vigil. Cosmic law cannot be stayed or changed, and man would do well to put himself in harmony with it.

Paramahansa Yogananda

The purpose of a law is to move us from complexity — in analyzing reams of empirical data, observations and information — to simplicity and predictability through a formulation that describes a relationship between a group of phenomena or variables. The language of science is principally mathematics, which is governed by its own set of laws used to quantify the formulation and relation.[2]

In Newton's laws of mechanics, for example, force is equal to mass times acceleration ($F = ma$). In Einstein's theory of relativity, energy is equal to mass times the speed of light squared ($E = mc^2$).

Both formulations greatly simplify the complexity that was previously required to describe the phenomenon, suggesting that the truth is always simple.

Evolutionary Perspective on Universal Laws

Knowledge is a process of piling up facts. Wisdom lies in their simplification.

MARTIN FISCHER

From the evolutionary perspective, the hard sciences such as physics, chemistry and biology have evolved a myriad of laws and theorems that reliably model events and predict specific outcomes of natural physical and artificial processes.

However, in examining the soft sciences related to human behavior, there emerged a very different story.

Auguste Comte, the nineteenth-century French philosopher also known as the father of Sociology, was inspired by Newton's discovery of the law of universal gravitation in the seventeenth century and suggested that Sociology's primary purpose should be to discover, using scientific methodology, the universal laws that govern human behavior. Nearly 200 years later, despite efforts by psychologists, psychiatrists, sociologists and social scientists, no one has discovered universal laws that govern human behavior.

The closest social scientists have come to a guiding principle of human behavior is that "a rewarded behavior tends to be repeated". The reason 'tends' is in the principle is that a rewarded behavior is not always repeated.[3]

Our search to that point suggested that, of the four domains of intelligence, the physical domain was subject to universal laws found by hard science, but the mental, emotional and spiritual domains were not necessarily subject to these same laws in quite the same way.

This indicated to us that, unlike other natural processes, humankind possessed the power of choice, or free will, which allowed it to both adhere to and align with universal laws, or to disregard and work against them.

Involutionary Perspective on Universal Laws

Many people today seek their own laws. Yet, in so doing, they often find only partial values of these Universal Principles. Others of us, seeking to restore feelings of comfort and security, are more committed than ever to uncovering the fundamental shared values [and universal principles] of all religions. The full value of these timeless concepts has been recorded similarly in all major religions since time immemorial. The principles of inner development are no different now than they were in the days of Jesus, Buddha, Mohammed, Moses or Confucius. These great masters offer similar messages that have not become less essential for people in the modern world. These principles extend beyond time and change. They establish a clearly marked path that will enable each individual to attain the peace and enlightenment that is their ultimate goal in life.

JEFFREY MOSES

Natural or universal law was first promoted in the West by Heraclitus in ancient Greece when he suggested that "a common wisdom pervades the whole universe." Aristotle agreed with Heraclitus that there existed "a rule of justice that is natural and universally valid."

Zhu-Xi, who was a Neo-Confucionist, suggested that all objects in nature were composed of two forces: *Li*, which is a universal law or principle, and *Chi*, which is the substance from which all material things were made. Chi could dissolve, but Li remained constant and indestructible. Zhu-Xi went on to suggest that "when one has investigated and comprehended the Universal or Natural Laws inherent in all animate and inanimate objects, one then becomes a Sage." From Zhu-Xi's perspective, seeking and understanding universal laws is one of the paths to wisdom.

Jeffrey Moses, in his book *Oneness*, has examined the world's wisdom traditions and found 64 common universal principles.[4] We have chosen three of his principles as an illustration of what constitutes a universal principle from these traditions: *There is One God*, *The Golden Rule,* and *As Ye Sow, So Shall Ye Reap*.

There is One God

- *Baha'i:* "He in truth, hath throughout eternity been one in His Essence, one in His attributes, one in His works."
- *Christianity:* "There is one God and Father of all, who is above all, and through all, and in you all."
- *Hinduism:* "He is the One God hidden in all beings, all-pervading, the Self within all beings, watching over all worlds, dwelling in all beings, the witness, the perceiver."
- *Judaism*: "The Lord is God in heaven above and on the earth beneath; there is no other."
- *Sikhism*: "There is but one God whose name is true. He is the creator, immortal, unborn, self-existent."
- *Sufism*: "All this is God. God is all that is."

The Golden Rule

- *Baha'i*: "Ascribe not to any soul that which thou wouldst not have ascribed to thee."
- *Christianity*: "Do unto others as you would have them do unto you, for this is the law and the prophets."
- *Confucianism*: "Tzu Kung asked: 'Is there any one principle upon which one's whole life may proceed?' Confucius replied: 'Is not Reciprocity such a principle? — what you do not yourself desire, do not put before others'."
- *Hinduism*: "This is the sum of all true righteousness — Treat others, as thou wouldst thyself be treated. Do nothing to thy neighbor, which hereafter, thou wouldst not have thy neighbor do to thee."
- *Islam*: "Do unto all men as you would they should do unto you, and reject for others what you would reject for yourself."
- *Jainism*: "A man should wander about treating all creatures as he himself would be treated."
- *Judaism*: "What is hurtful to yourself do not to your fellow man. That is the whole of the Torah and the remainder is but commentary."
- *Sikhism*: "Treat others as thou wouldst be treated thyself."

- *Taoism*: "Regard your neighbor's gain as your own gain; and regard your neighbor's loss as your own loss, even as though you were in his place."

As Ye Sow, So Shall Ye Reap

- *Buddhism*: "It is nature's rule, that as we sow, we shall reap."
- *Christianity*: "Whatever a man sows, that he will also reap."
- *Confucianism*: "What proceeds from you will return to you."
- *Hinduism*: "Thou canst not gather what thou dost not sow; as thou dost plant the tree, so it will grow."
- *Judaism*: "A liberal man will be enriched, and one who waters will himself be watered."
- *Sikhism*: "As a man soweth, so shall he reap."

• • •

Integrative Universal Framework and Methodology

We read Aristotle and Plato, Aquinas and Augustine, the Old Testament and the Talmud, Confucius, Buddha, Lao-Tzu, Bushido (the samurai code), the Koran, Benjamin Franklin, and the Upanishads — some two hundred virtue catalogues in all. To our surprise, almost every one of these traditions flung across three thousand years and the entire face of the earth endorsed six virtues: Wisdom and knowledge; Courage; Love and humanity; Justice; Temperance; Transcendence and Spirituality.

Martin E.P. Seligman

From our examination of the wisdom and mystic traditions, there emerged an involutionary story concerning the origin of universal laws as they related to the creation myths.

The story was this: Just as light passing through a prism is separated into the seven colors of the rainbow, the One Law that existed beyond Level III awareness descended — through the process of involution and manifestation — and diffracted or separated into seven Universal Laws. These descended

Table 7: Universal Laws and Wisdom and Mystic Traditions

Index	Universal Law	Scriptural Perspective
8	**Oneness**	"I and my Father are One." [John 10:30]; "Hear O Israel, the Lord our God is one Lord." [Mark 12:29]
7	**Love**	"Thou shalt love the Lord thy God with all thy heart, with all thy soul, with all thy mind…and thy neighbour as thyself."[1] [Mathew 22:37–38]
6	**Truth**	"…and the Truth shall make you free." [John 8:32]
5	**Will – Desire**	"Whatsoever you ask of the Father in my Name, He will give it to you." [John: 16:23]
4	**Harmony**	"Peace I leave with you, my Peace I give to you." [John 14:27]
3	**Cause and Effect**	"As Ye Sow, So Shall Ye Reap." [Galatians 6:7]
2	**Creativity**	Like begets Like. "And God created…every living creature…after their kind." [Genesis 1:21]
1	**Life**	"And God…breathed into him the breath of life." [Genesis 2:7]
	On the Law	"It is easier for heaven and earth to pass than one tittle of the Law to fail." [Luke 16:17]

[1] Love is both a Law and a Commandment, yet we chose it for its relative importance. This statement of loving God, neighbor and yourself is often called the "Whole Law" of the Scriptures. It is visualized as a love triangle with God at the top and self and others at two corners of the base. This triune relationship acknowledges the love of God as God as well as the love of God in you and in others. This principle applies to all relationships. So, what is the spirit of your relationship?

deeper into Level II and Level I awareness and diffracted even further to become the myriad of theorems and laws that govern our physical reality.

Just as in evolutionary theory, complexity moves towards simplicity through the discovery of universal laws that govern the natural world. In the involutionary theory, simplicity — as the One Spiritual Law — became seven laws, and then became a complexity of many, over the course of its descent into the natural world.

The question was: "What were the candidates for these eight universal laws?"

To answer this question we developed a methodology that first of all created a candidate catalogue of universal laws that ranged from the scientific to the wisdom and mystic traditions, much like Seligman's virtue catalogue. From this list, we took an integrative approach that utilized intuition and

Table 8: Levels of Awareness, Laws, Motivation and Domains

Index *Custodian*	Level of Awareness	Universal Laws	Maslow's Motivations[1]	4 Domains and 3 Levels of Mind
8	Four	**Oneness**	Unity in *Service* to All That Is	Cosmic Source
7	Three – Four	**Love**	*Enlightenment* Making a Difference	Spiritual Power
6	Three	**Truth**	*Transcendental Change*: Meaning and Significance	**Soul – Mind**
5	Two – Three	**Will**	Self Actualization	Will – Desire Choice – Need
4	Two	**Harmony**	*Transformational Change*: Relationships with Self/Others	**Heart – Mind**
3	One – Two	**Cause and Effect**	Self Esteem and Earthly Power	Emotional Power
2	One	**Creativity**	*Transactional Change*: Personal Growth and Achievement	**Body – Mind**
1	Null – One	**Life**	Survival, Security, Health	Physical

[1] Adapted from Richard Barrett's *Liberating the Corporate Soul*.

evaluation, information and inspiration, to suggest the names, sequence and hierarchy of the eight universal laws.[5] The results are shown in Table 7, with a Biblical scriptural perspective.

These eight laws are shown in Table 8 as they relate to Maslow's Need Hierarchy. Table 9 illustrates the eight universal laws and how they would be seen and experienced from the three levels of awareness.

The universal law that illuminates and governs the mechanistic level of awareness is the law of cause and effect. This law translates into a philosophy of "Do to others as they do to you" and demonstrates a transactional style of leadership. The universal law that illuminates and governs the organic level is that of harmony. The organic level law translates into the principle of "Do to others as you would have them do to you" and is a transformative style of leadership. The universal law that illuminates the wholistic level is love, which translates into a principle of unconditional compassion that can be stated as

Table 9: Universal Laws and Three Levels of Awareness

Index	Universal Laws	Level I Mechanistic	Level II Organic	Level III Wholistic
8	**Oneness**	Multiple Forms	Duality	Unity
7	**Love**	Eros	Phillia	Agape
6	**Truth**	Honesty	Relative Truth	Wisdom
5	**Will - Desire**	Sleeping Will	Personal Will	Higher Will
4	**Harmony**	Law and Order	Peace	Universal Peace
3	**Cause - Effect**	Karma[1]	Struggle - Flow	Grace
2	**Creativity**	Imitation	Innovation	Inspiration
1	**Life**	Physical Laws	Mental Laws	Spiritual Laws

[1] Karma is a Sanskrit word that in simple terms is defined as memory of past decisions that, through the operation and action of Universal Laws — as opposed to Divine Judgment — influence our present circumstances and life events. How we react or respond to the present event will set these Laws in motion that will inevitably and unerringly create our future. Thus our life and our destiny are interwoven into the decisions we make in the present moment.

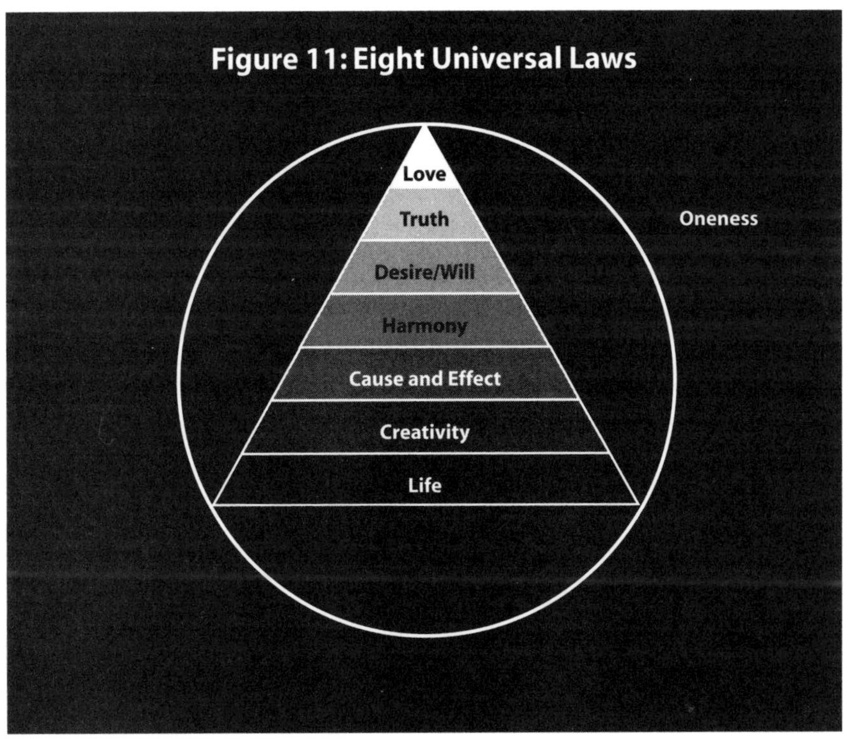

"Do unto others without expectation of return". This is the level that characterizes and informs transcendent, enlightened and integrative leaders.

In our experience of these universal laws, we have observed that there is a hierarchy wherein physical laws may be overcome by mental laws, and mental laws may be overcome by the spiritual laws. When higher-order law overcomes lower-order law, the result appears to our mechanistic eyes as a miracle.

In the physical domain, for example, the "miracle" of healing is called *spontaneous remission*. In the mental domain it is called *precognition, thought transmission* or *higher sensory perception*. In the emotional domain, it is the *empathetic wholeness* or oneness we at times experience with one another. If noticed and not dismissed or suppressed, these mysterious and extraordinary events can serve to resonate and awaken our awareness from the mechanistic to the organic, or from the organic to the wholistic.

These laws also act as a community in that even the smallest microscopic event contains the whole of the law. By effectively dealing with and seeking to understand the *smallest of things* that are out of alignment in our lives, we set in motion the solution to effect, affect and positively transform the *big things* in our lives. That is why it is often suggested in the wisdom traditions to "use what you have at hand, and the rest will be given to you."

The universal laws are activated by our conscious awareness of their existence on our life and leadership journey. If we choose to focus our attention and live only in the mechanistic paradigm, then only the three lower laws—of life, creativity, and cause and effect — will be consciously active.

If we choose to elevate our awareness and live in the organic paradigm, the fourth law of harmony is consciously activated and works in cooperation with the lower three laws that frame the mechanistic paradigm. The conscious activation of the law of harmony is felt as an awakening of the heart and begins a process of transformation that aligns and integrates our mechanistic attitudes and beliefs, transforming them in such a way that we can fully experience ourselves within the organic paradigm.

If we choose to continue our awakening and strive, through our intention and through focus of our attention, to live in the wholistic paradigm, the first law we consciously activate is the law of *Will-Desire*.

The conscious activation of the law of Will-Desire completes a phase of the transformative process and begins a phase of the transcendent process of integration. The choices we make to elevate and integrate our body, mind and heart at the mechanistic and organic levels will set up the potential for an internal struggle or battle that will be waged between our personal will and Higher Will, between our Personality and Universality, between our image of self and our Essence, and between our False Self and our True Self.

This is where most end their journey of integration. This is where many choose to step off the path. Without some supportive relationship or association with others who have walked this way before, it is not impossible, but very difficult to make the leap of faith across the gap between where we are and where our Ideal would like us to be.

If we choose to surrender our personal will to our *Higher Will* and choose in that moment to continue to respond as our Ideal rather than react as our Surreal or Real Selves, then the higher laws of Truth, Love and Oneness are activated in our conscious awareness and the full spirit and implications of the wholistic paradigm comes into existence for us. This is the realm from which we access higher sensory perception, knowledge, wisdom, original blessings and inspirations, which is the nature of our True Self.

In our own journey towards integration, by choosing to align our intentions, beliefs, feelings and behaviors with these universal laws, we experienced more peace, happiness and sense of *flow*. When we chose to not align our intentions with, but be in opposition to, these universal laws, we experienced more hardship, confusion and *struggle*. This is the blessing and the curse of free will.

Universal Laws: Virtues, Values and Variables

In the world of knowledge, the essential Form of Good is the limit of our inquiries, and can barely be perceived; but, when perceived, we cannot help concluding that it is in every case the source of all that is bright and beautiful—in the visible world giving birth to light and its master, and in the intellectual world dispensing, immediately and with full authority, truth and reason—and that whosoever would act wisely, either in private or public, must set this Form of Good before his eyes.

Plato, *The Republic*

A *value* is a principle, standard or quality that is considered worthwhile and valuable to individuals, cultures or societies.

Values can be understood at the mechanistic level of awareness as *variables*, because they are often situational, *values* at the organic level, since they are more stable, and *Virtues* at the wholistic level since they are considered eternal. Virtues are the highest and best that we can conceive and achieve in human conduct and behavior and are often related to holiness, sacredness and higher principles.

The concept of natural or universal laws had its origin with the ancients and influenced western civilization until the nineteenth century when it was replaced by the doctrine of utilitarianism. Jeremy Bentham, a British philosopher who proposed this doctrine, based utilitarianism on the premise that all human actions are motivated by a desire to obtain pleasure and avoid pain. In Bentham's view, the highest good in any given society is measured by the happiness of the greatest number of people.

Today, due to the crisis of trust in various sectors — government, financial, not-for-profit and corporate — there is an emerging interest in examining historical beliefs about natural or universal laws, a movement which could inform and transform our current ethical framework.

Ethical principles, sometimes called morals, historically developed along three standards of human conduct as being "the highest good." These three historical standards we found to be resonant with the three levels of awareness, if restated slightly and re-examined as follows:

- **Level I Awareness – Mechanistic**: Duty, Obligation, Physical Sensual Pleasure
- **Level II Awareness – Organic**: Happiness, Gratification, Mental - Emotional Pleasure
- **Level III Awareness – Wholistic**: Perfection as the fullest development of human potential

In the integrative framework, this would suggest that the authority for good conduct is the "Rule of Nature" in the mechanistic paradigm. The "Rule of Nature" is that human conduct conforms to the authority of nature, situation or need. The authority for good conduct in the organic paradigm is the "Rule of Reason and Intuition" in which human behavior arises from a balance that can exist between reason and intuition, thoughts and feelings, attitudes and emotions. Finally, the authority for good conduct in the wholistic paradigm is the "Higher Will" that can be found in the Scriptures of the wisdom and mystic traditions (outer journey), but which can also be perceived through personal revelation, inspiration, introspection and insight (inner journey).

Within our emerging Integrative Philosophy, we believe that eight core virtues are associated with the eight universal laws. From these eight core virtues, all other virtues, values and variables followed as the initial eight, through the process of involution, diffracted from the one to the seven, to the many.

In a methodology similar to the one that uncovered the universal laws, we collected a catalogue of Virtues and Values,[6] evaluating and sifting through them to find those that would resonate with the wisdom and mystic traditions and with current scientific and psychological thought — such as those found in Martin Seligman's work, *Authentic Happiness*.

Seligman, who founded the concept of Positive Psychology, identified six ubiquitous core virtues that spanned 3,000 years of time and involved diverse cultures. The six were: Wisdom and Knowledge, Courage, Humanity and Love, Justice, Temperance (self-control), Spirituality and Transcendence.

In examining Seligman's work, we felt he had found five of the eight core virtues in his investigations, however there were virtues that were missing

Table 10: Eight Universal Laws with Virtues

Index	Level of Awareness	Universal Law	Core Virtues	
			First Choice	*Second Choice*
8	Cosmic	Oneness	**Unity**	Spirituality
7	Wholistic – Cosmic	Love	Love	Mercy
6	Wholistic	Truth	Wisdom	Hope
5	Organic – Wholistic	Will – Desire	**Determination**	**Perseverance**
4	Organic	Harmony	**Peace**	Faith
3	Mechanistic – Organic	Cause and Effect	Courage	Honour
2	Mechanistic	Creativity	Temperance	Judgment
1	Animalistic – Mechanistic	Life	Justice	**Law**

from our Universal Integrative framework. We continued to search for the missing virtues in a way similar to Mendeleyev (1869),[7] who suggested that there were elements missing on the periodic table that were yet to be discovered by researchers. Our work further uncovered three other primary Virtues and rearranged, for clarity, Seligman's other associated higher values. Table 10 summarizes the results of our investigation of Core Virtues to date.

The Principle of Correlation

> *Jesus of Nazareth could have chosen simply to express Himself in moral precepts; but like a great poet He chose the form of the parable, wonderful short stories that entertained and clothed the moral precept in an eternal form. It is not sufficient to catch man's mind, you must also catch the imaginative faculties of his mind.*
>
> Dudley Nichols

There is a correlation among the three levels of awareness: By understanding Level I we can also begin to formulate an understanding and appreciation of Level II and Level III. This principle of correlation has been phrased in many ways in the wisdom traditions. For example, ancient Hermetic writings state it this way: "As above, so below. As within, so is it without."[8]

Teachers and Sages throughout the Ages have used this principle of correlation to share with others in lower levels of awareness their understanding of higher levels of awareness. They used stories, myths, allegories, poetry and metaphor in an attempt to bridge the gap between these different worlds in an effort to communicate, commune and awaken their listeners.

Jesus, for example, used the principle of correlation in his parables, which taught people about the nature of what he called the Kingdom of God (Level III or soul-mind awareness). One such parable was about a farmer, sowing seeds in his field, which spoke into the listeners' Level I awareness (body-mind), but was also simultaneously teaching them about the nature of Levels II (heart-mind) and III (soul-mind) awareness:

> A sower went out to sow. And as he sowed, some seed fell along the footpath; and the birds came and ate it up. Some seed fell on rocky ground, where it had little soil; it sprouted quickly because it had no depth of earth, but when

> the sun rose the young corn was scorched, and as it had no root it withered away. Some seed fell among thistles; and the thistles shot up, and choked the corn. And some of the seed fell into good soil, where it bore fruit, yielding a hundredfold or, it might be sixty fold or thirty fold. If you have ears, then hear. (Matthew 13:4–9, New English Bible)

In answer to his disciples' persistent questioning about what the parable of the sower really meant, Jesus explained that although many heard the parable, they did not necessarily understand it, saying, "He who has ears to hear, let him hear" (Mark 4:1–34) and he explained the parable privately to them this way:

> When a man hears the word that tells of the Kingdom, but fails to understand it, the evil one comes and carries off what has been sown in his heart. There you have the seed sown on the footpath. The seed sown on rocky ground stands for the man who, on hearing the word, accepts at once with joy; but as it strikes no root in him he has no staying power, and when there is trouble or persecution on account of the word he falls away at once. The seed sown among thistles represents the man who hears the word, but worldly cares and false glamour of wealth choke it, and it proves barren. But the seed that fell into good soil is the man who hears the word and understands it, who accordingly bears fruit, and yields a hundredfold or, it may be sixty fold or thirty fold. (Matthew, 13:18–23, New English Bible)

In this parable, Jesus suggests that there are four kinds of people in the world whom we would relate to the four domains of intelligence. The first kind are those who hear and don't understand (physical). The second are those who hear and are excited about what they have heard, but have no depth of understanding and when challenged, fall quickly away from the path (emotional). The third are those who hear but are distracted by temporal pleasures rather than continuing to walk the path (mental). And finally, the fourth kind of people are those who hear, understand and focus the light of their attention and the warmth of their compassion on the seed-thoughts of truth that have been planted in their hearts (spiritual). For this fourth group, the seed-thoughts will grow, flower, bear fruit and multiply, transforming their whole beings in the process of integration.

The principle of correlation can also be expressed in a metaphor of the Sun, Moon and Earth as the three levels of awareness. If Level III is the Sun and Level II is the Moon, then Level I awareness is the reflection of our Sun and the Moon on our Earth. The light from the One Source (Sun) at the superconscious level is reflected (diffracted through a prism) on the unconscious level (Moon) to illuminate our conscious level (Earth).

To become a perfect reflection of the Sun of our True Self, or the Moon of our Real Self, we must learn to quiet the chatter of our Surreal mind and allow it to become a perfect mirror.[9] We must learn to quiet the troubled waters of our emotional domain and allow it to become a perfectly still pond. With quietness of mind and stillness of emotions, we then become a perfect reflection of our True Self in the Earth. This is a natural process that, when accomplished, appears supernatural to the unawakened and uninitiated.

It is through this principle of correlation that science — which is focused primarily on the physical laws of the universe through evolution — and the wisdom and mystic traditions — which are focused on the spiritual laws of the universe through involution — can find common ground.

By seeking to understand and attune to the spirit that informs the stories, fables, myths and parables that are evident throughout history, the meaning and essence of that spirit — and its morals and lessons — can serve as guidelines and signposts for our journey of integrative life and leadership.

Integrative Transformative and Transcendent (ITT) Practices

> *Spiritual discipline is not a hard, formalistic compliance with law-like rules for living, but rather fluid, customized habits and practices that create an openness of mind, heart and spirit.*
>
> Mark D. Hostetter, CEO *Vinik Assett Management*

We have uncovered and experienced, in our journey, eleven integrative transformative and transcendent practices that are helpful in the process of integration. We would suggest that you search your own life experience for what the twelfth practice might be for you.

Table 11: Twelve Integrative, Transformative and Transcendent (ITT) Practices[1]

Practice	Description
1. Integration	Attunement, alignment, embodiment
2. Awareness	All domains (*PI, MI, EI, SI*)
3. Meditation	Inner power of silence
4. Observation	Witnessing of your life drama
5. Formulation	Ideal, personal vision, mission
6. Visualization	Images, associations and relations
7. Interpretation	Nightly dreams, visions, inspirations and intuitions
8. Concentration	The power of focus
9. Contemplation	Leading a reflective life
10. Application	Knowledge to understanding & understanding to wisdom
11. Relaxation	Stress management (physical, mental, emotional)

The 12th Practice: ______________________________

[1] Leonard, G., & Murphy, M. (1995). *The life we are given*. New York, NY: Putnam. George Leonard is an Aikido Master and Michael Murphy is the founder of Esalen in California. For over a year, they experimented with a group on implementing Integral Transformative Practices (ITP) that engaged all four domains. The result was success on multiple levels of being and awareness that included physical, mental, emotional and spiritual healing and growth. They worked with Ken Wilber of the Integral Institute to convert Wilber's theories and philosophy into practical applications. We have added Transcendent practices to the idea of Transformative practices to allow a connection, not just with Level I and II awareness, but with Level III awareness.

All these practices work in cooperation and in harmony with one another. However, we have learned that the best practice is the one that you begin to apply in your own life.

If you had time to perform only one practice daily, we would recommend that you habituate the practice of meditation that allows you an experience of the inner power of silence. This practice embodies relaxing the body, quieting the mind and stilling the emotions so that you may in time become a perfect reflection of your True Self.

If you had time for more integrative practices, the second practice we would recommend would be to consciously formulate, attune and work with an Image of your Ideal Self and use it in your waking life as a guide and a standard for making decisions in each of your present moments. The Ideal can further be integrated into your meditative practice as an Image, feeling, thought or intention before, during or after the silence. In this way, one of the personality fragments on your wheel of life begins to act as a place for your True Self to consciously reside; there is then the potential for experiencing a harmonizing and unifying resonance that serves to integrate your other personality fragments.

After formulating and working with an Ideal, and after beginning to meditate and act upon it, we have found the simplest avenue for awakening higher levels of awareness and our higher sensory perception is to remember, interpret and apply the lessons and advice offered to us in our nightly dreams.

Each of us dreams for about a third of our entire sleeping period, yet few of us, for a variety of reasons, pay attention to them. Our ability to remember our dreams is in direct proportion to our desire and motivation to do so. Once our barriers of ignorance or belief are overcome, a path is created between our three levels of awareness. Information from our daily life is then allowed to flow upwards through our awareness as we fall asleep, from Level I (waking) to Level II (dreaming) and Level III (deep sleep). This information is integrated, and then descends as we reawaken from Level III through Level II and into Level I awareness carrying new information. This new information may appear in many forms: as feelings, impressions, dreams, visions, inspirations, intuitions and insights. If we learn to pay attention to this inner information, interpret the language of our soul and develop this intimate inner relationship, our journey becomes less and less a path of struggle and more and more a path of flow.

A fourth application would be to consciously practice cultivating awareness, observation and reflection through examining your life history in the form of a life review. One purpose of the life review is to recall the presence of your True Self through remembering your past peak physical, mental, emotional and spiritual experiences.

The journey of integration, as German mystic Meister Eckhart suggests, is one of subtraction rather than addition. We were all innocent in the beginning and, over time, layers of life experience hid us from ourselves. Periodic life reviews help us recall those original experiences in which we knew and tasted our True Self, embraced our Calling and felt the joy and meaning of living our life's purpose, even if the experiences were only momentary.

In this way, the process of integration requires that we become a Master Detective for a time, acting as one who patiently and persistently unearths the mysteries of our life journey by finding and examining memory clues from our past and present and piecing them together in a way that will help us solve the puzzle of our lives: "Who are you, and what do you want?"

The Appendices contain four sections that you may find helpful in developing your own Integrative Practices. The first appendix is a Life Review Exercise that allows you an opportunity to engage in reflection by examining your life journey from the perspective of how your four domains of intelligence have evolved through your three levels of awareness. The second appendix is a simple Integrative Meditative Practice that focuses on your breath and on your Ideal during the inner silence. The third appendix offers guidelines for choosing and working with your vision and Ideal. The fourth appendix is a description and methodology that we have successfully used in awakening and working with participants' dreams.

When you begin the journey by focusing your attention and applying at least one of the ITT Practices, it will naturally awaken other suggested practices, in proportion to the strength of your desire and the level of awareness of your Ideal.

Integration Indicators: Staying on the Path

> *The spiritual awakening that is slowly taking place counter-culturally will become more of a daily norm as we all willingly break mainstream cultural taboos that silence or erase our passion for spiritual practice.*
>
> BELL HOOKS

What follows are ten Integration Indicators, or signs of flow that will help you recognize when you are firmly on the path of integration:

- *Increased energy:* Experiencing more energy and vitality and less burnout in life, love, work and play.
- *Finding hidden talents:* Acquiring and developing hidden creative talents such as intuition, heightened awareness, higher sensory perception, creativity, music, poetry, and the like.

- *Feeling balanced:* Recognizing in yourself a sense of balance across all four domains of intelligence and all three levels of awareness.
- *Awakening others:* Realizing a desire and ability to awaken others to their life and leadership potential, and helping them to develop that potential.
- *Noticing meaningful coincidence:* Experiencing frequent synchronicity in life, love, learning and leadership.
- *Self-discovery as an adventure:* Enjoying the mystery, wonder and excitement in life.
- *Living in the present moment:* Having no past fears or future worries, but living only in the peaceful present.
- *Experiencing your Higher Self:* Experiencing the active presence of a Higher Power, at a high level of awareness, which often results in higher sensory perception.
- *Living a purposeful life:* Finding purpose and meaning in everything.
- *Increased enjoyment:* Enjoying life, love, work and play to the fullest.

Separation Indicators: Leaving the Path

Of the thirty-six alternatives, running away is best.

CHINESE PROVERB

Below are five Separation Indicators, or signs of blockage that will help you recognize when you are straying from the path of integration:

- *Avoidance:* Consciously or unconsciously avoiding people, places, situations or circumstances that evoke strong emotional feelings.
- *Suppression:* Consciously withholding strong thoughts, feelings and actions.
- *Compromise:* Expressing suppressed thoughts to such a degree that there is a sense of guilt and remorse which in turn motivates one to make compromises that only serve to perpetuate the cycle of suppression and repression.

- *Repression:* Unconsciously withholding strong thoughts, feelings and actions; continual repression leads to abdication, the final step.
- *Abdication:* Fully abdicating (walking away from) personal responsibility for your life decisions and the natural consequences that follow; a state of blaming other people and circumstances in our lives for the way we are, based on a perception bound by our *image of self.*

Principles for Strengthening Relationships

> *All creation is governed by law. The principles that operate in the outer universe, discoverable by scientists, are called natural laws. But there are subtler laws that rule the hidden spiritual planes and the inner realm of consciousness; these principles are knowable through the science of yoga. It is not the physicist but the Self-realized master who comprehends the true nature of matter. By such knowledge Christ was able to restore the servant's ear after it had been severed by one of the disciples. All human ills arise from some transgression of Universal Law.*
>
> SRI YUKETSWAR

In our journey towards integration, we saw the emergence of twelve principles that align with universal laws. Although we knew many of them cognitively, until we consciously began the process of integration, we did not understand them from within all four domains of our intelligence and all three levels of our awareness. We use these twelve principles as touchstones, standards and guides of conduct, periodically reviewing our external and internal relationships and measuring ourselves against them. To date, we have identified eleven of the twelve principles. We are not certain of the twelfth principle, but intuitively know that it exists. We encourage you to find your own way of describing these suggested principles that is grounded in your own experience and is meaningful for you.

These principles are centered, activated and felt to flow from our souls into our awakened hearts. Because of this, we have come to describe these twelve principles as awakening, developing, living and leading from the heart.

Leading from the Heart

> *The heart aroused attempts to keep what is tried and true, good and efficient, at the center of our present work life, while opening ourselves to a mature appreciation of the hidden and often dangerous inner seas where our passions and our creativity lie waiting.*
>
> DAVID WHYTE

An integral part of walking the path of leadership is learning how to build and solidify relationships along the way. Here are the twelve principles for strengthening relationships that we call "Leading from the Heart":

- *Experience Oneness:* Strive to experience the interconnectedness of life; cultivate a unifying and abundant heart.
- *Be Compassionate:* Love one another; develop an unconditionally loving and caring heart.
- *Connect to Inner Wisdom:* Take the time you need to pause, reflect and introspect; grow a wise heart.
- *Live in the Present Moment:* Live in the now — not in the past, not in the future, but in the peaceful present; find your peaceful heart.
- *See the Good:* Look for the good, even in difficult situations; develop a positive, hopeful heart.
- *Practice Radical Honesty:* Tell the truth and by doing so, seek to create a truthful heart.
- *Live by the Golden Rule:* "Do to others what you want done to you"; develop a giving and forgiving heart.
- *Be Grateful and Appreciative:* Be grateful for all you have; cultivate an appreciative heart.
- *Keep your Word:* Maintain all agreements impeccably and with integrity; foster an integral heart.
- *Choose Full Responsibility:* Become fully responsible and accountable for all your decisions; create a responsible heart.
- *Commit to Lifelong Learning:* Learn from both micro and macro life events; cultivate a reflective heart.

- *The Twelfth Principle:* With an open heart and in a spirit of truth-seeking investigation, decide for yourself what the twelfth principle might be.

  The Twelfth Principle:

  ____

  ____

  ____

We encourage you to experiment and apply your understanding of these principles one at a time for a week at a time. After your experimental application, answer these questions: What did you observe? What did you think? How did you feel? What did you want? Record your answers daily, if possible. By faithfully and consistently journaling your experiences, you will be able to periodically review and monitor your ongoing process of application and integration.

These life experiments will help change your perspectives, beliefs and values, for we have learned that an experience of our knowledge helps shape our beliefs, and an experience of our beliefs helps build our faith. So, make haste slowly with intention, attention and determination to observe these principles as they manifest themselves fully within your integrative life and leadership journey.

• • •

Final Thoughts on Universal Laws

Metaphysics abstracts the mind from the senses, and the poetic faculty must submerge the whole mind in the senses. Metaphysics soars up to the universals, and the poetic faculty must play deep into the particulars.

GIAMBATTISTA VICO (1688–1744)

The Law of the Lord is perfect, converting the soul:
the testimony of the Lord is sure, making wise the simple.

PSALM 19:7

Seven of the eight universal laws, as they descend into the mechanistic paradigm, diffract further into the multiplicity of laws and theorems that define our known universe. The law of harmony, for example, can be separated further into the principles of *levity*, that can overcome the lower order law of gravity contained within the law of life; *balance,* that naturally arises when we integrate our *True Self* with our *Surreal Self*; *polarity,* that is seen as negative and positive, protons and electrons, light and darkness, life and death, yin and yang, feminine and masculine; and *attraction,* often phrased: "As a man thinketh in his heart, so is he."[10]

The laws and principles that govern the physical domain have a correlation with the laws and principles that govern the mental, emotional and spiritual domains. Seeking to understand these correlations will be the common ground where science and spirituality can dialogue and in time become one.

In his observations, Socrates suggested that the majority of people who chose to live their lives in vice rather than virtue did so out of ignorance about the existence and operation of universal laws and virtues, rather than from malicious intent.

By endeavoring to educate the existence of these universal laws, virtues and associated principles within our primary, secondary and post-secondary institutions, we will help our children meet life's many challenges and equip them with the necessary tools that will allow them to positively transform our third millennial world.

By further applying our highest understanding of these universal laws within our world governments, institutions and organizations, a new order can begin to emerge that is based on wisdom, understanding and awareness and not on cleverness, information and ignorance.

Through personal connection, thoughtful education, courageous and heartfelt application of these universal laws and principles in all facets of our life and work, each of us can become in time the fully human foundation upon which the coming age of wisdom, synthesis and integration may be built.

Chapter 7

Organizational Integration™: Building a Living Organization

One needn't go anywhere to find Corporate Soul. It doesn't exist in a secret text or a hidden monastery. Soul is where you are. And for most of the day, that means at work. As Jewish theologian, Abraham Joshua Heshel has said, 'God is hiding in the world and our task is to let the divine emerge from our deeds.' Leadership in this context begins by acknowledging the presence of soul. When it comes to awakening the Corporate Soul, leadership is based on understanding that the soul wants to shine through us and illuminate our work and workplaces.

ERIC KLEIN & JOHN IZZO

ONE OF THE FIRST QUESTIONS WE RECEIVED when we began our Integrative Leadership consulting, facilitation and coaching work was from a CEO of a major Canadian energy company, who asked us: "How do I build a Living Organization?" It was a fascinating question and one that we could not answer to our satisfaction at that time.

In the years that followed, his question rested gently in our hearts and minds, occasionally bubbling to the surface during other writing, research, facilitations and assignments.

At this point in our journey, we are now ready to offer some insights regarding this deeply penetrating and soul-awakening question.

We will share some reflections on life, death and rebirth, relating first to the individual and then the organization. We will then examine several perspectives on the impact of leadership on the culture of an organization. Finally, we will outline the rationale and suggest ways of applying the integrative life and leadership model to help co-create a Living Organization.

Life, Death and Rebirth

It's only when we truly know and understand that we have a limited time on earth
— and that we have no way of knowing when our time is up,
we will then begin to live each day to the fullest, as if it was the only one we had.

Elisabeth Kübler-Ross

In our journey of integration, we have often reflected on and experienced different aspects of life and death. For those who have witnessed the birth of their children or the death of a loved one, there is a sense of awe, mystery and wonder that is evoked by the presence of these two aspects of the law of life. We have sensed the presence of life as an animating principle that is active first at conception, then in the womb with the developing fetus, and then heard as the breath of life in the newborn's first cry. We have sensed this same animating principle in the dying moments of a loved one, as they exhaled their last breath and it departed to different shores, leaving only the body in its wake. This animating principle has historically been called many names, with our preference to name its presence the *spirit of life* and its absence the *spirit of death*.

First to the Individual

Death is not the greatest loss in life.
The greatest loss is what dies inside us while we live.

Norman Cousins

When an individual has the *spirit of life*, they are excited, enthusiastic, optimistic, committed, creative and alive. These enlivened individuals strive to live life to the fullest. When an individual does not have the spirit of life, they are dull, boring, mediocre, cynical, pessimistic, imitative, compliant, complaining and mundane. Consciously or unconsciously, these mundane ones have attuned to the *spirit of death* and, in doing so, have joined the ranks of the *living dead*.

In examining these two opposing types — committed and compliant, enthusiastic and mundane, excellent and mediocre — we learned that there were many factors that appeared in one type but not in the other. The key distinguishing factors were: perspective and attitude towards life, the presence or absence of an Ideal, personal vision and mission, and the ways in which each type handled and managed their fears.

The committed type acts with courage in the presence of fear, and this moves them beyond themselves and towards their Ideal Self. The compliant type acts with cowardice in the presence of fear that binds them to themselves and holds them hostage within their Surreal Self. This bondage leads to poor self-image, low self-esteem, and self-limiting attitudes and beliefs.

We examined a multitude of fears that serve to bind people to their Surreal Selves and prevent them from moving towards their Ideal Selves. In our examination we found that these fears fell into one of two categories: the fear of death or the fear of life.

The Fear of Death

I have absolutely no fear of death. From my near-death research and my personal experiences, death is, in my judgment, simply a transition into another kind of reality.

RAYMOND MOODY

The fear of losing our self-created Surreal Self or *image of self* often prevents us from fully engaging with life. In threatening situations, our instinct for self-preservation physically motivates us to preserve our *spirit of life*. This same instinct for physical self-preservation is triggered when we find ourselves in mentally and emotionally threatening situations. Our mechanistic reaction is to attack and defend, or else run and withdraw, when beliefs, values, thoughts or feelings associated with our *Surreal Self* are threatened. This fear of death often prevents us from choosing to voluntarily walk the path of integration.

One hopeful perspective on physical, mental and spiritual death was first shared by Dr. Raymond Moody[1] in 1975 in his book, *Life after Life*. In this groundbreaking book, Moody investigated and documented cases of people who had been pronounced medically dead (brain and heart) and who, minutes or hours later, were resuscitated or naturally returned to life. He called this event a Near Death Experience (NDE) and the survivors shared their experiences of the altered state of consciousness they had encountered while near death.[2]

Kenneth Ring[3] later investigated this phenomenon extensively by interviewing NDE survivors. In analyzing the reports from the survivors, he concluded that there were five temporal stages that characterized an NDE:

- A feeling of peace and contentment
- Detachment or separation of awareness from the physical body
- Entering a transition region of darkness
- Seeing a brilliant white light
- Passing through the light into another realm of existence

Survivors who passed through the light described the other realm of existence as transcendent and mystical in nature. They first encountered — whether non-believers, atheists, agnostics, humanitarians, or believers in various faiths — a Loving Being or Source of Light that radiated unconditional love, acceptance and forgiveness. The survivors then engaged in a life review, in which they re-experienced the good and the bad deeds they had done in their lives, both for themselves and others. They were then given — by their True Self — an understanding of their Ideal, Vision and Mission and were finally returned to their bodies to continue living their life in the earth.

Upon awakening, many survivors had a positive attitude, experienced many value changes, positively transformed and integrated their personalities, had a greater appreciation of life, and many of them began to diligently pursue a path of spiritual development in service to others. And interestingly, many survivors who had previously feared death, no longer did.

With modern advancements in medical technology, nearly 35% of those who have come close to death and returned have experienced one or more of the five stages that characterize a Near Death Experience (NDE). Recent polls suggest that 5% of the adult population in the United States, or 13 million adults, have had an NDE which included some or all of the five temporal stages.[4]

In our opinion, the NDE is an involuntary experience involving the three levels of awareness. The same patterns, processes and temporal stages in the NDE also were present in accounts of mystics who were engaged in deep meditation (Samadhi — deep sleep states), accounts of significant visions during sleep (deep dream states), and accounts describing peak transformative and transcendent experiences that we sometimes encounter in our normal life (deeply impacting waking states).

The same patterns and processes evident in the NDE — including mystic meditation and engaging in dream states and transformative waking states — are in fact suggested practices for walking the path of integration. These include: developing the practice of focusing your attention, concentrating or engaging in deep introspection on a subject (*separation from the body*); experiencing the power of silence through meditation (*separation from the mind*); consciously formulating and living your Ideal to set up the conscious conditions for an experience of your True Self (*as light, illumination, unity*); paying attention to your nightly dreams in such a way that a path opens between your conscious and unconscious through to your superconscious (*integration of daily experiences*); and performing periodic life reviews to measure — and correct — your daily actions against your Ideal (*reflection and application*).

We have learned that the best way to allow the spirit of life to return more fully to us is to confront our fears and false beliefs about death of the physical, mental and emotional aspects of ourselves.

It is true that "something" must die when one chooses to walk the path of integration, but we have discovered this "something" is our own self-created fears, worries, doubts and illusions about the nature of death and the nature of life.

The Fear of Life

> *Our deepest fear is not that we are inadequate. Our deepest fear is that we are powerful beyond measure. It is our light, not our darkness, that most frightens us. We ask ourselves, who am I to be brilliant, gorgeous, talented and fabulous? Actually, who are you not to be? You are a child of God. Your playing small does not serve the world. We are born to make manifest the glory of God that is within us. It is not just in some of us. It is in everyone. And as we let our own light shine, we unconsciously give other people permission to do the same. As we are liberated from our own fear, our presence liberates others.*
>
> MARIANNE WILLIAMSON

Our fear of death or contraction is what prevents us from allowing our awareness to elevate from the mechanistic to the organic paradigm. On the other hand, our fear of life or expansion is what prevents us from elevating from the organic to the wholistic paradigm.

The *spirit of life* is an expression of growth and change, and we often work in opposition to it, rather than in harmony with it. In our attempts to prevent negative change from encroaching into our world and upsetting any balance we may have created, we also prevent, in this same way, any positive change from entering our lives.

One way of dealing with this inherent fear of life is to link our growth to a higher purpose. If *pleasure* is the motivator of the mechanistic paradigm, and *gratification* is the motivator of the organic paradigm, then *altruism* is the motivator of the wholistic paradigm. Understanding these motivators can move us through our fear of life and allow the *spirit of life* to express more fully through us in service to others.

Another way to overcome our fear of life is to find something in our lives we would be willing to die for.

Would you be willing to die for your children? Your spouse? Your honor? Your country? Your beliefs? Your principles? Your work? For only when you have something in your life you are willing to die for, can you truly begin to live again.

Then to the Organization

The key characteristic of a Living Organization is its ability to continually transform in response to the changing business environment. Adaptation, empowerment and high performance are then their ways to endure.

William Guillory

There is a relationship between individuals and organizations. An individual is made up of structures, systems and internal and external relationships, as is an organization. An individual is born, moves through stages of growth, matures and dies, as do various segments within the life cycle of an organization. An individual is made up of trillions of cells each with a purpose, mission and role to accomplish for the sake of the greater good and in service to the spirit of life. An organization is made up of individuals, each of whom has a purpose, mission and role to perform for the sake of the overall good and in service to the organization's spirit and intent.

Individuals have personalities and organizations have cultures, with each potentially unaware of their characters or *essence*. This suggests that the same patterns and processes that allow individuals to find new life are the same patterns and processes that allow organizations to find new life.

When an organization has the *spirit of life*, there is high morale, strong team spirit, high performance and abundant creativity, which are positive attractors for success. When the *spirit of life* is missing from an organization, it is dispirited, weak, and negative, often exuding a toxic atmosphere that can be tasted and felt by those immersed in it, and these qualities are negative attractors for success.

In his book *Leadership and Spirit,*[5] Russ Moxley suggests that a lack of the *spirit of life* is what causes organizational cultures and constituents to:

- Use only the mental (head) and physical (hands) sources of energy at work.
- Consider work only as a "job".
- Promote a sense of separation, isolation, and fragmentation.
- Experience excessive internal competition, individualism and self-centeredness.

- Lack congruence between personal and organizational missions and values.
- Lack a sense of meaning and purpose.
- Feel drained of energy and suffer burnout and poor morale.
- View leadership as a role for the select few at the top of the organizational structure.

The natural questions that follow about how to build a Living Organization are: What conditions attract and allow the *spirit of life* to be present in an organization, and what conditions discourage it? What conditions allow the *spirit of life* to flourish and thrive, where elsewhere it merely exists and survives? And how can we bring the *spirit of life* back to an organization that may have lost, misplaced or forgotten it?

The simple answer to all of these questions is to first *transform* the organizational culture from mechanistic to organic and then *transcend* the organizational culture from organic to wholistic. However, in order to elevate the culture, one must first begin to reawaken and repopulate that culture with individuals who desire to truly *live* and not remain numbered among the *living dead*.

Leadership and the Organization

The most significant contributions leaders make are not to today's bottom line — they are to the long term development of people and institutions that adapt, prosper and grow.

Jim Kouzes & Barry Posner

Of the many perspectives and models of leadership we examined in our search for a foundational leadership model, we would like to share viewpoints from Goleman, Collins, Covey, Kouzes and Posner, and Cashman and discuss how they relate to Integrative Leadership™. We have chosen this sampling not only because of their popularity, but also because all of these leadership advocates and researchers have indicated that the style of leadership within an organization has a profound effect on organizational culture.

Goleman[6,7] identified six styles of leadership in his research and linked them to a lack or presence of emotional intelligence. These six styles are: Commanding, Pacesetting, Coaching, Democratic, Affiliative and Visionary. Most leaders develop one or two styles in the course of their career, but are undeveloped or lacking in the others. His philosophy is that the more of these six styles leaders develop within themselves—which demonstrate progressively higher levels of emotional intelligence—the more successful, flexible and adaptive those leaders will be to a rapidly changing business environment.

Goleman then went on to link leadership style to its impact on organizational climate and culture and determined that it was responsible for up to one third of bottom-line organizational performance and results.

If an organization is dominated by a leadership style of Commanding ("Do what I say") or Pacesetting ("Do what I do") — which we would classify as mechanistic — Goleman found these styles have long-term negative effects on the culture of the organization and negatively affect bottom-line results.

If the organization is dominated by a leadership style of Coaching ("Try this"), Democratic ("What do you think?") or Affiliative ("How do you feel?") — which we would classify generally as Organic — these styles have a positive impact on corporate climate, culture and the bottom line.

Goleman's Visionary ("Come follow me") style of leadership has the most positive impact, of all his styles, on culture and bottom line. We would classify this as the style that most closely approaches and connects with the wholistic paradigm.

Jim Collins, in *Good to Great*,[8] suggests that, of eleven companies he studied that underwent significant positive transformation and enhanced profitability, in all cases each company had in place what he called a "Level 5 Leader." He characterized this leadership style as "a paradoxical blend of fierce determination and humility." Despite Collin's own initial resistance to and reservations about this finding, the evidence suggested that Level 5 Leaders managed, led and were in large part responsible for the positive transformative cultural change and resulting extraordinary financial performance.

Collins' evolutionary model of leadership included, from the base of the triangle to the capstone: 1) Individual Contributors 2) Team Players 3) Managers 4) Effective Leaders and 5) Level 5 Leaders, which became the name for the style of leadership that emerged from his research.

What we found interesting is that coincidentally, Collins' Level 5 Leader corresponded to the fifth Universal Law of Will-Desire within our Integrative Framework Model. The Virtue we assigned as a first choice to this Law of Will-Desire was Determination, with a second choice of Perseverance. In the process of integration, in order to transcend from the organic to the wholistic paradigm, one must first cultivate personal will and then, in humility, surrender to Higher Will. This is one possible explanation for the paradox that Collins identified: "humility coupled with fierce determination." We would suggest that the successful organizational transformation that was orchestrated and led by those Level 5 Leaders was accomplished not in self-interest, but in selfless service to a higher purpose connected with the wholistic paradigm.

According to Collins' terminology, then, Integrative Leaders would be called "Level 6 Leaders". Although Collins did not understand what peculiar circumstances, life events and internal processes conspired to create Level 5 Leaders, our experience suggests that the process of becoming an Integrative Leader is one path to doing so. In this way, through the process of integration, the resulting Level 5 Leaders will help organizations move from 'Good to Great' while the resulting Level 6 Integrative Leaders will also help their organization, community or nation move from 'Good to Grace'.

Stephen Covey also believes that leadership style profoundly affects corporate culture. His approach to organizational leadership development is to first begin with the individual. Covey shares his groundbreaking book, *Seven Habits of Highly Effective People*,[9] with individuals to help them develop personal leadership. He then refers to the four domains of intelligence (physical, mental, emotional and spiritual) in relation to his "Four Roles of Leadership"[10] model as: Modeling, Aligning, Empowering and Pathfinding for developing team, organizational and community leadership.

To help participants in his leadership seminars internally validate the existence of the four domains of intelligence, Covey asks them to compare Gandhi and Hitler in terms of their leadership styles. We've adapted his question to conform with our Integrative framework as follows: "If the physical is characterized by Discipline, the mental by Mission and the emotional by Passion, what is the difference between these two leaders?" On reflection, one can see that both leaders displayed discipline and passion in attempting to fulfill their missions. On further reflection, what made them different from each other was their intention and the conscience (still small voice) that informed their actions in fulfilling their mission. Gandhi's intent was freedom through selfless service (wholistic paradigm), whereas Hitler's intent was power through self-service (mechanistic paradigm). Intention is an essential quality of the spiritual domain that can apply to any of the three levels of awareness.

Covey's "Principle Centered Leadership"[11] approach that originates from the inside out is generally resonant and congruent with our Integrative Leadership philosophy. In our view, Covey's 'Seven Habits' and 'Four Roles of Leadership' together comprise a transformative life and leadership model that *primarily* seeks to move leaders, individuals and their organizations from the mechanistic to the organic paradigm.

Kouzes and Posner, in their "Leadership Challenge,"[12] advocate that Leadership is comprised of five exemplary practices. These practices originate from themes extracted from a large cross-section of leaders' anecdotal 'Personal Best' stories they began collecting nearly 20 years ago. Their leadership research is ongoing and evolving, with hundreds of thousands of stories that validate their evolutionary, behavioral and empirical approach to leadership. The most recent edition of their work was published in 2002.

The five practices of the Leadership Challenge model are: Modeling the Way, Enabling Others to Act, Challenging the Process, Encouraging the Heart, and Inspiring a Shared Vision. Associated with these five practices are six behaviors (an outside-in approach) that align with each of their respective practices (30 behaviors in total). Kouzes and Posner have found, in their research and application of their leadership model, that leaders engaging in these five practices positively transform organizational culture.

We have correlated these five exemplary practices to the four domains of intelligence[13] as: Modeling and Enabling (physical); Challenging (mental); Encouraging (emotional); and Inspiring (spiritual). We have also correlated the five exemplary practices with two of the three levels of awareness as: mechanistic (Modeling, Enabling and Challenging) and organic (Encouraging and Inspiring). The Leadership Challenge model improves the culture and performance of existing mechanistic organizations (three practices) and also helps leaders transform their organizations from mechanistic to organic (two practices).

Kevin Cashman, in *Leadership from the Inside Out,*[14] has a slightly different perspective on leadership and corporate culture. Cashman suggests that leadership is "authentic self-expression that creates value." Regardless of leadership style, a successful leader needs to be aware of their strengths and weaknesses, continually remind themselves and others of what is important, and be able to serve multiple constituencies successfully (handle paradox and conflicting demands).

Whether leadership styles were mechanistic, organic or wholistic was not relevant, in Cashman's involutionary view. What was most relevant was performance achieved by being authentic and true to oneself (integrity), and through self-awareness and clear communication of needs, wants and desires by the leadership of the organization to their constituents. So long as the philosophy and approach of the Leader was clearly communicated and understood, constituents successfully performed and achieved within that resulting culture.

The many leadership models and approaches that we have examined through the perspective of our Integrative Model and Framework these past three years have been primarily focused on either improving the performance of an existing mechanistic organization or moving organizations from the mechanistic to the organic paradigm.

In the process of elevation and transformation, more of the *spirit of life* is able to penetrate, enliven and be felt in an organic organization than in a mechanistic organization. This is one way to create a more living organization than what existed before.

However, to fully experience a Living Organization, to feel what it means for the *spirit of life* to awaken, infuse, intermingle and inform all domains and all levels of awareness of the constituents and the culture, the applied leadership model must be able to help leaders and their organizations transcend from the organic to the wholistic paradigm.

The Integrative Leadership Model is capable of moving individuals and organizations choosing to engage in the process of integration, from the mechanistic to the organic, and from the organic to the wholistic paradigm by integrating all four domains of intelligence and three levels of awareness.

Co-Creating a Living Organization

All the conventional techniques in the world cannot produce fundamental change. Today's organizations are spiritually impoverished, and only when companies find ways to integrate personal beliefs with organizational values will meaningful change occur.

Ian Mitroff & Elizabeth Denton

Walking the path of Integrative Leadership is a process for creating living individuals and, by their association, Living Organizations. The universal laws of Love, Truth and Oneness govern the wholistic paradigm. By seeking to invite, resonate and align your beliefs and behaviors with these laws and with the virtues of wisdom, love and service, you begin to embody and become the change you seek to make in the world. In this way, from whatever level of awareness you may find yourself, the individuals and the organization surrounding you will begin to transform and transcend in a way that integrates the best of all for the good of all.

Integrative Leaders help co-create the conditions for the *spirit of life* to fully reside within the workplace. The resulting Living Organization is characterized by:

- The constructive use of the four domains of intelligence and all three levels of awareness in their relationships, systems and resulting structures.
- Work that is seen as a vocation or calling, with deep personal meaning and purpose for employees and associates.
- A deep sense of interrelationship and connectedness with others both inside and outside the organization.
- Knowing the best uses for competition, cooperation and collaboration.
- An alignment between individual and organizational intention, mission and values.
- Being populated with dynamic, passionate and energized employees and associates.
- All employees being engaged in responsive leadership from wherever they are in the organization.

The process of integration first begins with the individual, then the team and then the the organization. Ideally, the process begins with the Senior Executive.[15] Initially, the Executive needs facilitation, coaching, support and association for a time that is dependent on their desire to attune, embody and integrate the universal principles and practices of the path.

At some point during association, the process of integration becomes self-generating and self-guiding. The Executive body can then progressively move the integrative process into other areas of the organization, as they deem appropriate. In this way, senior leadership acts authentically by walking the path of integrative leadership before inviting others to embark on the journey.

In our opinion, the journey towards integration is one of invitation and not imposition. Not everyone within an organization needs to be alive to allow the *spirit of life* to enter and be present in that organization. We have found that only a few awakened Integrative Leaders can have a significant positive and enlightening impact on their organizations and communities.[16]

The competitive advantages, for those leaders who choose to embark on the journey of co-creating a Living Organization, include extraordinary results on multiple levels (financial, technical, environmental, social) for their constituents, shareholders, stakeholders, communities and, in time, for the very soul of humankind.

Final Thoughts on the Living Organization

> *The invisible threads of a compelling vision weave a tapestry that binds people together more powerfully than any strategic plan. And people, not the business plan alone, determine the outcome. Success depends on what an organization's people are about, what they do and how they work together.*
>
> GOLEMAN, BOYATZIS, MCGEE

The simple answer to the soul-penetrating question of "How do I build a Living Organization?" is to consciously begin the process of integration, looking first to the individual and then to the organization.

Through the principle of correlation, we can see that the same physical processes of digestion, assimilation, circulation and elimination that sustain the *spirit of life* within the body are also the same processes that sustain the *spirit of life* within an organization.

The blood that circulates and nurtures the body is organizational capital. The bones and muscles are its buildings, offices and structures. The nerves are the communication channels and pathways that send and receive signals to react or respond to a situation. The parasympathetic system is the unconscious and informal processes that keep an organization running smoothly despite structural barriers. The digestive system is where good aspects of internal and external communication and relationships are assimilated and bad aspects are eliminated.

The physical domain includes the structures of location, information and communication; the mental domain is the policy, procedures and best practices; the emotional domain is the morale, compassion and caring of an organization for itself and for others; and the spiritual domain is the residence of the organization's Ideal, vision, and wisdom and the universal laws and principles that constitutes governance of its Soul.

Through the principle of resonance, the Integrative Leaders of an organization, regardless of their formal position, have an impact on the climate, culture and bottom-line results. The Integrative Leader invites in the spirit, nurtures the ideas and feelings and holds the space for that *spirit of life* to be present in the organization's relationships, systems and structures.

Just as a farmer sets up the conditions for seeds to grow within his or her field, so too must an Integrative Leader set up the conditions for the seed-thoughts of love, truth, wisdom and service to grow within the hearts and minds of those choosing to co-create and sustain with them, a Living Organization.

Chapter 8

A Call to Oneness

I found no comfort in any of the philosophical ideas which some men parade in their hours of ease and strength and safety. They seemed only fair weather friends. I realized with awful force that no exercise of my own feeble wit and strength could save me from my enemies, and that without the assistance of that Higher Power which interferes in the eternal sequence of causes and effects more often than we are always prone to admit, I could never succeed.

WINSTON CHURCHILL

WE WILL CONCLUDE OUR TIME WITH YOU by sharing our reflections and experiences on living an integrative life, integrative love and integrative leadership. We will then share some final thoughts on a *Call to Oneness* that we sense is the underlying message arising from the unprecedented time of transition in which we are all living.

Reflections on an Integrative Life

Man does not weave this web of life. He is merely a strand of it.
Whatever he does to the web, he does to himself.

CHIEF SEATTLE

The first choice in living an integrative life is to consciously choose to live the life you've been given and not to merely exist within it. In making that choice, you are affirming a willingness to grow and change from being bound to your history into exploring the mystery of your own True Self. In making that choice, the path of how to bring more of the spirit of life into your world will become evident and apparent, for we have found that once invited, the spirit of life will conspire to bring you exactly what you need for your personal journey of integration.

The second choice in living an integrative life is to begin to see the world and everything in it as purposeful and meaningful. Engaging, developing and affirming this belief will awaken your natural curiosity to search for the purpose and meaning of your own life once again.

The third choice is understanding that we are perceiving as well as sense-making beings that continually make up stories from what we have experienced, observed or been taught in the past. These stories are the basis of our mental models and mind maps that serve to guide our life.[1] The integrative perspective would ask: "If you are going to make up a story about your life or about your world, why not make up a story that is filled with hope, wonder, love and truth rather than despair, mediocrity, fear and illusions?" The choice of which story we desire to guide, shape and inform our mental models is up to us.

The fourth choice is to pay attention to what we put in the gap between our expectations and reality, our vision and our experiences, our Surreal, Real and Ideal Selves. In each life event we face, we could choose to put in the Gap our fears, doubts and worries or our love, faith and confidence that all that was happening in that life event was purposeful and meaningful. Cultivating self-awareness and exercising our power of choice become essential ingredients for living an integrative life.

The fifth choice is to consciously formulate an Ideal that would serve to act as a new guide around which our life may integrate. In our work these past years, we have found that our Ideal (highest principles, virtuous conduct, noblest behavior) is interwoven with our past notions, experiences and beliefs about the nature of a Higher Power.

Recent polls have shown that 95% of Americans believe in the existence of a Higher Power and an alternate reality to the one we experience in normal life.[2] However, 76% of Americans are also pessimistic, skeptical and cynical.[3] They see the glass and their world as half empty rather than half full.[4] These two beliefs we see as contradictory and they have an impact upon our personal Ideal or what the mystics call our 'Image of God'.[5]

Joseph Campbell [6] suggested that we could determine a culture's Image of God by examining the structures those cultures built over time. In the villages, towns and cities he observed while touring Europe, each had built at their core, a Church or Cathedral. To him, the center of these villager's lives was the Power of God as embodied by the Church. Later in history he observed, it was palaces and government buildings that represented the power of Kings, Rulers and Ministers of that day. Today, if we examine the tallest structures and edifices in our cities, they are Banks, Financial Institutions and Corporate Offices that represent the power of money within the economic and business sectors. These have become the centers of our lives and represent the current 'gods' of our culture.

By examining who and what you surround yourself with and where you focus your attention, you will gain an understanding about the nature of your current Ideal and the Image of God that may be unconsciously guiding your life today.

Three Levels of Awareness, Ideal and Image of God

Every human life is a reflection of divinity and...every act of injustice mars and defaces the Image of God in man.

Martin Luther King, Jr.

God is infinite and without end, but the soul's desire is an abyss which cannot be filled except by a Good which is infinite; and the more ardently the soul longs after God, the more she wills to long after him; for God is a Good without drawback, and a well of living water without bottom, and the soul is made in the image of God, and therefore it is created to know and love God.

Johannes Tauler

From the involutionary perspective, in the beginning we were all made in the Image of God. Throughout recorded history many have tried to understand what this phrase truly meant. In our examinations, three perspectives and 'stories' on the Image of God associated with the mechanistic (literal), organic (meaning) and wholistic (spirit) paradigms emerged.

The god of the mechanistic paradigm is imaged as an old white haired and bearded man who sits on a throne in the far and distant kingdom of Heaven.[7] This god manifests into the world as a god of law, a law that is rigid, inflexible and somehow — and often incomprehensibly — just in his pronouncements. There is a fear associated, nurtured and maintained by those who worship this god that is sustained out of ignorance rather than knowledge. This god comes to earth infrequently (is transcendent) for if god is good, why would he associate with a world and a people that are in their very essence evil? But when he does come, he comes in retribution and punishment for all the evil humankind has done and continues to do to this very day.

Philosophers, theologians and great thinkers throughout history have tried to look beyond this literal interpretation of the Image of God and focused their attention on unraveling the meaning behind it.

From their perspective, the god of the organic paradigm is imaged as a great mind that wove the idea of the universe from his or her creative imagination or harmonious dreams. The earth, with its multitude of forms and expressions, is simply the product of this one great mind. Those who worship this god view it as one that is based on systems of belief. They subscribe to a doctrine that by simply understanding and applying reason and the laws that govern the mind, they will obtain dominion over their earth and all its multifaceted expressions. God may be present or absent from their day-to-day life dependent on their beliefs.

This organic god is a god of duality that sees all things as good or evil; light or dark; truth or lies; positive or negative; yin and yang; masculine and feminine (father-mother-god) and is the place where the hard sciences and various branches of philosophy, theology, wisdom traditions and mainstream psychology all remain mired, struggling on how best to deal with this paradox and resolve this god of duality. Those who worship this god bring clarity and illumination or more confusion and ignorance into their life, depending on their choices.

The mystics, enlightened and illuminated souls struggled to move beyond physical form (no-body), beyond mind (no-mind) and beyond desires (no-desire) in an effort to experience the spirit, intent and purpose of the Image of God that hid behind these three.

They found in their journey of integration that the Image of God of the wholistic paradigm is comprised of the light of Truth, the energy of Life and unconditional Love that is the fabric that serves and binds these two and all of creation together. They found this God is the place of all memory, all knowledge, all wisdom, all understanding, all virtue, and all inspiration. And they found that whoever chose, could attune to this Image of God, access these gifts of the spirit and allow them to flow through them in compassionate selfless service to others.[8]

From this perspective, it was not our physical being that was made in the Image of God, but our spiritual being that manifests within each of us as a living Spirit and living Soul.

Each of these three perspectives contains a portion of the truth of God as Law, God as Mind, and God as Spirit but only by attuning to an Image of God held in the wholistic paradigm can these three portions of truth be resolved into one.[9]

By consciously forming an Ideal that is the highest of which you can conceive; by engaging the four domains of intelligence so that you can imagine, feel, and strive to act as your Ideal in your day-to-day decisions, you can in time and patience become it.

Your Ideal should evolve and grow as you do. If your Ideal is not allowing you to experience more growth, joy, peace, love, harmony and a sense of wonder in your life, then it is a sign that the beliefs that inform your Ideal should be re-interpreted, re-examined and re-formulated so that you can resume your journey of living an integrative life once again.

• • •

Reflections on Integrative Love

We expect our wives or husbands or children (or friends or colleagues/those we work with) to make us happy by behaving the way our ego desires. We all want others to make us feel important, wise and attractive. So we spend twenty to fifty years living together — expecting and demanding many things from each other — but this has nothing to do with our experiencing our love and walking on the real spiritual path. When we truly love someone, we love the Light within that person. The process of enlightenment is the path of learning to appreciate the Light within both ourselves and those we love, and seeking to allow the full expression of our Self as well as the Self of others.

Swami Rama

The subject tonight is Love. And for tomorrow night as well. As a matter of fact, I know of no better topic for us to discuss until we all die.

Hafiz

If Life is the first Universal Law that we activate and consciously experience when we awaken into this world, then True Love is the last. Between the alpha of Life and the omega of Love, we live and move and have our being. If life is the question of "Who am I?" and "Where am I going?" then we have found, on our integrative journey, that Love is truly the answer. When our life and our Love merge and marry within our awakened heart, a critical phase of the process of integration is complete.

Ideally, during our life journey, the spirit of life evolves, rises and ascends toward Love and the Spirit of Love involves, falls and descends toward life. Intuitively and instinctively, we are aware of these two processes of evolution and involution active and moving within us for we often say someone has risen to the occasion or another has fallen in love.

Love then becomes the motivation for our life in all its many facets, flavors, colors and textures. In our search for wholeness from the world of fragmentation in which we are first born, the question becomes which love will complete and fulfill us? Is it the love of Eros, which is of the body-mind? Is it the love of Phillia, which is of the heart-mind? Or is it the love of Agape, which is of the soul-mind? In our journey towards living an integrative life, we have found that only the Love of our Soul and the Spirit of Love that resides within it can fulfill us and allow us to become whole.

Four Universal Laws govern our True Self: Will, Truth, Love and Oneness. These four Laws are resonant with four core Virtues of Determination, Wisdom, Divine Love and Unity. Three Universal Laws govern our Surreal or False Self: Life, Creativity and Cause and Effect. These three laws are resonant with three core Virtues of Justice, Temperance and Courage. One Universal Law governs our Real Self: Harmony that has the resonant core Virtue of Peace.[10] We have found that the only way to integrate our life and our love and find peace, harmony and balance in our life was to harmonize the state of higher Level III awareness and lower Level I awareness within our hearts.

The Music of the Spheres

Love led by the body is satisfying our appetites and sensualities.
Love led by the mind is indulging our fantasies.
Love led by the heart is gratifying our need for intimacies.
But Love led by our Soul is fulfilling our destiny.

Richard John & Lillas Marie Hatala

If we view these Universal Laws as the seven fundamental notes in music, then our Ideal is a note that we can sound that will be resonant or dissonant, in harmony or discord with the other Laws.

If our life motivation for love is sexual gratification, sensual pleasure, physical needs or lust, then the only notes that can be sounded are those that activate the three lower Laws. The higher order laws remain dormant within us and are not active under this focus and motivation. This is the process of transactional change that occurs within Level I awareness.

If our motivation for love is friendship, fellowship, heartfelt romance or intimate relationships, then the fourth Law of Harmony is activated and begins to play within our life. If we pay attention and are aware, we can either feel the resonance and harmony of these four notes being played together in our loving relationships, or feel the dissonance that something between these four notes is not right. Upon becoming aware of this dissonance, we can either choose to alter the frequency of the three lower notes to harmonize with the fourth as we would an eight-stringed guitar, or stop the fourth note from playing in our life.[11]

Choosing to alter the three lower notes becomes the process of transformation and growth within Level II awareness. Choosing to stop the fourth note from playing in our life is the process of sameness, mundaneness and mediocrity that often characterizes the majority of our life. This is the choice we make to remain in Level I awareness and also choose to suppress or repress the memory of Level II awareness. Through reflection with intention during a Life Review, this event would resurface and appear in our recollections as a peak experience of Level II awareness when compared to our overall life in Level I awareness.

If our motivation for love is selfless service to others by giving the best of the truth of our experience, wisdom, understanding, knowledge and love freely without expectation of return, then the upper notes or Laws in our body mind instrument are activated and begin to resonate with the remaining awakened Laws below them.

If we do not take the time to retune the strings of the other laws below it to harmonize with these upper notes, then the experience will be a fleeting momentary peak experience that will be lost through suppression to our unconscious memory. However, if we take the time to retune our other four strings (four lower Universal Laws) so that they play in harmony with the upper strings, then this becomes the process of transcendence that is led from within Level III awareness and impacts upon and helps us reshape Level II and Level I awareness.

The sustaining of this process of transcendence is seen by many as being "born again" to a new life from their old life in the earth. Those who have experienced the light of their True Self are irrevocably and undeniably changed. All the wisdom and mystic traditions point to this state of enlightenment and illumination as the goal of the process of integration.

Conscious formulation of our Ideal becomes an important catalyst and key for initiating and sustaining the process. If we imagine our Ideal Self as the 'lower C' note and our True Self as 'upper C' on a piano, then alignment becomes retuning our Surreal Self to 'Lower C' and our Real Self to 'Middle C' for total resonance and harmony of all Three levels of awareness to take place. In this way our Surreal, Real and True Self would be awakened, aligned, attuned and congruent. The mechanism that allows this to occur is conscious formulation of our Ideal.[12]

We can conceive of our Ideal, we can attempt to feel it and set the intention behind it, but if the note is not struck by our actions and behaviors that are aligned with our Ideal, then the process of integration cannot begin.[13]

The Integrative Transformative & Transcendent (ITT) practices that we suggest are designed to help gain an experience of our True Self. By concentrating, meditating and contemplating deeply within, we are consciously suppressing — by relaxing the body, quieting the mind and stilling the emotions — the three lower Laws from activating while we attune our awareness through our Ideal to our True Self. In this way we can gain an experience of the subtler notes of higher awareness that are usually drowned by the louder notes of lower awareness. In the practice of interpretation of our inspirations, intuitions, visions, inner locutions and nightly dreams, we are attempting to apply our inner messages in our outer life. This is the process of embodiment.

However, between these two, attunement and embodiment, we have found that there is a need for integration, which can only occur within a heart-mind that is awakened to all four domains of intelligence.

Our Heart is the Crossroads and Key to Integration

The marriage between the Spirit of Love and our spirit of life in the earth can only occur through an awakened heart, for the heart is the great crossroads in humankind, that is the pathway that unites the four domains and three levels of awareness.

RICHARD JOHN & LILLAS MARIE HATALA

Without all four domains of the heart awakened, engaged and developed, nothing meaningful happens. The process of our life evolving upwards to True Love or True Love attempting to descend through the heart to involve itself with our life is stopped. Without an awakened heart, there is no pathway for life to ascend and Love to descend in flow. Without an awakened heart, there is no place for the marriage between the spirit of life and the Spirit of Love to occur.

In the Eastern wisdom and mystic traditions, there is an image of the spirit of life as a serpent or snake called the Kundalini, that when awakened, evolves and rises in those who have prepared the way within themselves, along the tree of their life.[14] This rising of the spirit of life cleanses, imparts knowledge and inflames and purifies the heart-mind.

In the Western wisdom and mystic traditions there is an image of the Spirit of Love as a Dove called the Holy Spirit, that when invited, involves and descends from heaven into those who have prepared the way within themselves, that illuminates the mind and inflames the heart. This descent of the Spirit of Love cleanses, imparts wisdom and inflames and purifies the heart-mind.[15]

The tree of life has its roots and is fed from the earth and its boughs and branches grow into the heart (Four Lower Universal Laws). The tree of love has its roots and is fed from the heavens and its boughs and branches descend into the heart (Four Upper Universal Laws).[16] The Serpent in its upward evolution can initially only rise to the level of the heart (body-mind), later evolving a set of wings that would enable it to fly (heart-mind).[17] The Dove (Soul-mind) in its downward involution has the freedom to remain in the air or rest on the boughs of the tree of life (heart-mind), or descend to the very base of our being that is the first center and custodian of the Law of Life (body-mind).

The heart is the crossroads and the path for Love's descent and life's ascent. In our experience of the journey of integrating the spirit of life and Spirit of Love in our life, the Ideal marriage between these two forces is a marriage that occurs within an awakened heart.[18] When this marriage is allowed, when this union occurs, there is a peace that is felt that is beyond understanding.[19]

The evolutionary (Serpent-Life) aspect of the integrative process requires self-development, self-management and self-leadership. The involutionary aspect (Dove-Love) of the integrative process requires an invitation for our True Self to come, abide and help us live our life to the fullest and asks us, for it is never an imposition, to surrender our self-leadership to our Soul.

In our invitation to the Spirit of Love and our pursuit of self-development of our life, we found the journey of integration was only half as long as we originally thought. For each time we stepped toward Love in our life, Love also took a step towards us.

Without an experience of a natural love of the heart we cannot hope to experience a Divine Love in the earth. In order to enable you to integrate love into your journey of living an integrative life, the question becomes: "For what or for whom are you willing to open the door of your heart?"

The Eight Levels of Love

- Love is the power and spirit that sustains and maintains all of creation.
- Love is the life that one may experience if one so chooses in the earth.
- Love is the creative expression and fulfillment of all Soul desires.
- Love is the memory of all that has transpired that makes us special and unique.
- Love is the peace and harmony that is beyond all human understanding.
- Love is the will and desire to be of service to our Ideal, others and ourselves.
- Love is the truth that underlies all spiritual and earthly existence.
- Love is the Love for Love's sake alone.

There is love of course. And then there's life, its enemy.

JEAN ANOUILH

Reflections on Integrative Leadership

Whole people bring a kind of magic into the systems they are leading.

ELIZABETH & GUILFORD PINCHOT

We suspect that the best kept secret of successful leaders is love; being in love with leading, with the people who do the work, with what their organizations produce, and with those who honor the organization by using its work. Leadership is an affair of the heart, not the head.

JIM KOUZES & BARRY POSNER

The intentions of our leadership study, which began many years ago and evolved into the philosophy, principles and practices of Integrative Leadership, were three fold: simplicity, unity and service.

When we first approached our study, we found the complexity surrounding the idea of leadership development was immense and overwhelming. Our desire was to look for the truth that stood behind all these approaches — that we called a foundational model — and held a space in our conscious awareness for that model to be mentally built. Our search for this foundational model was guided by the principle that the truth is always simple. We also believed that each leadership development model — and the body of knowledge that informed that approach — contained a portion of the truth, but none that we found in our life and leadership journeys to that date, as yet contained its full measure.

Our second intention was to find the underlying common ground or unity that informed and was the framework on which the various approaches to leadership development could be understood, displayed and valued. Our aim was to establish an integrative *context* by which we could evaluate individual leadership model *content*. A short time into our study, we encountered a fundamental duality in the various leadership approaches that could be generally characterized as scientific on the one hand and spiritual on the other.

The scientific evolutionary leadership (outside in) models included trait, behavioral, and contingency models as just a few of the many available categories in which to place external observations and interpretations of leadership development. The spiritual involutionary leadership (inside out) models were more principle-centered and highly influenced by the various authors' religious perspectives, heritage and history.[20]

Between these two fundamental approaches there was a Gap. The scientific leadership models were more focused on analysis, pragmatism and external observations, whereas the spiritual leadership models were more focused on idealism, virtue and internal perceptions.

We observed that the forces of separation that were keeping these models and approaches apart were centered in the mechanistic paradigm and were based in fear.[21] The forces of integration that were seeking to unify these models and approaches were centered in the wholistic paradigm and were based in love.

Our search for unity uncovered for us a third approach to leadership that involved awakening, developing and understanding the organic paradigm which is the means to bridge the Gap between science (mechanistic) and spirituality (wholistic). The practice of attuning to our Ideal (wholistic) and embodying our Ideal (mechanistic) we found could only be integrated in an awakened heart. Awakening, nurturing and developing the heart of leadership is the key to unifying these two historical approaches to leadership development.[22, 23]

Our third intention was to be of service in sharing our emerging understanding and application of the evolving philosophy, principles and practices of the foundational model for others and ourselves in two ways. The first was to add value to the body of knowledge and practice of leadership that would be simple and unifying and be applicable to individuals, relationships and organizations to allow them to experience more of the spirit of life and to live that life more abundantly. The second was to first work with individuals; then to work with families, teams and groups; and finally to work with organizations and local, regional, national and global communities to help them become more integrated.

In the past three years our search for a foundational model of leadership became the philosophy, principles and practices of Integrative Leadership™. And the process of integration that characterizes Integrative Leadership we often refer to as 'walking the path'.

All management and leadership models were built with the intent to foster knowledge and understanding and leader development. Some were built to help people evolve from being individual contributors to team players to managers (mechanistic). Others were built to help individuals evolve from managers to effective leaders (organic).

Integrative Leadership was co-creatively built to help provide an integrative context for the many existing leadership models. It was co-creatively built to help individuals move through the entire spectrum and evolution of life and leadership; from personal and interpersonal relationships, to becoming individual contributors, team players, and managers within organizations (mechanistic to organic). And it was co-creatively built to illuminate a path for effective leaders to become good leaders and, if they desired, to in time and patience become Great Leaders (organic to wholistic).

Integrative Leadership development begins by answering "Which of the four domains of intelligence will lead you?" It begins by answering "Which of the three levels of awareness will inform and guide you?" It begins by exercising our power of choice in answering "Whom or what are you willing to serve?" And it ends by being fully integrated in the integrative principles and practices that nurture and sustain an awakened heart.

All leadership development is about understanding our relationship with ourselves and with others. Integrative Leadership is about understanding our relationship with ourselves and our relationship with others, but also understanding our relationship with the Spirit that energizes, animates and seeks to inform our Ideal.

The Soul of Leadership as the Sun

Integrative Leadership is the perfect marriage
of the Sun of our Soul and the fire in our belly.

Richard John & Lillas Marie Hatala

The Soul of Leadership[24] has three aspects that, when awakened, conform to the three Higher Laws held within the wholistic paradigm. These three are Mind as Truth or Wisdom (Light); Spirit as Divine Love or Agape (Love); and Higher Will as Original Creativity (Life). The highest Spirit or motivation that can inform our Ideal of Integrative Leadership is Agape and the symbol that most closely reflects Agape in our world is the Sun.[25]

If we examine the qualities of the Sun, we can begin, through the principle of correlation, to gain a sense of what an experience of the Spirit of Love or Agape might be like. Here is one perspective on the relationship between our Ideal as the Sun and the Spirit of Love:[26]

> The Sun is the source of light, warmth and energy that falls on and sustains all of earthly creation as does the light, warmth and Spirit of Love. There are no favorites or special places where the Sun will shed its light, just as the Spirit of Love holds no favorites but loves all souls with a love that is the same. The Sun is totally giving of itself for the sake of others, as is the Spirit of Love.
>
> The Sun does not judge on whom, where or what its life-giving light and warmth should fall. It does not withhold itself from some and give itself to others in a random and precocious way, but is constant, consistent and purposeful in the fulfillment of its covenant of sustaining the spirit of life in service to humankind. In this same way, the Universal Laws are as the Sun in that they are constant, consistent and purposeful in maintaining order, balance and harmony for the evolution of the soul of humankind.

> The Sun is a sphere that appears to have no beginning and no end for one can travel many paths on its surface and each path will bring one back to where one began. In this same way, the Spirit of Love has no beginning and no end for each may choose a unique path to walk to experience the many facets and faces of Love Divine, but all paths will in time lead one back to the beginning of All That Is.
>
> The Sun is a symbol of wholeness and perfection whose light is sourced from within. Our soul is wholeness and perfection whose light, love and life come from within.
>
> From the earth, the Sun is seen as a circle or a wheel that revolves and draws an arc across the heavens. The Spirit of Love is also seen as a circle or wheel that in time and patience will revolve and evolve all souls back to their One True Source.
>
> And we were made in the Image of God and our Soul can be as the Sun in the earth.[27]

If we imagined that each of us is a solar flare that emanates from the surface of the Sun, some of us would be large and brilliant, others would be more moderate, and still others would be relatively small. And yet each expression, no matter how large or small, would be unique, brilliant and beautiful regardless of color, shape, nature or size. If we could imagine drawing a line inwards from each soul expression from the surface of the sun, we would find that all souls would be connected at the core.[28]

The essence of the Soul of Integrative Leadership would then be the Ideal Spirit of "loving for Love's sake alone". The Universal Law that informs and guides our leadership practices and behaviors would be Oneness and the Virtue would be unity. Our efforts as Integrative Leaders would be to serve, collaborate and willingly develop others knowing in their hearts that "as one of us gets better, so do we all."

The Ideal of Relationships

Art is not necessary at all. All that is necessary to make this world a better place to live in is to love—to love as Christ loved, as Buddha loved.

Isadora Duncan

If the symbol of our Ideal Spirit of Integrative Leadership is the Sun, then the image of our Ideal integrative relationship is an equilateral triangle that is set within that Sun. At the peak of the triangle we would place the Spirit of the Relationship and at the corners of the base we would place Self and Others.

In our journey towards integration, we found that each relationship that we encountered was not a dyad (me and you, us and them, individual and

Figure 12: The Image of Ideal Relationship

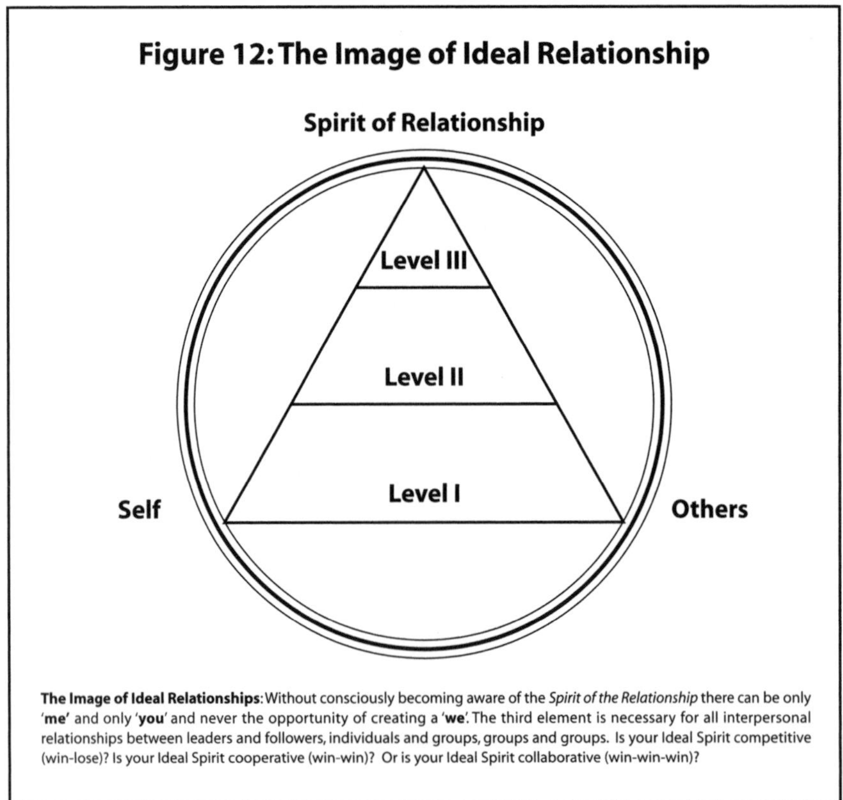

The Image of Ideal Relationships: Without consciously becoming aware of the *Spirit of the Relationship* there can be only '**me**' and only '**you**' and never the opportunity of creating a '**we**'. The third element is necessary for all interpersonal relationships between leaders and followers, individuals and groups, groups and groups. Is your Ideal Spirit competitive (win-lose)? Is your Ideal Spirit cooperative (win-win)? Or is your Ideal Spirit collaborative (win-win-win)?

group) but rather an implicit or explicit triad. The triad consists of three entities: Self, Others and the Spirit of the Relationship.

The Ideal Spirit of any relationship is Agape or "unconditional love" that is contained within our True Self and resonant with our Ideal Self. The wisdom and mystic traditions are in relative agreement as to the priority of relationship within this love triangle[29] which is to first call, invite or invoke the Ideal Spirit of the Relationship to be present during any encounter, engagement or exchange.[30] In this way, that Ideal Spirit will descend and be present and resonate within the space you hold between you and them. Invitation is a simple practice that, if habituated, helps ensure success in walking the path of integrative life and leadership.[31]

The second priority within this triangular relationship is for others then self, or for self then others, which dynamically changes as the exchange, discussion or dialogue proceeds.

The triangle of love is a drama that takes place within the awakened heart of an Integrative Leader. The Universal Law that governs any relationship is Harmony and the associated principle that guides that relationship is, "Do unto others as you would have them do unto you".

If there is a sense of imbalance, of giving more than taking, of sacrifice of self to the other, or winning more than your fair share in the negotiation, it is a signal that the balance and harmony is no longer present and needs to be re-established before the exchange continues. If a negotiation is concluded and an agreement is reached with this sense of imbalance in place, then the Law of Cause and Effect beneath the Law of Harmony will be activated and Justice will be restored, in one form or another and at one time or another, for we know from experience that 'what goes around, comes around'.

Table 12 displays the Dimensions of Relationship and the three levels of awareness. The Ideal Relationship is shown within the framework of the wholistic paradigm. These associations can act as a guide for self-awareness as to how you are managing and leading your own intimate, family, work or social relationships.

All relationships are formed based upon their spirit, intent, purpose and motivation. Once formed and with agreements at one or more levels of awareness in place, the relationship becomes an entity with a life of its own. The relationship has the attributes of the four domains of intelligence imparted to it by the participants. These four domains are seen as the spirit

Table 12: Dimensions of Relationships and the Three Levels of Awareness

Dimensions of Relationship	Level I Mechanistic	Level II Organic	Level III Wholistic
Nature and Type	Surreal Relationship	Real Relationship	Ideal Relationship
Spirit of Relationship	Competition	Cooperation	Collaboration
Speaking Style	Debate	Discussion	Dialogue
Listening Style	Attentive	Active	Empathetic
Intention	Conversation	Communication	Communion
Thinking	Serial	Associative	Unitive
Outcome	Lose – Lose, Win – Lose	Win – Win, No Deal	Win – Win – Win
State of Will	Sleeping Will	Personal Will	Higher Will
Agreements	Physical Contracts	Heartfelt Promises	Spiritual Covenants
Motivation	Needs	Desires – Wants	Higher Will
Attitude	Criticism	Acceptance	Appreciation

of the relationship; the ideas and memories of that relationship; the attitudes and emotions evoked by that relationship; and the behaviors, needs and wants of the participants within that relationship. In time, the relationship can take on a kind of personality, character and spirit dependent on the investments made by each of the participants. The relationship can be sparsely fed due to lack of interest and desire and merely survive among the 'living dead', or it can be generously nurtured, become vibrant and alive with the active presence of the spirit of life.[32]

The choice of birth, survival, growth, decline or death is fully dependent on the intentions, attentions, motivations and actions of those involved within that relationship. And it is fully dependent on the sensitivity to the wants, needs and desires of those others as they bear witness to the truth of their experience of that relationship.

The Integrative Leader is one who desires the highest good and the best for themselves, for others and their Ideal Spirit. In this way, any relationship that mutually fulfills these desires would be a win-win-win. Integrative

Leaders desire the best for all concerned, but are also aware of and sensitive to others needs and desires.

Whether there is a concern or need by those others of survival, security, self-esteem or self worth associated with the mechanistic paradigm: Whether there is an unfulfilled desire for belonging, achievement or expression associated with the organic paradigm: Or whether there is an unfulfilled desire and need for freedom, love, spiritual worth and unity associated with the wholistic paradigm, the Integrative Leader is awake, aware and sensitive to these needs, wants and desires.[33]

Once identified, the Integrative Leader has the capacity to connect with inner wisdom, reflectively evaluate, sense and become aware of their own and others feelings, and then has the courage to respond with the best of intents in doing the best for all for the highest good of all, which is the process of integration and wholeness in motion.

• • •

I try to give to the poor people for love what the rich could get for money.
No, I wouldn't touch a leper for a thousand pounds;
yet I willingly cure him for the love of God.

Mother Teresa

Love is life. All, everything that I understand, I understand only because I love. Everything is, everything exists, only because I love. Everything is united by it alone. Love is God, and to die means that I, a particle of love, shall return to the general and eternal source.

Leo Tolstoy

Love feels no burden, regards not labors, strives toward more than it attains, argues not of impossibility, since it believes that it may and can do all things. Therefore it avails for all things, and fulfils and accomplishes much where one not a lover falls and lies helpless.

Thomas à Kempis

He who is in love is wise and is becoming wiser,
sees newly every time he looks at the object beloved,
drawing from it with his eyes and his mind those virtues which it possesses.

Ralph Waldo Emerson

A Call to Oneness

And Jesus said to them: 'When you make the two into one, and when you make the inner like the outer and the outer like the inner and the upper like the lower; and when you make male and female into a single one so that the male will not be male nor the female be female; when you make an Eye in the place of eyes, a Hand in the place of a hands, a Foot in the place of feet, an Image in place of an image, then you will enter [the primordial state of perfection or] the Kingdom of God.'

Gospel of Thomas: 22: 4–7

The Call to Oneness that is resonating on the earth at this time is a call to integrate our fragmented selves, our fragmented families, our fragmented organizations, our fragmented communities, our fragmented nations and our fragmented world. It is a Call to heal our fragmented collective intentions, motivations, beliefs and actions. And it is a Call to seek to be the best that is above us and within us for ourselves and in service to all those others with whom we share our world.

Our response to this resonant call was to begin our search for a foundational model of life, love and leadership that would be simple, unifying and be of service for those desiring to unite rather than divide, join rather than part, integrate rather than separate.

Our intention in our study was to help individuals and organizations experience more of the *spirit of life* in their lives, more of the *spirit of love* (Agape), more of the *spirit of truth* (Wisdom), and achieve more of an understanding of the *spirit of law* (Logos) and its role in governing our universe and all things in it.

These four faces of our Image of God became the four domains of our intelligence. The three-fold nature of our Image of God became the three levels of our awareness.[34] The power of creation that is within the very 'Word' of our Image of God became the power of our choice. And the spirit that united these within us and outside of us into one cohesive and congruent whole was the *Spirit of Oneness* that stood behind and informed us through our Ideal that, in our journey of evolution, involution and integration, became our true Image of God.

"And we were all made in the Image of God and our Soul can become as the Sun in the earth."

This is the integrative life and leadership model that resides within an integrative framework that we have been granted the grace to rediscover. We uncovered this model by patiently peeling back the layers of our current time and human history to find it externally, while also patiently peeling back the layers of our Surreal and Real Self, to discover that the model also existed within. In that moment of discovery, our outside story and our inside story became One. Our hope is that, in your journey, it will also do so for you.

We believe that Integrative Leadership™ is the foundational model of life, love and leadership that captures the spirit, pattern and structure and informs, much like Platonic Forms,[35] all other spiritual, conceptual and practical leadership models in current and historical times. It is a gift that was given to us from the *Spirit of Oneness* to aid the soul of humankind in this time of transition from the mechanistic to the organic paradigms.

We invite you to examine, experience and determine for yourself whether this Integrative Life and Leadership model is true or not by testing its validity and applicability within your own life.

We know from our experience, that each individual who willingly steps on the path of integration is honored and their step will cause a ripple in our collective sea of thought and energy that will, in time, touch every soul with a touch that will lift us from within.

We began this work by asking: "Who are you?" From the multiple perspectives we've seen within our search and personal journey, we would suggest that you are a child of God that through the journey of integration can become a Son or Daughter of the Most High. But only if you want to: and only if you choose. For this Call to Oneness that is resonating across the face of the earth and within the hearts of humankind is not an imposition, but rather an invitation into a personal and intimate relationship with your Image of God.

The Eight Universal Laws in this work are self-evident, observable, unchangeable, immutable and whether we believe in them or not, they govern every aspect of our existence. Through ignorance of these Laws, our culture, society and modern day civilization has chosen to break us and our world against them, rather than understand, cooperate and work in harmony with them.

An internationally sponsored project to study these Universal Laws and disseminate their unbiased, objective and non-sectarian research and information to the world could be the spark of truth that would burn down a forest of barriers, ignorance, biases and prejudices within our fragmented society.[36] The removal of these barriers and acceptance of Universal or Natural Laws again as they once were, would be a step closer to Unity and would lay the foundation on which the Age of Wisdom, Synthesis and Integration could be built.

Education, however can only give us information and knowledge. Only through personal application can that knowledge be transformed into understanding. Only through deep reflection, focused attention with highest intention, can that understanding be transformed into inner wisdom. And it is wisdom that will help bring a peace of heaven into our earth.

The hopeful sign for us within this time of transition is that even one small lit candle can illuminate a large darkened room. Only a handful of honest men and women can save a city. And only a few awakened and integrating souls can help awaken many.

In our work we found that we often stood on the shoulders of giants, and we are in awe and wonder at being given that honor, grace and privilege.

May the spirit of love and the spirit of peace be your constant companions on your journey of integrating life, love and leadership.

The breezes at dawn have secrets to tell, don't go back to sleep!
You have to ask for what you really want, don't go back to sleep!
You know, there are those who go back and forth
over the threshold where the two worlds meet,
and the door, it's always open, and it's round,
don't go back to sleep!

Jalal al-Din Rumi

Epilogue

John and Mary Three Years Later

The total fulfillment of one's potentialities, which usually generates happiness, depends on the simultaneous presence of two processes. The first is the process of differentiation, which involves realizing that we are unique individuals, responsible for our own survival and well-being, who are willing to develop this uniqueness, wherever it leads, while enjoying the expression of being in action. The second process involves integration, or the realization that however unique we are, we are also completely enmeshed in networks of relationships with other human beings, with cultural symbols and artifacts, and with the surrounding natural environment. A person who is fully differentiated and integrated...has the best chance of leading a happy, vital and meaningful life.

MIHALY CSIKSZENTMIHALYI

Mary's Story

THE EIGHTH INTEGRATIVE COACHING SESSION, where Mary reported successfully speaking the "truth of her experience" to her husband Ron, and where she was about to introduce the process of integration to her whole family, was the final formal session that Lillas and Mary had in that first phase of her integrative journey. However, Mary kept in touch through periodic lunches and correspondence in order to update us on her ongoing challenges and progress on the path.

Mary continued to move rapidly on the path of integration in a way that could only be characterized as being in the flow.[1] All the things that she had perceived as being wrong in her 'old life' were now going amazingly and synchronistically right as every segment of her 'new life' underwent integration.

Ron and Mary embarked on an incredible and intense intimate integrative relationship journey for the following six months, in which they unraveled issues of being dependent, as they had been in the past, to being independent from one another as people, and finally, to being interdependent, where they each saw themselves as two whole people who were choosing to be together because they wanted to and not because they had to. Their process was open and, at times, brutally honest and emotionally impacting, with many past issues that surfaced dealt with in the moment in accordance and in alignment with their combined relationship Ideal.

Their three young adult children were deeply affected by witnessing the process of integration and the support, communication and Ideals that Ron and Mary both modeled. Independently and individually, each of the three began to adopt the ITT practices and practiced them with Ron and Mary almost every evening and morning. They each began, in their own way, to use the twelve principles of strengthening relationships with their friends and significant others, with many fascinating stories emerging from their experiments. They also began applying their understanding of the principles to their own intimate relationships saying "I want to have the kind of intimate relationship that you two have," which was a source of immense satisfaction for Ron and Mary, given where they had been — and now were — in their intimacy.

Mary continued her "telling the truth" experiments at work with both internal and external relationships, using wisdom, compassion and service to others as her guide. In fact, many of those stories became legendary and were incorporated as standards of excellence within the corporate mythology. So successful were her experiments, that within a year of embarking on her journey, she was promoted to Senior Vice President of Human Resources for SBT Corporation, reporting directly to the President and CEO. Mary became known, within and outside the corporation, as the "heart" of her organization.

We were called to SBT by Mary 18 months later to discuss applying Integrative Leadership ™ to the entire organization. SBT was in the midst of acquiring and merging with yet another international retail chain, and Mary had discussed with the President that it would be an ideal time to adopt the practices of both organizations and incorporate them within the Integrative Model and Framework to produce a third culture that would blend the best of both organizations. The President had agreed with her suggestion and approach saying, "We want more people like you that are helping us build a Living Organization."

We had never applied the Integrative Leadership Model to such a large organization before. We custom-tailored the approach, in dialogue with Mary and the senior Executive and other constituents, and co-developed a program that suited their combined needs. The I.L. program would be invitational and fully supported and sponsored by the President and CEO. Candidates were required to submit a situational profile essay stating their intention and reasons for entering the program.

The structure and delivery of the I.L. programs would take place over a twelve-month period and involve several strategies: five-day intensive sessions every quarter, a weekly newsletter about the process and essentials of integration, weekly coaching sessions by teleconference, and weekly meetings with Integrative Support Group members both electronically and face to face. We also developed distance-learning modules that were interactive and allowed people to input experience-based stories of 'integration in motion' that would help to build the new corporate mythology.

The first cohort was comprised of the senior Executive and senior managers of the organization. We felt that until they personally experienced and were comfortable with the process, we would not offer it to anyone else in the organization. Within three months of their pilot integrative journey, the senior participants experienced so many breakthroughs in their life and leadership experiences, that the Integrative Leadership program was unanimously adopted as a company-wide initiative.

Cohorts were no larger than 24 people, with one cohort starting every three months. By word of mouth and through recommendations by past participants, the program became known as one that supplied both personal and corporate competitive advantage. As a consequence, the I.L. program had a long waiting list. The integrative program was self-administered and self-generated by the Corporation. Those involved in ongoing learning and development were invited first to participate in the Integrative Leadership program, to give them an experience of the process of integration before they were allowed to teach and facilitate others.[2]

At Christmas, Mary sent us a card with a picture of her, Ron and the family on a Caribbean cruise. She thanked us once again for inviting her on the journey of integration and attached this note:

"Ron and I have never been better. I always suspected, but never would have believed that the support and love of another human being was so important to life and leadership success. I knew that behind every successful woman, there was a supportive significant other, but I had never fully experienced it until now. Ron has grown to be the companion I've always longed and yearned for. My *fantasies* of Paul from ten years ago have become my *realities* with Ron today. I would have never expected it. It is a loving surprise and I am in awe over what an amazing adventure this integrative journey truly is! Life just keeps getting better and better..."

She went on to say: "I don't know if you remember our last coaching session from many years ago, Lillas, where I shared with you a poem from Ron to me. He is writing poetry continuously now and is set to publish his first volume in the next six months. Can you imagine? An engineer writing poetry! He asked me to pass this poem on to you and Rick as a gift for inclusion in your upcoming book, if you so choose. Blessings in peace, from all of us to all of you, signed Mary."

We smiled when we saw that Ron had coincidentally and synchronistically given his poem the same title that we had given the last chapter of our book on Integrative Leadership: "A Call to Oneness."

• • •

A Call to Oneness

As with one voice they all had cried:

'O Lord, when will we with certainty know
the power and beauty of our own Soul?'

And to them all the Lord replied:

When the seeds of truth that I have sown,
Blossom and bear fruit inside your bones.

When all that is outside is found within,
When your bodies and minds are purged of sin.

When you have given all you have received,
When your gaining exceeds the losses grieved.

When all that is earthy has become Divine.
For you and for all, this is the final Sign.

Then my children you will surely know,
The nature and beauty of your own Soul:

I in you and you in Me.
Together you and I will be,
Truthful. Joyous, Peaceful and Whole,
When my Love you know your Soul.

John's Story

When my patients lose sight of their significance and are disheartened by the effort of the work we are doing, I sometimes tell them that the human race is in the midst of making an evolutionary leap. Whether or not we succeed in that leap, I say to them, is your personal responsibility. And mine. The universe, this stepping stone, has been laid down to prepare a way for us. But we ourselves must step across it, one by one.

M.Scott Peck

From the day Rick and John were together in the mountains, John began to earnestly and methodically change his whole approach to life and leadership. Rick continued to spend time each month in integrative coaching sessions, the number dependent upon what John needed in terms of support for his journey.

Physically, John put himself fully under the guidance and care of the medical team at the IMI and followed their advice impeccably. There were four areas that his team at the IMI wanted to restore and balance within his body, and by association, his mind. The four areas to be awakened and attuned were John's systems of circulation, assimilation, relaxation and elimination.

The IMI initially prescribed a new diet, vitamins and minerals that were kinesiologically tested before being administered, an exercise regime, and eight 12-oz. glasses of water each day. The new diet eliminated red meats from John's diet (although he could still eat fish, fowl and lamb) and prescribed percentages of daily fruits, almonds and vegetables designed to move his body's acid-alkaline balance from 70% acid and 30% alkaline at present (which they told him was a toxic environment that supported disease) to 20% acid and 80% alkaline in the future (which supported a healthy life-giving environment). To help in relaxation and circulation, John attended massage and acupressure treatments (to balance out his blocked Chi) three times per week, began a regimen of walking five kms per day increasing to 10 kms per day over six weeks, and T'ai Chi classes several times per week (to balance out his blocked Chi mentally and spiritually).

The worst thing for John was that his IMI team suggested 24 colonic (deep bowel irrigation) treatments over the space of eight weeks as an initial phase of tuning up his body's elimination system.

"Getting a colonic has got to be one of the worst experiences of my life," John commented one day during a coaching session. "Everybody can watch those tubes flushing out all that yuck stuff from your colon. One lady, by watching those tubes, could tell me what I had for supper four days ago." Rick remembered the feeling of being pumped up and flushed out during his last colonic treatment and just smiled in empathy at John's comments.

Mentally, John began to deeply examine his mental models and mind maps from the perspective of his Ideal of *living integrity*, asking himself the question: "Which of my beliefs and behaviors support my Ideal and which ones don't?" Some of what he found in observing his own behavior (standing aside and watching oneself go by) and reflecting on his life surprised him for they were beliefs that he had created in the distant past that were no longer serving him.

"It's like when you have installed a program on your computer that you are no longer using, but it continues to run in the background and causes your screen to go funny at times or makes your other programs not work properly," John shared one day. "I think everyone would benefit by examining what is on their mental computer and putting into the trash bin what they're no longer using."

Emotionally, John found something in his life that gave him a sense of joy, bliss and flow. He had browsed through the music store, as Rick had suggested, on their return from the mountains. He chose a keyboard and synthesizer combination and had it delivered to his home the next day. John seemed to gain great enjoyment in playing, creating melodies and lyrics and singing his own original compositions.

Spiritually, John began the practice of concentration, visualization, meditation, and contemplation daily. Although it was initially hard for John to sit still, quiet the mind and calm his emotions, with practice and repetition he got better at it. He also rediscovered his Christian roots that he had neglected since his youth and began to explore and reclaim their meaning. He began a practice of reading Scripture, attending church services, joining an evening discussion group and was even thinking of joining the church choir.

From a family perspective, John had taken another several weeks before working up the courage to speak the truth about his infidelity while in the FSU with his wife Diane. She did not seem surprised about his story, nodded, thanked him, hugged him and went out for her evening social work appointments.

"I asked her forgiveness and she gave it to me," John said in describing his truth-telling session, "but it felt mechanistic and not from her heart. The only thing she seemed to be really concerned about was whether I had blood tests after my affairs and was clean of any sexually transmitted diseases."

His family success story was with his two young adult children. Since his release from *Crisis Energy*, he was spending as much time as he could getting to know them better. What amazed him after investing the time in their relationship was how wonderful they truly were.

In the past five years he had traveled so extensively overseas that he did not know who they were anymore. And the truth was, he had admitted, that he probably never did know them since he had been sound asleep inside the mechanistic paradigm. Whenever he was at home in the past, his relationship with them had been 90% critical and 10% positive.

"Now I apply the principle of looking for the good, and not the bad as I had in the past, using your formula "seven strokes to every poke' and I can't believe the difference it has made in our relationship. With this new attitude, I'm sharing more with them and they with me than I have or they have with anyone. Diane used to tell me that we lose our influence over our kids after the age of 4 or 5. From personal experience, I know that is not true. You can always start a loving, honest, open relationship with them at any age and at any time."

John made a date with each of his kids separately once a week and did whatever they wanted, from going bowling to seeing a movie, theatre, or hiking in the mountains. During the experience, they would talk about life, love and share their insights, often laughing and joking about their stories.

Six months later, Rick observed that John was looking better and younger than in the past ten years. When John visited his family doctor, he also commented on how good John looked, took more blood tests and scheduled John for an MRI that week.

Sometime later, they met again and his doctor said, while shaking his head: "I don't know what you're doing John, but whatever it is, keep it up. Your cancer seems to be in the process of shrinking and clearing itself up. I' don't know why or how. But you're on the road to — what we would sometimes whisper in our profession — *spontaneous remission*. So whatever you're doing to help this come about, don't stop. Just keep doing it."

John was very happy, went home and shared what he thought was good news with Diane. She thought about his news for a while and then said matter-of-factly that she was leaving him. John was shocked and asked her why, when he was spending time with the kids as she had always wanted, trying to improve himself as she had always wanted, trying to broaden his interests from single-mindedly focusing on work as she had always wanted. Why pick this particular time to leave?

Diane replied that she had been thinking about it for some time, that she felt their relationship was dead and had been for many years, and that if he was getting better and wasn't going to die, then it was time for her to leave. And she did.

Initially, John went through the five stages of death and dying again over the loss of Diane. Their two children surprisingly decided to stay with John in the family home rather than move in with their mother. A month after Diane's departure, John's perspective on their separation had changed.

"Diane gave me a great parting gift, Rick. She told me her truth. I knew somewhere in my being that our relationship was dead, but no one ever named it. We had a marriage contract that said we would be together until death "did us part." Well, our relationship was dead. Neither one of us had the courage to say that it was dead until Diane stood up and said it a month ago. Initially I was angry, but now I'm grateful and appreciative and know that something good will come from all of this."

The last time we saw John was several years later while we were facilitating an Integrative Leadership program for a small company at a beautiful Chateau nestled within the mountains beside a glacier-fed lake. After supper, we went into the lounge to debrief and relax and there was John, playing his keyboard and singing a love song. We were surprised to see each other and during his break he sat at our table and gave us an update on living an integrative life.

John looked great, happy, smiling and bubbling with enthusiasm and said, "It's such a lovely and unexpected surprise to see you both."

We learned that John's passion for music had grown over time and that he had produced his first CD and gave us a copy. He was consulting part-time to the energy industry as an advisor on corrupt business practices in the FSU and often worked overseas. He loved his kids deeply, and both were now in University. Occasionally, he would indulge his passion and perform his music live in the mountains.

"Oh, I have something for you both. I found a prayer that is perfect for those walking the path of integrative life and leadership. I hope you don't mind. It's a little crinkled. I use it as part of my meditation practice, but I've memorized it now." We thanked him for the CD and his prayer. John got up to play his next set and said, "I've been meaning to call you and tell you, but never seemed to have the time..." He paused, looking awkward. "I want to thank you for awakening me and showing me the path. I use the principles every day. For every decision I make, I consider my Ideal. I feel the presence of my Soul in my music, my children and my life. I'm happier now than I've ever been and I know I would not be alive today if it were not for you. Thank you for helping me to find and live my life again."

When he left, we looked at each other and both of us were quietly weeping, not in sadness, but from the peace and joy that resonated within our hearts.

A Prayer on the Path

Lord, make me an instrument of your peace.
Where there is hatred, let me sow love;
Where there is injury, pardon;
Where there is doubt, faith;
Where there is despair, hope;
Where there is darkness, light;
Where there is sadness, joy.

O Divine, Master, grant that I may seek not so much
To be consoled as to console;
To be understood as to understand;
To be loved as to love.

For it is in giving that we receive;
It is in pardoning that we are pardoned;
And it is in dying that we are born to eternal life.

Saint Francis & Saint Clare of Assisi

Endnotes

Introduction

1. Carl Jung originally wrote in German. His work has been translated into English and has certainly captured the literal aspects of his work, but may not — depending on the level of awareness of the translator — capture his full meaning and intent. Our sense is that the fuller meaning of his personality type categorization of introvert and extrovert is related to the overarching meta-forces of involution and evolution. Introvert (involutionary) and extrovert (evolutionary) are merely specific cases within the human sphere of influence of these meta processes and forces that work within every aspect of our universe. One possible resolution would be to utilize an awakened and integrative thinker, who is fluent in German and English, to review Jung's material and render an expert and informed opinion on our intuitive perspective asking: What was Jung's possible meaning and intent between the meta-force of involution and his personality type of introvert? And the same question involving evolution and extrovert.
2. Pfeffer, J., & Sutton, R.I. (2000). *The Knowing-Doing Gap: How Smart Companies Turn Knowledge into Action*. Watertown, MA: Harvard Business School Publication Corporation. We have extended Pfeffer and Sutton's concept and included the third dimension of Being to conform with the three levels of awareness within the Integrative Framework Model.
3. Warren Bennis uses the phrase: "The Crucible of Leadership" to describe extremely difficult situations as transformational learning opportunities. Bennis, W.G., & Thomas, R.J. (2002). The crucibles of leadership. *Harvard Business Review*, 80(9):39–45. Watertown, MA: Harvard Business School Publication Corporation.
4. Both Ken Wilber, who is one of the leading integral philosophers, psychologists and thinkers of the past century, and David Hawkins, a psychiatrist and profound consciousness researcher, suggest 85% of the global population is "asleep" and

15% as "awake" (as of 2001). Wilber's work can be found at <**www.integralinstitute.org**> and Hawkins's landmark work, *Power vs. force: The hidden determinants of human behavior*, is in the references.

Chapter 1

1. Edwin Hubble proposed the "Big Bang Theory" in 1924, and first published his ideas in 1929. Here is Pablo G. Ostrov's perspective and history of the Big Bang Theory: "After having elaborated the General Theory of Relativity, Einstein was determined to use it in order to understand what the cosmos was like. His calculations indicated that the universe could not be stable: It should be either expanding or collapsing. As Einstein *believed* that the universe was stable, he proposed the existence of a force opposed to gravity that would enable the universe to be stable. The physicist and mathematician Alexander Friedmann kept on working in the right direction, accepting the consequences of General Relativity and elaborated, in 1922, models that described the universe in expansion. The vision of the cosmos we had at the beginning of the twentieth century was that we were part of a flat system that contained all the stars. In 1924 the astronomer Edwin Hubble discovered that certain astronomic objects known as 'spiral nebulae' were in fact other galaxies (in those days they would use the term 'island universes') each one formed by thousands of millions of stars located at enormous distances. In the following years he studied their distances and velocities and discovered that the galaxies were getting further from one another: In other words he discovered that the universe was expanding (paradoxically, Friedmann's works were not known in the west until 1935)." <**http://www.stillmoving.ca/hst/EdwinHubble.html**>
2. Darwin, Sedgwick and Henslow: Charles Darwin, John Henslow and Adam Sedgwick were friends and consulted one another frequently as Darwin was formulating his theory of evolution. As described in the 2001 edition of *Encarta Encyclopedia*.
3. Covey, S.R. (2001). Presentation for a major Oil and Gas Company and the Calgary Community. Calgary, AB. [We were participants.]

Chapter 2

1. Bronowski, J. (1974). *The ascent of man*. Boston, MA: Little Brown & Company. This was also a wonderful series made for public television in the late 1970s as well as a beautiful description of the evolution of humankind.
2. The phrase "Chief Misunderstanding about Life" is one coined by the Russian Spiritual Teacher, Georgi Gurdjieff as quoted by one of his students: Ouspensky, P.D. (1949). *In search of the miraculous*. London, UK: Harcourt, Inc. Georgi Gurdjieff (1877–1949), was a Greek-Armenian religious teacher and mystic. Gurdjieff suggested that we were comprised of a central core around which our various sub-personalities revolved like the spokes on a wheel. The core that informed our sub-personalities was not our Ideal in the sense of our Wholistic or Level III awareness, but rather from our Mechanistic or Level I awareness. Our "Chief Misunderstanding about Life," such as "peace at all costs", "no one understands me" or "extreme individualism" as was his pronouncement one evening to his student, Ouspensky, was what prevents us from walking the path of integration. We will use this concept from Gurdjieff in formulating and building a model of Integrative Leadership in Chapter 4. Here is a sample quote from Gurdjieff that is fascinating if it can be unraveled: *"A man may be born, but in order to be born he must first die, and in order to die he must first awake. If a man dies without having been awakened he cannot be born. If a man is born without having died he may become an 'immortal thing'. Thus the fact that he has not 'died' prevents a man from being 'born'; the fact of his not having awakened prevents him from 'dying'; and should he be born without having died he is prevented from 'being'."*
3. Easwaran, E. (1991). *Meditation*. Tomales, CA: Nigiri Press.

Chapter 3

1. Kübler-Ross, E. (1997). *On death and dying*. New York, NY: Scribner. Elisabeth Kübler-Ross's classic stages of response to dealing with death and dying are: 1. Shock and Denial; 2. Bargaining; 3. Anger; 4. Sadness and Depression; and 5. Acceptance and Moving On.
2. Kurzweil, R. (1998). *The age of spiritual machines: When computers exceed human intelligence*. New York, NY: Texere Publishing. Ray Kurzweil, US author and developer of such technologies as the Kurzweil reading machine for the visually

impaired and the voice recognition software that appears in Microsoft Corporation's *Windows 98*. Kurzweil is a futurist who has a model of technology development that speaks of the rate and speed of change. From his book: "A thousand years ago, a paradigm shift required a few hundred years. Today, a paradigm shift is measured in years. The World Wide Web didn't exist in anything like its present form just a few years ago. Kurzweil's Law indicates that paradigm shift rates are currently doubling (that is, the paradigm shift time is halving) every decade. This means that the 21st century will see about 20,000 years of progress, with 'year of progress' defined as the amount of progress we make in one year now, in the year 2000."

3. Collins, J.C., & Porras, J.I. (2000). *Built to last*. New York, NY: Harper-Collins Publishers Inc. Collins investigated 18 companies that had significant, long-term sustainable growth that exceeded 50 years. These companies, including IBM, Proctor & Gamble, Motorola and 3M Company, had an interesting characteristic of a strong core culture, values and beliefs that were rock steady and stable, whereas all around this core was allowed to change and adapt to a changing business environment. This philosophy allowed these companies to be built to last. The Image that Collins and Porras used to illustrate their findings was the Chinese symbol of the Yin and Yang. For them this symbol embodied the paradox of stability in the midst of change and continuous change in the midst of stability.
4. Ken Wilber calls this new age the *Age of Synthesis*, Stephen Covey the *Age of Wisdom*, and Anderson and Ray the *Age of New Enlightenment* (see reference list). Diane Dreher calls it the *New Renaissance*. We have chosen to call it *the Age of Integration.*
5. Campbell, J. (1990). *The hero with a thousand faces*. Princeton, NJ: Princeton University Press (first published in 1949). Campbell (1904–1987) was featured in a PBS series called "The Power of Myth" with Bill Moyers which was completed three months before he died in 1987 at the age of 83. His perspective in seeing the common themes across diverse cultures, mythic and mystic traditions that could aid us in our own life journey was refreshing. When asked what advice he would give to youth, his answer was "Follow your Bliss," explaining that if you follow your bliss, the money, relationships and opportunities will come. "Simply follow your Bliss."

Chapter 4

1. Zaleznik, A. (2004). Managers and leaders: Are they different? *Harvard Business Review*, 82(1):74–81. Watertown, MA: Harvard Business School Publication Corporation.
2. Wilber, K. (2003). *Introduction to integral theory and practice*. A paper available from the Integral Institute website: <**www.integralinstitute.org**>. Wilber did an extensive analysis of spirituality across over 300 cultures and felt that there were only two dimensions necessary to express all varieties of spiritual experience. The first dimension was inner versus outer; the second dimension was individual versus group (or community). The combination of these two dimensions becomes Wilber's four-quadrant model: 1. inner-individual [I], 2. outer-individual [IT], 3. inner-communal [We], 4. outer-communal [ITS]. The majority of people consider spirituality to involve the inner quadrant 1 and 3 while also considering science to involve outer quadrants 2 and 4. Quadrants 1 and 3 are about subjective experiences, whereas Quadrants 2 and 4 are about objective experiences.
3. de Bono, E. (2001). *Six thinking hats*. London, UK: Penguin.
4. Jung, C.G. (1923). *Psychological types*. New York, NY: Harcourt Brace. [H.G. Baynes 1921 translation, Chapter 10]. See also: *Modern man in search of a soul*. (1933). New York, NY: Harcourt Brace; and *Memories, dreams and reflections*. (1963). London, UK: Collins & Routledge & Kegan Paul.
5. Gardner, H. (1995). Reflections on multiple intelligences: Myths and messages. *Phi Delta Kappa*, 77(11): 200–209. The seven original intelligences proposed by Gardner in 1983 and the two others in 1999 can be grouped into the four domains of intelligence. Our suggested grouping is **Physical Intelligence**: Body-Kinesthetic. **Mental Intelligence**: Logical, Linguistic, Naturalistic. **Emotional Intelligence**: Musical, Interpersonal, Visual-Spatial. **Spiritual Intelligence**: Intrapersonal, Metaphoric.
6. The **Life Force** has many names in history. In Yogic traditions, it is called *prana*. In Chinese traditions, it is called *Ch'i*. It has also been called *anima*, *animating principle* and *orgone energy*. Henry Bergson, the French philosopher, called it the *élan vital* that was the immaterial essence that helped push evolution ever forward. We describe the life force as the *spirit of life* in Chapter 7: Building a Living Organization.

7. Sheldrake, R. (1987). Mind, memory and archetype morphic resonance and the collective unconscious. *Psychological Perspectives 18*(1):9–25; *18*(2):320–331; *1988 19*(1):64–78. Sheldrake is a theoretical biologist whose 1981 book, *A new science of life: The hypothesis of formative causation* (New York, NY: Tarcher) caused a storm of controversy. His four essays are classics on his theory of Morphogenic field. In essence, he is saying that we live in a *sea of thought* that has impressed upon it the collective memory of all things and all human memory. We are accessing this collective consciousness or memory all the time as well as adding to it. This connection influences our development and evolution. In his words: "Such an encompassing perspective is part of a very profound paradigm shift that is taking place in science: the shift from the mechanistic to an evolutionary and wholistic world view."
8. Judith, A. (1996). *Eastern body western mind: Psychology and the chakra system as a path to the self*. Berkley, CA: Celestial Arts. See Judith for sensations, feelings and emotions. There are many interpretations of the chakras or spiritual centers of the body. The following are where you can begin your search: Sharamon, S., & Baginski, B. (1991). *The chakra handbook*. Twin Lakes WI: Lotus Press; another introductory interpretation and links to power and healing is Myss, C. (1996). *Anatomy of the spirit*. New York, NY: Three Rivers Press. The history of the concept of spiritual centers is ancient: "The concept of spiritual centers can be found in the art of antiquity, from glowing globes on people's heads in Egyptian art to third eyes on the bodies (even on the palms of hands) in classical Asian art. The first formal mention of spiritual structures, including energy centers and pathways, appears in Patanjali's Yoga Sutras, c. 300 BC. He reveals six centers and an ultimate luminescence that occurs around the top of the head. These centers are depicted in two ways: as *chakras* (literally, 'spinning wheels') and as *padmes* (literally, 'lotuses'). Therefore, one may understand that the spiritual centers are both energy vortexes that generate movement as they are stimulated (as a spinning wheel), and enlightenment complexes that unfold as they grow (as an opening lotus)."
9. Goleman, D., Boyatzis, R., & McKee, A. (2002). *Primal leadership: Realizing the power of emotional intelligence*. Boston, MA: Harvard Business School Press.
10. American Association of Clinical Endocrinologists. Website: <**www.aace.com**>. There are links to many other sites for review and for the most current research on the endocrine system.

11. The exception of the endocrine glands is the pancreas that also secretes into the intestines. There is a debate as to which endocrine gland represents the second, or navel, center in the literature. At this time, the least controversial seems to be the pancreas.
12. Pert, C. (1997). *Molecules of emotion: Why you feel the way you feel*. New York, NY: Scribner.
13. Lamsa, G.M. (Ed.). (1936). *The holy bible: The book of revelations*. San Francisco, CA: Harper & Row Publishers. The seven churches (Revelations 1:4, 1:11), seven angels (Revelations 1:20), seven stars (Revelations 1:20), seven seals (Revelations 5:1, 5:5, 6:1), seven plagues (Revelations 15:1, 15:6, 15:8, 21:9), seven horns (Joshua 6:4), and seven crowns (Revelations 12:3) are suggested to be associated with the seven spiritual centers of the body.
14. Maslow, A. (1998). *Maslow on management*. New York, NY: John Wiley & Sons.
15. Hawkins, D.R. (2002). *Power vs. force: The hidden determinants of human behavior*. Carlsbad: CA: Hay House.
16. Watson, J. (1913). Psychology as the behaviorist views it. *Psychological Review*, *21*:158–177.
17. Story sourced from the Zoroastrian tradition almost 2,500 years ago. The Zoroastrian wisdom tradition, in addition to suggesting that love is the power of integration and fear is the force of separation, contains a version of the golden rule as follows: "Do not unto others whatever is injurious to yourself." Shayast-na-Shayast 13.29. This story can also be found in the aboriginal traditions.
18. **The Seven Deadly Sins & Virtues:** The seven deadly sins are pride, envy, gluttony, lust, anger, greed and sloth. The seven virtues that counteract these are humility, kindness, abstinence, chastity, patience, liberality (giving) and diligence, respectively. According to theology, practicing and embodying the seven virtues will overcome the existence within us of the seven deadly sins.
19. **The Fruits of the Spirit:** Galatians 5:22–23; "The fruit of the Spirit is love, joy, peace, longsuffering, gentleness, goodness, faith, meekness, temperance."
20. Kushner, L. (1998). *Invisible lines of connection: Sacred stories of the ordinary*. New York, NY: Jewish Lights Publications. Drawing on personal stories to illustrate that the micro events of our lives yield macro lessons for living, Rabbi Kushner, through a series of stories, illustrates the principle of interconnectedness and develops one of Emmon's principles of spiritual intelligence which is the ability to sanctify everyday experiences. For example, in his story about doing the hokey pokey with his children when young, he concludes, "So that's what

it's all about! You put your whole self in, you take your whole self out; you put your whole self in and you shake it all about. The idea is that by doing whatever you're doing with all of you, you can then take all of you out. The trick is how to do both.

21. References on mystics:
    - Underhill. E. (1960). *The essentials of mysticism and other essays*. New York, NY: Dutton. [first published 1920].
    - ———. (1913). *The mystic way: A psychological study in Christian origins*. London, UK: Dent.
    - ———. (1948). *The cloud of unknowing: The classic of medieval mysticism*. New York, NY: Harper. [first published 1912].

    All three books by Underhill are classics in the field.
    - Merton, T. (1967). *Mystics and zen masters.* New York, NY: Farrar, Straus and Giroux. St. John of the Cross, the companion of St. Theresa of Avila, speaks about the 'dark night of the soul' which resonates with Warren Bennis's 'crucibles of leadership'. For a more complete bibliography on mysticism, you might begin at <**http://www.ccel.org/u/underhill/mysticism/mysticism1.0-BIBLI OGR.html**>

    Some further selections on mysticism follow:
    - Blumenthal, D.R. (1978/1982). *Understanding Jewish mysticism: A source reader.* (2 volumes). New York, NY: Ktav Publishing.
    - Bridges, H. (1970). *American mysticism: From William James to Zen.* Lakemont, GA: CSA Press.
    - Butler, D.C. (1967). *Western mysticism: The teaching of Augustine, Gregory, and Bernard on contemplation and the contemplative life.* (3rd edn.). London, UK: Constable.
    - Dasgupta, S. (1927). *Hindu mysticism*. New York, NY: Ungar. [Reprinted in 1959].
    - de Marquette, J. (1949). *Introduction to comparative mysticism.* New York, NY: Philosophical Library.
    - Jones, R.M. (1909). *Studies in mystical religion*.London, UK: Macmillan & Co. Ltd. [Reprinted in 1970].
    - Knowles, D. (1964). *The English mystical tradition.* London, UK: Burns & Oats.
    - O'Brien, E. (1964). *Varieties of mystical experience: An anthology and interpretation*. New York, NY: Mentor-Omega.
    - Parrinder, E.G. (1976). *Mysticism in the world's religions.* London, UK: Sheldon Press.

- Peers, E.A. (1951–60). *Studies of the Spanish mystics*. (3 volumes). London,UK: S.P.C.K.
- Scholem, G.G. (1961). *Major trends in Jewish mysticism* (3rd edn.). New York, NY: Schocken.
- Stace, W.T. (1961). *Mysticism and philosophy.* London, UK: Macmillan.
- Suzuki, D.T. (1957). *Mysticism: Christian and Buddhist*. New York, NY: Harper. [Reprinted 1971].
- Underhill, E. (1930). *Mysticism: The nature and development of man's spiritual consciousness. (12th Rev. edn.)*. London, UK: Methuen & Co. Ltd. [Reprinted 1961].
- Zaehner, R.C. (1969). *Hindu and Muslim mysticism*. Oxford, UK: Oneworld. [first published 1960].

  There are many websites for mystic quotations. Begin with this one: <**http://www.digiserve.com/mystic/index.html**>
- Kirkpatrick, S.D. (2000). *Edgar Cayce: An American prophet*. New York, NY: Riverhead.
- Yogananda P. (1961). *Autobiography of a yogi.* London, UK: Rider. [first published 1948].
- Sugrue, T. (1984). *There is a river: The story of Edgar Cayce*. Virginia Beach, VA: A.R.E. Press. [first published 1943].

  All three are good examples of mysticism in the 20th Century.

22. Hendricks, G., & Ludeman, K. (1997). *The corporate mystic: A guidebook for visionaries with their feet on the ground*. NY, New York: Bantam.
23. **Perspectives on Spiritual intelligence:**
    - Emmons, R.A. (1999). *The Psychology of ultimate concerns: Motivation and spirituality in personality*. New York, NY: Guilford.
    - Wolman, R.N. (2001). *Thinking with your soul: Spiritual intelligence and why it matters*. NY, New York: Harmony Books.
    - Simpkins, C. <**www.clive.co.za**>
    - Leavy, J., & Leavy, M. (2003). Personal correspondence on spiritual intelligence for inclusion in an article on 'Spiritual Intelligence' or 'On Becoming an Integrated Leader'.
    - Litchfield, B. (1999). *Spiritual intelligence*. Urbana-Champaign, IL: University of Illinois, <**http://www.uinc.edu/ro/ICF5/Papers/Spiritual_Intel.pdf**>. Contact B. Litchfield via e-mail: <**B-litch@uiuc. edu**>

24. Damasio, A.R. (2003). *Looking for Spinoza: Joy, sorrow, and the feeling brain.* Orlando, FL: Harcourt. See also Damasio, A.R. (1994). *Descartes' error: Emotion, reason, and the human brain.* New York, NY: Putnam. Ledoux, J. (1998). *The emotional brain: The mysterious underpinnings of emotional life.* Clearwater, FL: Touchstone Books.
25. Persinger, M.A. (1996). Feelings of past lives as expected perturbations within the neurocognitive processes that generate the sense of self: Contribution from limbic libility and vectorial hemisphericity. *Perceptual Motor Skills, 83*(12):1107–1121. Ramachandran, V.S., & Blakeslee, S. (1998). *Phantoms in the brain.* London, UK: Fourth Estate.
26. Llinas, R., & Ribary, U. (1993). Coherent 40 Hz oscillation characterizes dream state in humans. *Proceedings of the National Academy of Science,* 90 (March): 2078–2081. Singer, W., & Gray, C.M. (1995). Visual feature integration and the temporal correlation hypothesis. *Annual Review of Neuroscience 18*:555–586. Singer, W. (1999). Striving for coherence. *Nature 397*(6718):391–392.
27. Barrett, R. (1998). *Liberating the corporate soul.* Woburn, MA: Butterworth-Heinemann.
28. Consciousness researchers such as Charles T. Tart have suggested up to twelve levels of consciousness of which the seven lower are a portion. Ken Wilber has suggested nine to twelve states of consciousness in his integral evaluations. David Hawkins indicates over twenty different quantum states of consciousness in his map of consciousness.
29. Capra, F. (1975).*The tao of physics.* London, UK: Wildwood House. See also Capra, F. (1989). *Uncommon wisdom.* New York, NY: Bantam. The Socrates quote is sometimes attributed to Aristotle, Plato's student.
30. The Seeker Fish story is an ancient fable that has been resurrected as a common spiritual myth today to help explain why we cannot see evidence of spirit or consciousness since we are immersed in it. It is similar and corresponds to not being able to see the forest for the trees.
31. Platonic forms are Ideals that exist in the same regions as Sheldrake's Morphogenic fields and Jung's collective unconscious. In Plato's view, all circles that we perceive *here* are reflections of an Ideal circle (or sphere) that is *there. Here,* we suggest, is Level I awareness. *There* is Level III awareness.
32. Palmer, P. (1998). *The courage to teach: Exploring the inner landscape of a teacher's life.* San Francisco, CA: Jossey Bass. Parker suggests that a "community is an outward and visible sign of an inward and visible grace, the flowing of personal

identity and integrity into the world of relationships" (p. 90). Parker goes on to say that to teach, or to lead, is to be in a place where a *community of truth* is practiced. This community of truth is where people can share who they truly are and how they truly feel about an issue or subject with total listening by the community without recrimination or judgment. The only way we have found to build a community of truth is to have the courage to listen deeply to another, then to be radically honest and have the courage to speak our truth without fear into their listening.

33. Mishlove, J. (1975). *The roots of consciousness: The classic encyclopedia of consciousness studies.* New York, NY: Marlowe & Company. This is a classic treatment of the evolution of consciousness research from ancient to modern times. Two areas to point out for review: The first, Mishlove's summary of Arthur Young's Reflexive Universe, is exceptional (see pages 369–373). In Mishlove's words: "Young's work cannot be considered a theory in the strict scientific sense. It is larger than a theory; it is a model of reality that goes beyond science. The potential value of such a worldview, paradigm or model for the scientific endeavor is heuristic: it suggests new avenues of inquiry. In this sense, Young's approach has been an inspiration to a generation of scholars working on the leading edge of consciousness exploration." Young influenced many individuals in the past thirty years including Kenneth Pelletier, Stanislav Grof, Frank Barr and Saul-Paul Sirag. The work of Saul-Paul Sirag deserves special attention. Sirag's work involves relating through the principles of symmetry, geometry and mathematics hyper-dimensionality, hyperspace and consciousness that could lead to a link between science in its search for the unified field theory (uniting relativity's gravity with quantum mechanics) and spirituality (as experienced by the mystics) and its search for the unified field theory of consciousness or God. Mishlove's suggests that Sirag's work is promising. In his words on pages 367–368, "Sirag's model of consciousness, as presented in the Appendix — 'Consciousness: A Hyperspace View,' (pages 375–418) — could be called a Pythagorean approach to consciousness, since Sirag's strategy is to look to mathematics for an appropriate structure to describe the relationship between consciousness and the physical world. He finds that unified field theories of the physical forces depend fundamentally on mathematical structures called *reflection spaces*, which are hierarchically organized in such a way that an infinite spectrum of realities is naturally suggested. "This situation is natural because mathematicians have discovered that the hierarchical organization of reflection

spaces also corresponds to the organization of many other mathematical objects — e.g. catastrophes, singularities, wave fronts, and contact structures, error correcting codes, sphere packing lattices and, perhaps surprisingly, certain regular geometric figures including Platonic solids. It is generally believed by physicists working on unified field theory that space-time is hyper-dimensional, with all but four of the dimensions being invisible. The reason for this invisibility is a major subject of research. Beside space-time dimensions, there are also other internal (or invisible) dimensions called *gauge* dimensions. The reality of these *gauge* dimensions is also a topic of controversy and research. In Sirag's view, both the extra space-time dimensions and the gauge dimensions are real. This provides scope for considering ordinary reality a substructure within a hyperdimensional reality. This idea has, of course, been suggested before — e.g. it is implicit in the *Parable of the Cave* of Plato. The difference in Sirag's approach is that the structure of the hyperspace is defined directly by the properties of physical forces. A further innovation in Sirag's approach is that his version of unified field theory embeds both *spacetime* and *gauge* space in an algebra whose basis is a finite group. This group, which directly models certain symmetries of particle physics, is a symmetry group of one of the Platonic solids — the octahedron. Thus, it is a mathematical entity contained in the reflection space hierarchy. In fact, the reflection space corresponding to the octahedron is seven-dimensional and is also a superstring-type reflection space, so that a link with the most popular version of unified field theory is provided. The central postulate of Sirag's paper is that this seven-dimensional reflection space is a universal consciousness, and that individual consciousness taps into this universal consciousness (Note: Which is resonant with Jung's *Collective Unconscious*, Sheldrake's *Morphogenic fields*, de Chardin's *Noosphere,* among many others). This implies that the high level of consciousness (we would say awareness) enjoyed by humans is due to the complex network of connections to the underlying reflection space afforded a highly evolved brain. Moreover, the hierarchy of reflection spaces suggests a hierarchy of realms (or states) of consciousness. Each realm would correspond to a different unified field theory with different sets of forces. In fact, the seven-dimensional reflection space is contained in an eight-dimensional reflection space (Note: which would align with the eight universal laws suggested as the integrative framework within which we play our game of life, love, learning and leadership. See Chapter 6: Guidelines), and contains a six-dimensional reflection space, so that there would be a realm of consciousness directly "above" ordinary reality, and a realm of consciousness directly "below" ordinary reality. In principle, the relationship between the different forces in these different realms could be worked out in detail, so that precise predictions could be made. Sirag believes that this hierarchy of realms of consciousness is analogous to the spectrum of light discovered in 1864 by James Clerk Maxwell in his electromagnetic theory of light, which unified the forces of electricity and magnetism. Maxwell had no way of directly testing his theory, which proposed the reality of frequencies of light both higher and lower than ordinary light. He boldly proposed the existence of invisible light, simply because his equations contained the higher and lower frequencies. Similarly, in the unification of all the forces, we can expect something new to be described, which could be the analog of light. Sirag proposes that this new thing be consciousness, and that since the mathematics of the unification gives reflection space a central role, the hierarchy of reflection spaces suggests a hierarchy of realms of consciousness." Sirag further suggests that of the Platonic forms, the octahedron (two four sided pyramids joined at the base) and cube belong in the same symmetry family all placed within a three dimensional spherical universe. The framework model of integrative life and leadership contains these images of hierarchy as a triangle, structure as a cube and community as a sphere as representations of this hyperdimensional view of consciousness. The Platonic forms, geometric shapes and images that we have chosen to visually depict our unified model of life and leadership is resonant with current scientific thought and aligned with the concepts and images presented in many of the ancient wisdom and mystic traditions.

34. Ni, Hua-Ching (1979). *The complete works of Lao Tzu: Tao Teh Ching & Hua Hu Ching*. Los Angeles, CA: SevenStar Communications Group, Inc. Of the many translations we have researched of Taoist thought, Ni's translation of the work of Lao Tzu is the most clear and resonant. Ni's interpretation of this universal integrative model begins on page 187, Axiom 61 of the Hua Hu Ching: "The ancient sages also expressed the development of the universe numerically. The number one represented the Subtle Origin, while two represented the duality of yin and yang, and three the trinity of yin, yang and their integration as *T'ai Chi* (three levels of awareness), which brings forth life. These are considered the three main categories of the universe. The number four represents the four basic forces (four domains of intelligence) of the universe which are variations of yin and yang: the strong force which was referred to as 'old yang'; the weak force which was

called 'old yin'; the heavy force which was called 'young yang'; and the light force which was called 'young yin'. For a force to be strong does not necessarily mean that it is heavy, nor is a weak force necessarily light. It is possible for a force to be both light and strong, or weak and heavy. These four forces may be considered parallels to what modern physics terms 'strong nuclear force', 'gravity', 'weak nuclear force' and 'electromagnetism'. The harmonization of these four forces creates a fifth, united force, a *T'ai Chi* (heart mind), which is the harmonizing force of the universe, a common field. These four forces manifested as water that symbolized the strong force (emotional) characterized by aggregation, contraction, collection and condensation. Fire symbolized the weak force characterized by expansion, disaggregation, dispersion, dissipation (mental). Wood symbolized the light force characterized by explosion and dynamism (spiritual). Metal symbolized the heavy force characterized by gravity (physical). The inherent nature of these four different forces battle and conquer each other, while earth, the fifth force, symbolizes the united, harmonized and neutral force among them." To complete the Taoist perspective on this universal model, the three levels of awareness are referred to as the *Yu Ching* (wholistic), *Shan Ching* (organic) and *T'ai Ching* (mechanistic). This taken from page 197, Axiom 62 of the Hua Hu Ching: "The total reality of the universe is energy; it is called 'prime energy' or 'prime chi'. Two divisions of this energy occur: the heavy, physical energy of the earth (mechanistic) and the light, spiritual energy of heaven (wholistic). The three divisions of this energy are the physical (mechanistic), the spiritual (wholistic) and a combination of the two (organic). Human life represents one whole category of the natural energy flow. The ancient developed ones used the three divisions of energy to distinguish the energy in an individual human being: spiritual energy being centered in the head (soul mind), physical energy in the belly (body mind), and harmonized energy in the heart and mind (heart mind). Spiritual energy is not equally pure at all levels, and each of the Three Main categories has its own purity (which from our perspective would mean one can integrate around a mechanistic idol/image, an organic idea or a Wholistic Ideal): *Yu Ching*, *Shan Ching* and *T'ai Ching*. As we have already seen, these unified energies can be applied to both the macrocosm and the microcosm. To the ancient achieved ones, the purity of the three different levels was the goal of personal achievement (walking the path of integration). One who achieved himself spiritually attained the range of *Yu Ching* (Level III awareness: enlightenment); one who achieved himself by attaining the wisdom that is connected with universal mindedness or universal heartedness attained the range of *Shan Ching* (Level II awareness) and one who achieved himself by refining his sexual energy attained the range of *T'ai Ching* (Level I awareness: embodiment). The one who achieved himself with all three (by walking the path of integration within Level II awareness), expressed in an integral and virtuous life (informed and led from Level III awareness), attained the Universal Integral Way (and became an Integrative Leader).

35. See Edward de Bono's *Six thinking hats* in the references. Also discussed briefly in the section on Multiple Perspectives in the early part of Chapter 4 of this book.
36. Dickens, C.J.H. (1812–1870). *A christmas carol* (1843). A classic tale and parable that is a must-read for those desiring to reawaken their three levels of awareness. We would also recommend Alistair Simms' 1952 film version of *A Christmas Carol*. Despite all the movies made before it and after it, this version is the one that most closely captures the spirit and meaning of Dicken's original written work. Here is a quote from Dickens on change: *"If a man habituated to a narrow circle of cares and pleasures, out of which he seldom travels, steps beyond it, though for never so brief a space, his departure from the monotonous scene on which he has been an actor of importance would seem to be the signal for instant confusion. The mine which Time has slowly dug beneath familiar objects is sprung in an instant; and what was rock before, becomes but sand and dust."*
37. **A Brief History of Dream Work:** Our present understanding of nightly dreams and visions and their interpretations comes from a rich history of inquiry. The dream state is one of the three universal states of consciousness with waking and deep sleep the other two states. Dreams were first discussed in **ancient Egypt** over 5,000 years ago where thousands of dream interpreters and dozens of temples were erected to the Egyptian god of dreams, Serapis. To the Egyptians, a dream was a message from the gods. Dream incubation, where one posed a question to oneself, three times just before one fell asleep, slept in the temple, and then expected an answer to their question in ones dreams, originated in Egypt. One famous Egyptian dreamer was Thutmose IV (1450 BC) who dreamt that the spirit of the Sphinx came to him in a dream and asked him to be the one to return her to her former glory. Thutmose honored her request and applied it by undertaking a massive excavation and repair project to remove the sands that had built up around the Sphinx (only her head was visible at the time) and repaired the damage wrought by the sands of time. The **ancient Chinese** felt there were two parts to our soul: material and spiritual (Hun). The material

soul stayed with and animated the body, but the Hun was free during sleep to travel to other places and other dimensions beyond our physical world. The ancient Chinese felt that the sources for dreams were from ordinary physical stimuli, astrological influences from the stars and the Hun's experiences in other dimensions. Meng Shu (640 AD) was the first to chronicle and codify Chinese beliefs and methods of dream interpretation. In **ancient India**, their belief was that the soul left the body during sleep. Dreams were a reflection and a mirror of our present life circumstances that, if extrapolated, were also presented in the dream as precognitive experiences. Some concepts about dreams from the Vedas (1500–1000 BC) are: If you dream of Elephants that is a lucky omen and if you dream about Donkeys it is an unlucky omen. (Note: This adds a new perspective to the Democrats and Republicans in the United States.) Bad dreams could be met and overcome through a series of rituals, and we had a series of dream periods during sleep. The earliest dream period upon falling asleep saw the furthest into the future. The latest dream period just before awakening, saw the nearest (hours or days) into the future and should be the one interpreted first. In **ancient Greece,** the earliest concepts were that a dream was a visitation from the gods of Olympus. Individuals would remain where they were (bedroom for example) and the gods would visit them and deliver a message as they slept. Later, around 500 BC, person's beliefs changed to allow a person's soul to travel to other places, times and dimensions. In Greece's golden age, there were over 600 temples to the Greek god of dreams and healing, Asklepios. This is where the ancient Egyptian art of dream incubation was refined to the degree that an individual who had a problem or question could ask someone else to dream for them on their problem while that other slept in Asklepios's temple. Hippocrates, the father of medicine, used patient's dreams as a diagnostic indicator for their health in body, mind and soul. Plato believed in three levels of awareness: physical awareness, mental awareness and what he called, "divine madness." On the one hand, Plato was cautious about the messages received in one's dreams for he felt that on occasion "In all of us, even in good men, there is a lawless, wild beast nature that peers out in sleep." On the other hand, Plato also felt that man was capable of high dreams sourced from their divine nature when man had sufficiently cultivated his reason to align with higher reason. Aristotle, Plato's student, rejected the possibility of a divine origin to man's dreams, primarily based on the fact that he witnessed all the movements and actions of dreaming when animals slept. If animals could dream, went his reasoning, who are not even close to the divine, then dreams must be from our animal and not our divine natures. This philosophy and doctrine would heavily influence western societies view of the importance of dreams and dream interpretation for 800 years. In the **Biblical Traditions,** there are over 70 passages in Scripture that describe and refer to dreams. In Job (33:12) for example: "God speaks to man in a dream, in a vision of the night when deep sleep falls upon men, he opens their ears." And in Joel (2:28): "I will pour out my spirit on all flesh; your sons and daughters shall prophecy; your old men shall dream dreams and your young men shall see visions." One of the most famous dream interpreters in the Old Testament was the Prophet Daniel and his interpretation of King Nebuchadnezzar's dream of impending madness. This was an interesting story, for the King called over 300 of his magicians and soothsayers together and asked for an interpretation of the dream that had awoken him in the night screaming. However, he refused to tell them the dream. It was so important to him, that he wanted his magicians to tell him the dream he had (testing their authenticity to see if they could walk their talk) and also the interpretation. For the soothsayers and oracles who came forward and could not first tell the King his dream before offering the interpretation, the King vowed to put them to death. Daniel took up this life and death challenge, went into the silence, successfully apprehended the dream and then told the King the divine interpretation, which resonated truth for the King. Joseph, one of Isaac's twelve sons who was sold into slavery by his brothers, also was a famous dream interpreter. When the Pharaoh had a dream that disturbed him greatly, it was Joseph who correctly interpreted and applied the dream as seven plentiful bountiful years of the harvest where they should store grain followed by seven years of famine where the stored grain should be given to the people to sustain them. For this dream interpretation and the wisdom to apply it, Joseph was made Regent, second only to the Pharaoh in power over all of Egypt. In the **New Testament** the first notable dream was Joseph the Carpenter who was the fiancé of Mary (the eventual mother of Jesus) and his dream where an angel spoke to him and suggested that he should marry Mary, even though she was pregnant, and he did. Others were the three Wise Men dreaming that they should not return to King Herod to tell him that the Messiah was born in Bethlehem, and they didn't: Joseph's dream where he was told by an angel to take Mary and the child Jesus to Egypt to save Jesus from King Herod's madness and wrath, and they left and spent five years in Egypt: Peter's dream about what food he could eat in the house of the Roman Cornelius which allowed, not just the Jews, but gentiles to become brothers and sisters in Christ. In the **Islamic/ Arabic Traditions**, dreams were an experience obtained from the world of images (mental realms), a world that had a separate reality to our physical waking state that could be reached and mastered through training and development. The most famous dream of Islamic history was Mohammed's night journey (Lailetal-Miraj) which was his great dream of initiation into the mysteries of heaven, hell and humanity that birthed the Muslim faith. Mohammed worked with his disciples on dreams and, by the 11th Century AD, dream interpretation flourished in Islamic society. The early **Church fathers,** Clement, Origen, Synesius, Constantine all believed that in sleep, man became receptive to the holy spirit and that dreams were "presentations of symbols that revealed the nature of the non-physical world." As we entered the Dark Ages in Europe — what the Taoist Masters called the Age of Confusion — Aquinas (1220 AD), who was educated in the Aristotelian perspective, dismissed dreams being the result of physical processes such as digestion and belittled their importance. Many subsequent philosophers accepted Aquinas's view of dreams and dreaming. For example, Thomas Hobbes felt that dreams were merely the "distemper of the inner parts". Martin Luther, who was instrumental in the Christian Reformation, was unable to discern the source of his dreams as Satan or God. Because of this uncertainty, Luther determined to throw his dream baby out with his unconscious bathwater and willed himself to stop dreaming. As a result, he advised all his followers to do the same, and many of them still do. **Twentieth Century Perspectives:** In 1900, Freud published his landmark "The Interpretation of Dreams" which reawakened the importance of dreams and their connection to waking states for 20th Century humankind. Freud used dreams to heal neurosis and other forms of mental illness. He believed that our unconscious was the storehouse and repository of repressed sexual needs, aggressions and self-preservation. He believed we repressed these violent tendencies to keep them from our waking state. It was our unconscious, the source of our dreams, that could reveal and conceal our hidden urges, appetites and desires. In the dream states, Freud believed that our conscious suppression was bypassed, and that our seething cauldron of beastly nature was occasionally released during our dreams, similar to a Freudian slip during our waking states. For Freud, dreams were a safety valve or release mechanism that allowed people to have healthier waking psyches. However, Freud also felt that dreams were deceptive and were not to clarify, but to disguise our deepest desires, urges and abhorrent needs. Carl Jung, a student of Freud in the beginning, who later broke away to form his own psychoanalytic theory in the end, took a healthier approach and view towards dreams and human nature. He believed that the purpose of dreams was to help awaken the dreamer to an aspect of themselves that they were consciously unaware of (a blind spot). By making us aware of these deep seated issues, we then had an opportunity to deal with them in a healthy way. For Jung, dreams were a mechanism to enhance our growth (individuality) and lead us to balance, wholeness and integration. Jung described three levels of awareness; conscious, subconscious and collective unconscious that not only linked us to the mind and memory of all of humanity, but also the mind and memory of the Divine. Jung was instrumental in bringing Eastern Wisdom Traditions (I Ching) and the original Biblical perspectives on dreams and dreaming into Western Civilization's awareness in the 20th century. Post World War II, **Sleep Laboratories** developed that attempted to correlate physiologic effects (EEG, ECG, REM) to the dreaming state while we slept. Stephen Laberge took this one step further, and began to investigate individuals in his sleep laboratories who experienced a lucid state while in the dream (awake in the dream). In his work, Laberge came full circle to align with ancient Tibetan Buddhist teachings that our awakening and path to enlightenment and integration could begin by cultivating the ability to become and remain awake while in our dreams. From the **Integrative Perspective and Framework,** we would suggest that the value of your dreams and dream interpretation is directly related to your world view or paradigm. If you are mechanistic, then your dreams will be about the body and waking state events. If you are organic, then your dreams would be about the body, heart and mind and the meaning behind the events in your life. If you are wholistic, then your dreams could be sourced from any level and from any dimension of your being, including the Divine, for it is your beliefs that will keep you fragmented or help to make you whole. However, wholeness only occurs if your Ideal is set firmly within, and resonant with, the universal principles and virtues of the wholistic paradigm.

38. **Jesus comforting his Disciples:** (John 14:1–4). "Do not let your hearts be troubled. Trust in God; trust also in me. **In my Father's house are many mansions** (rooms); if it were not so, I would have told you. I am going there to prepare a place for you. And if I go and prepare a place for you, I will come back and take you to be with me that you also may be where I am. You know the way to the place where I am going." We would interpret this as trusting in Spirit as

well as trusting in the mind of the Christ embodied by Jesus. Jesus suggests that there are many levels of awareness (rooms), many states of consciousness (mansions) and that through the life of Jesus in modeling the pattern of the Christ as his Ideal, that place in consciousness will be prepared for all to follow and abide (collective unconscious).

39. **Gurdjieff's Four-Domain Metaphor: (Carriage, Horse, Driver, Master)**: Georgi Gurdjieff. (1950). *Beelzebub's Tales to his Grandson*. Arkana, NY: Viking Penguin. Gurdjieff related a metaphor early in the 20th century that involved the four domains, or what he called the four bodies within man. In paraphrasing his metaphor: 'A carriage driver forgets his duty, obligation and life purpose, drives up to the neighborhood pub and drinks himself silly for days and days on end. Meanwhile, the horse is suffering from lack of food and water, accepting handouts and kindness from passing strangers in order to continue to live. The carriage is suffering from lack of attention and is in need of repair. One day, the driver wakes up, realizes he has been drunk these past days, leaves the pub, feeds and grooms the horse, repairs the carriage and then begins to set off on a journey towards his goal (Ideal). Only when he is moving in the direction of his hearts desire, does the Master come. First the Master walks beside the carriage for a time, then opens the carriage door and allows himself into his rightful place to aide the driver in finding his direction and his purpose in life.' This metaphor can also be found in the *Katha Upanishad* and Plato's *Phadreus*. Gurdjieff and his student, Ouspensky, just before WW I had the following conversation about his metaphor and the mechanized nature of man and the possibility of a unified man: "According to an ancient teaching, traces of which may be found in many systems, old and new, a man who has attained the full development possible for man, a man in the full sense of the word, consists of four bodies. These four bodies are composed of substances which gradually become finer and finer, mutually interpenetrate one another, and form four independent organisms, standing in a definite relationship to one another but capable of independent action." He goes on to say that the first body is like a machine that is his mechanized nature. However, "...in this second body, under certain conditions, a third body can grow, again having characteristics of its own. The consciousness manifested in this third body has full power and control over the first two bodies; and the third body possesses the possibility of acquiring knowledge inaccessible either to the first or to the second body. In the third body, under certain conditions, a fourth can grow, which differs as much from the third as the third differs from the second, and the second from

the first. The consciousness manifested in the fourth body has full control over the first three bodies and itself. These four bodies are defined in different teachings in various ways. The first is the physical body, in Christian terminology the 'carnal' body; the second, in Christian terminology, is the 'natural' body; the third is the 'spiritual' body; and the fourth, in the terminology of esoteric Christianity, is the 'divine' body. In theosophical terminology the first is the 'physical' body, the second is the 'astral,' the third is the 'mental,' and the fourth the 'causal' body. In the terminology of certain Eastern teachings the first body is the 'carriage' (the body), the second is the 'horse' (feelings, desires), the third the 'driver' (mind), and the fourth the 'master' (I, consciousness, will). Such comparisons and parallels may be found in most systems and teachings which recognize something more in man than the physical body. But almost all these teachings, while repeating in a more or less familiar form the definitions and divisions of the ancient teachings, have forgotten or omitted its most important feature, which is: that man is not born with the finer bodies. They can only be artificially cultivated in him, provided favorable conditions both internal and external are present." From: <**www.cassiopaea.org**>

40. **Archetypes:** An archetype is defined as a model or type after which other similar things are patterned. The first of something would be an archetype or prototype. Archetypes are related to and synonymous with Platonic forms. A paradigm is defined as an archetypal example or pattern that provides a model for a process or system. Carl Jung used the concept of archetypes in defining what lay in the realm of the collective unconscious that at times, informed our dreams. The following from Encarta: "Jung made a distinction between the personal unconscious, the repressed feelings and thoughts developed during an individual's life, and the collective unconscious, those inherited feelings, thoughts and memories shared by all humanity. The collective unconscious is made up of what Jung called *archetypes,* or primordial images, that manifest themselves symbolically in religions, myths, fairy tales and fantasies."

41. **Joan of Arc, Saint**. (1412–1431): From Encarta: "French military leader and heroine. Inspired and directed by religious visions, she organized the French resistance that forced the English to end their siege of Orleans (1429). The same year she led an army of 12,000 to Rheims and had the dauphin crowned Charles VII. Captured and sold to the English by the Burgundians (1430), she was later tried for heresy and sorcery and was burned at the stake in Rouen. She was canonized in 1920." Throughout history, the Church has had difficulty with

individuals such as Joan of Arc who were connected inwardly (attunement) and bore witness to their truth (embodiment). In each of the many cases we examined, there was a conflict between the existing order and institution and the new and deeply personal revelation that caused confusion. The confusion always revolved around whether to kill these self-actualized individuals or to canonize them. Unfortunately for Joan of Arc, she was killed and then much later made a saint. Our society and civilization wrestles with these same issues within our transition from the Age of Confusion, to the Age of Enlightenment to our current emerging Age of Integration. Our hope is that in our current transition, the clarity will help bring peace in the midst of paradox, and not more unrest, mistrust and unjust violence towards the innocent.

42. McMillin, D.L., Richards, D.G., Mein, E.A., & Nelson, C.D. (1999). The abdominal brain and enteric nervous system. *The Journal of Alternative and Complementary Medicine*, 5(6): 575–586. This article contains the theory of the abdominal brain/mind first proposed by Byron Robinson nearly 100 years ago. The following is an extract from the article: "American physician Byron Robinson, a medical doctor, did extensive research and writing culminating in his impressive work, *The Abdominal and Pelvic Brain* (Robinson, 1907). The premise of Robinson's book is that the abdominal viscera contain a vast and complex nervous system, which influences, and to a great degree regulates, the vegetative process of the abdominal viscera. Robinson was not alone in his fascination with the nervous system of the abdomen. At about the same time that Robinson was discovering the 'abdominal brain,' British physiologist Johannis Langley of Cambridge University recognized that 'the nervous system of the gut was capable of integrative functions independent of the central nervous system' (Gershon et al., 1994, p. 424). It is now known that the human GI system, deprived of CNS innervations, is capable of coordinated digestion, mobility, secretion and absorption (Davenport, 1978). Langley labeled the brain in the gut the enteric nervous system, the term now used for this system."

43. Armour, J.A. et al. (1997). Gross and microscopic anatomy of the human intrinsic nervous system. *Anat Rec*. 247:289–98. Armour found 14,000 to 40,000 neurons in the human heart. Neurons were known to be in animal hearts as early as 1977. Here are two perspectives on the heart. Ali Quasimi: "The actual physical heart in our breast beats at about 100,000 times a day, pumping two gallons of blood per minute, 100 gallons per hour, 24 hours a day, seven days a week, 365 days a year for an entire life time! The vascular system that sends this life-giving blood

is over 60,000 miles long: it is more than two times the circumference of the earth." And from Virginia Essene: "Amazing recent evidence indicates that the heart begins to beat in the unborn fetus even before the brain is formed so it appears that the heart truly holds primary status as the initiator of human life. Even so, scientists have yet to discover what causes the human heart to automatically begin this essential *auto-rhythmic* beating function that grants us physical existence. Although previously unknown, neuroscientists have now discovered that there are over 40,000 nerve cells (neurons) in the heart alone, indicating that the heart has its own independent nervous system sometimes called 'the brain in the heart.' In addition, the heart has an electromagnetic energy field 5,000 times greater than that of the brain and this field can be measured with magnetometers up to 10 feet beyond the physical body. This provides support for the spiritual teachings that indicate we humans have energy fields that constantly intermingle with each other, enabling healing (or negative) thoughts to be extended and exchanged." (From: Essene, V. *Science and spirituality: How are your brain and heart connected to god?* <**http://www.experiencefestival.com/i/topic/articles/article/1961**>

44. Bennis, W.G., & Thomas, R.J. (2002). The crucibles of leadership. *Harvard Business Review*: 80(9):39–45. Watertown, MA: Harvard Business School Publishing Corporation.
45. Sui, R.G.H. (1979). *The craft of power*. Toronto, ON: John Wiley & Sons.
46. ———. (1980). *The transcendental manager*. Toronto, ON: John Wiley & Sons.
47. Young, A.M. (1974). Prologue for a new religion consistent with the findings of science. *Nous Newsletter*. <**http://www.arthuryoung.com/barr.html**>. See also Young, A.M. (1976). *The reflexive universe: The evolution of consciousness*. New York, NY: Delacorte Press.
48. Sui, R.G.H. (1981). *The master manager*. Toronto, ON: John Wiley & Sons.
49. Collins, J. (2001). *Good to great: Why some companies make the leap...and others don't*. New York, NY: HarperCollins Publishers Inc.
50. References on the Will:
    - Assagioli, R. (1973). *The qualities of will*. Baltimore, MD: Penguin.
    - ———. (1972). *The act of will*. Baltimore, MD: Penguin.
    - Ferrucci, P. (1982). *The will: What we may be*. Los Angeles, CA: Tarcher.
    - James, W. (1967). *The dilemma of determinism*. J.J. McDermott, (Ed.). New York, NY: Random House.

51. Maltz, M. (2002). *The new psycho-cybernetics: The original science of self-improvement and success that has changed the lives of 30 million people.* Paramus, NJ: Prentice Hall.
52. The Myth or "Parable of the Cave" is contained in Plato's *Republic* as a dialogue between Glaucon and Socrates. You can see the full Platonic Parable at the following website: <**http://www.geocities.com/Athens/Acropolis/3497/cave.html**>
53. Bohm, D. (1980). *Wholeness and the Implicate Order.* New York, NY: Routledge.
54. **Acupuncture:** Acupuncture is an ancient Chinese medical practice that dates back 4,000 years. Acupuncture is based on the theory that there are special meridian lines and points on the body that are connected energetically to our internal organs. Vital energy called *Ch'i* flows along these meridian lines. According to the theory, diseases are caused by interrupted energy flow. The inserting and twisting of a needle or applying pressure (acupressure) to the 360 meridian points along the body helps restore normal energy flow, and therefore health, to the body. Acupuncture is practiced in most hospitals in China, and private practices in Japan, United States and Canada among other countries. For more information on Acupuncture, you can begin your search here: <**http://www.medicomm.net/Consumer%20Site/am/accupuncture.htm**>
55. Jensen, B. (1931). *The science and practice of iridology: A system of analyzing and caring for the body through the use of drugless and nature cure methods.* Escondido, CA: Self-Published. From the Foreword, Bernard's perspective is that "...by examining the markings and signs in the iris of the eye, the reflex condition of the various organs of the body can be determined. Iridology is the science of determining acute, sub-acute, chronic and destructive stages in the affected organs of the body through their corresponding areas in the iris. Drug deposits, inherent weaknesses and living habits of the patient are also revealed in the iris of the eye." Iridology is practiced extensively in Europe and the C.I.S., but is only available as an alternative diagnostic tool in private practices in the United States and Canada.
56. **Reflexology:** Reflexology is a healing system in which specific points on the feet or hands, known as reflex points, are manipulated to bring about changes in other parts of the body. These reflex points are believed to correspond to every major organ, gland and area of the body. Reflexology was introduced in the early 1920s as Zone Therapy and is based on the principle of many ancient Asian medicine practices in which a life force circulates throughout the body connecting

one part to another. When this energy or life force is blocked, disease develops. By stimulating the reflex points on the feet or hands, energy flow is thought to be restored in the body that would assist it in its natural ability to heal itself.

57. **Morihei Ueshiba** (1883–1969) founded the Japanese martial art of Aikido, which in Japanese means "way of harmony" (**Ai**-union, harmony; **Ki**-vital breath, energy; **Do**-way), in 1925 shortly after having a spiritual awakening, insight and vision. The vision prompted him to move away from the art of war as practiced by the samurai, such as *jujutsu*, and develop Aikido as the art and practice of peace. To help establish and develop his art, Morihei began a school in 1928 and combined Zen teachings with his past experience in martial arts and integrated them into one harmonious philosophy on the art of living. Aikido, that consists of over 700 moves to control or throw an opponent, is non-combative based on the principle of forming a harmonious relationship with one's opponent. The movement and blending of *Ki*, the vital energy that is centered in the abdomen or body-mind, becomes an important aspect of the way of Aikido. His students called Morihei the Great Teacher and there are many stories written and told about his life. Morihei had cultivated the ability to see his opponents' intention as a white light that emanated from them. In his words: "It was...just a matter of clarity of mind and body. When the opponent attacked, I could see a flash of white light, the size of a pebble, flying before the sword...all I did was avoid the *streams of white light*, and in that way I avoided the sword that followed it." Morihei also describes other occasions "when the center of Ki is concentrated in one's mind and body" (attunement, alignment, embodiment) and he could intuitively see the thoughts and violent intentions of an opponent. In Inner Mongolia in 1924, when Chinese Nationalists attacked his party, Ueshiba avoided oncoming bullets by merely shifting his body in what others called a "beautiful and harmonious dance". When asked how he could avoid the bullets at almost point blank range, he replied: "When the machine gun was firing at me, I could see *streams of white light* that marked the path that the gunners thoughts and the bullet *intended* to follow. I simply avoided the light, and in that way, avoided the bullets." His axiom evolved from these personal experiences of spirit in motion as: "Spirit (as the light) goes first, then the mind (as the thought), then the body (as the action or bullet)." From 1925 to his death in 1969, Morihei developed an integrative philosophy. Here are a few of his sayings: 1. The Art of Peace begins with you. Work on yourself and your appointed task in the Art of Peace. Everyone has a spirit that can be refined, a body that can be trained in some manner, a suitable path to follow. You

are here for no other purpose than to realize your inner divinity and manifest your innate enlightenment. Foster peace in your own life and then apply the Art to all that you encounter." 2. "One does not need buildings, money, power, or status to practice the Art of Peace. Heaven is right where you are standing, and that is the place to train." 3. "Eight forces (as polarities of the four domains of intelligence) sustain creation: Movement and stillness, Solidification and fluidity, Extension and contraction, Unification and division." For more principles that form the foundation of Aikido's integral philosophy, see <**http://www.cs.ucsd.edu/users/paloma/Aikido/artpeace.html**>

58. Tolle, E. (2004). *The Power of now: A guide to spiritual enlightenment.* Palo Alto, CA: New World Library.
59. **Distance to Mars:** Mars, in August 2004, at a distance of 35 million miles was the closest it has been to the Earth for 60,000 years. From August onward it began to move away from us again. The next closest planet is Venus, which is 14 minutes away at the speed of light.
60. **Luke:** 11:33: "No one **lights** a lamp and puts it in a place where it will be **hidden**, or under a bowl. Instead he puts it on its stand, so that those who come in may see the **light**." Sage advice for those desiring to move from the mechanistic to the organic.

Chapter 5

1. Zohar, D., & Marshall, I. (2001). *SQ: Connecting with your spiritual intelligence.* London, UK: Bloomsbury.
2. Goleman, D., Boyatzis, R., & McKee, A. (2002). *Primal leadership: Realizing the power of emotional intelligence*. Boston, MA: Harvard Business School Press.
3. Farr, J.N. (1998). *Supra-conscious leadership: New thinking for a new world.* Research Triangle Park, NC: Research Triangle Publishing.
4. Kouzes, J.M., & Posner, B.Z. (2002). *The leadership challenge: How to keep getting extraordinary things done in organizations*. San Francisco, CA: Jossey-Bass.
5. Hill, N. (1987). *Think and grow rich*. NY, New York: Ballantine. A classic treatment of the formula of success by changing your thinking, that was influenced by studying men like Andrew Carnegie, Thomas Edison, Henry Ford among others who formed Master Mind Groups to help ensure each other's success in life and work. First published in mid 20th Century.

6. Hedva, B. (2001). *Betrayal, trust and forgiveness: A guide to emotional healing and self-renewal*. Berkley, CA: Celestial Arts. Betrayal is one form of challenge and awakening to the individual who has chosen to walk the path of integration. From Egyptian Mythology, according to Hedva, there are five ways that this awakening could occur: 1. Bliss, Joy and Love; 2. Self Discipline; 3. Studying with an Awakened Teacher; 4. Crisis, Trauma and Tragedy (as in Betrayal); and 5. Self Study, Introspection, and Self Awareness. Hedva's purpose in her work is to elaborate on the issue of trauma, betrayal and crisis as a stage of awakening to the path of integration. Her work is to help show how people often inadequately cope with betrayal and to describe a process that may help individuals overcome betrayal that often prevents connecting and acting in alignment with their True Self. The five stages that we experience, according to Hedva, once we have had a betrayal are: 1. Separation in relationship; 2. Purification; 3. Symbolic Death; 4. New Knowledge (or Perspective) and; 5 Rebirth. The First Stage of betrayal is a separation from ourselves or a significant and meaningful relationship (work, social, intimate, other). The Second Stage of betrayal is called Purification, and is a series of five phases. In Purification, we initially experience righteous resentment of the betrayer and ask, "How could they do that to us given all that I have done for them? I would never do to them, what they have now done to me." The next phase is the projection of the shadow side of ourselves onto our betrayer. This is all our negative ideas about the incident and who has done this to us before all mixed up in this shadow side projection. The third phase is that we become cynical about people and life and begin to generalize that all men, women, supervisors, managers, organizations are truly like our betrayer and should not be trusted. This is the root of bias, prejudice and bigotry. The fourth phase is self-betrayal where we stop believing in our dreams and stop trying to become a better person in alignment with our True self. The fifth phase is entering suspicion and fear of others that forces us to try and control and manipulate our environment and others to protect ourselves from future betrayals, pain and hurt and the resulting loss of relationship. The Third Stage of betrayal is called Symbolic Death where we experience the five phases of Elisabeth Kübler-Ross's work on death and dying. These are: 1. Denial; 2. Anger and resentment; 3. Rationalization; 4. Depression; and finally, after some time, 5. Acceptance of the situation as it is. The Fourth Stage of betrayal, once we have accepted the situation as it is, is the acquisition of new knowledge, wisdom or inner learnings and insights about our situation and our life. Hedva uses the acronym T.R.U.S.T.

to bring home what we should do in this Fourth Stage of the process: T-Truth and a need to be true to your own self; R-Relax, release and receive wisdom from your inner intuitions; U-Use your intuition and your inner and outer resources, beginning with what you have in hand; S-Speak your truth in that you should use what you know and take a stand creating your personal sacred space that cannot be violated externally again. T-Turn Inward and try to live life as best as you know to do in the moment again and always try again. The Fifth Stage Hedva calls creative rebirth and follows the sequence of natural birth in the earth of a child. These five phases are: 1. Insemination; 2. Gestation; 3. Labor; 4. Transition; and 5. Rebirth. At rebirth, our new life is reborn from an inner connection with our soul. Our new life has the promise of new teachings within it. When we act from a point of trust of our inner spiritual natures, True Self or Essence, we have compassion for others and let go of the need to be right; we have intuitive awareness about our position and role in life and understand that all is happening to us for our higher good; we allow ourselves to experience creative self-expression in truth and integrity; we have the ability to act on our commitments and experience freedom for perhaps the first time in our lives. Hedva's final healing acroncym is T.R.U.S.T. again, but with a different twist: This time it is T-Truth, R-Release Righteousness, U-Understand the Higher Good (Intuition); S-Start to fulfill your dreams with commitment; and T-Trust the process of your life that will lead you to freedom.

7. Pannett, A. (2000). Facing and managing change. *New Law Journal Practitioner*, *150*:466
8. Anderson, D., & Anderson, L.A. (2001). *Beyond change management: Advanced strategies for today's transformational leaders*. San Francisco, CA: Jossey-Bass.
9. Chopra, D. (2000). *How to know God*. Toronto, ON: Harmony Books.
10. Goleman, D., Boyatzis, R., & McKee, A. (2002). *Primal leadership: Realizing the power of emotional intelligence*. Watertown, MA: Harvard Business School Publishing Corporation.
11. Kouzes, J.M., & Posner, B.Z. (2002). *The leadership challenge: How to keep getting extraordinary things done in organizations*. San Francisco, CA: Jossey-Bass.
12. Good resources for working on your mission statement are: Jones, L.B. (1997). *The path: Creating your mission statement for life and work*. El Paso, TX: Candlestick Publishing; Covey, S.R. (1989). *The seven habits of highly effective people*. New York, NY: Fireside; Thurston, M. (1995). *Soul-purpose: Discovering and fulfilling your destiny*. New York, NY: St. Martin's Press; Cashman, K.(2003).

Awakening the leader within. Hoboken, NJ: John Wiley & Sons; Senge, P., Kleiner, A., Roberts, C., Ross, R. & Smith, B. (1994). *The fifth discipline fieldbook*. New York, NY: Bantam-Doubleday-Dell Publishing Group; Bolles, R.N. (2000). *What color is your parachute?* Berkley, CA: Ten Speed Press. [Especially Appendix E. Bolles updates Parachute annually].

13. Myers Briggs Type Indicator (MBTI) a personality profile based on Carl Jung's theories and developed into an instrument by Katherine Briggs and Isobel Myers Briggs. Palo Alto, CA: Consulting Psychologists Press Inc. <**www.mbti.com**>. In addition to integrative MBTI personality type profiles, the ILI is currently developing Integrative Character Type Profiles (ICTP) with 8 dimensions and Integrative Universal Type Profiles (IUTP) with 4 dimensions. These tools will help individuals, groups and organizations determine where they are within the evolutionary and involutionary journey of personal and organizational integration.
14. Maltz, M. (2002). *The new psycho-cybernetics: The original science of self-improvement and success that has changed the lives of 30 million people*. Paramus, NJ: Prentice Hall.
15. Research into EQ Assessments is still relatively new. EQ Map by Q Metrics <**www.qmetricseq.com**>; ECI by Goleman and Boyatzis can be found at <**ei.haygroup.com**> and Bar-on EQ-I at <**www.learninnng2lead.net**> are emerging instruments.
16. Dalton, M. (1999). *The learning tactics inventory*. San Francisco, CA: Jossey Bass and the Center for Creative Leadership.
17. Bodhidharma was the first missionary to bring Buddhism to China in the 6th Century AD. As found in: Pine, R. (1987). *The Zen teachings of Bodhidharma*. New York, NY: North Point Press. Bodhidharma said: "Only one person in a million becomes enlightened without...help." "Bodhidharma (6th century), semi legendary Indian Buddhist monk, 28th in the line of transmission from the disciple Kasyapa (a student of the Buddha) and the founder of the Zen school of Buddhism. He is said to have come from somewhere near Madras, India. In 520 he traveled to Guangzhou, China, and then went to a monastery near Luoyang in eastern China where his teachings emphasized meditation. His actual role in the emergence of Zen is obscure, but legends abound of his spiritual determination. Bodhidharma is credited with being the founder of Shao-lin boxing. In Japan, where he is called Daruma, he is considered the protector of households, political campaigns, and businesses." *Encarta Desk Encyclopedia* (1998).

18. **Seven Elements correlated with three Wisdom & Mystic Traditions:** The seven elements of becoming an integrative leader is a journey that is evident and resonant within many of the world's wisdom and mystic traditions. We will examine briefly three paths: Tibetan Tantra Buddhism, The Path of Israel and the Path of Yoga (Patanjali's Eight Limbs of Yoga). **The Buddhist Path of Tibetan Tantra**: (Principle source: Powers, J. (1995). *Introduction to Tibetan Buddhism*. Ithaca, NY: Snow Lion Productions. pp. 219–282, 424.). "The term *tantra* refers to the systems of practice and meditation derived from esoteric texts emphasizing cognitive transformation through visualization, symbols and ritual." Powers overview is based principally from the Gelupka School, but is also applicable to Sakya, Nyingma and Kagyu Schools of Tibetan Buddhism. "Tantra is viewed as the supreme of all Buddhist teachings and the shortest and most effective path to Buddhahood. Tantra emphasizes the path of the Bodhisattva (an enlightened teacher who chooses to remain among the people to help show them the way), which leads to the supreme goal of Buddhahood and the central importance of compassion (emotional intelligence) and wisdom (mental intelligence), which is the primary motivation for pursuing enlightenment." According to Lama Thubeten Yeshe, enlightenment is a path of transformation from "an ordinary, limited and deluded person trapped within the shell of petty ego (body-mind, mechanistic) into a fully evolved, totally conscious being of unlimited compassion and insight (soul-mind, wholistic)." Whereas on the classical Mahayana path it can take eons of time to be freed from mechanistic illusion, adherents of the tantra path claim that those practicing 'highest yoga tantra' can become Buddhas (or their Ideal) in as little as one human lifetime. The Dalai Lama further suggests "one must in the end engage in tantra in order to become a Buddha." It seems that all roads and all schools of Tibetan Buddhism eventually lead to the tantra path (walking the path of integration). The tantra path is for individuals who have "greater compassion and intelligence" than the more common adherents of the sutra path. Those walking the tantra path are individuals who are *altruistic* and have a pure desire sourced from the heart to embody the perfect union of "method (practices) and wisdom (truth)" in service to others. The four paths of tantra are Action Tantra (ritual action), Performance Tantra (concentration, ritual action), Yoga Tantra (visualization, concentration, ritual action) and Highest Tantra Yoga (intention, concentration, visualization, sacred action), which correspond to the four domains of intelligence. Those following the tantra path do not deny desires, wants and needs, but merely redirect these energies

(winds) towards becoming their Ideal or Image of God, which in the Tibetan Buddhist tradition, is to become Buddha-like. The traditional method of teaching is a guru-disciple or teacher-student relationship. The guru or teacher helps the student successfully reach the highest levels of realization by guiding the student around pitfalls, warning them of danger, and correcting their errors. In this way, the teacher skillfully helps their students to actualize (not just realize) their Buddhahood. The lineage of the guru (source of teachings) is very important as a guarantee of the authenticity of the teachings. Tibetan Buddhism is a traditional system. Teachers and Leaders are revered, not necessarily for their innovations, but how closely they approximate the ideals of their respective traditions. Therefore, faith in the guru, regardless of the character or faults that may be displayed, becomes important in the path of tantra. The preliminary tantric practices are: deciding to take refuge which means refuge in associations (Samgha), refuge in truth (Dharma) or refuge in spiritual awareness (Buddha nature) that is motivated by fear, faith or compassion; prostration which is learning humility and admitting that one does not truly know; special meditation where one visualizes light entering the top of the crown of the head and downward immersing the whole body in light; Mandela offerings where the student sees, inwardly and outwardly, the unity in the inner circle, square, and outer circle that awakens and embodies the phrase "I in you and you in me"; guru yoga where one seeks and is taken in by a guru or teacher. The formalization of the guru teacher relationship is by initiation on the path through four rituals: vase, secret, knowledge and word. The fourteen vows (their opposites would be the downfalls of the path of tantra) are: 1. Honor the guru; 2. Support the teachings of the guru and the Buddha that informs them; 3. Cooperate in peace and harmony with other followers of the path; 4. Work for the benefit of all sentient beings without exception; 5. Practice celibacy from earthly intercourse; 6. Support the paths of other systems of thought (other religions, philosophies, paths); 7. Keep honored and secret the path of tantra ('don't feed pearls of wisdom to those who are ignorant of the path'); 8. Honor the five aggregates that make up our psycho-physical-perceiving natures; 9. Have Faith that following the path of tantra will lead to the desired goal; 10. Act creatively, constructively and positively when a potentially disastrous situation is seen from whatever level of awareness; 11. Maintain balance in all perceptions and viewpoints (not advocating or adopting extremes); 12. Teach others who have a heart and soul desire to know the path the way of the path of tantra; 13. Willingly participate in all levels of life, learning and love; 14. Honor the spirit of light, love, life and law in all beings (especially women). An **Integrative Perspective on the Path of Tantra:** The tantra path is about becoming your Ideal (Buddha) and not merely studying, observing and analyzing the traits, characteristics and behaviors of your Ideal. The path of tantra engages the four domains of intelligence and three levels of awareness by aligning need, desire, choice and volitional intention. Formulating an Ideal (in tantra, this is known as Deity Yoga where one visualizes and imagines oneself as the Ideal of the Buddha) is to imagine, feel, think of yourself as the Ideal and then to act like it in the moment. It is motivated by a desire to help all sentient beings to also be free from bondage and illusion and become awakened and enlightened (as one of us gets better through our help and support so do we and so do we all…). The path of integration is embodied by aligning our compassion (emotional intelligence) and wisdom (mental intelligence) with an altruistic intent (spiritual intelligence), and then acting like it in the moment (physical intelligence). Through ritual and sacred actions (right action), concentration (right thought), visualization (right image and desire) one can realized their intention of becoming the best for oneself, others and the world as an Integrative Leader (or Bodhisattva) that can teach others the do's and don'ts of the path. Integrative Leadership is the perfect union of the male and female principles within and outside of us, not in the earth as a sexually motivated act, but rather as a spiritually motivated act within our life and work as everyday spirituality. Your relations and associations are important on your personal process of integration (Samgha), which will either help or thwart your walk along the path. **The Path of Israel:** (Principal Source: The New Jerusalem Bible.) The children of Israel (sometimes referred to as the children of light) trace their history to Adam and Eve (the primordial earthly parents evident within many wisdom traditions but called different names). Much later, after the destruction of the world by flood and the saving of a select few (Noah and the Ark), the story of Abraham and his wife Sarah, the earthly father and mother of Israel, begins. Abraham, against all odds given his and Sarah's age and barrenness, gave birth to Isaac (Hebrew tradition) and Ishmael (Arabic tradition). Ishmael went on to give birth to all of the Arabic race whereas Isaac's son Jacob then gave birth to twelve sons, one of whom, Joseph, becomes the second most powerful person in Egypt, next to the Pharaoh. During a time of famine in the lands of Egypt and surrounding area, Jacob and his family come to stay with Joseph. In time, their descendents are slowly enslaved by the Egyptians for nearly 400 years. In enslavement of the children of Israel, Moses is born, is miraculously saved from the Pharaoh's decree that all the male children of the Hebrews should be slain, is picked up from the waters of the Nile by a Princess of the Egyptian Court, grows up as an Egyptian Prince, becomes aware of his heritage at about the same time as the Egyptians do, is banished to wander in the desert for 40 days and nights, ends up in the lands of Midean, marries and becomes a Shepherd in service to the Sheik of Midean. Later, Moses climbs the Holy Mountain of God (Mount Sinai), hears the voice of God and is called into service to free the children of Israel from Egyptian bondage. Through a series of miracles (10 plagues, Cyclone of Fire, parting of the Red Sea, manna from heaven) he manages to free them, feed them, and lead them through the desert to the Mountain of God (Mount Sinai). Moses climbs the mountain again while Joshua stands guard at the base of the mountain, and apprehends the Ten Commandments (God had to give His commandments to Moses twice...), which God strongly suggests, through Moses, should be used as a guide for the children of Israel for their life on earth and for their collective journey towards the Promised Land (heaven on earth). These Ten Commandments are the basis and inform the ethical, moral and legal systems of much of the western world. The Ten Commandments are (the order varies depending on Hebrew or Christian perspectives): 1. I am the Lord your God. You shall have no other gods before me; 2. Don't use God's name in vain; 3. Keep the Sabbath day holy; 4. Honor your mother and father; 5. Don't kill; 6. Don't commit adultery; 7. Don't steal; 8. Don't bear false witness (lie); 9. Don't covet your neighbor's property (greed); 10. Don't covet your neighbor's wife (lust). However, many of the children of Israel could not clearly understand how to apply these ten principles in everyday life. To help them, Moses appointed judges and counselors over the people to help their interpretations. In this way, rules and regulations were created to guide the children of Israel on how to live by the ten commandments in their normal everyday life. Today there are thousands of rules, regulations and man-made laws governing how humankind must live these ten ethical and moral principles (whether Jewish, Christian, Muslim). **Integrative Perspective on the Path of Israel:** If we examine the historical story as an allegorical and metaphorical story of the children of Israel, then their micro-journey can shed light on the macro-journey of the soul of humankind. The transformative process would be ignorance in bondage, awakening, chaos, death, releasing the old, visioning the new, and ascending to a new level of awareness. The primordial awakening is first in Abraham, his connection with God so great that when God orders him to kill his only son, Isaac, Abraham is willing to do it. For his faith and obedience, God fulfills the promise to Abraham to make his descendents as numerous on the earth as the grains of sand are on a beach. Later, the awakened will as Abraham, falls asleep over time to eventually find itself enslaved in an unfamiliar and foreign land (the many gods of Egypt). Then Moses is born as a sleeping infant that, in time, awakens first to personal will (as the Prince of Egypt) and then to Higher Will (as Moses the Deliverer and Lawgiver). A part of our nature apprehends the Universal Laws from Level III awareness (God) and then comprehends through Level II awareness (Moses), finally reaching its final descent as communication to our Level I awareness (people). The one law that is stated "I am the Lord your God" and "Know O Israel the Lord thy God is One" was first given as the ten ethical and moral principles to Moses, then later as the many rules and regulations through their teachers, lawyers and judges, to the children of Israel. Whenever personal will awakens, it is first seen as *negation*, then *negotiation* and finally *affirmation*. The Ten Commandments, if examined, contain three affirming and seven negating ethical and moral principles that could be characterized as the *don'ts* of the path. For 2,500 years, we, as a civilization and a society, have been negotiating with these ten ethical principles to understand what they mean for our and others' lives. For example, the commandment not to kill does not seem to apply to plants, insects, fish, animals or various categories of humans in the world, for when one nation is at war with another, when military or police are sanctioned to use lethal force against an aggressor, or when our judicial system condemns a criminal to death, we use this principle as a *variable* (situational) rather than a more permanent *value* or eternal *Virtue.* Today, in the coming Age of Integration, we are moving from nearly 2,500 years of negotiation towards affirmation of these same ten principles. In this way, our third millennial transition would suggest rewording the ten original Mosaic commandments from being *don'ts of the path* into *do's of the path*. One suggested rewording of the ten commandments are as follows: 1. There is and ever will be, only One Spirit, One Mind, One Family of God, and we are all children of that One Source; 2. Use the power of choice, voice and creation only for Good; 3. Keep every moment of every day holy by living in the present sacred moment; 4. Honor all those who choose to do the will of God (Higher Will) above others' (sleeping will) or their own (personal will); 5. Give the *spirit of life* to all things and all people (do no harm); 6. Have spiritual, physical, mental and emotional communion with the Divine daily; 7. Give the best of who you are to others: For it is better to give than to receive and one can only keep that which one freely gives away; 8. Tell the truth to all people, at all times and under all circumstances as best you are able; 9. Bear witness to the spirit of generosity with your life and leadership; 10. Be generous to all whom you meet for as you do it to others, it will also be done to you. **The Path of Yoga:** (Iyengar, B.K.S. (1966, 2001). *Light on Yoga.* London, UK: Thorsons). Yoga, which is Sanskrit for union, is one of the six classic systems of Hindu philosophy, which suggests that through the practice of certain disciplines, one may achieve liberation from the limitations of flesh, the delusions of our senses, and the pitfalls of thought, and attain a perfect union with the object of knowledge (God). It is ultimate knowledge (wisdom, truth) and not feats of asceticism, clairvoyance or the working of miracles, that is the ultimate goal of all yoga practices. Yoga doctrine insists that physical, mental and emotional training is to be used only as a means to a spiritual end, which is defined as union with the Divine and All That Is (Atman and Brahman becoming One). Those who practice Yoga are called Yogi's (male) or Yogini's (female). Yoga is thought to be over 5,000 years old with the first philosophical foundation for Yoga built in the second century BC by Patanjali in his *Yoga Sutra*'s. Patanjali divided the practice of Yoga into eight steps, stages or limbs that would move the student, initiate or adept of Yoga towards freedom, liberation, enlightenment and Mastery. The eight limbs of Yoga are: self control (yama, inner observances: non-violence, truth, non-stealing, continence [celibacy, religious study, self-restraint], non-coveting), outer observances (niyama: purity, contentment, austerity, study of the True Self, dedication to the Lord), postures (asana), regulation of the breath (pranayama), restraint of the sense (pratyahara), steadying of the mind (dharana), meditation (dhyana), and profound contemplation (Samadhi). Achieving Samadhi liberates the True Self from the illusions of sense and the contradictions of reason, leading to an inner illumination. Time is required, perhaps several lifetimes, to achieve liberation and self-realization from the world of phenomena, thoughts of self and the spirit's entanglement with matter. Those who travel this path are said to achieve remarkable capacities: insensitivity to heat or cold, injury, temporal pleasure or pain; almost supernatural mental and physical capabilities; and the ability to distinguish and name the subtlest elements of matter, thought and energy. **Integrative Perspectives on the Path of Yoga:** There are seven schools of Yoga, many of which can be correlated to the four domains of intelligence:

Hatha or Karma Yoga (physical intelligence), Jnana and Mantra Yoga (mental intelligence), Bahkti or Devotional Yoga (emotional intelligence) and Raya or Raja Yoga (spiritual intelligence). In addition, the three levels of awareness can be related to Tamasic (mechanistic), Rajasic (organic) and Satvic (wholistic). The ITT practices include the key elements of the eight limbs of Yoga which are designed to move our awareness in an evolutionary path from the asanas to Samadhi. In the involutionary process of integration that we call Christian Union, our awareness would also move from Samadhi or deep contemplation and descend towards embodiment of the Ideal Christ-like behaviors in the world. In this way, the path of Yoga and the path of Christian Union, through integration, can become one.

Chapter 6

1. McArthur, B. (1993). *Your life: Why it is the way it is and what you can do about it. Understanding the universal laws*. Virginia Beach, VA: ARE Press.
2. **Science & Mathematics:** Mathematics is considered the science of relations. It is a science that draws necessary conclusions using symbolic logic that is viewed as an exact theory of logic. Mathematics was first historically developed 4,000 years ago in Babylonia and Egypt where it was used for arithmetic, measurement and geometry. Some 2,500 years ago, the ancient Greeks (Thales, Pythagoras, Euclid) built on the Babylonians' and Egyptians' mathematical works by developing logical structures, definitions, axioms and proofs. For much of the first millennium, the Hindu's ruled and advanced our knowledge of mathematics, giving way to Islamic mathematicians around 900 AD. The Islamic mathematicians extended the Hindu decimal system to include decimal fractions, square and cube roots of numbers, algebraic polynomials, plane and spherical geometry and numbers theory. In 1500 AD, Western Europeans first began to emerge as mathematicians, rising to new mathematical heights by the 17th and 18th Centuries with the addition of logarithms (Napier), number theory (Fermant), analytic geometry (Descartes), probability theory (Pascal) and the crowning achievement of mathematical theory of the Age of Enlightenment, differential and integral calculus (Newton). Since that time, spurred by the development of digital computer technology in the second half of the 20th Century, humankind has seen the greatest mathematical advances in recorded

history. Here is Leonardo da Vinci's perspective on science and mathematics and William James's perspective on mathematics and the Ideal: "...for no human inquiry can be called science unless it pursues its path through mathematical exposition and demonstration." Leonardo da Vinci (1452–1519). "The union of the mathematician with the poet, fervor with measure, passion with correctness, this is surely the Ideal." William James.

3. Bushe, G. (2000). *Clear leadership. How outstanding leaders make themselves understood, cut through the mush and help everyone get real at work*. Palo Alto, CA: Davies-Black Publishing.
4. Moses, J. (2002). *Oneness: Great principles shared by all religions*. New York, NY: Ballantine.
5. Hatala, R. (2003). The universal principles and practices of walking the path of integrative leadership. Unpublished paper. Calgary, AB: Integrative Leadership Institute.
6. Hatala, R. (2003). Virtue and value-centered approaches to integrative life and leadership. Unpublished paper. Calgary, AB: Integrative Leadership Institute.
7. Mendeleyev, D. (1869). Discovery of the Periodic Law of the Elements that led to development of the Periodic Table containing over 100 elements today. "As a result of discoveries in atomic theory, scientists in the early 19th century could determine the relative weights of atoms of elements. In 1864 British chemist John A.R. Newlands listed the elements according to increasing atomic weights and noted that some properties recur at every eighth place, but his discovery of periodicity went unnoticed. The periodic law was developed independently by Russian chemist Dmitry Mendeleyev in 1869 and German chemist Julius Lothar Meyer in 1870. Each realized that some elements were not yet discovered, and that vacant places must be left in any classification. Later, elements were discovered that fit into these vacant slots, confirming the periodic law. Since its original formulation, the periodic law has been extended to a family of elements, the noble gases, that were unknown until the 1890s. The law has also been interpreted in terms of the Bohr theory (1913) of the structure of the atom." (*Encarta*: 2001)
8. Holmes, E. (1938). *The science of mind*. New York, NY: Dodd, Mead & Company.
9. Walker, B. (1992). *Hua hu ching: The unknown teachings of Lao Tzu*. New York, NY: Harper Collins Publishers. Lao Tzu regarding being mirrors for one another: "When one gives whatever one can without restraint, the barriers of individuality break down. It no longer becomes possible to tell whether it is the student

offering himself to the teacher, or the teacher offering herself to the student. One sees only two immaculate beings, reflecting one another like a pair of brilliant mirrors." (Walker, 1992, axiom 73).

10. Allan, J.R. (2001). *As a man thinketh.* London, UK: Executive Books. This is a classic inspired by the Scriptural quotation on the power of thought where 'we become what we think about.' From Allan: "All that a man achieves and all that he fails to achieve is a direct result of his own thoughts." Although his book, *As A Man Thinketh*, has inspired millions around the world and been a major influence in the self-improvement industry, very little is known about its author, James R. Allen. He was born in Leicester, England in 1864 and worked as a personal secretary for an executive of a large English corporation until 1902. At the age of 38 he 'retired' to writing and moved with his wife to a small cottage at Ilfracombe, England. He penned more than 20 works before suddenly passing away at the age of 48. *As A Man Thinketh* has influenced many contemporary writers including Norman Vincent Peale, Earl Nightingale, Denis Waitley and Tony Robbins, among others. His 'little volume,' as he called it, has been translated into five major languages, inspiring millions of readers to recognize that man's visions can become reality, simply through the power of thought. This book is also available as a free download from <**http://www.asamanthinketh. net**>

Chapter 7

1. Moody, R.A. (1975). *Life after life.* New York, NY: Bantam.
2. Moody, R.A. (2001). *Life after life: The investigation of a phenomenon — survival of bodily death. (2nd Edn.)* San Francisco, CA: Harper.
3. Ring, K. (1985). *Heading toward omega: In search of the meaning of the near death experience.* New York, NY: William Morrow. What is important from our perspective is that the stages of the typical or characteristic Near Death Experience or NDE are similar to the stages that we have experienced in walking the path of Integrative life and leadership. The NDE is considered non-pathological by the DBM-IV because of the positive affects on the person experiencing the NDE. Survivors usually return with a positive attitude, value changes, personality transformation, spiritual development and a new appreciation for life. This extract from Ring, pages 15–58: "The typical near-death survivor emerges from his

experience with a heightened sense of appreciation for life, determined to live life to the fullest. He has a sense of being reborn and a renewed sense of individual purpose in living.... He is more reflective and seeks to learn more about this core experience. He feels himself to be a stronger, more self-confident person and adjusts more easily to the vicissitudes of life. The things that he values are love and service to others; material comforts are no longer so important. He becomes more compassionate toward others, more able to accept them unconditionally. He has achieved a sense of what is important in life and strives to live in accordance with his understanding of what matters."

4. The statistics on NDE's can be found at the following website: <**http://www.virtualcs.com/blackboard/lessons/types/ndetype.htm**>
5. Moxley, R. (2000). *Leadership and spirit: Breathing new vitality and energy into individuals and organizations*. San Francisco, CA: Jossey-Bass.
6. Goleman, D., Boyatzis, R., & McKee, A. (2002). *Primal leadership: Realizing the power of emotional intelligence*. Watertown, MA: Harvard Business School Publishing Corporation.
7. Goleman, D. (2000). Leadership that gets results. *Harvard Business Review 78*(2):78–79. Watertown, MA: Harvard Business School Publishing Corporation.
8. Collins, J. (2001). *Good to great: Why some companies make the leap...and others don't*. New York, NY: HarperCollins Publishers Inc. *Article*: Maney, K. (2004). True believers ignite super sales rate for *Good to Great. USA Today*, May 18, Section B: 1–2. "Good is the enemy of Great" is the opening line of Jim Collins' book, *Good to Great*, that at first appears to be about business but turns out to be about much more. With 1.5 million copies sold since publication in September 2001, it has already exceeded sales of Tom Peter's *In Search of Excellence* (1982, Sales: 1.4 million copies). *Good to Great* is based on five years of research by Collins and 20 business students (that he affectionately calls his 'chimps') where they investigated 1435 companies on the Fortune 500 list of companies from 1965 to 1995. They found in their research 11 companies had decent results for years and then shot skyward — showing sustained great results. The secret of this sustained great performance and general applicability is, in Collins' words: "Our work is about greatness and the difference between great and good. We used a wonderful data set called 'companies' to try to get at these principles", but they are applicable in personal as well as organizational life. The seven step process that Collins identified as the way to move from good (organic) to great (wholistic) is as follows: 1. Install a Level 5 Leader as moral and positional head of the

organization; 2. First ask who should be in subsequent organizational positions of leadership, then what they should do; 3. Confront the brutal facts, yet never lose faith; 4. Figure out the one thing the organization does best (hedgehog concept) and then do it; 5. Create a culture of discipline; because great organizations build strong cultures that guide every member's actions; 6. Add technology accelerators that support the vision of the organization; 7. The flywheel: keep pushing the organization in the same direction, building momentum with every action and decision. The seven step process is dependent on one singular factor, and that is installing Level 5 Leaders who have the organization's interests above their own. Collins admits he does not know the peculiar set of life circumstances and life changing events that create Level 5 Leaders. All he knows is that they are necessary for sustained success to occur in these 11 organizations. The process of integration is a method to create Level 5 and Level 6 Integrative Leaders. We would suggest that Collins' seven steps could be expanded and rephrased as follows using the Integrative life and leadership Framework: 1. 'First to the individual, then to the organization.' Level 5 and 6 Leaders arise from individuals who consciously choose to walk the path of integration. Once they are in the self-generating phase of the process of integration, install them as the moral and positional heads of companies that desire to move from good to great; (wholistic paradigm); 2. First who, putting people first into positions of influence (organic paradigm); 3. And then determine what (mechanistic paradigm); 4. Tell the truth (confront the brutal facts of the situation); 5. While keeping the faith; (in the vision, principles, purpose of the organization). 6. Look for the good: Find what you do well; talents, skills, abilities, products and then choose to do more of it; 7. Cultivate a culture of discipline where you keep your word and do what you say you will do, impeccably; 8. Determine who or what you will serve. All else, whether technology, ideas, feelings, actions become servants to that Ideal Spirit, Vision or Mission; 9. Overcome past habits and inertia by continuing to experiment and move towards your Ideal: 10. Pay Attention to 'life as your teacher' and be willing to change your reactions to responses in order to align with your personal and organizational Ideal; 11. Attune to and embody your Ideal-Vision daily; 12. Reflect and integrate your life experiences and events within an awakening and growing heart. This 12 step process of personal and organizational integration cannot occur without an Integrative Leader. That is why we continue to suggest that any meaningful change must 'first occur to the individual'.

9. Covey, S.R. (1989). *The seven habits of highly effective people.* New York, NY: Fireside. With over 14 million copies sold worldwide and translated into over thirty languages, this is a very influential work. The *Seven Habits* were sourced from a review of literary sources on the topic of success which were published between 1760 to 1960 and distilled by Covey into the Seven Habits. The first three habits have to do with personal independence and are: 1. Be Proactive; 2. Begin with the End in Mind; 3. Put First Things First. The second three habits deal with interdependence while in relationship with others and are: 4. Think Win-Win; 5. Seek First to Understand, Then to be Understood; 6. Synergize (Higher Order Thinking). The seventh habit was 'Sharpen the Saw' which meant to balance and nurture the four domains of intelligence: physically, mentally, emotionally, and spiritually. Habit 5, 'Seek first to understand...' is originally sourced from the Prayer of St. Francis written 800 years ago that begins: "Lord make me an instrument of your peace..." This suggests the mystics, like St. Francis of Assisi, understood the principles of success and effectiveness a very long time ago and we are just rediscovering them in our day. It is interesting to note that Covey chose Seven Habits, which have a coincidental relationship with the seven levels of consciousness found in the Eastern and Western Wisdom traditions. Within our Integrative Framework, Habits 1, 2, 3 resonate with Level I awareness or the Mechanistic paradigm. Habits 4, 5 resonate with Level II awareness or the Organic paradigm. Habits 6, 7 resonate with the Wholistic paradigm. Regarding the Eight Universal Laws, Habits 1 and 3 resonate with the Law of Creativity; Habit 2 with the Law of Cause and Effect; Habits 4 and 5 with the Law of Harmony; and Habits 6 and 7 with the Law of Will-Desire. The transition between transaction and transformation occurs with Habit 2, 'Begin with the end in mind.' The transition between latter transformation and initial transcendence occurs with applying Habit 6, 'Synergize' and Habit 7, 'Sharpen the Saw'. After 15 years where 7 habits seemed sufficient, Stephen Covey is releasing in November 2004, his new book called, *The 8th Habit. The 8th Habit* is about developing a new habit, a new paradigm and a new skill set that he feels will be required for the coming age of wisdom. He describes it as moving from effectiveness to greatness and it involves "finding your voice and inspiring others to find theirs". This will allow individuals to lead a more balanced, integrated and powerful life. In the Integrative Framework, Covey's *8th Habit* resonates with the Fifth universal principles of will/desire and is fundamentally organic in nature and transformative, not transcendent, regarding change.

10. Covey, S.R. (2002). *Four roles of leadership*. [seminar] Calgary, AB: University of Calgary. As we shared in the footnotes to Table 6, Chapter 4, we would attribute Covey's four roles of leadership of Modeling, Aligning, Empowering and Pathfinding differently in relationship to the four domains of intelligence.
11. Covey, S.R. (1992). *Principle-centered leadership*. New York, NY: Fireside.
12. Kouzes, J.M., & Posner, B.Z. (2002). *The leadership challenge: How to keep getting extraordinary things done in organizations*. San Francisco, CA: Jossey-Bass.
13. Hatala, R. (2002). Comparison of various leadership models to integrative leadership. Unpublished paper. Calgary, AB: Integrative Leadership Institute.
14. Cashman, K.(1998). *Leadership from the inside out*. Minneapolis, MN: TCLG Publishing.
15. We suggest that *Ideally*, Integrative Leadership is a process that can begin from the top down starting with the Executive and then cascading to others within the organization. However, we have been both participants in and witnesses to situations where an individual or group within a mechanistic organization can awaken the Organic paradigm beginning from the bottom or middle. Integrative Leadership is not about position, but rather about intention, attitude, moral authority and belief. That is why we suggest that meaningful change first happens to the individual, then group, then organization. Pilot programs are just as effective in one segment of an organization as an individual applying behavioral change in one segment of their personality wheel. Covey describes this process in "Living the Seven Habits" where 80 people transformed an entire organization from the bottom up.
16. This principle is reflected in many wisdom traditions as: 'only one small lighted candle is needed to illuminate a very large darkened room ' (Buddhism); 'only ten honest men can save an entire city full of sinners (darkness) (Old Testament: Sodom & Gomorrah); 'only one enlightened soul is needed to awaken many sleeping souls' (Hinduism). In the mystic traditions we have also seen it phrased, 'only a little leaven is needed to leaven the whole lump'. Dr. David Hawkins *(Power vs Force)* also views this as correct suggesting that one individual at 500 level on his map of consciousness can awaken and illuminate thousands of people who are at 200 level consciousness.

Chapter 8

1. Bushe, G. (2001). *Clear leadership*. Palo Alto, CA: Davies Black Publishing. Clear perception and an integral communication model that engages the four domains of intelligence to eliminate interpersonal and corporate 'mush'.
2. Gunther, M. (2001). God and business. *Fortune*, 144(1): 58–70. *Article synopsis*: "Bringing spirituality into the workplace violates the old idea that faith and fortune don't mix. But a groundswell of believers is breaching the last taboo of corporate America." *Article excerpt*: Many executives that are acting as a vanguard of a diverse counter-culture bubbling up all over corporate America who want to bridge the traditional divide between spirituality and work. Highlights from the article are: 1. A conference at the business School of Santa Clara University, a Jesuit institution in Silicon Valley, begins with the chime of a Tibetan bowl, a reading from the Sufi mystic Rumi, and a few moments of silent meditation. Executives, academics and theologians discuss such topics as how to find one's true calling. "There are two things I thought I'd never see in my life," says Andre DelBecq, a management professor and organizer of the event, "the fall of the Russian Empire and God being spoken about at a business school." 2. The spiritual revival in America is indicated in various polls "that suggest 95% of Americans say they believe in God; in much of Western Europe, the figure is closer to 50%." 3. "When the Gallup Poll asked Americans in 1999 if they felt a need to experience spiritual growth, 78% said yes, up from 20% in 1994; nearly half said they'd had occasion to talk about their faith in the workplace in the last 24 hours." 4. "'Spirituality in the workplace is exploding,' declares Laura Nash, a senior research fellow at Harvard Business School who has followed the topic for a decade." 5. "Now more and more people are willing to talk about bringing faith to work, but are choosing their words carefully. To avoid tripping over dogma, they speak of 'spirituality' and 'meaning' not of religion and God. And with good reason: One survey of executives found that more than 60% had positive feelings about spirituality and a negative view of religion."
3. **Force for Change:** In their 2001 work, *The cultural creatives*, (New York, NY: Three Rivers Press), Anderson and Ray report that 24% of the American population or 50 million people represent a force for change in this time of transition. As a group, The Cultural Creatives believe in the interconnectedness of life, humanity, human potential and ecology among other characteristics and qualities. We, as do Anderson and Ray, see them as a force for transforming the Mechanistic to the

fully Organic paradigm. The Cultural Creatives are one source that can help build a firm foundation for the coming Age of Integration and Wisdom.

4. **Cynicism and Optimism:** The prevailing cynicism is why we feel it is important that work such as Seligman's 2003 *Positive psychology and authentic happiness* (New York NY: Free Press) that advocate a positive, hopeful, optimistic view (which can be learned) of life and leadership is important in this time of transition. During his tenure as President of the American Psychological Association, Seligman was motivated to found Positive Psychology by examining his own field of endeavor: "What he discovered was shocking, with broad implications. From 1970 to 2000 there were 45,000 studies conducted on depression, psychosis and other forms of mental illness. During that time a mere 300 studies on topics related to human joy, mental health and well-being. Seligman had not expected to find such a focus on illness in the research and he concluded that the field of psychology had veered far from its original goals — to identify what is best in humans — to heal the sick and help people live better, happier lives." In his successful leadership coaching practice, Kevin Cashman found that focusing on improving leaders' weaknesses produced small returns compared to identifying their strengths and alignments and building on them. The difference between these two approaches in adding value to them and their organization was as much as a factor of ten times improvement. David Cooperrider's *Appreciative Inquiry* approach influences organizations to "fan what is good in an organization" and not focus an organization's attention and critical thinking on what is wrong. This body of knowledge, which is fifteen years old, is having success in transforming organizations from the Mechanistic to the Organic paradigms. In the wisdom and mystic traditions, this ancient principle was stated as: 'when one focuses on the light, the shadows fall far behind. So face the light.' The Integrative life and leadership principle that captures all these approaches to personal and organizational life and leadership is 'Look for the Good'.
5. **Two Creation Stories:** In the Bible, there are two creation stories. The first creation story (Genesis 1:26–31) suggests that Adam and Eve were created in God's Image (*Image of God*) and were the crown of creation. Later, (Genesis 2:7–9), Adam was made out of the dust of the earth and was a caretaker of the Garden of Eden. Afterwards, when Adam was lonely, God made from his side (rib) his companion Eve. The first creation story is thought to be in the heavens as Souls. The second creation story is thought to be on the earth as man and woman.

6. Campbell, J. (1987). *The power of myth*. PBS Documentary.
7. **A Place Called Heaven:** The Heavens are sometimes what we term the sky with its sun, moon and stars, comets and galaxies. In Christianity 'Heaven' is defined as the home of God, angels, spiritual beings, celestial powers, redeemed souls, holy men and women and the communion of saints. It is also defined as an "eternal state of communion or everlasting bliss" in relationship with God. In Islam, it is unrestricted and inexhaustible joy resonant with the physical senses. In Buddhism, heaven is called *Nirvana* where one realizes the extinction of all desires and experiences union with the Creator achieved through successive transmigrations. In Greek Mythology, heaven was a place on Mount Olympus (highest point of Greece) where Zeus, the King of the Greek Gods, had his throne. Zeus or the Roman equivalent, Jupiter, was probably the origin of the Image of God as an old man with a white beard who is sitting on a throne in heaven. This image was later used by Michelangelo in his famous painting of the ceiling of the Sistine Chapel in the 16th Century AD. In Norse mythology, heaven was called *Asgard* where Odin, the King of the Norse Gods who was another bearded white haired old man, made his home. Heaven would be most closely associated with Level III awareness or the highest level of the Wholistic paradigm within our Integrative Philosophy.
8. **Enlightened Souls who have returned** in service to humankind to help awaken them to their True Self is evident within all the wisdom and mystic traditions. In Islamic tradition, the Sufi Mystics such as Kabir, Rumi, Hafiz are examples of Enlightened Souls who through their poetry and life attempted to awaken us to the reality of Level III awareness and unify the separations within religions within Level I awareness by living in their hearts. In Buddhism, Enlightened ones are called Bodhisattvas, of which in Tibetan Buddhism, today's 14th Dalai Lama is a representation. In Hinduism, they would be called reincarnations of Rama or Krishna that came from Brahma to show us that our Atman and Brahman can become one. These souls are sometimes termed Mahatmas (great soul), as Gandhi was called in his time by his people in India, or Saints. The doctrine and dogma of Christianity established in the Council of Nicea in the 4th Century AD eliminated the idea of reincarnation in favor of the doctrine of resurrection. The Church however, does acknowledge that the Holy Spirit and the Mind of Christ can be methods of connecting to the Divine Spirit and Mind of God as embodied by His Son, Jesus. St. Paul in Scripture suggested that we should 'put on the mind of the Christ' so that we could be more like him. Thomas Kempis espoused

this view in his 'Imitation of Christ'. St. Francis of Assisi walked in the footsteps of the Lord by connecting to the Spirit and Mind of Jesus Christ and founded the Franciscans. St. Francis Xavier, whose body still lies uncorrupt in Goa, India, over 500 years after his death, did this for the Jesuits. Mother Theresa would be a modern day example of a living saint and a great soul who has come to show us the way back to relationship with the true Image of God through her selfless service to humanity regardless of race, color or creed.

9. **Holy Trinity:** These three images of *God as Father*, *God as Mind* and *God as Spirit* are seen as the Holy Trinity of Father, Son and Holy Spirit in the Christian traditions. God as Father is associated with the Laws of Life, Creativity and Cause and Effect and the virtues of justice, temperance and courage. God as Mind is associated with the Law of Harmony and the virtues of peace, harmony and faith that is seen as one who has a pure or Sacred heart. God as Spirit is associated with the Laws of Will, Truth, Love and Oneness and the virtues of determination, wisdom, love and unity and is embodied as someone who is wise, truthful and compassionate. The sequence of events according to involutionary theory was that Spirit moved first, then the Mind, then the Body. The First Cause is then in Spirit. The Pattern is in the Mind. And the results or effects occur in the physical or Body. For other associations to this Christian Trinity, see Table 6 in Chapter 4: Building a Model of Integrative Leadership.

10. **Virtue and Vice:** Aristotle divided morality or the search for the good of human conduct as intellectual morals and emotional morals. The intellectual morals were changeless and included principles such as Wisdom and Truth. We would equate these with the sixth, seventh and eighth Universal Laws of Truth with its virtue of Wisdom, Love with its virtue of Divine Love and Oneness with its virtue of Unity. The emotional morals were seen as duality along a continuum between virtue and vice. For example, courage was one polarity with cowardice the other and our conduct lay somewhere along the continuum between these two. In a similar way, Justice would be one polarity and injustice would be the other: Temperance one pole and intemperance (lack of self-control, rage, irrational behaviors) would be the other. We found in our examinations, that this duality between truth and lies, love and hate existed from the first to the fourth law. Once personal will was surrendered to Higher Will within the fifth Law of Will-Desire, the duality was resolved into Oneness.

11. **String Theory:** The eighth note of oneness is the harmonious playing of the seven other Universal Law notes that reside within the body, mind, heart and

soul. St. Augustine and Thomas Aquinas both suggested that Moses' Ten Commandments were 'first written in men's bodies, minds and hearts before they were written on tablets of stone'. The stone tablets were simply an external reminder of what was all ready written within humankind, but lay dormant as potential without conscious activation or awareness. The metaphor of the 'Strings and Attunement' is found in Buddhism. When the first Buddha, Siddhartha Guatama, came to the realization that a string that is too loose or too tight cannot play or sound its note, he awakened and realized that the path of asceticism — the total denial of body appetites and desires — was not the way to enlightenment and neither was the path of excess indulgence. What he realized was the middle way for those desiring to walk the path of integration. In practicing the middle way, our actions, habits, beliefs, attitudes and passions are not too tight and not too loose, allowing us to experience the journey of integrating life and love without becoming a part of it or denying its existence. In this way, you can be 'in the world but not of it.' We are extending the metaphor of the 'Strings and Attunement' to include the idea of harmony between the Eight Universal Law Strings of Attunement and their associated notes in walking the path of integration. This metaphor is also resonant with Super String Theory that is a way to unify disparate forces. The four forces of gravitation, electromagnetic forces, and weak and strong nuclear forces are evident in all material interactions and are aligned and correlated to the four domains of intelligence. Can you relate intuitively which force relates with which Domain?

12. **Virtues, Values, Variables:** We can try to attune and integrate around common activities or variables in the mechanistic paradigm, common values in the organic paradigm and common virtues in the wholistic paradigm. Common activities with others that are pure self-interest are only resonant with the lower three laws or strings on our body-mind instrument and are variables. Values can begin to integrate the mechanistic personality with the organic character with the four lower laws. In the character-based organic paradigm, self-interest can be blended with common interest. In our society, we are always suspicious of which interest will prevail in our political, corporate or institutional leaders. Since 85% of our culture is currently mechanistic, then it is safe to assume that self-interest will predominate, feeding cynicism and skepticism within our society. Within the organic paradigm, we can attune and integrate the four lower laws around common values, but the question becomes, as in King Arthur's Court, Knights of the Round Table, and Parsifal's quest of the Holy Grail: 'Whom does it serve?'

The fundamental question for us all in life and leadership is then: 'Whom do you serve?' For example, you and I can work together, play together, understand one another because of common values, but we can both be either working for an International Criminal Organization or be monks within a Buddhist Monastery. The question of 'Whom do you serve?' is fundamental for moving our awareness from Value-Centered to Virtue-Centered Leadership.

13. **Attunement and Change:** The concept of retuning the notes within this metaphor means to consciously alter our perspective about life; examine and alter our beliefs about life; change our attitudes about life; and consciously and willingly transform ourselves from our Surreal to our Real Self. Balance is achieved by attempting to live and embody the Law of Harmony as "Do unto others as you would have them do unto you". In a similar way, when the fifth note that is the Law of Will-Desire is sounded in our journey and personal will and Higher Will are engaged, then its note will bring to our awareness the dissonance and misalignment of the lower four notes or laws. This allows us an opportunity to correct knowledge, understanding, beliefs and values as this engagement moves through competition, cooperation and into the final harmony that is felt as collaboration.
14. **Spiritual Centers, the Spine and Tree of Life:** The Eastern traditions view the seven spiritual centers as located in the etheric body that connects to the nervous system (brain and spinal column) in seven places: Crown (top of the head), Spiritual Eye (between the eyebrows), cervical, dorsal, lumbar, sacral and coccyx. The Kundalini is imaged as a serpent that is coiled three times at the base of the spine and is waiting to be awakened through spiritual practices that include meditation. This serpent is like an intelligent fire that seeks out our seed thoughts and desires hidden within the body and heart mind and inflames and gives them life. This is an evolutionary awakening of knowledge without wisdom and we would not advise anyone to attempt a Kundalini awakening without the guidance of a qualified teacher.
15. **Christian Union vs Eastern Yoga:** Of the Western Traditions, Christianity most graphically describes this process. The image of the Dove is first encountered at the river Jordan when Jesus asked John the Baptist to baptize him in accordance with the law. At first John was reluctant, knowing who Jesus truly was, but baptized Jesus anyway. A dove descended from heaven and anointed Jesus and a voice said: "This is my Beloved Son in whom I am well pleased. Listen to Him". Later, after the crucifixion and resurrection of Jesus, the Holy Spirit descended

on the Apostles like tongues of flame on the crown of their heads, and they began to prophecy, speak in tongues and heal. This is an involutionary awakening of wisdom, love and truth. We would encourage everyone to invite and invoke the presence of the God of their understanding into every aspect of their journey of integration from wherever they are in terms of Levels of Awareness or in the process of awakening and developing their four domains of intelligence.

16. **Eight Universal Laws:** From our Integrative Model, the Eight Universal Laws are comprised of One Law that through its descent, diffracted into Seven Universal Laws that currently form the framework for consciousness. From the perspective of the seven, the Three Upper Universal Laws are Love, Truth, Will-Desire and the fourth is Harmony. The Three Lower Universal Laws are Life, Creativity and Cause and Effect and the fourth is Harmony. Our two natures of spiritual and physical, serpent and dove, angel and devil, spirituality and materiality, join and co-mingle and attempt to blend in the heart through the Law of Harmony. The heart (subconscious mind) is also the cross and the crossroads between our physical, mental, emotional and spiritual natures. This is why it was said by Jesus that a man cannot serve two masters (body-mind or soul-mind), but needed to pick one to serve. And also said that 'as a man thinketh in his heart, so is he'. The question would be: 'Who have you chosen to serve within your integrative journey? Is it your body-mind, heart-mind or soul-mind?'
17. **Winged Serpent:** The winged serpent can be seen within many cultures and traditions. The most famous depiction is the Caduceus, which is an ancient Greek word that means herald or badge of rule. Hermes, the messenger of the Greek Gods and son of Zeus, had this symbol on his staff. It is interesting to note that it is comprised of two snakes intertwining eight times along a central shaft ending up facing each other with two angel wings behind them. In the Yogic tradition, there are three roads on which the life energy moves: *Ida* (feminine-negative), which rises; *Pingala* (masculine-positive), which falls; and the *Sushumna*, which is the energy superhighway that runs along our spine from our coccyx to our brain. This is also symbolized as the feminine and masculine energies, *Shakti* and *Shiva*, one descending and one ascending that both meet in the heart. Metaphorically the *Caduceus* is a symbol of that relationship with the spine and the Eight Universal Laws that are associated with our body-mind instrument. Hippocrates (c. 400 BC) who is known as the father of western medicine and the Hermetic symbol of the Caduceus were both adopted as symbols of our modern medical profession; one as an oath and the other as an image. The winged serpent

is also evident in the ancient Mayan culture as a symbol of *Quatzlcoatl*, the red-haired, white-skinned and tall prophet who came to unify the people under Natural Laws. The winged serpent is also seen carved on temples at Teotihuacan — site of the Pyramid of the Sun and the Moon — located about 30 kilometers north of Mexico City. The Teotihuacans, a theocracy, built a city that contained a University or School called "The City of the Gods" or the city where 'Man became God-Man'. This was suspected by some researchers to be the first North American site of the ancient School of the Prophets originally founded by Melchizadek, the High Priest of Salem and a friend of Abraham. The School of the Prophets was rebuilt and active at the time of Samuel, Elijah, Elisha and was located at Mount Carmel near Haifa, Israel. No one is sure where this School of the Prophets has gone and its whereabouts remain a mystery to this day.... Back to the winged serpent; it was known as the flying dragon of European mythology and was seen as an evil, demonic or satanic force that needed to be subdued by the will of man (St. George slaying the Dragon for example). In China, the Dragon is one of the animals of their astrological calendar and is revered, honored and paraded in the streets during many of their festivals and celebrations. What is your reaction, response or association to flying snakes versus flying doves?

18. **Heart Marriage:** The wisdom and mystic traditions encourage a practice of purifying and cleansing the heart to make it a fit place for our Image of God to come and reside. In Scripture, it is phrased 'Seek and ye shall find; knock and the door will be opened' on the one hand and 'I wait patiently at the door and knock' waiting for you to open it so that I may come in and abide with you on the other. Both perspectives and actions are necessary for the journey of integration, our evolutionary desire to seek the truth and love of the Divine and our involutionary desire that in humility invites the Divine into our life. The door that needs to be opened in either case is the door of our heart. Tantric Yoga is the force for evolution and Christian Union is the force for involution with both ending their journey in the heart. In Revelations this ideal marriage of the tree of life and the tree of love is seen as 'the Tree that has roots on both sides of a river'. The river would be the *river of life* that runs through an awakened heart and the *tree* planted with roots on both sides of the river means in heaven as the *tree of love* and in the earth as the *tree of life*.
19. **"The Peace that Passeth Understanding"** (John 14:27). Also in the Old Testament: "The wolf and the lamb shall feed together and the lion shall eat straw like the bullock." (Isiah 65:25). Also "The wolf shall dwell with the lamb, and the

leopard shall lie down with the kid; and the calf and the young lion and the fatling together." (Isiah 11:6). The leopard, lion, wolf all represent and are symbolic of the characteristics of our body-mind, human nature, Level I awareness or mechanistic paradigm. The lamb, kid, calf, fatling all represent the innocence and virtue of our soul-mind, spiritual nature, Level III awareness or wholistic paradigm. These two natures will, at some point in time, be peacefully co-existing with one another. Even though they were former enemies, they will now be friends. What is interesting is that innocence prevails over the savage aspect of our human nature, and the lion will 'eat straw with the lamb' (non-violence, peace). This union will first happen in the heart of each individual, and then later manifest within the coming Age of Wisdom, Synthesis and Integration as Peace for the soul of humankind. This time of transition is the movement between our old mechanistic paradigm and the new emerging organic paradigm.

20. **Resources for Spiritual Leadership** (partial list):
    - Baron, D., & Padwa, L. (2000). *Moses on management: 50 leadership lessons from the greatest manager of all time*. New York, NY: Pocket Books.
    - Conger, J.A., and Associates (1994). *Spirit at work: Discovering the spirituality in leadership*. San Francisco, CA: Jossey-Bass.
    - De Pree, M. (1997). *Leading without power: Finding hope in serving community.* San Francisco, CA: Jossey-Bass.
    - ———. (1989). *Leadership is an art.* NY, New York: Bantam Doubleday Dell Publishing. [A classic simple and spiritual treatment involving the art of leadership.]
    - Metcalf, F., & Gallagher-Hateley, B.J. (2001). *What would Buddha do at work? 101 answers to workplace dilemmas*. Berkley, CA: Ulysses Press.
    - Greenleaf, R. (1977). *Servant leadership: A journey into the nature of legitimate power and greatness*. New York, NY: Paulist Press. [Reprinted 1983, 1997].
    - Griffin, E. (1993). *The reflective executive: A spirituality of business and enterprise.* New York, NY: Crossroad.
    - Jones, L.B. (1995). *Jesus, CEO: Using ancient wisdom for visionary leadership.* New York, NY: Hyperion.
    - Kouzes, J., & Posner, B. (2004). *Christian reflections on the leadership challenge.* San Francisco, CA: Jossey-Bass.
    - Nouwen, H.J.M. (1989). *In the name of Jesus: Reflections on Christian leadership.* New York, NY: Crossroad.

- Palmer, P.J. (1996). Leading from within: Spirituality and leadership. *Noetic Sciences Review 40*(Winter): 32–40.
- ———. (1990). *Leading from within: Reflections on spirituality and leadership*. Washington, DC: Potter's House Book Service. [Appears also as Chapter 2 in Conger's *Spirit at work*).
- ———. (1993). *To know as we are known: A spirituality of education*. San Francisco, CA: Harper.
- Rafik , I., Badawi, B., & Badawi, J.A. (1999). *Leadership: An Islamic perspective*. Beltsville, AL: Amana Publications.
- Thompson, C.M., & Johnson, R.A. (2000). *The congruent life: Following the inward path to fulfilling work and inspired leadership*. San Francisco, CA: Jossey-Bass.
- Whyte, D.(1996). *The heart aroused: Poetry and the preservation of the soul in corporate America*. New York, NY: Currency Doubleday.

21. **Forces of Separation based on Fear**: In the course of our work, we sometimes encountered fear at the very idea of bringing spirituality into the workplace. Negative reactions were initially based on confusing religion with spirituality, and then limiting beliefs that a person's spirituality is an aspect of our deep inner Secret Self or Private Self and is not part of our Public Self. When we describe spirituality in the workplace and in Integrative Leadership development as 'telling the truth', 'being compassionate and caring' and 'being of highest service to others' calmness returns. Academically, in traditional leadership research, there was a Chinese wall between the secular and the sacred. Today there is a growing movement to involve spiritual leadership models in our mundane world and also a movement to evolve secular leadership models and elevate them to include the spiritual domain. Involution and evolution are struggling in this time of transition to become One.
22. **Emotional Intelligence (EI)**: The development of emotional and social intelligence in the past 70 years is a key aspect of awakening the heart of leadership. Baron Eqi is the oldest instrument for testing emotional intelligence developed in the 1980's. Mayor and Salavoy coined the term *Emotional Intelligence* (EI) in 1990 but are treating and developing it as an intelligence similar to mental intelligence or IQ (that was first developed by Alfred Binet in 1905). The popularization of EI occurred in 1995 with Daniel Goleman's book of the same name. We view this movement as the management and leadership evolution of allowing hands, heads and now hearts into the workplace and it is a wave that is washing over many organizations worldwide. This conscious movement will

facilitate the process of integration and is a key to Integrative Leadership development. According to Goleman, EI has four dimensions: self-awareness and self-management (Self): social awareness and relationship management (Others). There are 20 competencies that Goleman has associated with these four dimensions that are: **Self-Awareness**: 1. Emotional Self-Awareness; 2. Accurate Self-Assessment; 3. Self-Confidence; **Self Management**: 4. Self-Control; 5. Trustworthiness; 6. Conscientiousness; 7. Adaptability; 8. Achievement Orientation; 9. Initiative; **Social Awareness**: 10. Empathy; 11. Organizationally aware; **Relationship Management**: 12. Developing Others; 13. Service Orientation; 14. Leadership; 15. Power and Influence; 16. Communication; 17. Catalyzing Change; 18. Conflict Management; 19. Building Bonds; 20. Collaboration-Teamwork. Goleman, who first wrote a book on meditation in 1980 must have a similar view to our perspective, given his competencies above, of the heart-mind as the bridge between the body-mind and soul-mind.

23. **The Heart of Integrative Leadership**: The three concepts of attunement to our True Self, embodiment of our Ideal Self and integration within the heart of our Real Self are foundational and have been discussed for millennia. Here from Jeffrey Moses' "Oneness" are extracts from the world's wisdom traditions on the importance of the heart: "If we keep unperverted the human heart — which is like unto heaven and received from the earth — that is God" (Shintoism). "God is concealed in every heart, his light is in every heart" (Sikhism). "Know ye not that ye are the temple of God, and that the Spirit of God dwelleth in you?" (Christianity). "God is the light of all lights and luminous beyond all darkness of our ignorance. He is the knowledge and the object of knowledge. He is seated in the hearts of all" (Hinduism). "The heart of him who knows, and so believes with full assurance, is the throne of God" (Islam). "May He abide always within my heart, The Supreme Self, the One God of all gods" (Jainism).
24. **The Soul of Leadership**: Deepak Chopra began working several years ago with the Kellogg Business School at Northwestern University and delivered a program called "The Soul of Leadership". The ILI's program is called "Awakening the Soul of Leadership" that is facilitated through an Integrative Model and Framework. In Chopra's program, he suggested that there are seven needs or motivations within every relationship between leaders and followers and understanding how a leader should respond [*we would suggest react from the past or respond to your Ideal*] to those needs is important. The Maslow's motivation or needs hierarchy was correlated with Chopra's seven responses. We have positively correlated

Chopra's approach to the Eight Universal Laws that comprise the Integrative Leadership Framework Model and his approach and philosophy is congruent. Here are the ten key points from Chopra's perspective on the "Soul of Leadership": 1. Leaders and followers co-create each other; 2. A leader is the symbolic soul of the group; 3. Inner qualities determine results; 4. A multitude of responses must be known to a leader; 5. A leader must understand the hierarchy of needs; 6. For every need, the right response can be found; 7. Understanding need and response leads to success; 8. Great leaders are those who can respond from the higher levels of spirit; 9. Leaders give of themselves; 10. A leader must be comfortable with disorder. A few final thoughts from Chopra: "Wisdom traditions define truth as a single spark that burns down the whole forest. If the leader is willing to be that spark, others will see it within him. Craving direction, they will value what he offers, which is the first step toward valuing it in themselves." And finally, "There is always a jumble of needs and responses that must be sorted out. Otherwise, groups will be crippled in turmoil. Fear and survival, competition and creativity, vision and love make their own demands. Each has a voice, whether we hear it or not. Yet underneath there is only one voice, the silent whisper of spirit, which understands everything."

25. **Agape as the Sun**: Since earliest times, the Sun has been worshiped as a god by many cultures. The Egyptian sun god *Ra* is an example. In Egyptian history there was an anomaly under the leadership of one Pharaoh around 1350 BC where monotheism replaced the polytheism of the traditional and historical Egyptian many gods. This pharaoh was named *Akhenaton* and he ruled with his Queen, *Nefritiri*. Akhenaton built an entire city downriver from Luxor honoring the God *Aton*. *Aton* was believed to be the One source of all life, all knowledge and all wisdom and was imaged, symbolized and represented as the Sun. On Akhenaton's death, Egypt reverted back to polytheism and discarded the new city, with the monotheistic experiment lasting perhaps 30 years. Jesus spoke of *Agape* as "the sun shining and the rain falling on the just and the unjust alike", implying that life, light and love are given freely to everyone regardless of moral character or conduct to do with as they please. However, from Jesus's Integrative perspective, he reminded people also that there are consequences in accordance with Universal Law of every action we undertake, every thought we think and every desire we feel for "Like begets like", "As a tree falls, so shall it lie" and "as you sow, you will reap" and so on.
26. **Sons** (Suns) **and Daughters** (and other Suns) **of God**: God as Mind was the 'Son of God' (or Sun of God as the Light of God) that was born of the God of Spirit. It

was the only begotten Son for, according to the Law of Oneness, there is only One Mind of which all of us are but individualized aspects that can draw from it and contribute to it (collective unconscious). The idea that Jesus Christ is the only begotten Son of God is a fusion between the person and form of Jesus (mechanistic) and the Pattern of the Christ (organic) that is contained within the One Mind and available (as a potential that needs to be activated in sounding the higher note) to us all. For Jesus said "don't you know that in the Scriptures it states that you are all Gods: Sons and Daughters of the Most High". So the common medium is not the person of Jesus, but the Mind of God as the pattern found in the Christ. Each of us contains a portion of superconscious or Divine Mind, although we may be unaware of it. This portion or spark of the Divine is our heritage from being born first as spiritual beings and then later as physical beings. From this perspective, we are all Children of God striving through the process of involution and evolution, to become His/Her/All That Is's rightful Son or Daughter. This perspective can help build common ground between all the differences that are evident and seeking to divide rather than join the various wisdom and mystic traditions. These differences are based on mechanistic and organic perspectives, and not a wholistic perspective. So if Jesus the person became the Christ or pattern or Mind of God whose Source was God as Spirit then Moses the person became the Christ or pattern or Mind of God whose Source was God as Spirit (I AM that I AM) as well. Regardless of the name, person or form, whether Buddha, Krishna, Moses, Socrates, Mohammed, Lao-Tzu, Confucius or whatever your composite Ideal of the highest good can be, each in some way and to some degree can attune you to the Mind of God or pattern whose source is the God of Spirit. Each of us as a person can become John the Christ or Mary the Buddha (using our case examples) if we so desire. This is a life-giving, optimistic, integrative and hopeful perspective that can help unify in spirit rather than divide in duality of the organic (good versus evil) or divide in the multiple forms, traditions and rituals that the world's wisdom and mystic traditions adhere and follow. One Spirit. One God. One Source. One Cause. And we are all children of that One Source. Oneness.

27. Hatala, R. (2001). *Recalling the children of light*. Unpublished Manuscript. Calgary, AB: Integrative Leadership Institute.
28. **Sun, Water and Waves**: The metaphor of the sun and 'Soul-ar' flares is also found in the wisdom and mystic traditions as the metaphor of the ocean and waves. Each of us is a wave on the Ocean of Spirit that can look across to all the other waves and believe we are all separate existences, each unique, each very

individual. But if we were to dive into the depths of our being, into the depths of the Ocean, we would see that each separate wave is a part and owes its existence from the very same Source which in this case is the Ocean of Spirit. The Ocean of Spirit can exist without the waves, but the wave of our existence cannot exist without the loving presence of the Ocean of Spirit. The greatest error or sin — which is an Anglo-Saxon word in archery meaning 'missing the mark' — is that we often unwittingly take our relationships for granted; are not grateful for and appreciative of the people we cherish most in our lives; and often forget the spirit of life that allows us to have those relationships. Consciously thanking the universe for your life daily is one way not to take your life and your Source for granted.

29. **The Whole Law**: The whole of the Law of the Prophets within the Old and New Testament and many of the wisdom and mystic traditions is to "Love God with all your heart, mind and soul and your neighbor as yourself". This can be imaged as a Love Triangle within a circle. The circle or sphere is a representation of the Law of Oneness within which all our relationships are formed. For we know that it is 'in God we live and move and have our being…' If you have difficulty with this concept, remember the seeker fish story...
30. **Invitation and Invocation:** The concept of invitation and invocation of the Spirit of God as Truth, Love, Life or Unity has its roots in all wisdom and mystic traditions and many cultural traditions in various forms. In western civilization over the past 50 years, this common practice at gatherings and functions has slowly been suppressed, repressed, ignored or abandoned. We would suggest, based on the principle of resonant communication, a reawakening to the importance of this simple practice and advocate its use in everyday life, love, work and play. For us, this is the number one candidate for the 12th ITT practice that we utilize many times during a normal day.
31. **Holding the Space**: William Isaac, who specializes in Dialogue, describes this concept of "holding the space" in his work (see References). We feel it is more than the Spirit (Level III) or energy; it is more than simple thought (Level II); it is about holding the intention, thought, feeling and by your action (speaking, acting, doing), you strike the note of trust, truth, love, unity in the mechanistic that will resonate for yourself and others at Level I awareness. This is an important and useful concept in dialogue coupled with invitation and invocation.
32. **Living Relationships**: This concept of the four domains of intelligence and three levels of awareness associated with relationships is also applicable to families, groups, tribes, teams, organizations, nations and our global community.

33. **Maslow's Needs Hierarchy Revisited:** Maslow's Needs Hierarchy, as well as being related to the Three levels of awareness can also be related to the Eight Universal Principles starting from the lowest or base as 1. Life: Safety, Security, Survival; 2. Creativity: Achievement; 3. Cause and Effect: Self Esteem; 4. Harmony: Belonging; 5. Will-Desire: Expression; 6. Truth: Freedom; 7. Love: Love; and 8. Oneness: Spiritual Worth.
34. See Chapter 8, Note 9 on page 298.
35. **Platonic Forms**: Platonic forms, as we discussed briefly in Chapter 4, were Ideal Forms that existed in what was resonant with Jung's Collective Unconscious, Sheldrake's Morphogenic fields, or de Chardin's Superconscious. This etheric realm, which has been described in the mystic traditions as the 'skein of space and time', is known in the Eastern Traditions as the 'akasha', the place that is the memory of the mind of the Divine. All our intentions, thoughts, feelings and actions are recorded in the Akashic Records (memory of the Divine) that is called in Christianity, 'God's Book of Remembrance' upon which we all will be judged, not externally, but by our own soul. It is from this Book that people who experience a Near Death Experience (NDE) have an experience of their Life Review and are able to 'read' their life story. Returning to Platonic forms: from Plato's perspective, all that we see of a 'square' here in Level I awareness, is an imperfect representation of the Ideal Square in our collective unconscious at Level III awareness. In a similar way, the Integrative Leadership model is the imperfect representation here of the perfect model of the journey of integrative life, love and leadership, that we feel is aligned with the truth and is the model that informs all others. We have tried to show this in relating Integrative Leadership to a few of the more popular leadership models available in Chapter 7: Building a Living Organization.
36. **Multinational Interdisciplinary Research (MIR) Project on Universal Laws:** One suggestion would be to establish a Multinational Interdisciplinary Research (MIR) Project on Universal Laws funded by the United Nations (or other Consortium of International Organizations) that would combine the best minds and the best understanding of the Laws of Science, Wisdom and Mystic traditions, Philosophy and Positive Psychology among other disciplines, with a purpose to conduct research, study and produce a body of knowledge and understanding of these Universal Laws. Their findings would result in a non-denominational, non-sectarian *Integrative Framework of Universal Laws* that are congruent, self-evident and harmonious across all history and current scientific understanding

and research. From the work of the MIR could flow the R&D for an Education Project (curriculum and materials) that could be incorporated and integrated within our primary, secondary and post-secondary institutions. This Education Project would teach the existence, understanding and operation of these Universal Laws and associated Virtues, principles and practices. From MIR could also flow methods of helping governments examine their codes, rules, regulations and practices that would more closely align with these Universal Laws so that their practices would truly become "best practices," policies and procedures, regulations and codes. From MIR could also flow Organizational Integration Guidelines (profit and not for profit) that would help organizations who desire to transform themselves from the Mechanistic to the Organic paradigms or from Organic to Wholistic paradigms. The MIR would help facilitate the change of our global socio-economic-framework from 85% Mechanistic to 50% Organic-Wholistic in the next decade. Understanding Universal and Natural Laws and Virtues would help inform our Ethical and Moral principles and reshape the guidelines for their implementation and use in our culture, society and civilization. We would be interested to hear your interest in helping to fund or participating in the MIR Project on Universal Laws (coincidentally MIR means *peace* in the former Yugoslavia).

Epilogue

1. Csikszentmihalyi, M. (2003). *Good business: Leadership, flow and the making of meaning*. New York, NY: Viking. Csikszentmihalyi is the proponent of 'Flow' and what it means to be in that state. Our process of flow we call "Awakening the Soul of Leadership" within the Integrative Leadership Model which is transcendent in nature and serves to integrate our three levels of awareness and four domains of intelligence.
2. This description is not an actual case study of applying the Integrative Leadership Model to an organization, but our Ideal of how we would envision doing so if we were asked. We are in the process of developing the methodologies, protocols and regimen to do so with our work on Organizational Integration™ scheduled for publication within the next three years.

Appendices

Appendix A

Experiencing a Life Review

History repeats itself, and that's one of the things that's wrong with history.

CLARENCE DARROW

One who forgets history is doomed to relive it.

OLD HEBREW SAYING

Introduction

Living a reflective life is an important practice of walking the path of integration. This as an opportunity to reflect on the highs (peak experiences) and lows (death dealing experiences) of your life from the perspective of the Four Domains of Intelligence: physical, mental, emotional and spiritual and the Three Levels of Awareness (conscious, unconscious, superconscious) as Low, Medium, High. The following questions may help prompt your life review.

Physical Domain

- When was I healthiest and most fit?
- When was I most sick or ill?
- Who or what is my ideal physically?

Mental Domain

- When did I have an "ah-ha" moment when I felt I truly understood a problem, challenge or situation?

- What have I learned and applied in the course of my life and work?
- When did I feel the least smart?
- Who or what is my ideal mentally?

Emotional Domain

- When was my heart first broken?
- When did I first fall in love with life, a thing, an animal, or another person?
- Who or what is my ideal emotionally?

Spiritual Domain

- When did I have a deeply impacting vision, dream, insight or intuition?
- Have I ever had a sense of something happening and it did?

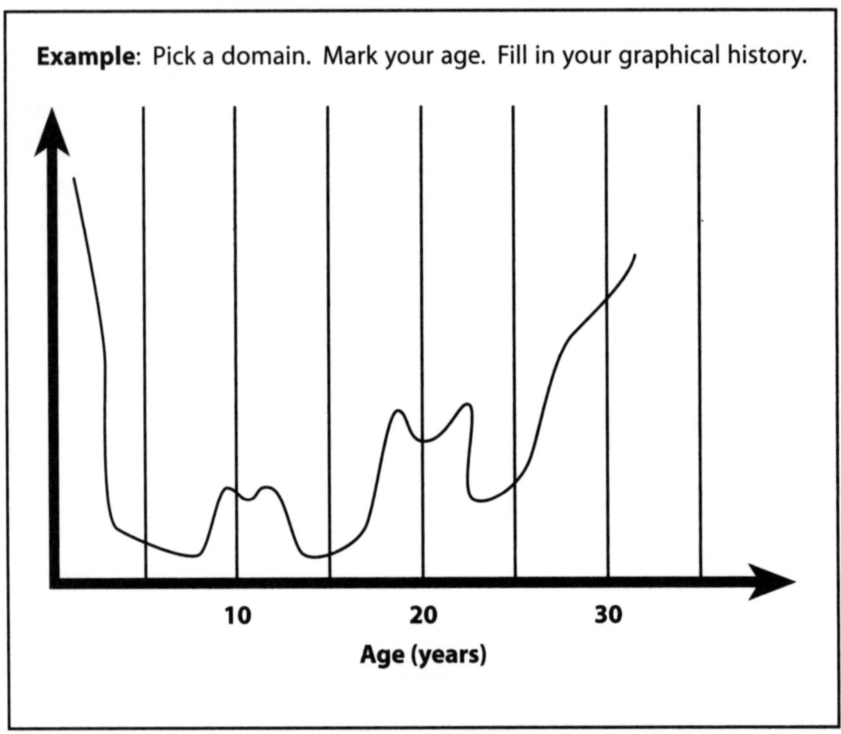

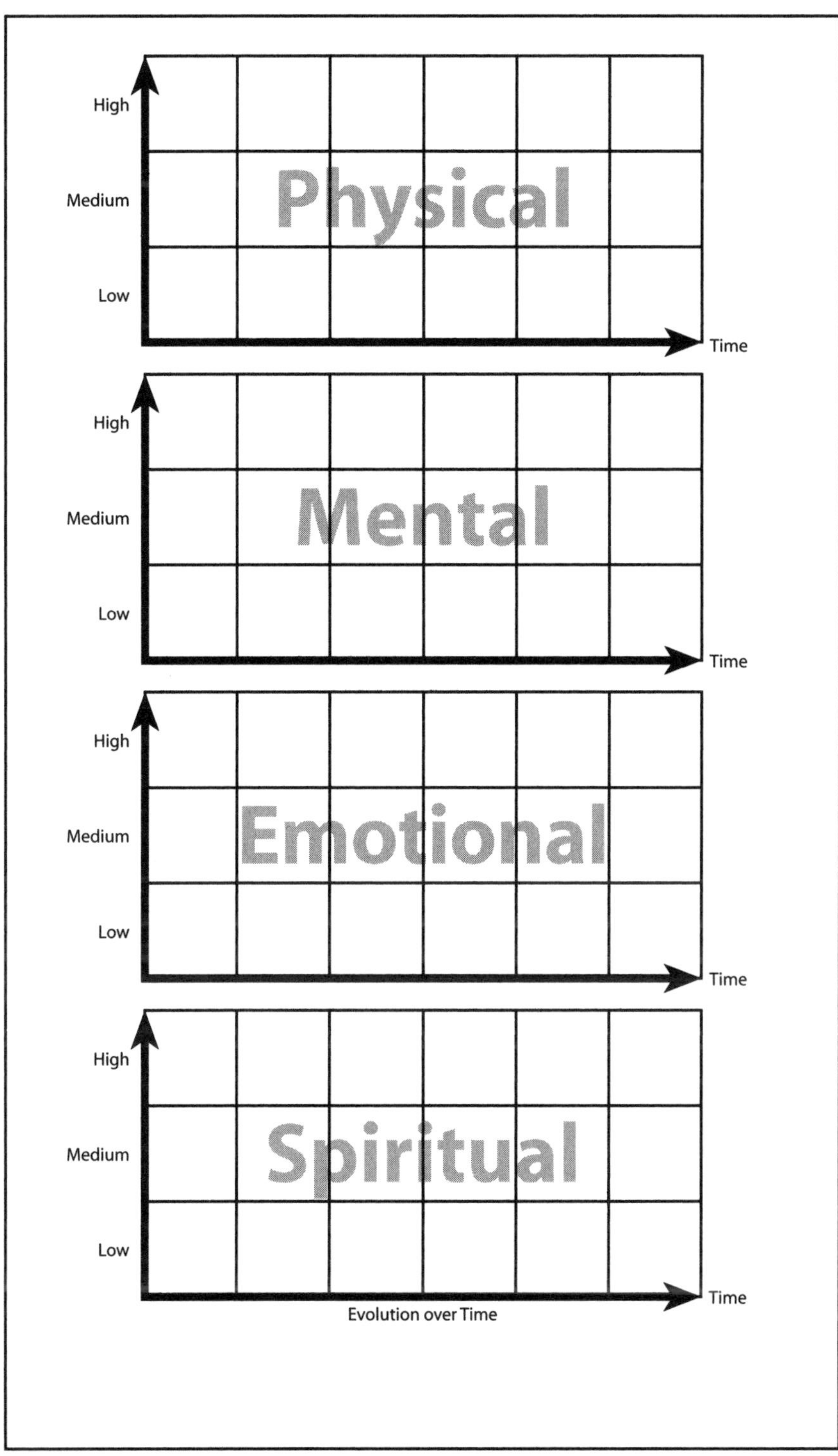
High
Medium
Low
Physical
Time
High
Medium
Low
Mental
Time
High
Medium
Low
Emotional
Time
High
Medium
Low
Spiritual
Time
Evolution over Time

- When did I experience deep synchronicity or meaningful coincidences?
- Have I ever experienced a deep connection or communion with another person, place or thing?
- When did I have an experience of higher sensory perception. For example: telepathy, clairvoyance, clairaudience, clairsentience, inner voice, out-of-body experience, telekinesis or manifestation.
- Who or what is my ideal spiritually?

Methods of Sharing Your Life from the Four Domains

- Telling a story.
- Acting out portions of your story.
- Writing a poem or sharing a poem that has meaning.
- Writing or sharing a piece of music that has meaning.
- Drawing a picture, painting or sketch about it.
- Can you imagine other creative ways to share the sacred events of your life. Take a moment to reflect, then write them down here:

Appendix B

Meditation: The Inner Power of Silence

Health, a light body, freedom from craving, a glowing skin, sonorous voice, fragrance of body; these signs indicate progress in one's practice of meditation.

SHVETASHVATARA UPANISHAD, 2:12

Relaxation, Concentration, Visualization, Meditation, Contemplation

Introduction

Although meditative practices are relatively new in Western cultures, there is a keen and growing interest in learning about relaxation, concentration, visualization, meditation, and contemplation. This developing field:

- Is backed by 25 years of study (Benson et al, 'Relaxation Response' and today, many others) and 2,500 papers to date.
- Offers opportunities for growth and insight for those in positions of leadership.
- Is an experience of the inner power of silence as conscious sensory deprivation. This allows your awareness to move within rather than remain without.
- Originated in spiritual and mystic traditions in both East and West.

Meditation has been used successfully to:

- Relieve chronic pain, promote healing and reduce effects of stress.

- Control certain autonomic functions of the body (*breath, heart rate, immune system*).
- Enhance problem solving, decision-making and creativity.
- Access your inner wisdom, connect to your intuition and stimulate spiritual growth.
- Contribute to the overall quality of your life and enliven intimate relationships.

Meditation is an integrative tool that helps connect your purpose, desires, thoughts and actions with all domains, all levels and all perspectives.

Five Steps Towards the Inner Power of Silence

Step 1: Preparation

- Choose an appropriate environment for your experience.
- Assume a comfortable physical position (sitting comfortably upright with spine erect).
- Physically relax the body by whatever method (stretching, yoga, light exercise)
- Mentally, relax the body and the mind (visualization exercise)
- Focus on your intention for meditating (Quiet, Question, Connection)
- Use ritual, prayer or affirmation to convert your personal space into sacred space.

Step 2: Concentration

- Focus on your breathing. Initially, don't try and control, simply pay attention to it.
- With each inhalation say "I am" and with each exhalation say "One". "One" can be replaced by your Ideal, Virtue or other personally meaningful or resonant word.
- Later, try and count to three mentally on the in-breath, hold in your comfort zone, then release to the count of three.

- Later still, try and extend the counts from three, to four, to six moving with your comfort zone.

Step 3: Detachment and Self Observation

- Adopt a passive, "let it happen" attitude.
- If distracting thoughts enter, acknowledge them, smile and let them pass.
- Refocus on observing the breath, saying your *word or phrase*, letting go and releasing.

Step 4: Meditation & Contemplation

- Empathetically listen for the *still small voice* of inner wisdom that speaks from within.

Step 5: Give the Good Away

- In concluding, let the sense of love, peace, wonder, energy or joy you felt move from you to all the others you would honor and positively think about in your life, love, work or play.

Five Steps along the Inner Path

- **One-Minute Relaxation** **(Physical Intelligence)**
- **One Minute Concentration** **(Mental Intelligence)**
- **One Minute Visualization** **(Emotional Intelligence)**
- **One-Minute Meditation** **(Spiritual Intelligence)**
- **One Minute Contemplation** **(All Four Intelligences – Unity)**

Notes on Your Personal Experience:

Appendix C

Reflecting on Your Vision and Ideal

Vision is the art of seeing the invisible.

JONATHON SWIFT

I am not bound to win. I am bound to be true.
I am not bound to succeed, but I am bound to live up to the light that I have.

ABRAHAM LINCOLN

Vision

- Is written down and reviewed daily
- Is is written in the present tense
- Covers all aspects of life, love, work and play
- It is about *who* and *what* it is we want to be
- Captures our hopes, wishes, dreams and desires
- Is the future we want to create for ourselves
- Has a hint of uniqueness
- Is a source of enormous energy
- Has positive compelling pull to the future

1. What is one hope, wish, dream or desire you have for yourself?

____

2. What is your vision for the kind of person you want to be?

____

Reflecting on Your Ideal

3. What is the Ideal in and for your life? Engage the Four Domains of Intelligence in describing your Ideal physically, mentally, emotionally and spiritually.

- What would my Ideal look like physically?
- How would my ideal behave?
- What would it act like?
- What would it feel like to be my Ideal?
- How would others feel around me when I am my Ideal?
- What would I think about as my Ideal?
- What would others think about my Ideal?
- What is the purpose and intent of my Ideal? For me? For others?

4. In one word, describe how you would like to be viewed by yourself and by others?

---

5. From the table *Finding Your Ideal Core Value: Positive Attractor*, opposite, choose three Values. What do you value the most? From the three Values you've chosen, put them in order of priority and select only one Core Value. Compare the Core Value you have chosen with your single word from Question 4 above in the exercise Reflecting on Your Ideal and answer the question below as best you can in this moment:

- What do you most want to model and represent in this world?

- See page 328–329 for further ideas on working with your Ideal Core Value.

Finding Your Ideal Core Value: Positive Attractor

Appreciation	Assertiveness	Beauty	Caring	Caution
Charity	Citizenship	Cleanliness	Commitment	Compassion
Competition	Confidence	Consideration	Cooperation	Courage
Courtesy	Creativity	Critical Thinking	Curiosity	Detachment
Determination	Dignity	Diligence	Discretion	Duty-Obligation
Enthusiasm	Equality	Excellence	Fairness	Faith
Flexibility	Forgiveness	Freedom	Friendship	Generosity
Gentleness	Genuineness	Gratitude	Helpfulness	Honesty
Honor	Hope	Humanity	Humility	Humor
Idealism	Industry	Ingenuity	Innovation	Integrity
Interest in World	Joy	Judgment	Justice	Kindness
Levity	Love	Loyalty	Materiality	Mercy
Moderation	Modesty	Nobility	Open mindedness	Optimism
Orderliness	Originality	Passion	Patience	Peace
Perseverance	Personal Truth	Positive Attitude	Prudence	Purity
Relationships	Relative Truth	Reliability	Respect	Responsibility
Safety	Security	Self-control	Self-discipline	Self-worth
Sense of Purpose	Serenity	Service	Simplicity	Spirituality
Tact	Teamwork	Temperance	Thankfulness	Tolerance
Transcendence	Transformation	Trust	Trustworthiness	Truth (fullness)
Understanding	Unity	Wholeness		

Appendix D

Awakening the Dreamer

An uninterpretted dream is like an unopened letter from your soul.

RABBI HISADA, *Babylonian Talmud*

Introduction

- Dreams are integrative and the easiest way to tap into our Unconscious Mind.
- Everyone dreams, but we often choose not to remember them (see recall techniques).
- About 30% of our sleep time is used in dreaming (1.5–2 hours per night)
- Three universal states of consciousness: Waking, Sleeping and Dreaming.
- Historically, dreams are used for teaching, guidance, problem solving, healing and prediction.
- Often answers to problems or challenges can be found in intentional dreaming or incubation.

Five Steps in Working with the Dreamer

Step 1: Preparation

- Keep a journal, notepad or recording equipment beside your bed.
- Be open and have a positive attitude towards receiving a helpful, hopeful dream.
- Repeat, three times, in hypnogogic state, your intent for dreaming.

Step 2: Recording and Observing

- Don't move on awakening. Reflect on your feeling, thoughts, images.
- Capture the key words and connections.
- Record and retell the details of the dream upon full awakening.

Step 3: Working with Your Dreams

- **Theme**: of the dream or dream segment: What is going on? What is the action?
- **Feelings**: How did you feel in the dream? Upon awakening?
  - *Theme* and *Feelings* often set the context of the dream in your life
- **Images and Symbols**: Amplify and associate with your images and symbols:
  - **Literal**: Things and people are really what they are.
  - **Cultural**: Things and people are associated with our culture.
  - **Archetypal**: Things and people have in-depth cross cultural meaning.

Step 4: Formulate a Preliminary Understanding of the Dream

- Reflect on the elements of Step 3 above.
- Is there a moral? Is there a message? Is there a common theme? Is the dream compensatory (opposite of waking life)? Is the dream another perspective on an existing relationship or situation in your life? Does it creatively solve a problem? Does it show you possible consequences of a decision? Is Higher Sensory Perception operating in the dream? Could the dream be precognitive? If none of the above, is it simply a rehash of past events?

Step 5: Application

- What is the dream asking me to look at in my life?
- What should I pay attention to? What am I missing while awake?
- Ask for a clarification if you did not get it the first time around...

Note: Most dreams are about different aspects of one's self and the images and symbols are often not literal, but cultural or archetypal.

References on Dreams

Todeschi, K.J. (2000). *Dream interpretation (and more) made easy*. New York, NY: Paraview Press.

Farady, A. (1972). *Dream power: Learn to use the vital selfknowledge that lies stored in your dreams*. New York, NY: Berkley Books.

Laberge, S. (1997). *Exploring the world of lucid dreaming*. New York, NY: Ballantine Books.

Dream Recall Techniques and Approaches

- **Write out your purpose**: Why do you want to remember your dreams? Clarify your purpose and intent.
- **Go to bed early**: Getting full night's sleep can sharpen your recall. Your longest dream period is typically at the end of the sleep period.
- **Pre-sleep suggestion**: Just before falling asleep at night, repeat to yourself a suggestion such as "I will remember my dreams upon awakening." This is also the time for asking for guidance on a challenge you are facing in your life. Repeat the request, suggestion or question to yourself three times while falling asleep.
- **Paper and Pen/Recording Equipment by the bed**: Have something nearby to record your dreams immediately upon awakening.
- **Don't move upon awakening**: Lying still upon awakening enhances transfer of memories.
- **Record key words and images**: Record any fragments of a dream. This recollection will help recall the rest.
- **Relive the dream in reverse**: Often we recall the end of the dream. Start at the end and successively ask, "What happened before this?"
- **Record your feelings**: If you don't remember the images, remember how you felt when you awoke. Lousy or good? This tells about the context and the theme of the dream.
- **Regularly share and listen to dreams**: By sharing your dreams with others, we can develop a sense of community or family with others.

- **Learn to wake in the night**: Recalling a dream can be enhanced by waking when it is over. A preliminary period of using an alarm or drinking water before bed can train us to awaken at the appropriate time.
- **Have a partner watch for REM**: Another person watching you sleep can awaken you either during or shortly after a REM period.
- **Act on your dreams**: The real interpretation of a dream is an application in daily life. By acting on the message of the dream and weighed against our conscious principles and values, our relationship with our unconscious or inner self is enhanced.

Finding Your Ideal Core Value: Positive Attractor

Table 1 opposite represents the Wholistic; Table 2 the Mechanistic and Table 3 the Organic paradigms. Where were your three core values? Were they one from each table, or spread between the three tables? This will help indicate where you are in beginning your journey of Integrative Life and Leadership.

Finding Your Ideal Core Value: Positive Attractor

Table 1				
Commitment	Detachment	Determination	Flexibility	Freedom
Humility	Patience	Idealism	Responsibility	Purity
Cleanliness	Excellence	Hope	Nobility	Tolerance
Truth (fullness)	Understanding	Perseverance	Transcendence	Passion
Integrity	Kindness	Originality	Genuineness	Love
Forgiveness	Sense of Purpose	Mercy	Spirituality	Unity
Joy	Wholeness	Service		

Table 2				
Safety	Security	Assertiveness	Creativity	Honesty
Modesty	Orderliness	Reliability	Self-discipline	Tact
Charity	Confidence	Courage	Courtesy	Dignity
Diligence	Enthusiasm	Equality	Honor	Justice
Loyalty	Moderation	Relationships	Respect	Self-worth
Curiosity	Caution	Materiality	Judgment	Citizenship
Temperance	Self-control	Interest in World	Critical Thinking	Personal Truth
Duty-Obligation	Industry	Discretion	Competition	

Table 3				
Caring	Compassion	Consideration	Cooperation	Faith
Friendship	Generosity	Gentleness	Helpfulness	Peace
Serenity	Positive Attitude	Simplicity	Thankfulness	Gratitude
Trust	Trustworthiness	Ingenuity	Humanity	Fairness
Prudence	Appreciation	Beauty	Humor	Levity
Open mindedness	Optimism	Relative Truth	Teamwork	Transformation
Innovation				

References

Anderson, D., & Anderson, L.A. (2001). *Beyond change management: Advanced strategies for today's transformational leaders*. San Francisco, CA: Jossey-Bass.

Anderson, P., & Ray, S. (2001). *The cultural creatives: How 50 million people are changing the world*. New York, NY: Three Rivers Press. [Division of Random House].

Barr, F. (1983). The theory of evolutionary process as a unifying paradigm. Article found at: <**http://www.arthuryoung.com/barr.html**>

Barrett, R. (1998). *Liberating the corporate soul*. Woburn, MA: Butterworth-Heinemann.

Bennis, W.G., & Nanus, B. (1997). *Leaders: Strategies for taking charge*. New York, NY: Harper.

Bennis, W.G., & Thomas, R.J. (2002). The crucibles of leadership. *Harvard Business Review, 80*(9): 39–45. Watertown, MA: Harvard Business School Publication Corporation.

Blanton, B. (1996). *Radical honesty: How to transform your life by telling the truth*. New York, NY: Bantam-Doubleday-Dell.

Bronowski, J. (1974) *The ascent of man*. Boston, MA: Little Brown & Company.

Brown, L. (2001). Leading leadership development in universities. *Journal of Management Inquiry, 10*(4):312–323.

Brown, L., & Posner, B. (2001). Exploring the relationship between learning and leadership. *The Leadership and Organizational Development Journal, 22*(6): 274–80.

Brown, L., & Hatala, R.J. (2003). Walking the path of integrative leadership. *Canadian Association of University Continuing Education Conference Proceedings*. May 28–29, 2003, Calgary, AB: University of Calgary.

Bushe, G.R. (2001). *Clear leadership: How outstanding leaders make themselves understood, cut through the mush and help everyone get real at work*. Palo Alto, CA: Davies-Black Publishing.

Cashman, K. (2003). *Awakening the leader within*. Hobeken, NJ: John Wiley & Sons.

———. (1998). *Leadership from the inside out*. Minneapolis, MN: TCLG Publishing.

Charan, R., Drotter, S., & Noel, J. (2001). *The leadership pipeline: How to build the leadership-powered company*. San Francisco, CA: Jossey Bass.

Cherniss, C., & Goleman, D. (2001). *The emotionally intelligent workplace*. San Francisco, CA: Jossey Bass.

Chopra, D. (2000). *How to know God*. Toronto, ON: Harmony Books.

———. (1994). *The seven spiritual laws of success*. San Raphael, CA: Amber Allen Publishing & New World Library.

Cleary, T. (1992). *The essential tao: An initiation into the heart of taoism*. Edison, NJ: Castle Books.

Collins, J. (2001). *Good to great: Why some companies make the leap…and others don't*. New York, NY: HarperCollins Publishers Inc.

Cooper, R.K., & Sawaf, A. (1996). *Executive EQ: Emotional intelligence in leadership and organizations*. New York, NY: Penguin-Putnam Inc.

Cooperrider, D., Sorensen, P., Yaeger, T., & Whitney, D. (2001). *Appreciative inquiry: An emerging direction for organization development*. Champaign, IL: Stipes Publishing.

Covey, S.R. (1992). *Principle centered leadership*. New York, NY: Fireside.

———. (1989). *The seven habits of highly effective people*. New York, NY: Fireside.

Dalton, M., Swigert, S., Van Velso, E., Bunker, K., & Wachholz, J. (1999). *The learning tactics inventory: Facilitators guide*. San Francisco, CA: Jossey-Bass.

De bono, E. (2001). *Six thinking hats*. London, UK: Penguin.

De Mello, A. (1998). *Awakening: Conversations with the master*. Chicago, IL: Loyola Press.

Damasio, A.R. (2003). *Looking for Spinoza: Joy, sorrow, and the feeling brain*. Orlando, FL: Harcourt.

Easwaran, E. (1991). *Meditation*. Tomales, CA: Nigiri Press.

Emmons, R.A. (1999). *The psychology of ultimate concerns: Motivation and spirituality in personality*. New York, NY: Guilford.

Farr, J.N. (1998). *Supra-conscious leadership: New thinking for a new world*. Research Triangle Park, NC: Research Triangle Publishers.

Gardner, H. (1995). Reflections on multiple intelligences: Myths and messages. *Phi Delta Kappan, 77* (November 11):200–209.

Goleman, D. (1997). *Emotional intelligence: Why it can matter more than IQ*. New York, NY: Bantam.

Goleman, D., Boyatzis, R., & McKee, A. (2002). *Primal leadership: Realizing the power of emotional intelligence*. Watertown, MA: Harvard Business School Publishing Corporation.

Guillory, W.A. (2000). *The living organization: Spirituality in the workplace*. Salt Lake City, UT: Innovations International.

Hammond, S.A. (1998). *The thin book of appreciative inquiry*. Plano, TX: Thin Book Publishing.

Hatala, R.J. (2004). *Virtue and value-centered approaches to integrative life and leadership*. Unpublished paper. Calgary, AB: Integrative Leadership Institute.

———. (2003). *The universal principles and practices of walking the path*. Unpublished paper. Calgary, AB: Integrative Leadership Institute.

Hatala, R.J., & Brown, L.M. (2001). *The theory and practice of integrative leadership*. Unpublished paper. Calgary, AB: Integrative Leadership Institute.

Hatala, R.J., & Hatala, L.M. (2003). *On becoming an integrated leader*. Article available from <**www.banffcentre.ca**> under leadership development. Banff, AB: Banff Centre for Management.

Hawkins, D.R. (2002). *Power vs. force: The hidden determinants of human behavior*. Carlsbad: CA: Hay House.

Hedva, B.(2001). *Betrayal, trust, and forgiveness: A guide to emotional healing and self-renewal*. Berkley, CA: Celestial Arts.

Hendricks, G., & Ludeman, K. (1997). *The corporate mystic: A guidebook for visionaries with their feet on the ground*. New York, NY: Bantam.

Hitt, J. (1999). This is your brain on god. *Wired Magazine, 7*(11): 120–132.

Hubble, E. (1929). *The expanding universe: The big bang theory.* Information can be found at the following website: <**http://www.stillmoving.ca/hst/EdwinHubble.html** >

Isaac, W. (1999). *Dialogue and the art of thinking together*. New York, NY: Doubleday.

Iyengar, B.K.S. (2001). *Light on yoga*. London, UK: Thorsons.

———. (1993). *Light on the yoga sutras of patanjali*. London, UK: Thorsons.

James, W. (1910). *Varieties of religious experience*. New York, NY: Putnam. (reprinted in 1935).

Judith, A. (1996). *Eastern body western mind: Psychology and the chakra system as a path to the self*. Berkley, CA: Celestrial Arts.

Jung, C.G. (1961). *Memories, dreams and reflections*. Glasgow, Scotland: Collins.

———. (1954). The gifted child. In William McGuire (Ed.) *Collected works*. Princeton, NJ: Princeton University Press, 17:249.

———. (1933). *Modern man in search of a soul*. New York, NY: Harcourt Brace.

———. (1921). *Psychological types*. Zurich, CH: Rascher. [H.G. Baynes translation in 1923, Chapter 10].

Kirkpatrick, S.D. (2000). *Edgar Cayce: An American prophet*. New York, NY: Riverhead.

Kisshomaru, U. (1987). *The spirit of aikido*. Translated by Taitetsu Unno. Tokyo, Japan: Kodansha International Ltd.

Klein, E., & Izzo, J.B. (2000). *Awakening the corporate soul: Four paths to unleash the power of people at work*. London, UK: Fair Winds Press.

Kouzes, J.M., & Posner, B.Z. (2002). *The leadership challenge: How to keep getting extraordinary things done in organizations*. San Francisco, CA: Jossey-Bass.

Krass, P. (Ed.). (2001). *The little book of business wisdom: Rules of success from more than 50 business legends*. New York, NY: John Wiley & Sons.

Kubler-Ross, E.(1997). *Living with death and dying*. New York, NY: Simon & Schuster.

Kyle, D. (2003). *The four powers of leadership: Cultivating presence, intention, wisdom and compassion*. Deerfield Beach, FL: Health Communications.

Lamas, G.M. (1933). *Holy bible: From the ancient eastern text*. San Francisco, CA: Harper & Row Publishers. [Reprinted in 1977].

Lao-Tze. (500 BC). The tao te ching: Very great leaders. In T. Cleary, (Ed.). *The essential tao (axiom 17)*. New York, NY: Castle Books.

Ledoux, J. (1998). *The emotional brain: The mysterious underpinnings of emotional life*. Clearwater, FL: Touchstone Books.

Leonard, G., & Murphy, M. (1995). *The life we are given*. New York, NY: Putnam.

Levey, J., & Levey, M. *Wisdom at work*. Berkley, CA: Conari.

Litchfield, B. (1999). *Spiritual intelligence*. Urbana-Champaign, IL: University of Illinois, Illini Christian Faculty. Contact e-mail: <**B-litch@uiuc.edu**>

Llinas, R., & Ribary, U. (1993). Coherent 40Hz oscillation characterizes dream state in humans. In *Proceedings of the National Academy of Science, 90* (3):2078–2081.

Maltz, M. (2002). *The new psycho-cybernetics: The original science of self-improvement and success that has changed the lives of 30 million people*. Paramus, NJ: Prentice Hall.

Maslow, A. (1998). *Maslow on management*. New York, NY: John Wiley & Sons.

Mitroff, I., & Denton, E. (1997). *A spiritual audit of corporate America: A hard look at spirituality, religion and values in the workplace*. San Francisco, CA: Jossey-Bass.

Moses, J. (2002). *Oneness: Great principles shared by all religions*. New York, NY: Ballantine.

Moxley, R. (2000). *Leadership and spirit: Breathing new vitality and energy into individuals and organizations*. San Francisco, CA: Jossey-Bass.

Owen, H. (1999). *The spirit of leadership: Liberating the leader in each of us*. San Francisco, CA: Berrett-Koehler.

Palmer, P. (2000). *Let your life speak: Listening to the voice of vocation*. San Francisco, CA: Jossey-Bass.

Pannett, A. (2000). Facing and managing change. *New Law Journal Practitioner, 150*: 466.

Persinger, M.A. (1996). Feelings of past lives as expected perturbations within the neurocognitive processes that generate the sense of self: Contribution from limbic libility and vectorial hemisphericity. *Perceptual Motor Skills, 83*(12): 1107–1121.

Pert, C. (1997). *Molecules of emotion: Why you feel the way you feel*. New York, NY: Scribner.

Pine, R. (1987). *The zen teachings of Bodhidharma*. New York, NY: North Point Press Publishing.

Ramachandran, V.S., & Blakeslee, S. (1998). *Phantoms in the brain*. London, UK: Fourth Estate.

Reany D. (2002). S.R. Covey: Author seeks leadership based on principles. *The Winchester Star*. October 2, 2002. <**http://www.winchesterstar.com/TheWinchesterStar/021002/Area_leadership.asp**>

Ribary, V., & Llinas, R. (1991). Magnetic field tomography of coherent thalamocortical 40Hz oscillations in humans. *Proceedings of the National Academy of Science, 88*:11037–11041.

Seligman, M. (2003). *Positive psychology and authentic happiness*. New York, NY: Free Press.

Purohit, Shri Swami, (1935). *The bagavad gita: The gospel of the lord Shri Krishna*. New York, NY: Vintage Books Edition/Random House. [Reprinted in 1977].

Singer, W. (1999). Striving for coherence. *Nature 397*(6718): 391–392.

Singer, W., & Gray, C.M. (1995). Visual feature integration and the temporal correlation hypothesis. *Annual Review of Neuroscience, 18*: 555–586.

Smith, H. (1986). *The religions of man*. New York, NY: Harper & Row.

Sui, R.G.H. (1981). *The master manager*. Toronto, ON: John Wiley & Sons.

———. (1980). *The transcendental manager*. Toronto, ON: John Wiley & Sons.

———. (1979). *The craft of power*. Toronto, ON: John Wiley & Sons.

Suler, J. (2001). *Bringing online and offline living together: The integration principle.* Available at: <**http://www.rider.edu/~suler/psycyber/integrate.html**>

———. (1999). Cyberspace as psychological space. In *The psychology of cyberspace.* Available at: <**www.rider.edu/users/suler/psycyber/psycyber.html**>

Teilhard de Chardin, P. (1955). *The phenomenon of man*. New York, NY: Perennial Press. [Reprinted in 1976].

Thurstan, M. (1995). *Soul-purpose: Discovering and fulfilling your destiny*. New York, NY: St. Martin's Press.

Walker, B. (1992). *Hua hu ching: The unknown teachings of Lao Tzu*. New York, NY: Harper Collins Publishers.

Whitteveen, H.J. (1997). *Universal sufism*. Shaftesbury, UK: Element Books Ltd.

Wilber, K. (1998). *The essential Ken Wilber*. Boston, MA: Shambhala Publications.

———. (2004). Papers available from the Integral Institute website at <**www.integralinstitute.org**>

Williamson, M. (1992) *A return to love*. New York, NY: Harper Collins.

Wilson, E. (1982). *The wisdom of Confucius*. New York, NY: Avenal Books.

Wolman, R.N. (2001). *Thinking with your soul: Spiritual intelligence and why it matters*. New York, NY: Harmony Books.

Yogananda, P. (2001). *Autobiography of a yogi*. Los Angeles, CA: International Publications Council of Self Realization Fellowship.

Young, A.M. (1976). *The reflexive universe: The evolution of consciousness*. New York, NY: Delacorte Press. Reprints available from <**www.arthuryoung.com**>

———. (1974). Prologue for a new religion consistent with the findings of science. *Nous Newsletter*. <**http://www.arthuryoung.com/barr.html**>.

Zaleznik, A. (2004). Managers and leaders: Are they different? *Harvard Business Review, 82*(1):74–81. Watertown, MA: Harvard Business School Publishing Corporation.

Zohar, D., & Marshall, I. (2001). *SQ: Connecting with your spiritual intelligence*. London, UK: Bloomsbury.

Key Personal Integrative References

Ask yourself if you could take only ten books from all the ones you have read or owned that would guide you on your next life on the far and remote side of the world, the solar system or universe, which books would they be? Write them down in the space provided on this and the next page.

-
-
-
-
-
-
-
-
-
-

•

After you have thought of ten titles and written them down, consider that you now have room for only five books, which five would they be? Place a check mark next to the five titles you would take. Subsequently you must now choose three of the five. Place an X by these three titles. Finally, circle one of the three titles that has been a companion on your life journey to date. This should be the book that has resonated most with your theory of practice of life, love, learning and leadership.

My Theory of Practice
Integrating My Life, Learning, Love & Leadership

Bibliography

Bass, B.M. (1990). *Bass & Stogdill's handbook of leadership (3rd Edn.)*. New York, NY: Free Press.

Berry, I. (2001). *The age of wisdom*. Article available from <**http://www.ianberry.au.com/article4.html**>

Briskin, A. (1998). *Stirring of soul in the workplace*. San Francisco, CA: Berrett-Koehler Publishing.

Bukkyo Dendo Kyokai (BDK) [Society for the Promotion of Buddhism]. (1966). *The teaching of Buddha*. Tokyo, Japan: Kosaido Printing Company.

Cady, H.E. (1923). *Lessons in truth: A course in twelve lessons in practical christianity*. Unity Village, MI: Unity Books

Capra, F. (1989). *Uncommon wisdom*. New York, NY: Bantam.

———. (1975). *The tao of physics*. London, UK: Wildwood House.

Deming, E. (2001). In J. van Reenen (Ed.). *Work and productivity in the 21st century*. Alberquerque, NM: University of New Mexico, UNM Libraries.

Chopra, D. (1997). *The path to love: Renewing the power of spirit in your life*. New York, NY: Harmony Books.

Clark, G. (1946). *Walter Russell: The man who tapped the secrets of the universe*. Waynesboro, VA: University of Science and Philosophy. [Reprinted in 2000]

Conger, J.A., & Benjamin, B. (1999). *Building leaders: How successful companies develop the next generation*. San Francisco, CA: Jossey-Bass.

Csikszentmihalyi, M.(2003). *Good business: Leadership, flow and the making of meaning*. New York, NY: Viking.

De Mello, A. (1992). *One minute nonsense*. Chicago, IL: Loyola Press.

Goddart, M. (1999). *Bliss: 33 simple ways to awaken your spiritual self*. Emmaus, PA: Daybreak Books.

Jaworski, J. (1996). *Synchronicity: The inner path of leadership*. San Francisco, CA: Berrett-Koehler.

Jones, L.B. (1997). *The path: Creating your mission statement for life and work*. El Paso, TX: Candlestick.

Kegan, R. (1998). *In over our heads*. Cambridge, MA: Harvard University Press.

Kotter, J. (1999). *What leaders really do*. Cambridge, MA: Harvard Busines School Press.

Kovess, C. (2000). *Passionate performance*. Sydney, NSW: Information Australia.

McCauley, C., Moxley, R., & Van Velsor, E. (Eds.). (1998). *The centre for creative leadership: Handbook of leadership development*. San Francisco, CA: Jossey Bass.

Mezirow, J., & Associates. (2000). *Learning as transformation: Critical perspectives on a theory in progress*. San Francisco, CA: Jossey-Bass.

Mishlove, J. (1993). *The roots of consciousness*. New York, NY: Marlowe & Company.

Myss, C. (1996). *Anatomy of the spirit*. New York, NY: Three Rivers Press.

Noble, K.D. (2001). *Riding the windhorse: Spiritual intelligence and the growth of self*. Creskill, NJ: Hampton Press.

O'Neil, J. (1997). *Leadership aikido: Six business practices to turn around your life*. New York, NY: Harmony Books.

Osborne, M.P. (1996). *One world, many religions: The ways we worship*. New York NY: Alfred A. Knopfe.

Pierce, G.F.A. (2000). *Spirituality at work: Ten ways to balance your life on the job*. Minneapolis, MN: Augsburg Press.

Raka, R.(1906). *Raja yoga or mental development*. London, UK: Yoga Publication Society. [Reprinted in 1934].

Secretan, L. (1999). *Inspirational leadership: Destiny, calling and cause*. Toronto, ON: Macmillan.

Senge, P., Kleiner, A., Roberts, C., Ross, R., & Smith, B. (1994). *The fifth discipline fieldbook*. New York, NY: Bantam-Doubleday-Dell Publishing Group.

Sharamon, S., & Baginski, B.(1991). *The chakra handbook*. Twin Lakes WI: Lotus Press.

Sinetar, M. (1986). *Ordinary people as monks and mystics*. New York, NY: Paulist Press.

Tucker, G. (1987). *The faith-work connection: A practical application of christian values in the marketplace*. Toronto, ON: Anglican Book Centre.

Vaill, P. (1999). *Spirited leading and learning process wisdom for a new age*. San Francisco, CA: Jossey-Bass.

Watkins, J., & Mohr, B. (2001). *Appreciative inquiry: Change at the speed of imagination*. San Francisco, CA: Jossey Bass.

Watson, J. (1913) Psychology as the behaviorist views it. *Psychological Review, 21*:158–177.

Whitney, D., & Trosten-Bloom, A. (2001). *The power of appreciative inquiry: A practical guide for positive change*. San Francisco, CA: Barrett Koehler.

Yukl, G.A. (1994). *Leadership in organizations*. Englewood Cliffs, NJ: Prentice-Hall.

Zaehner, R.C. (1957). *Mysticism: Sacred and profane*. London: Oxford University Press.

Zenger, J., Ulrich, D., & Smallwood, N. (2000). *Leadership: The new leadership development*. Alexandria, GA: Training and Development.

Index

C

F

G

J

K

L

T

W

Y

Z

About the Authors

RICHARD JOHN HATALA is a Professional Engineer (PEng) with a twenty five year career in the energy industry; 15 years as an evolving corporate intrapreneur and 10 years as an entrepreneur, founder, President and CEO of several domestic and international energy and service related companies. Rick is a life-long student of history, depth psychology, martial arts, management, leadership and the world's wisdom and mystic traditions. Currently he is the Executive Director of Integrative Leadership International Ltd.

LILLAS MARIE HATALA is a Certified Human Resource Professional (CHRP) with a Masters Degree in Continuing Education and a 28-year career in Human Resource Management and Leadership development. Lillas is currently Director of Business and Leadership programs at the University of Saskatchewan <**www.learntolead.usask.ca**>. In addition to her work life, Lillas is a dedicated meditation practitioner, Yoga Instructor and mother of five children.

Together, Rick and Lillas are dedicated to helping people awaken, nurture and integrate the leader within, discover and live their life's purpose, bring forth their unique gifts, talents and capabilities, and appreciate and bring out the highest potential in others. They are keynote speakers, authors, facilitators, consultants and coaches and have worked with thousands of leaders worldwide. They are co-founders of Integrative Leadership International, Institute and Foundation whose purpose is to help individuals and organizations become integrated.

Integrative Leadership International Ltd.

THE PURPOSE OF INTEGRATIVE LEADERTSHIP INTERNATIONAL (ILI) LTD., is to "help individuals and organizations become integrated." The book, *Integrative Leadership*, is the foundational philosophy, principles and practices that form the *heart* of ILI. From this foundational work, seminars, workshops, longer-term educational programs, consulting and coaching protocols, associations and other publications follow.

The vision of the ILI is to become the resource of choice in Canada and internationally for integrative leadership, philosophies, thought, approaches, frameworks and practices.

Integrative Leadership International is the commercial arm of a three-fold organization. International's commercial operations are associated with two other entities that are focused on educational endeavors (Institute) and charitable activities (Foundation). *IL International* conducts and facilitates public speaking, programs, seminars, workshops, coaching and consulting within all aspects of the evolving integrative model and framework for individuals, groups and organizations. The *IL Institute* is involved in ongoing research, development, education, publication and production involving all aspects of the process of integration. The *IL Foundation* supports — financially, intellectually and emotionally — individuals, institutions and not-for-profit organizations whose purpose and intent are aligned and support integration and not separation, unity and not division, a coming together rather than a breaking apart within local, regional, national and international communities in which the ILI operates.

For more information on the on-going work of the ILI, please visit our website at: <**www.integrativeleadership.ca**>

Contact Information for ILI

Integrative Leadership International, Institute or Foundation
P.O. Box 22204, Bankers Hall
Calgary, AB, Canada T3A 1P1
Phone: (403) 651 • 8351 or (306) 244 • 0934
Toll Free: 1 (866) 616 • 0934 / Fax: (306) 244 • 1379
E-Mail: iliinfo@integrativeleadership.ca
Website: www.integrativeleadership.ca

Forthcoming Publications from the Integrative Leadership Institute

April 2005

Lessons on the Path: Weekly Reflections and Applications on the Art of Living Integrative Life, Love and Leadership

A collection of 52 weekly lessons on the path of integration written by Richard John and Lillas Marie Hatala. Each weekly reading includes comments and perspectives from subscribers to the original newsletter, journal sections for the individual choosing to walk the path of integration as well as further observations, reflections, inspiration, information and application of the lesson.

September 2005

A Field Guide to Integrative Life and Leadership

The *Field Guide* is the practical and pragamatic guide to applying integrative leadership principles and practices in your everyday life and work. The guide contains advice, suggestions and inspirations that relate to the methods used to successfully walk the path and fully experience the process of integration.

For information or advance ordering,
please visit <**www.integrativeleadership.ca**>